WITHDRaWN

A THICKNESS OF PARTICULARS

A THICKNESS OF PARTICULARS

THE POETRY OF ANTHONY HECHT

JONATHAN F. S. POST

OXFORD
UNIVERSITY PRESS

OXFORD
UNIVERSITY PRESS

Great Clarendon Street, Oxford, OX2 6DP,
United Kingdom

Oxford University Press is a department of the University of Oxford.
It furthers the University's objective of excellence in research, scholarship,
and education by publishing worldwide. Oxford is a registered trade mark of
Oxford University Press in the UK and in certain other countries

Published in the United States of America by Oxford University Press
198 Madison Avenue, New York, NY 10016, United States of America

British Library Cataloguing in Publication Data
Data available

Library of Congress Control Number: 2015941921

ISBN 978–0–19–966071–1

Printed and bound by
CPI Group (UK) Ltd, Croydon, CRO 4YY

For Susan
In memory of her mother Lydia Gallick (1913–2015)

Preface

A Thickness of Particulars: The Poetry of Anthony Hecht grew out of a long period of intensive work devoted to preparing an edition of Hecht's *Selected Letters*, which appeared in 2013, published by the Johns Hopkins University Press. Before and concurrent with that project, I had the pleasure of teaching Hecht's poetry for a few years at Yale and many at UCLA to undergraduates and graduate students alike; and long before that, as a graduate student, I had the opportunity to study with Hecht in a seminar on William Butler Yeats and Theodore Roethke at the University of Rochester in 1972. I also house-sat while Hecht and his family were away for a semester at Harvard, and although I can't claim any special knowledge or "ensorcelment," as Hecht might say, emanating from the walls of his well-decorated, spacious upstate home, I made certain use of the many volumes in the Oxford poetry series in his downstairs den for which I remain still grateful. Nor can I trace, precisely, in this book more than a few points in the years of friendship that followed until his death in 2004. Probably the most important was developing an ear for the distinctive sound of his voice, the layering of (at times gleefully boyish) humor that infiltrates his verse and offsets and further enriches the darker broodings for which his poetry has become justly famous. Hecht was always reticent about discussing his poetry, modest to a fault I now rue. Sensing this, I was reluctant to ask him many questions. We often exchanged our writings but usually in printed form, an exchange I valued for, among other reasons, allowing a friendship to continue to flourish while living on opposite coasts.

In any event, the best preparation for understanding his writings, I came to discover, lay elsewhere, but it was in accord with the same advice he frequently gave to younger poets setting forth: to read, and in my case also to teach, as much poetry as possible, which I did, initially with concentration on the poets of the English Renaissance—as it was then called—and the seventeenth century: Shakespeare, Donne, Herbert, Milton, and Marvell, in particular, whose poetry in large quantities Hecht had committed to memory and, as was true with many poets of his generation, was foundational to much of his own work. But, of course, this marked only a beginning with regard to a poet who possessed a special knack for summoning spirits from the "vasty deep" in strikingly new and original ways, as Christopher Ricks has deftly explored of late.[1]

My own study draws frequently on Hecht's letters, and as a consequence, it offers something of a biographical context for understanding his poetry, but its general purpose is not biography per se.[2] That large project is being pursued by David Yezzi. Mine is intended to form, rather, an introduction to the poetry, attentive to its particular riches, with an eye toward the whole career, and making special use of the letters and his other critical writings as they cast light on these features. This includes *Anthony Hecht, in conversation with Philip Hoy* (1998), Hecht's highly illuminating "autobiography," a work I read immediately upon publication but whose charms are such that I returned to it only after having drafted my thoughts on a particular section. Although there have been a number of specialized studies of Hecht's writings, and, of course, many reviews, there has been no book-length study of the career—and indeed none was possible until recently, since Hecht was active as a poet right up to his death in 2004.

Besides taking advantage of the letters, I have also made use of the extensive materials in the Hecht Archive at Emory University, including drafts of some of the poems. Although my study is meant to provide an overview of the poet, and thus has a chronological cast to it, it also includes several chapters offering thematic angles. One of these is on the subject of ekphrasis. With good reason, Hecht has been called "our most painterly poet,"[3] a term that simultaneously reminds us of the significant place works of art have in his poetry as well as his own penchant for language often as steeped in color—in the rhetorical sense—as it is exact in its phrasing. A second chapter traces the wide

---

1. Ricks, *True Friendship: Geoffrey Hill, Anthony Hecht, and Robert Lowell under the Sign of Eliot and Pound* (New Haven, CT: Yale University Press, 2010).

2. For the convenience of the reader, I have included page references to those letters included in my edition of *The Selected Letters of Anthony Hecht* (Baltimore, MD: The Johns Hopkins University Press, 2013), abbreviated hereafter as *SL*. Those without page references are to letters that either remain in private hands or are in the Hecht Archive and noted as such.

3. Robyn Creswell, "Painting and Privacy: On Anthony Hecht," *Raritan* 21 (Winter, 2002), 20.

arc of Shakespeare's influence on Hecht's poetry. Other ancestral writers could have filled this role; Hecht was among the most deeply allusive poets of his generation, and, consequently, many authors, ancient as well as modern, make more than cameo appearances in my study. But Shakespeare is his most frequent point of reference, even more so than scripture—with allusion or echo often entailing resonances beyond citation. Indeed, Don Paterson, in his *New Commentary on Shakespeare's Sonnets*, recalls an amusing incident in which Hecht is said to have attributed his affectedly English accent—always surprising to a first-time listener—to his having "read a great deal of Shakespeare as a young man."[4] Hecht was a spell-binding, beautifully articulate reader of poetry, it should be said, although I am hardly the only person to say so, and Shakespeare, or rather Shakespeare as spoken on the stage in the mid-twentieth century, served not simply as a model for utterance but played into the shaping of individual poems themselves, indeed into helping Hecht navigate a crucial junction in his mid-life shift toward writing longer poems of a dramatic character as well as serving as a point of departure for one of his great, sustained comic flights in "Love for Four Voices" and the shorter, more intimate "Peripeteia," certainly among the finest love poems of its generation.

One of the benefits of reading published reviews of *The Selected Letters* is hearing from others about their response to Hecht. On the subject of Hecht and war, Colm Tóibín gets it just right. Quoting Randall Jarrell's remark in a review of Marianne Moore that "the real war poets are always war poets, peace or any time," Tóibín then applies that observation to a more obvious candidate, Hecht.[5] I take the point to be not that war is the only topic for a war poet but that a war poet can never be free of the subject, regardless of contemporary events. Oblivion is not to be hired. And so it is with Hecht. I have tried to give particular substance to this view by having his much anthologized poem, "The Book of Yolek," serve as a brief P.O.E. (point of embarkation) for this study. Only one other poem receives a single chapter,

4. Paterson, *Reading Shakespeare's Sonnets: A New Commentary* (London: Faber and Faber, 2010), 158–9. The anecdote is attached to Paterson's reading of Sonnet 53, which also spurred the observation that "*Millions of Strange Shadows*, incidentally, is one of Anthony Hecht's finest books" (158–9). For a slightly different account of the origins of his accent see Hecht's interview with J. D. McClatchy in the *Paris Review*, 108 (Fall, 1988), 163–4.

5. Tóibín, *London Review of Books*, 8 August 2013, 22.

"The Venetian Vespers," also by consensus one of Hecht's masterpieces and, in the eyes of some, "one of the finest narrative poems of the late twentieth century";[6] but I am taken by another reviewer singling out "Green: An Epistle" as Hecht's best poem. At the very least, the roiled, personal musings in this poem mark a threshold on the way to an extraordinary stretch—and stretching—of verse in the mid-1970s, as Hecht began to explore the resources of the longer interior monologue.

Hecht once commented to his Oxford editor, Jacqueline Simms, that he thought *The Venetian Vespers* was his best book up to that point.[7] I am not sure what book, if any, he might have nominated at the end of his life. Hecht could be quite Solomonic on the potential need for self-deception as one aged, as he revealed at some length in a letter to the literary scholar and critic, Eleanor Cook, in which he was responding to a review that had classified his work under the title "Old Guys":

> But as I stand tip-toe upon the threshold of my seventy-fifth year I have managed to preserve the comforting conviction that my work continues to improve. Doubtless there is a self-serving element in this, and it is possibly a simple delusion, since few writers could endure if they thought they were losing their abilities. And God knows it has happened to many. Wordsworth at the end grew weak; after the *Quartets* Eliot wrote little of merit in the way of poetry. Delmore Schwartz sank into oblivion, John Crowe Ransom stopped writing, and Dylan Thomas took to drink, while Hemingway, fearing the loss of his gifts, and suspecting self-plagiarism, took his own life. The catalogue is long and depressing, so it's no mystery that most writers refuse to see their own weaknesses. At the same time, there are the heartening instances of Hardy and Sophocles. Of course, there is a built-in danger to the conviction that one is getting always better. It means that as one comes to think less and less well of one's early work, put into the shade [by] this happy progressive view, that one may be right: the early work, of which one was once so proud, may not be so good after all, and two hideous conclusions may be drawn from that. The first is that the present state of excellence may not be so great if it is merely an improvement upon what went before; and secondly, that the illusion of present merit may be just as temporary as one's view of the past. The whole puzzle does not abide much thinking on.[8]

Whether or not later Hecht is right about "later Hecht," I have, nevertheless, dedicated significant space to his later poetry, in part because it

6. Robert B. Shaw, *Blank Verse: A Guide to its History and Use* (Athens: Ohio University Press, 2007), 195.

7. Letter, AH to Jacqueline ("Jackie") Simms, 28 April 1980.

8. Letter, AH to Eleanor Cook, 9 January 1997 (*SL*, 281–2).

remains, next to his earliest verse, probably the least familiar to readers but contains, as I kept rediscovering, many wonderful poems, as how could it not? Hecht readers will know "Proust on Skates" and "Sarabande on Attaining the Age of Seventy-Seven," but "Envoi," a poem favored by John Ashbery? Or "Prospects," perhaps stirred into being by his renewed collaboration with the engraver Leonard Baskin? Or the gorgeous ekphrasis "Matisse: Blue Interior with Two Girls— 1947"? Or later still, some of the smaller lyrics in *The Darkness and the Light* (2001), which, as Hecht's last published volume of poetry, marks the outer edge of my own book : "A Certain Slant," "Memory," "Lot's Wife," or "Illumination"—to name but a few? With Hecht, it is always about the individual poem, the "thing itself," to adopt the New Critical phraseology current when he set out to become a poet under the guidance of John Crowe Ransom and Allen Tate—a concept he never forgot. But I think there can be little doubt that *The Hard Hours* was the crucial, indeed critical, book in his career. It may be "a rather bleak note" on which to end a seminar, as Hecht once remarked to David Lehman in 1980,[9] but it remains a stirring, searing reading experience nearly a half-century later, putting to use an understanding of Robert Lowell's *Life Studies* in its own highly original way. It deserves being recovered as fully as possible. What's interesting, indeed inspiring, about Hecht's career, is that he didn't stop with this book, nor the next, or the next. Within the high terms he set for art, he kept developing, although to my thinking his middle years represented his most fertile period and, in the eyes of some, was unmatched by any poet writing in North America.

As with any poet of merit, it is through their work they must survive. The main knock against Hecht is that he is or can be "too poetic," an odd criticism to make of poetry when you think about the alternative. This general criticism usually devolves into a subset of attitudes: that his poetry is too formal; too interested in occasionally elaborate diction; too "closed" or balanced in its harmonics; too severe in tone and subject. Hecht certainly loved words in all sorts of shapes and sizes; puns, too, or paronomasias, to use the more dignified term for wordplay, but he also knew when not to use them; and though he experimented with many kinds of verse over his life, he never forsook the challenge of complicated patterns, even if he could make them seem simple, as in the case of the last poem in his final collection: " 'The Darkness and

9. Letter, AH to David Lehman, 15 December 1980 (*SL*, 187–8).

the Light are both alike to Thee.'" Hecht also possessed an especially fine ear for sound, for the musicality of a phrase, a quality that is sometimes turned against him as "eloquence," but only if you fail to hear the complicating counter patterns of speech. In this regard, he understood better than most poets of his era, the dilemma, the creative tension, at the heart of classical rhetoric: that while it valued the commonality of experience as poetry's subject, it understood that strangeness is often what dazzles and transports the listener.[10] And with other gifted poets of his generation, he had a great talent for rhyme and its many possibilities. He and John Hollander initiated the small craze for "jiggery-pokery," double dactyls, which swept through the 1960s, and it reminds us of his capacity for light verse. What is sometimes seen as Hecht's limitations, in other words, I embrace as opportunities for further exploration. If the study has a single goal it is the same as with most books of literary criticism: to initiate or otherwise stimulate a critical conversation that its author feels to be worth having. But poetry lives in the details, and so this is a book ultimately about poems: trying to hear them right, to think their thoughts, to read them as part of a life fully engaged in their writing throughout the second half of the twentieth century.

To that end, I have taken a line from one of Hecht's poems as the book's main title. "A thickness of particulars" appears near the end of "A Transparent Man," a fairly late dramatic monologue spoken by a dying woman, modeled in part on Flannery O'Connor. Hecht often selected this poem to read, and he did so at the last poetry reading of his I attended when he was in Los Angeles to receive the Los Angeles Times Book Prize for his *Collected Later Poems* in the spring of 2004. I suspect among the reasons he was drawn to the poem was that it expressed a view of looking at the world, and at art, that was central to his own, in much the same way that "At the Fishhouses" is crucial to Elizabeth Bishop's aesthetic. As is often the case with Hecht, the

---

10. See Catherine Nicholson, *Uncommon Tongues: Eloquence and Eccentricity in the English Renaissance* (Philadelphia: University of Pennsylvania Press, 2014), esp. 4–11 and 59–71. Hecht belonged to, if not the last, then one of the last generations that assumed knowledge of Classical literature, including rhetoric, as foundational to the school curriculum. Among his many poems reflecting a broad understanding of the Classical past, his late poem, "The Mysteries of Caesar" in *Flight Among the Tombs* (1996), is built out of classroom exercises studying Latin, its humor (and pathos) emerging from the clash between the desire for the "laws of common intercourse" and the verbal eccentricities and barbarisms realized in student efforts at translation.

full weight of a phrase can only be measured in the context of the preceding lines, in this case spoken near the end of the poem:

> But this last week it seems I have found myself
> Looking beyond, or through, individual trees
> At the dense, clustered woodland just behind them,
> Where those great, nameless crowds patiently stand.
> It's become a sort of complex, ultimate puzzle
> And keeps me fascinated. My eyes are twenty-twenty,
> Or used to be, but of course, I can't unravel
> The tousled snarl of intersecting limbs,
> That mackled, cinder grayness. It's a riddle
> Beyond the eye's solution. Impenetrable.
> If there is order in all that anarchy
> Of granite mezzotint, that wilderness,
> It takes a better eye than mine to see it.
> It set me on to wondering how to deal
> With such a thickness of particulars,
> Deal with it faithfully, you understand,
> Without blurring the issue.

Since I will be looking at these lines in more detail in Chapter 8, let me note here that I take the last sentence, in all its deliciously spacious musing and evident humility, to be not a dissuasive but a call, a credo, applicable to poet and critic alike, and also, of course, a warning about the difficulty of getting things right.

Acknowledgments

A number of people have contributed to the completion of this study. It is a pleasure to acknowledge them individually. Helen Hecht read through the entire manuscript, several sections more than once, always with a discerning eye, and I am grateful for her many suggestions and improvements. For years, I have been quietly pilfering phrases and ideas from my UCLA colleague, Stephen Yenser. I cannot imagine this book without thinking of the generous support, advice, and criticism he offered at nearly every stage of this project. So, too, J. D. McClatchy brought his fine intelligence and publishing expertise to bear on making this the best book it could be about a poet we both knew and admired. With readers as astute as these, it is easy to feel spoiled.

I owe as well a large debt of gratitude to Mary Jo Salter ever since we first met in Bogliasco, Italy, in 2004. More immediately, I thank her for inviting me to explore some ideas about Hecht in her graduate writing seminar at the Johns Hopkins University and for passing on several of her own stimulating, unpublished talks on Hecht. I also wish to thank Philip Hoy for many exchanges over the years, in which he generously shared his rich understanding of Hecht the person and the poet.

For helpful comments and encouragement, sometimes in the service of answering specific queries, it is a pleasure to acknowledge the following people: Albert Braunmuller, Gregory Dowling, Irving Feldman, Dana Gioia, Achsah Guibbory, Judith Herz, Langdon Hammer, Adam Hecht, Kimberly Hedlin, Christopher Hodgkins, John Irwin, Gabriel Josipovici, John Kerrigan, Cameron Macauley, Michael North, Diederik Oostdijk, Conor O'Sullivan, Christopher Ricks, Helaine Smith, David Sofield, the late Jon Stallworthy, Richard Strier, Chris Van 't dack, Robert Watson, Irving Weiss, Stephen Werner, and Richard Wilbur. A chance conversation with my UCLA colleagues, Joel and Joan Aberbach, directed me to their cousin, Jack Terry, a survivor of the Flossenbürg Concentration Camp. I am grateful for several telephone conversations and email exchanges with him.

Portions of this book had an earlier life as lectures or talks. A version of Chapter 1, "The Sestina and the Tattoo," was presented at a conference on Renaissance Poetic Forms at Wolfson College, Oxford. Chapter 5 on "The Venetian Vespers" was initially aired at a joint UCLA–Warwick University Conference in Venice, Italy. And a shorter version of Chapter 7, "*Shecht*speare," was given first at the Renaissance Society of America, and, in a more expanded form, at the Folger Shakespeare Library in Washington DC. For inviting my participation, I want to thank, respectively, Elizabeth Scott-Bauman and Benjamin Burton; Peter Reill and Jacqueline Labbe; Kimberley Johnson; and Stephen Enniss. A second fellowship from the Bogliasco Foundation allowed an opportunity to conceive of the book as a whole and the welcome leisure to write. I wish to thank in particular Ivana Folle and Alessandra Natale for their generous hospitality and friendship. I first learned of the Foundation's glorious Liguria Study Center from the person who is the subject of this book.

Closer to home at UCLA, Lynda Tolly remains the nonpareil of librarians, rarely defeated by a query, and Jeanette Gilkison continues to be the most unflappable and resourceful of office administrators. Much of this book was written while Ali Behdad was chair of the Department of English. I thank him for creating a climate conducive to research and teaching. I am equally grateful to the Friends of English, which helped pay for permissions for the artwork, and to Grant Rosson, who prepared the Index and read through the manuscript with care and intelligence. For many years, Hecht's writings featured regularly in my undergraduate and graduate seminars on poetry: I remain grateful to the students in those classes for their valuable responses in person, on paper, and, in one case, on film. I also want to thank the UCLA Academic Senate Research Committee for helping to fund the research for this book, in some cases allowing me to follow in the poet's footsteps to distant sites that were important sources of inspiration to him. The staff at the Robert Woodruff Rare Books Room at Emory University, where the Hecht Archives are stored, was invariably helpful. This book could not have been written without their services. I wish to thank as well Heather Kendall of the Burton Barr Library in Phoenix, Arizona, for making available the library's copies of the beautiful Gehenna Press editions of the Baskin–Hecht *Presumptions of Death* and *Florilegium*.

It has been a true gift to work again with Jacqueline Baker, Senior Commissioning Editor for Literature at Oxford University Press, and Rachel Platt, Senior Assistant Commissioning Editor. They make publishing a book not only possible but pleasurable.

This book is dedicated to Susan Gallick, my partner in all things, in memory of her mother, Lydia Gallick. Among her many attributes, she made it possible for both her daughters, Jeanne and Susan, to attend the University of California, Berkeley.

Chapter 1 appeared in *The Yale Review* 103 (July, 2015). A considerably revised version of Chapter 2 appeared also appeared in *The Yale Review* 100 (April, 2012). An early version of Chapter 5 was published in *The Johns Hopkins Review* 3.2 (Spring, 2010). I wish to thank the editors of both journals.

Unless otherwise noted, all quotations from Hecht's poetry are taken from *The Collected Earlier Poems* (New York: Alfred A. Knopf, Inc., 1990) and *The Collected Later Poems* (New York: Alfred A. Knopf, 2003).

The author would like to acknowledge permission to quote from the following poems:

"The Dover Bitch," " 'More Light! More Light!,' " "A Hill," " 'It Out-Herods Herod. Pray You, Avoid It,' " "Peripeteia," "The Deodand," "Claire de Lune," "The Ghost in the Martini," "The Venetian Vespers," "Behold the Lillies of the Field," "The Vow," "Rites and Ceremonies," "The Gardens of the Villa d'Este," "A Deep Breath at Dawn," "Sestina d'Inverno," "Still Life," "A Letter," "Double Sonnet," "To a Madonna Ex-Voto in the Spanish Style (After Baudelaire)," "The Man Who Married Magdalene," "The Origin of Centaurs," "Ostia Antica," "Message from the City," "Green: An Epistle," "Apprehensions," " 'Auguries of Innocence'," "Black Boy in the Dark," " 'Dichtung Und Wahrheit'," "A Birthday Poem," "The Grapes," and "The Seven Deadly Sins" from COLLECTED EARLIER POEMS by Anthony Hecht, copyright © 1990. Used by permission of Alfred A. Knopf, an imprint of the Knopf Doubleday Publishing Group, a division of Penguin Random House LLC. All rights reserved.

"The Book of Yolek," "The Transparent Man," "Devotions of a Painter," "See Naples and Die," "Meditation," "A Love for Four Voices," "Envoi," "Eclogue of the Shepherd and the Townie," and "Curriculum Vitae" from THE TRANSPARENT MAN by Anthony Hecht, copyright © 1980, 1981, 1982, 1986, 1987, 1990 by Anthony Hecht. Used by permission of Alfred A. Knopf, an imprint of the Knopf Doubleday

Contents

List of Illustrations

I

"The Book of Yolek," the Sestina, and the Tattoo

In one of his letters, Anthony Hecht took the occasion to remark:

My poetry is coming slowly. Producing it, even in small quantities has always been for me a painful and laborious process. (I mean painful here not in the sense of unpleasant to do, but only difficult in the extreme.) I have picked a particularly hard job for myself in deciding to write a sestina—which is a very strict and old verse form dating back to the 12th century.[1]

Anyone familiar with Hecht's poetry will hardly be surprised by these observations. Early Hecht's reputation for writing slowly was legendary: although his productivity would improve with age, he would still publish only seven books of verse over the course of more than fifty years of writing. And legendary, too, was his lifelong devotion to poetic form. As fate might have it, in fact, the last essay in his final book of essays, *Melodies Unheard: Essays on the Mysteries of Poetry* (2003), bears the title "The Music of Forms." Perhaps the only unusual feature about the letter is its date. Addressed to his parents, the letter was written while Hecht was still a twenty-year-old undergraduate at Bard, thus lending a precocious touch to the parenthetical distinction involving the word "painful." It is also, as it happens, the last surviving letter before Hecht would (like many young men in the United States) prematurely conclude his studies and enlist in the army in the spring of 1943. Two painful years later, painful now embracing both meanings, difficult as well as unpleasant, Hecht would find himself in Europe, at the front, as part of the final campaign against the German forces.

---

1. Letter, AH to Parents, 10 March 1943 (*SL*, 17).

A copy of the official "Story of the 97th Infantry Division" in the Hecht Archive at Emory University charts the troops' movement that spring. Landing first in France on 2 March 1945, the division passed quickly through Belgium, before crossing slowly through Germany into Czechoslovakia; then, cutting a narrow turn, it circled back through Germany on the way to returning to Le Havre and departing for Boston on 16 June. April was the cruelest month in terms of actual combat, as the Allied forces encountered significant German resistance in the Ruhr Valley. Never singled out by name in the official "Story," Hecht nonetheless received the "Combat Infantryman Medal" on 20 April, as he reported to his parents, "an award whose meaning I do not entirely understand myself."[2] But it is possible that early May was equally, if not more, painful. In spite of the German surrender on 7 May, Hecht had been among those involved in the discovery and liberation of the concentration camp at Flossenbürg in late April, again not mentioned in the official "Story." Flossenbürg was located in Bavaria, on the Czech border, and had been founded in 1938 to help with the Reich's massive building projects. At its maximum, in mid-March 1945, Flossenbürg held about 53,000 prisoners, but after forced evacuations by the SS in light of the approaching Allied powers—what Primo Levi characterized as "the murderous and apparently insane transfers with which the history of the Nazi camps came to an end during the first months of 1945"[3]—the camp population at Flossenbürg dwindled to about 1500 at the time of the initial discovery and liberation beginning on 23 April. Some 200 of the prisoners would die shortly thereafter, thus further winnowing the number of potential "bearer[s] of secrets"—to use Levi's phrasing again.[4]

2. Letter, AH to Parents, 20 April 1945 (SL, 43).
3. Primo Levi, The Drowned and the Saved, trans. Raymond Rosenthal (New York: Vintage, 1989), 14.
4. Levi, The Drowned and the Saved, 14. Estimates are from the United States Holocaust Memorial Museum. "The Holocaust." Holocaust Encyclopedia. <http://www.ushmm. org/wlc/en/?ModuleId=10005143>. Accessed on 13 May 2012. A detailed history of Flossenbürg can be found in Alicia Nitecki and Jack Terry, Jakub's World: A Boy's Story of Loss and Survival in the Holocaust (Albany: State University of New York Press, 2005). A careful treatment of Hecht's time in the military, responsive to the gaps in the record, can be found in Geoffrey Lindsay, "Anthony Hecht, Private First Class," The Yale Review 96.3 (July, 2008), 1–26.

In the form of an anonymously authored personal diary, also in the Hecht Archive, the Company C "Action Report" gives a slightly different, more detailed, version of events witnessed on 29 April:

We started walking this morning to N. Losimtal, Czech., a distance of about 5 miles, arriving there at 0930. The Second Platoon did not go with the rest of the company, but instead returned to guard the concentration camp at Flossenberg. The company was to send out patrols to contact Able company. Eight hundred of the sixteen hundred political prisoners in the concentration camp were sick from typhus. When the first outfit arrived, men were found dying at the rate of 80 per day. When we arrived the Medical Corps and the Camps hospital had cut this death rate down to 30 per day. What I actually saw is hard to explain. Bodies of once healthy men were now skeletons of bones covered with taut, yellowish colored skin. Many had died with their eyes wide open staring into space as if they were seeing over and over again all the torture the Germans had put them through—their mouths open, gasping for that last breath that might keep them alive. All of them were nude and as they died fellow prisoners carried them through the fence to the incinerator where they were stacked. The stench was unbearable.

Temporarily assigned to the Counter Intelligence Corps during this period, Hecht used his rudimentary interpretive skills to interrogate captured prisoners. He also interviewed concentration camp survivors. In part because of censorship regulations, Hecht's letters home are necessarily reticent about what he witnessed. Some twenty years later, Hecht's close friend during the war, Robie Macauley, remarked in a letter of 8 August 1976 to the *New York Times* that these were "the most horrifying days of my life."[5] There is every reason to believe that Hecht thought the same.

The enforced disjunction between attempting to master a form as complicated as the sestina and going off to war might have had heroic precedent to it: "'Tis time to leave the books in dust / And oil th' unused armour's rust," remarked Andrew Marvell in "An Horatian Ode Upon Cromwell's Return from Ireland," a poem later Hecht knew and admired. But for the student-soldier Hecht, doing battle—to use

---

5. Letters to the Editor, *New York Times* (1923–Current file); 8 August 1976; ProQuest Historical Newspapers *New York Times* (1851–2006), 169. I want to thank Cameron Macauley, Robie Macauley's son, for this reference. In an email to me of 15 August 2011, Cameron Macauley remarked that "to my knowledge [my father] never spoke of Flossenbürg or wrote of it at any other time besides this letter to the NY Times and one written to his brother of 14 May 1945."

Paul Fussell's decidedly unheroic title of his war memoir[6]—necessarily entailed lingering regrets for the literary life lost. Hecht's letters home are studded with quotations and allusions from favorite authors, especially Shakespeare, and, with each passing month in uniform, regret would occasionally swell to incorporate the realization of his having forsaken—or been forsaken by—the muse altogether. And yet, as it turned out, what was forsaken was not forgotten, nor was the memory of what he had witnessed. Some twenty-five years later, around the time Macauley made his rare reference to concentration camps in his letter in the *New York Times*, the now established poet Hecht can be found musing over the verse form again. In the volume appropriately titled *Millions of Strange Shadows* (1977) appears an earlier poetic shadow, his first published sestina bearing the seasonal title "Sestina d'Inverno."

Oddly, or perhaps not, Hecht had managed to avoid or repress, when few poets did, the fashion for this complicated pattern in the 1950s. The sestina, we are reminded by Edward Brunner, was especially popular with poets raised on New Critical principles valuing the artifice of verbal complexity, and the sestina's structure was certainly complex, indeed perhaps only surpassed in this regard by its near cousin, the canzone.[7] The list of its practitioners in the 1950s is long, and in some cases impressive, with Elizabeth Bishop being among them. Yet Hecht was out of step on this front, as he was on some others during these two decades, as he sorted through his literary models and mentors, war memories, occasional depression, and an unhappy, failing marriage. But, then, as if to make up for this gap or lapse, he wrote a second sestina fairly soon after the first, this one called "The Book of Yolek." Although not published in a collection of verse until 1990 in *The Transparent Man*, it had been completed almost a decade earlier. As Hecht noted in a September 1981 letter to Jacqueline Simms, his literary editor at Oxford, "I enclose, as you kindly requested, the fruits of this summer," which included not just "Yolek" but also "Devotions of a Painter" and "Meditation"—the latter two resulting from an idyllic vacation to Venice and the Veneto, whereas, "Yolek," by contrast, "got

---

6. Hecht favorably reviewed Fussell's book, *Doing Battle: The Making of a Skeptic*, for *The Washington Post* (29 September 1996), and noted that "everything Fussell writes here bears out with the almost uncanny precision of memory recovered from determined suppression the outlines of my own life."

7. Brunner, *Cold War Poetry* (Urbana: University of Illinois Press, 2001), 160–4.

finished just before I had to plunge into the thickets of academic chores and leave all thought of writing poetry behind."[8]

More evidently "painful" in both subject matter and formal difficulty than either of these poems, "Yolek" required a return to war memories of the most brutal kind, and even to memories preceding the war itself, back to childhood, recollections also further seasoned by his recent experiment with the form in "Sestina d'Inverno" and by his knowledge of the form as descending in English from Sidney's double sestina, "Ye Goteherd Gods,"—Empson's reading of it is important here—and as further described by the Elizabethan rhetorician George Puttenham, and as practiced by several of Hecht's contemporaries, Elizabeth Bishop and James Merrill, two of the poets who most seriously engaged Hecht's thinking in the 1970s.

This aggregation of sources and influences (and there are others) might seem a perfect recipe for writer's block, and it perhaps was for Hecht at an earlier point in his career. But here the different strains are fully assimilated, the overall vision of the poem too strongly motivated to be knocked off its rails. The poem is thirty-nine lines, as the rules of the sestina form require, with an epigraph in German from Martin Luther's translation of John 19:7 (we have a law, and by that law he must die). The poem deserves quoting in full:

> Wir haben ein Gesetz,
> Und nach dem Gesetz soll er sterben.

> The dowsed coals fume and hiss after your meal
> Of grilled brook trout, and you saunter off for a walk
> Down the fern trail, it doesn't matter where to,
> Just so you're weeks and worlds away from home,
> And among midsummer hills have set up camp
> In the deep bronze glories of declining day.

> You remember, peacefully, an earlier day
> In childhood, remember a quite specific meal:
> A corn roast and bonfire in summer camp.
> That summer you got lost on a Nature Walk;
> More than you dared admit, you thought of home;
> No one else knows where the mind wanders to.

> The fifth of August, 1942.
> It was morning and very hot. It was the day

---

8. Letter, AH to Jaqueline Simms, 17 September 1981 (*SL*, 190).

They came at dawn with rifles to The Home
For Jewish Children, cutting short the meal
Of bread and soup, lining them up to walk
In close formation off to a special camp.

How often you have thought about that camp,
As though in some strange way you were driven to,
And about the children, and how they were made to walk,
Yolek who had bad lungs, who wasn't a day
Over five years old, commanded to leave his meal
And shamble between armed guards to his long home.

We're approaching August again. It will drive home
The regulation torments of that camp
Yolek was sent to, his small, unfinished meal,
The electric fences, the numeral tattoo,
The quite extraordinary heat of the day
They all were forced to take that terrible walk.

Whether on a silent, solitary walk
Or among crowds, far off or safe at home,
You will remember, helplessly, that day,
And the smell of smoke, and the loudspeakers of the camp.
Wherever you are, Yolek will be there, too.
His unuttered name will interrupt your meal.

Prepare to receive him in your home some day.
Though they killed him in the camp they sent him to,
He will walk in as you're sitting down to a meal.

Only six months earlier, Hecht had described his "Sestina d'Inverno,"
about the winter weather in Rochester, New York, as "a rather bitter
sestina about this neck of the woods"[9]—and indeed, the word "bleak"
appears in the opening line of the poem, whose first two stanzas will
give a flavor of the poem:

Here in this bleak city of Rochester,
Where there are twenty-seven words for "snow,"
Not all of them polite, the wayward mind
Basks in some Yucatan of its own making,
Some coppery, sleek lagoon, or cinnamon island
Alive with lemon tints and burnished natives,

And O that we were there. But here the natives
Of this grey, sunless city of Rochester
Have sown whole mines of salt about their land

9. Letter, AH to Timothy Healy, SJ, 14 January 1981 (SL, 190).

> (Bare ruined Carthage that it is) while snow
> Comes down as if The Flood were in the making.
> Yet on that ocean Marvell called the mind...

Whatever bleak snowy reality underlies the circumstances of its making, this earlier sestina is generally comical in effect, and its evident wit reminds us of an important playful strain in Hecht's verse. The image of salt, used to melt the ice and snow on the streets, for example, gives rise to the parenthetical aside "Bare ruined Carthage that it is," referring at once to Shakespeare's great sonnet of seasonal change (73) in the famous allusion to "Bare ruined choirs where late the sweet birds sang," but now applied to a city, where, like Carthage, there is no prospect of seasonal change at all. And yet, to look beyond the allusion, if the quality of sameness is true of the city, part of the comedy involves the word "Rochester" itself, one of the terminal words that shifts shape, morphing socially upward into the "Earl of Rochester" and then descending downward to the "Rochester / Gas and Electric Co." There is also Hecht's further play with the form. If the "one thing indisputable" about Rochester is "snow," then one of the equally indisputable things about a sestina is the recurrence of the chosen terminal words, which includes, in this case, the word "snow" itself. The snow it snoweth every stanza.

Some years later with the authority of the Renaissance rhetorician George Puttenham behind him, Hecht pointed to the great challenge posed by the form of the sestina. Monotony, Puttenham recognized, will "try the makers cunning."[10] Against the evident sameness of nature (the Rochester weather) stands the poet, whose art continually seeks to reconfigure reality to meet the mind's desire to escape to an island fantasy. There is something of a bravura performance here, a "trial," in fact, in the sense of meeting a challenge posed by both nature and art; and just as Hecht refers at one point to how "the youthful natives, / Unable to conceive of Rochester, / Made love, and were acrobatic in the making," so the same may be said about the acrobatic poet, who not only employs "making" as one of the stanza's terminal

10. Hecht, "Sidney and the Sestina," in *Melodies Unheard: Essays on the Mysteries of Poetry* (Baltimore, MD: The Johns Hopkins University Press, 2003), 66, originally published in Jonathan F. S. Post, ed. *Green Thoughts, Green Shades: Contemporary Poets on the Early Modern Lyric* (Berkeley: University of California Press, 2002), 41–58. The whole essay, plus examples, provides an illuminating gloss on Hecht's understanding and deployment of the sestina.

words but conceived of their order in such a way that "making" serves as the poem's last word. Making do with bad weather and making art out of it are the conditions which inspire this elegant, amusing poem. The penultimate stanza rarely fails in a poetry reading to raise a smile, especially the first and last lines:

> The one thing indisputable here is snow,
> The single verity of heaven's making,
> Deeply indifferent to the dreams of the natives
> And the torn hoarding-posters of some island.
> Under our igloo skies the frozen mind
> Holds to one truth: it is grey, and called Rochester.

"The Book of Yolek" represents another kind of response altogether; indeed, one from an altogether different part of the mind and universe. "It is the most terrifying sestina I know," observes one critic not readily given to superlatives: "it is perhaps the most unbearable in the language."[11] As a poet, Hecht thrived on contrarieties, like Yeats before him, and yet the radical change in tone, subject matter, and execution in this second sestina is still a bit unnerving. The poem is nothing if not scrupulously exacting, indeed hair-raising, in its *concentration* on the event at hand.[12] The six terminal words are of the most ordinary kind: meal, walk, to, home, camp, and day. The time of the year is summer, nothing so unpleasant as winter; and to meet the challenge of monotony (and to "try the makers cunning"), Hecht resorts to the simplest of strategies and yet one of the most difficult feats to accomplish with a sestina. Tell a story.[13] Sestinas want to repeat, not to go forward. In this case, the story is one Hecht found in the *Anthology of Holocaust Literature*, written by Hanna Mortkowicz-Olczakowa, titled "Yanosz Korchak's Last Walk," a moving account of the famous Polish educator's

---

11. William Logan, "When Beauty Shows No Mercy," *New York Times Book Review* (7 July 1990), 27.

12. My use of the italicized "concentration" is meant to pick up on Hecht's double sense of the word as glossed in his letter to David Havird, 30 December 1997: "The sort of devoted concentration that [Auden and Simone Weil] identify with prayer is virtually impossible to distinguish from what Hannah Arendt recognized as the banality of evil...Technocrats are skilled at 'concentration'" (*SL*, 291). One of the accomplishments of "The Book of Yolek" is, in fact, to distinguish between these very different ideas: one associated with the creation of meaning through art, the other with the destruction of life.

13. My thoughts here have been influenced by Hecht's comments in "Sidney and the Sestina," 77.

decision to remain with the children in his Jewish Orphanage in the Warsaw Ghetto rather than forsake them when the opportunity arose, as indeed it did when they were rounded up by the Nazis and taken to the Treblinka Extermination Camp.[14] With the examples of Sidney's double sestina and of Bishop's "A Miracle for Breakfast" in mind, Hecht chose (or determined) to recount a narrative about innocence and experience, with the focus on the child, as Bishop had done in her "Sestina," but now to widen the horizon beyond the house or "home," and to make the story also include the speaker, indeed to implicate him in the narrative, to make him and his terrible memories as much the subject as Yolek himself, and to make the recursive form of the sestina include both shock and a sense of the inevitable.

Later asked to comment on his much anthologized poem, Hecht remarked that "the form, by its insistent repetitions, lends itself particularly well to an obsessiveness, a monomania, a kind of hypnotic fixation on some idea or feeling."[15] Its merciless logic reflects the systematic extermination of the Jews and it also slowly envelopes the speaker, whose use of the casual "you" at the idyllic outset establishes a tone of familiarity with the unidentified subject of address. But after the pivotal third stanza, the speaker's haunting memories of the past, linking him with the child Yolek, become his obsession as well, reminding us in the process of the shadowy soldier Hecht now thinking back "about that camp, / As though in some strange way you were driven to," a fusion amplified in intensity as the season of memory approaches yet again, enacting yet another version of repetition exacted by the form.

In composing "The Book of Yolek," Hecht thought carefully, then, not only about form but also the related topic of narrative. Earlier drafts of the poem show he initially planned to begin with what is now the third stanza, establishing the historical occasion at the outset, in the manner of his source: "It was the 5th of August 1942," something of a flat opening, at which point the poem also bore the title, "The Law," and two of the terminal words were "children" and "breakfast," later replaced by "home" and "meal," respectively. At some point in the process, Hecht decided to change the poem's narrative strategy and

14. Jacob Glatstein, Israel Knox, and Samuel Margoshes, eds., *Anthology of Holocaust Literature* (New York: Atheneum, 1973), 134–7.

15. Jonathan N. Barron and Eric Murphy Selinger, eds., *Jewish American Poetry: Poems, Commentary, and Reflections* (Hanover: University Press of New England, 2000), 80–3.

to begin with the summer camp memories, with the terminal words now assuming their present order, and the drafts showing many small changes in diction and phrase. A side note on the first stanza said "camping in Rockies," but Hecht clearly decided not to designate a specific place for the camp, however much memories of his own pre-war experience as a camper in the 1930s might have influenced his later thinking.[16] In the poem, Hecht wanted to keep the images general, especially at the outset, and then to suggest, in the second stanza, slightly more specific (and portentous) recollections, as they begin to crowd the speaker's thoughts, although again, these are of a generally recognized order. Then occurs the shift to the newly placed third stanza, which in draft begins, "It was the fifth of August 1942," and the story seemingly gets underway. But even now the line wasn't quite right. The shift in focus was not sufficiently absolute, and Hecht crossed out the first two words, leaving only the date of the event itself on the page, now a matter of historical fact only, the year made even more numerically (and visually) explicit by his already having determined to spell out the day of the month. Hecht has suspended the date from the logic of temporality, memorialized it, chiseled it into our memories as it has become so in his and in history. It becomes a kind of strange, numerically exact (and numerically perfect) pentameter tattoo.

And now the story does get underway ("It was morning and very hot"), as one meaning of camp seems to mutate effortlessly, but with hideous efficiency, into its opposite. From here on, the drama is achieved largely by shifting focus onto the speaker's intensifying identification with Yolek, which grows through the recollection of specific details, now amplified through the judicious addition of simple adjectives and phrases ("meal," becomes "small, unfinished meal," "walk" becomes "that terrible walk"—and so on), and the speaker's own, rather precarious hold on reality this time of year, unable as he is to protect himself from the memories relentlessly associated with Yolek's death: "the smell of smoke, and loudspeakers of the camp." Indeed, Hecht's substitution of "loudspeakers" for "watchtowers" in the final version furthers the assault on his senses in the last stanza and on his own feelings of

16. The entire early chronicle of his camp letters forms a fascinating, further autobiographical context for this poem. For a sampling see *SL*, 3–12. See also Emily Leithauser, "Anthony Hecht's Little Book," *The Hopkins Review* 7 (Summer, 2014), 336–45, an essay carefully attuned to Hecht's revisions and the poem's tonal complexities, especially at the close.

helplessness in the face of such memories. Only in the envoy does the speaker seem to recover a sense of equanimity, a release from this "hypnotic fixation." In part this happens through the new orientation of the terminal words, now compressed into three lines, as the form dictates, but also because such compression underscores the creation of a new community here, with Yolek appearing as a kind of Elijah figure at Passover, a symbol and source of endurance in the future, especially as remembered in the Haggadah. I am quoting from Herbert Bronstein's 1974 *Passover Haggadah*, for which Hecht helped with the text and wrote a brief note on the spiritual significance of Passover:

This man of mystery became associated with the End of Days, with the Messianic hopes of our people. The prophet Malachi promised that Elijah would come to turn the hearts of parents to children, and the hearts of children to parents, and to announce the coming of the Messiah when all mankind would celebrate freedom.

Hence, he has a place in every Seder. We open the door that he may enter, and set a cup of wine to represent the final Messianic promise for us and for all peoples: "I will bring you into the land."[17]

But the sestina's compression also requires a further accounting of events, a recounting of responsibility: "Though they killed him in the camp they sent him to, / He will walk in as you're sitting down to a meal." The moral determination quietly sounded in the penultimate line, blazingly simple in its certainty, suggests a speaker who has come to terms momentarily with the past—his past. And yet at the same time, the final line of the poem insists that Yolek, through the silent, ghostly figure of Elijah, persists into the indefinite future, just as for every reader of the poem, his "terrible walk" will be recalled, again and again.

With regard to contemporary influences, I suspect that the example of Merrill's ingenious sestina "Tomorrows" underlies, although for completely different reasons, the transposition by Hecht of the most insignificant of words—"to"—into the ominous sounding ordinal "1942" in the very next line: a gap in significance encouraged by the gulf separating one stanza from the next, indeed the world of golden memories, where the mind can wander, from the brazen world of Nazi Germany, when idylls of any kind are no longer possible. It might be

17. Herbert Bronstein, ed., *A Passover Haggadah* (1974; rev. edn. New York: Central Conference of American Rabbis, 1982), 68. Leonard Baskin produced the drawings. Hecht's note is on p. 17.

the case as well that Merrill's recently published "Book of Ephraim" in his *Divine Comedies* (1976) pointed Hecht in the direction of finally deciding on "The Book of Yolek" as the title of his poem, but, again, with a different, memorializing purpose in mind. Hecht's earlier title of "The Law" gives too much space to a general idea better expressed with "concentrated" irony in the added epigraph from Martin Luther's translation of John into German: "We have a law and by that law he must die." The line refers, of course, to the indictment of Jesus, one often used, in turn, as a justification for killing Jews—hence its painfully ironic, Germanic place in a poem about anti-Semitism. Another possible title had been "Via Dolorosa" (a phrase that appears in the prose source), but it too was scratched out, perhaps because the parallelism threatened to subordinate Yolek's story to that of Jesus and to reproduce the very circumstances Hecht was seeking to redress. Perhaps, too, for similar reasons, Hecht dispensed with "breakfast" in favor of "meal," in order to avoid the miraculous, Eucharistic suggestions he saw in Bishop's sestina.

In any event, Hecht's chosen title imposes an element of Hebraic solemnity fully appropriate to the occasion, a title that distinguishes his poem from Geoffrey Hill's well-known, seasonally similar holocaust poem, "September's Song," first published in 1968, but which seems to have left little mark on Hecht's poem. Hill writes as an outsider in this poem, as indeed he must,[18] about an unnamed child, in which the only tangible connection is their common birth dates. His terse compacted ironies and structured gaps insinuate the indescribable nature of the subject matter, of which, to add only a further distancing note, the poet is fully aware of his own self-interested status as an elegist. By contrast, "The Book of Yolek" is an "interior monologue," a personal remembrance of a named other by an author implicated in the events.[19] Difficult in the writing, painful in subject matter, it is a means whereby art, using one set of laws, might counter what another kind of law had condemned: a form to act as a counterweight to the "close formation"

---

18. Gareth Reeves, "'This is plenty, this is more than enough,' Poetry and the Memory of the Second World War," in Tim Kendall, ed., *The Oxford Handbook of British and Irish War Poetry* (Oxford: Oxford University Press, 2007), 584–5.

19. In response to Harry Ford's puzzlement over the poem's speaker, Hecht wrote: "it is an interior monologue, and the speaker's mind wanders in the course of the poem, turning from personal recollection to matters of which he has read." Letter dated 1 September 1989.

that spelled the death of the Jewish children. Hecht praised Bishop in "Sestina" for deftly removing "herself except as the artificer of the work," but his way, his via dolorosa, in his sestina was to include elements of his own biography in the poem. Not that these interfered with his manifest control of the form, or the pressure he could exert on the most minute of details, even perhaps hinting at Yolek's continuing presence in the poem. His name keeps reappearing as an anagram in each stanza, made out of the final letters of the terminal words (*y, o, l, e, k*), but without ever quite spelling out his name in the manner of an acrostic.[20]

All the more remarkable to think, then, that if "Yolek" was the last poem finished before Hecht began the teaching semester in early September 1981, he must have been working on it in the August heat. It was also, as it turns out, the last of several important poems Hecht wrote with a German setting, "Rites and Ceremonies" and " 'More Light! More Light!' " having appeared in *The Hard Hours* (1967). Although he would continue to write poems about World War II—most notably "Sacrifice" in *The Darkness and the Light* (2001)—"The Book of Yolek" laid this specific ghost to rest, and along with it Hecht's experimentation with the sestina form, it too having been interrupted by war, as was true for his subject, but in Hecht's case, possible to recover and to finish in the name of art.

In its mixture of pity and terror, "The Book of Yolek" rarely fails to move an audience to renewed contemplation of the gravity of a little boy being led off to camp and, in the process, to assert the significance of poetry for its ability to concentrate thought and feeling in a small space. "Mine is the task to find out words / For their memorial sakes," Hecht wrote, without bravado (although with some irony since he was utilizing a hymn form made popular by Isaac Watts), in the aptly titled "Persistences," published a few years before he composed "The Book of Yolek." The latter poem seems in many ways the fulfillment of this task, now going one step further. It names

20. Jeff Balch raises this interesting possibility in a letter to Hecht, now in the Hecht Archive, dated 26 January 2003. Although responding to Balch's letter, Hecht did not speak of this matter, thus leaving it very much in the realm of mystery. The substance of Balch's argument and his exchange with Hecht are reported, along with a few errors of fact (Hecht had not been thinking about Yolek since 1942 but only sometime after 1973), in his brief essay, "Receiving Yolek: A New Look at Anthony Hecht's Holocaust Sestina," *Jewish Currents* (September 2007), 32–3.

and memorializes an otherwise lost child, indeed even nearly lost to his sympathizers who might be led to focus on the more famous Yanosz Korchak but not the child. "I have no words, only tears reading 'The Book of Yolek,'" reported one boyhood survivor from the concentration camp at Flossenbürg.[21]

And as great poems often do, this one tells us much in little: about the significant place of form in Hecht's poetry, whether as an abstract principle sometimes associated with a Platonic notion of beauty and perfection or, in the particular, with the process of composition itself, a "shaping activity" as Coleridge emphasized, in which an idea is coaxed into being by certain laws, a favorite word of Hecht's, yielding verse of a beautifully firm but flexible order.[22] The poem also points to the habitually dialectical quality of Hecht's thinking. For one kind of "camp," there is always another; one version of a sestina is ghosted by a second; a poet possessed by the beauty of form in numbers is equally possessed, but in an altogether different sense, with a "numeral tattoo." What is habitual can become mechanical but rarely so with Hecht. The road from "Sestina d'Inverno" need not automatically lead to a Sestina d'Inferno.

21. Email to me dated 31 March 2013, from Dr Jack Terry, the "Jakub" of *Jakub's World: A Boy's Story of Loss and Survival in the Holocaust.*
22. In her wonderfully open-ended account of form, Angela Leighton reminds us that "there are more than twenty dictionary definitions of the word, among them shape, design, outline, frame, ideal, figure, image, style, genre, order, etiquette, body, beauty, mould, lair, print-type, format, desk, grade, class." *On Form: Poetry, Aestheticism, and the Legacy of a Word* (Oxford: Oxford University Press, 2007), 2. I would hazard that all but the last three find a place in Hecht's thoughts, just as at one point or another he seems to have participated, either as practitioner or critic, in almost every account of "form" enunciated from the mid-eighteenth century to the present. A brief survey of Hecht's comments about form scattered throughout his writings, both critical and poetic, early and late, ranges, in the first category, from his earnestly learned 1950 Columbia University Master's thesis, "Poetry as a Form of Knowledge," largely New Critical in focus, with its emphasis on structure, texture, and the "dramaticality" of poetry, to his more spaciously conceived A. W. Mellon Lectures on the Fine Arts (1992), published in 1995 as *On The Laws of the Poetic Art*, and continuing on to his final essay "The Music of Forms." To these more generalized discussions, we can add any number of critical essays on specific topics, including those on rhyme, the sestina, and the sonnet in *Melodies Unheard*. As for poems that become little "ars poeticae," the possibilities for reflection (and self-reflection) on form are nearly endless. A list of the most important moments include (at least portions of) "The Gardens of the Villa d'Este," "A Hill," "The Cost," "Peripeteia," "The Transparent Man," "Matisse: Blue Interior with Two Girls—1947," "Proust on Skates," "An Orphic Calling," and "The Plastic and the Poetic Form (Goethe)."

So, too, "The Book of Yolek" points to a further constellation of related subjects: the ongoing place of war and suffering in his poetry, of course, as well as the role of memory more generally in his verse, its Wordsworthian pleasures of events recollected in tranquility, but also the ensuing nightmares, and of the complex relationship in his verse between narration and detail, in getting that difficult balance right, whether in the highly structured form of a sestina or the longer narrative poems of his middle and later years. And the poem reminds us, perhaps most significantly, of Hecht's complex identity as a culturally assimilated—and at times not so assimilated—Jewish American poet: a poet who could borrow a form rooted in Provençal France in the middle ages, that flowered in English in the Renaissance and became especially popular in the 1950s era of New Criticism, and yet could be turned in an altogether new and different direction as memory, compulsion, and aptitude required—in this case to incorporate no less a subject than the Holocaust. At the same time, for all his sympathy and understanding of Jewish customs and beliefs, one of the sacrifices this poet of Jewish birth refused to make was the sacrifice of art to ideology, of poetry to identity politics. In the initial sunlit preference for the poetic artifact following World War II, Hecht was slow to embrace his identity as a Jewish poet, as Chapters 2 and 3 will reveal; but having said that, I have little doubt that Hecht would, like some others of his generation of writers—again Bishop and Merrill spring to mind—prefer to think of himself as a poet without the accompanying adjective.

To some degree Hecht's is a story similar to that of many educated American poets who came of age in the immediate aftermath of World War II: how to absorb, rechannel, or reject the influence of the great generation of modern poets who were, in some cases, still living presences or only recently deceased—Yeats, Eliot, Pound, Frost, Stevens, and Williams—but in a context now that included Auden, whose powerful poem, "The Shield of Achilles," was one of many to make a lasting impression on Hecht, and the emerging Robert Lowell and Elizabeth Bishop. But matters of influence and reciprocation also necessarily came to involve the loose community of supremely talented poets born, like Hecht, in the 1920s, who learned much from each other and perhaps, of equal importance at least to Hecht, helped to sustain a belief in the value of traditional forms of poetic expression. I am thinking especially of Richard Wilbur, James Merrill, and John

Hollander, whose skill with formal verse, like Hecht's, remains unsur-
passed in the latter part of the twentieth century and yet who are
remarkably different from one another. But I am already getting ahead
of myself and had better return to the story itself, when Hecht was
lingering in Japan at the end of the war.

2

Circa 1950

Eclectic Hecht among the Nightingales

"As I recall," Hecht wrote to his parents in a letter dated 17 January 1946, while stationed in Japan:

Milton wrote a sonnet upon becoming twenty-three years old. Not only did he write a sonnet, but the damned thing has become immortal. Besides this, he'd written plenty of immortal stuff before he ever became twenty-three. Take the "Hymn on the Morning of Christ's Nativity," written, I believe, at the age of nineteen. Yet I, a dull and muddy-mettled rascal, peak like John a'dreams, unpregnant of my cause, and can write nothing, no, not for a world, upon whose property and most dear life a damn'd defeat was made. Ah, it cannot be but I am pigeon-livered, and lack the gall to make oppression bitter. For if I would, oh, what would come of it?[1]

Hecht had good reason to be thinking of Milton on this occasion. A day earlier, on 16 January, he had turned twenty-three, and if several allusions to Milton were not weight enough for a young poet eager to test his wings, his vivid impersonation of Hamlet ("O, what a rogue and peasant slave am I") only leant a further dampening touch of vexation to his disgruntled musings. To think that a war had been won, on your behalf, and yet not to have had the opportunity to write anything of consequence, beyond the odd article for *Stars and Stripes*, this was to feel a lack well beyond the usual case of authorial anxiety with regard to past poets. I doubt Hecht would have been much cheered at the time to learn that Milton wrote his "Nativity Ode" not at age nineteen, as he believed, but at twenty-one, indeed as a kind of parallel celebration of his and his Savior's December birthdays, or to be

---

1. Letter, AH to parents, 17 January 1946 (*SL*, 66).

e subject of Milton's sonnet also expressed a similar
lated poetic career.

out, Hecht was shortly to be discharged from the army,
ch of the same year. He would soon begin a lengthy
ship, including stops at Kenyon (where he studied under
John C. we Ransom, Allen Tate, and William Empson, and perhaps
first encountered Robert Lowell), Iowa (briefly, where he met Flannery
O'Connor), New York University (Tate again), Columbia (for the
MA), and the American Academy in Rome (as its first Fellow in
Literature in 1951), before he eventually published his first collection
of poetry, *A Summoning of Stones*, some eight years later in 1954. He
was still only thirty-one, hardly long in the tooth. Milton would be
thirty-seven when his first book of poems finally appeared. But compared to some of his contemporaries and friends, such as Richard
Wilbur and James Merrill, Hecht was unquestionably a late bloomer.
Wilbur had already published his second book, *Ceremony and Other
Poems* (1950) well before Hecht had completed his first, and Merrill,
younger than Hecht by a few years, was also already in print, first with
the limited edition publication of *The Black Swan* in 1946, and then
more substantially and widely with *First Poems* in 1951. As early as
November 1950, Hecht confided in a letter to Wilbur that he had
come down to the island of Ischia off the coast of Naples "hoping to
work hard and get a book of poems finished by spring."[2] But it would
require several more years of work before he would have a manuscript
to send to Allen Tate for his scrutiny.

Many years later, offering encouragement to a younger poet, Hecht
recalled the problems associated with putting together this first volume
of poetry:

I remember the curious anguish that went into the assembly of my own
first book. I would write a couple of new poems, and deem them better
than anything written previously. So when I began to think in terms of a
book I would cut out the earliest work to make room for the later, not so
much out of eagerness to avoid having a book too long, but to avoid invidi-
ous comparisons (as I imagined) between early work and late. This process
went on for an embarrassingly long time. Each new poem was, as it were, the
death of an earlier one...[3]

2. Letter, AH to Richard Wilbur, 15 November 1950 (*SL*, 88–9).
3. Letter, AH to B. H. Fairchild, 7 June 1993 (*SL*, 254–5).

Among the poems cut were several early war poems, "To a Soldier Killed in Germany" and "A Friend Killed in the War," and a curious poem bearing the more obscure Hardyesque title "Once Removed," in which the speaker confronts, rather histrionically, a nightmarish wasteland of sorts:

> The air was convulsed, the water split its face on the stones,
> And the bitter weather rounded about my soul;
> And nothing at all was there to interpret the groans
> Or the palsy of the trees.
> And seeing this broken landscape tied by the wind together,
> I wanted to drop down on my paper knees,
> And become some wind-bitten plant, and bend in the weather,
> And I wanted to scream.[4]

What these early poems have in common is an uncomfortably visceral, mannered response to violence, as in these lines from "To a Soldier Killed in Germany":

> What wonder hit you, turned you inside out,
> Shaking all wonders from you at one blow?
> You could not doubt it was an honest ghost
> Because it killed all doubts, gave you that most
> Terrible killing wound. You could not know
> Doubt is the wound we cannot do without.[5]

Or in the sestet to the sonnet from "A Friend Killed in the War":

> In the clean brightness of magnesium
> Flares, there were seven angels by a tree.
> Their hair flashed diamonds, and they made him doubt
> They were not really from Elysium.
> And his flesh opened like a peony,
> Red at the heart, white petals furling out.[6]

One can certainly understand why a poet, especially a poet who spent a year at the American Academy in Rome, might wish to exclude these from a first volume of poems. Each is embarrassing in a different way—the poet with the "paper knees," an imaginary

---

4. *The Kenyon Review* 9 (Spring, 1947), 222.
5. *The Kenyon Review* 9 (Spring, 1947), 223.
6. Originally published in *Furioso* (Spring, 1948), I quote from the reprinted version in *Poetry* 198 (September, 2011), 447–8, introduction by David Yezzi, 441–4.

review might say of the first, the student of stichomythia in the second, the practitioner of the pretty metaphor of the third, one abruptly concluded by a shocking floral deflowering. Yes, stilted and awkward in their attempt to deal with violence; and yet in some ways, I wish these poems had been included for the same reasons Hecht wished to keep them out: because, in not belonging, they hint at a substrata of raw experience that forecast the writer Hecht would become in *The Hard Hours* better than many of the poems in *A Summoning of Stones*, although he certainly couldn't see so at the time, in 1954.

Hecht's first book of poems is very much of a piece: highly polished, stylistically inventive, now even a collector's item, having never been reprinted in full; and it is of interest today largely for what it tells us of Hecht's development as a poet in the 1950s—his affiliations, his friendships, his poetic models, what he took with him, and what he had to leave behind. At the time of its completion, Hecht remarked to Allen Tate in January 1952: "At last I think I have got enough for a book. It's about time, I suppose, but I'm rather glad I've taken this long. The book will represent quite a variety of style and development, and if this is good for nothing else, it may keep me from being 'typed' as a poet with a specialized talent."[7] In the early 1950s, it would not have occurred to Hecht (or to many east coast poets at the time apart from the emerging Creeley–Olson circle) that an interest in formal variety would, in fact, lead him to be later "typed" as a "formalist," which in turn would be used to reduce him, in the eyes of some, to "a specialized talent." In "A Little Cemetery," a group of unpublished "epitaphs" dating from the 1960s, Hecht can already be found kicking against this attempted reduction: "Here lies a poet briefly known as Hecht, / Whose verse was damned as being 'too correct' / By diverse rhapsodes whose unlettered song / Was fluent and conspicuously wrong." But in the letter to Tate, Hecht was thinking, rather, of the stylistically varied landscape of poets represented individually and collectively by Yeats, Auden, Eliot, Stevens, Hardy, Herbert, Donne, Dylan Thomas, and, among other possibilities, the "dolce stil nuovo of Dante and his friends," as he noted in a letter to Howard Moss in 1953.[8]

---

7. Letter, AH to Allen Tate, 2 January 1952 (*SL*, 97).
8. Letter, AH to Howard Moss, 4 December 1953.

Arthur Mizener rightly recognized *Stones* at the time for what it was—its eclectic status belonging to a "period style":

> We have, after all, been living for nearly half a century in an almost continuous poetic revolution, a preservation of the dialect of the tribe by drastic surgery. During the last decade or so, this revolution has been slowing down; as it does, poets become more interested in mastering the established style and using it than in making a new style for themselves. In poets like Mr. Hecht, and say, Mr. Wilbur, the period style seems to be emerging pretty clearly. It is an eclectic style, a composite of means developed by earlier 20th Century poets.[9]

Mastery is surely what we meet right off in *Stones*. The collection is introduced by the highly acrobatic "Double Sonnet," as if Hecht, the poet, were summoning Mozart, the musician, writing a Sonata for two pianos or four hands. (A reference to Mozart's *Figaro* will appear later in the collection; to piano playing in "Double Sonnet.") The 28-line poem is constructed not by appending two sonnets of fourteen lines apiece—nothing so simple as that—but by stitching together two Petrarchan octaves out of just two rhymes and a single sentence on the courtly topic of love, which turns out to have art as its real subject; followed by a second single sentence to make up the twelve-line, double sestet, the first with a *c-d-e* rhyme, the second reversing the order, *e-d-c*. For the full effect, and surely it is the full effect that is important, the poem needs to be presented in its entirety:

> I recall everything, but more than all,
> Words being nothing now, an ease that ever
> Remembers her to my unfailing fever,
> How she came forward to me, letting fall
> Lamplight upon her dress till every small
> Motion made visible seemed no mere endeavor
> Of body to articulate its offer,
> But more a grace won by the way from all
> Striving in what is difficult, from all
> Losses, so that she moved but to discover
> A practice of the blood, as the gulls hover,
> Winged with their life, above the harbor wall,
> Tracing inflected silence in the tall
> Air with a tilt of mastery and quiver
> Against the light, as the light fell to favor
> Her coming forth; this chiefly I recall.

9. Mizener, "Transformations," *Kenyon Review* 16 (Summer, 1954), 479.

> It is a part of pride, guiding the hand
> At the piano in the splash and passage
> Of sacred dolphins, making numbers human
> By sheer extravagance that can command
> Pythagorean heavens to spell their message
> Of some unlooked-for peace, out of the common;
> Taking no thought at all that man and woman,
> Lost in the trance of lamplight, felt the presage
> Of the unbidden terror and bone hand
> Of gracelessness, and the unspoken omen
> That yet shall render all, by its first usage,
> Speechless, inept, and totally unmanned.

Many years later, fellow poet John Hollander remembered having been "impressed at the time by the artful, imaginatively purposeful 'Double Sonnet.'"[10] For Mizener, the literary critic, the poem served mainly as evidence of the "composite" style, audible in this case in the echo from Hart Crane in the lines about the hovering gull. (Mizener had already mentioned a more general debt owed by the practitioners of the "period style" to Wallace Stevens' habit of elevated, continually dilated sentences, as found in this poem.) If one wanted to look further back in time, a reader might sense in the poet's "recall" a recollection of Thomas Wyatt's famous poem, "They flee from me who sometimes did me seek."[11] Although the poem concludes with a disconcerting reference at the end to "the presage / Of the unbidden terror and bone hand / Of gracelessness," which are in turn attributed to "pride," mentioned in the first line of the sestet, the consequences are felt in the realm of art only, of which

---

10. Hollander, "On Anthony Hecht," *Raritan* 17 (1997), 140.
11. To take a wider and more detailed look at the collection's composite style: along with the reference to Crane, Mizener noted echoes of Yeats and Stevens in "A Poem to Julia," to which one could add by way of echo or allusion, Dylan Thomas and George Herbert in the neatly shaped stanzas of "La Condition Botanique" and "The Gardens of the Villa d'Este," the latter a poem that pays tribute as well to some of Auden's essayistic poems, such as "In Praise of Limestone," with its characteristic turn of address at the end to another who hadn't yet figured into the poem; and Auden again from "Musée des Beaux Arts" in "At the Frick"; Allen Tate, not of "The Ode to the Confederate Dead," which is too serious for this volume (although not for "Rites and Ceremonies" in the next), but the urbane quatrains of "Mr Pope" in Hecht's "Samuel Sewall"; Tate's student Robert Lowell in the strenuous use of syntax and adjective in "A Valentine" ("February; the untented blizzard treads / Against us, and again the poor must heel / Into the weather with embattled heads"); and even Pound imitating the troubadours in "Imitation"; and Eliot in "Whispers of Immortality" on Webster in "The Place of Pain in the Universe."

this poem is a prime exhibit and demonstration, and not the "unbidden terror" of war.

In the right hands, Hecht's, that is—and Mizener recognized Hecht's talent—what is highly wrought could also be readily reshaped. Even by the standards of "Cold War" poetry's devotion to artifice, one of the more astonishing effects of *Stones* is the elaborate construction of stanzas, especially in those poems associated with gardens. "La Condition Botanique," for instance (the Stevensian French is misleadingly local) serves as an excuse to wander through a wide variety of vegetal locales and effects, from "Ischian springs" to "Brooklyn's botanical gardens," with the ever abundant imagination of the poet producing amply rounded stanza after stanza, nineteen in all, only to be visually topped by the more exquisite topiary of "The Gardens of the Villa d'Este," a poem based on the famous locale just outside of Rome. Eight lines apiece per stanza, instead of six, the poem has more room for expansion and contraction, which it does with mathematical precision by adding and then subtracting one foot per line, as in the following sample:

> But, ah, who ever saw
> Finer proportion kept. The sum
> Of intersecting limbs was something planned.
> Ligorio, the laurel! Every turn and quirk
> Weaves in this waving green and liquid world to work
> Its formula, binding upon the gland,
> Even as molecules succumb
> To Avogadro's law.

This is a poem for the eye as well as the ear. As is true with garden wandering more generally, it matters less where we step and more where we pause to take in the view. Hecht is addressing in this stanza the famous sixteenth-century Italian garden designed by Pirro Ligorio, plucking a few leaves from Andrew Marvell's "The Garden" along the way, which is also written in perfectly proportioned stanzas of a different order, as is true for the more distantly meandering patronage poem, "Upon Appleton House."[12] Here, in Hecht, the rhyme scheme is part

---

12. Further evidence of Hecht's long-standing interest in Marvell's two poems can be found in two critical studies, "Shades of Keats and Marvell," and "Houses as Metaphors: The Poetry of Architecture," both collected in *Obbligati: Essays in Criticism* (New York: Atheneum, 1986), 230–60 and 290–326, respectively.

of the fine symmetry, going up and down the scale, step by step (*a, b, c, d, d, c, b, a*), as the poet registers a sense of continuous movement and delight in what he sees in this profusely baroque garden of "waving green and liquid world"—the latter made in reference to belaureled Ligorio's clever and abundant use of water throughout the garden. Neither garden poem, "Villa d'Este" or "Botanique," has much of a message beyond exhibiting the poet's already considerable descriptive ability, mixed with erudition—who is Avogadro, non-Italians might ask?—although "La Condition Botanique" skates close to the subject of war in a few places in the process of asking "But what's become of Paradise?" In "Villa d'Este," that question becomes the underlying condition for discussions of aesthetics:

> It was in such a place
> That Mozart's Figaro contrived
> The totally expected. This is none
> Of your French Topiary, geometric works,
> Based on God's rational, wrist-watch universe; here lurks
> The wood louse, the night crawler, the homespun
> Spider; here are they born and wived
> And bedded, by God's grace.

As close as they are in look and subject matter, the two garden poems, in their differences, hint at a universal law underlying *Stones* and the eclectic style more generally: that no two poems shall be formally identical, not even in the case of sonnets. Indeed, the concept of the "Double Sonnet" gets redirected into the center of the collection, where there are two sonnets, almost doubles of each other, one called "Katharsis" the other "Imitation," as if representing two sides of an Aristotelian coin. But not only do they not mirror "Double Sonnet" in their two-ness, but they differ subtly from each other formally, for while Hecht replicates the rhyme scheme in the octaves, he varies them in the sestets. Elsewhere we discover a variety of poems in different sizes and shapes: songs, verse epistles, meditations, arranged, though, not according to genre or kind but more along the lines of a poetic miscellany, in which the jostle of one poem against the other is part of the "design." "To call the stones themselves to their ideal places, and enchant the very substance and skeleton of the world" is the brave epigraph to the collection from Santayana. The elegantly Yeatsian meditation, "A Poem to Julia," appears next to the more rowdy "Song of the Beasts"; "Japan" is a poem away from "La Condition Botanique."

"The Place of Pain in the Universe" fronts up against the more apparently ethereal "As Plato Said," a poem that turns out, however, to be
about the compelling law of erotic love in the world. This, in turn, is
followed by the corrective "Discourse Concerning Temptation."

A composite indeed, the stones are many, their Orphic summoner
single, but how singular the mosaic? In identifying Hecht as part of the
emerging period style, Mizener mentions Richard Wilbur, no doubt
in part because of Wilbur's precocious visibility with his first book,
The Beautiful Changes and Other Poems (1947). And "eclectic" that volume certainly is. From the start, Wilbur seems to have understood the
lyric as representing variety, a mix of poems that might individually
end, as Frost famously noted, "in a clarification of life—not necessarily
a great clarification, such as sects and cults are founded on, but in a
momentary stay against confusion."[13] Frost made that remark in 1939,
as World War II was closing in, and Wilbur, who was deeply influenced
by Frost and who fought on the European front, took the poet's remark
as his personal poetic credo in the immediate aftermath of the war,
beginning in 1947, and continuing through *Ceremony* (1950) and
beyond. "Cicadas," the first poem in *The Beautiful Changes*, in fact,
pays double homage to Frost. It sounds like colloquial Frost from the
start, "You know those windless summer evenings, swollen to stasis /
by too-substantial melodies." And it makes appealing the modesty of the
cricket's "song": "This thin uncomprehended song it is / springs heal-
ing questions into binding air," the poem enwrapping the song to
serve as a momentary stay against confusion.

From the start, too, among his contemporaries, Hecht admired no
poet more than Wilbur, admiration that deepened into a friendship and
occasional imitation that would last for half a century and be formally
capped by writing ballades for each other late in life: Hecht while
introducing Wilbur for a reading at the Library of Congress in 1993,
Wilbur in celebration of Hecht's eightieth birthday in 2003. Indeed,
Irving Weiss, living in the town of Forio on the island of Ischia in the
early 1950s when Hecht was there, much later recalled Hecht's early
admiration for Wilbur's "Tennysonian fluency" as well as Hecht's familiarity with Dylan Thomas' "reading performances and escapades."[14] And

---

13. Frost, *Collected Poems, Prose, and Plays* (New York: Library of America, 1995), 776–8.
14. Email, Irving Weiss to Jonathan Post, 10 July 2011. Weiss notes the adjective Tennysonian
    is his, but it seems perfectly apt, especially since Hecht describes Tennyson as a source
    for Wilbur's fluency in "Richard Wilbur," *Obbligati*, 135.

in the 1950 letter to Wilbur already cited, the two poets can be seen exchanging praise for each other's work which had appeared together in an issue of *Poetry*: Wilbur for two poems that became part of *Stones* ("To Phyllis," the final poem in "Songs for the Air," and "Alceste in the Wilderness"); and Hecht for "Castles and Distances" and "A World without Objects is a Sensible Emptiness," both to appear shortly in *Ceremony and Other Poems*. The former, in its combination of fluency and stanzaic shapeliness, left its mark on Hecht in his artfully fanciful foragings in "Villa d'Este."

In certain ways, it's possible to chart early parallels between the two along the path suggested by Mizener. Their formal variety and technical skill, versed in the rich tradition of the English lyric, speak of their coming of age as American poets under the rising sign of Auden, who had moved to the United States in 1940 and whom Wilbur was later to commemorate, in ways Hecht surely would approve, for sustaining "the civil tongue / In a scattering time."[15] As part of the overall lyricization of poetry, there can be little question that formal variety emerges as a feature of their interest in similar topics.[16] Music and art, songs and paintings, are chief among them, as well as an interest in landscape, especially gardens—all serving, in one way or another, as metaphors for talking about poetry. Along with the usual seasonal poem ("Springtime," from the French of Charles d'Orléans, and "Spring for Thomas Hardy" by Hecht; "Winter Spring" and "Praise in Summer" by Wilbur), there are odd meditations on airy topics, as in the case of Wilbur's "Sun and Air" and Hecht's "Songs for the Air or Several Attitudes about Breathing." The lyrics of each are occasionally shadowed by memories of war. In *The Beautiful Changes*, we see the subject directly addressed in Wilbur's well-known poem in *terza rima* "First Snow in Alsace," but also as deflected into other topics in this collection, as in the case of "Up, Jack," which is about Falstaff's famously playing dead in the climactic battle scene involving Hotspur at the end of Shakespeare's *1 Henry IV*. Hecht mixed moods on this topic: the more comical or festive in "Drinking Song," the more serious and apprehensive in

15. "For W. H. Auden," in Wilbur, *New and Collected Poems* (San Diego: Harcourt, Brace, Jovanovich, 1988).

16. This process receives much coverage in Virginia Jackson and Yopie Prins, eds., *The Lyric Theory Reader: A Critical Anthology* (Baltimore: Johns Hopkins University Press, 2014), 1–8 ("General Introductions"); and, more immediately relevant to Wilbur and Hecht, 159–65 ("Anglo-American New Criticism").

"A Deep Breath at Dawn"—to which we will return later in this chapter—and "Christmas is Coming."

Still, for all their similarities, few would confuse the first books of each. With regard to poetic influences, Frost would go on to play a part in later Hecht, but not in this first volume, and never the Frost that caught Wilbur's attention from the beginning, the ventriloquized, New England-sounding nature poet of "Cicadas." And while both poets drew on Stevens, it was largely a different Stevens in each case. For Wilbur, it was the dandified poet having fun with the imagination that appealed to him. Although the figurally fanciful Stevens was important to Hecht (as in "Seascape with Figures"), he was nonetheless drawn to the more philosophical and solitary Stevens—the Stevens whose amatory repression was worth poking fun at in "Divisions upon a Ground" (the title later changed—and the only change Hecht made in the 1967 reduced regathering of *Stones*—to "Le Masseur de my Soeur," to recollect Stevens' "Le Monocle de Mon Oncle"), and yet also the Stevens who could be solemnly invoked in the final poem of the volume, "A Lesson from the Master." As time went on, these differences in influence would continue, but in the case of Hecht the matter of influence itself would become more pronounced and inclusive, spreading its mantle to include writers ranging widely across the canon of literature in English, past and present, as distant in time as Shakespeare and as diverse and immediate as Eliot, Lowell, Bishop, and Merrill.

Wilbur's first book has rightfully become something of a landmark in the history of twentieth-century lyric poetry. It captures perfectly the post-World War II, New Critical mood with its concentrated focus on the poem as a detached aesthetic object worthy of repeated readings. On its own, *The Beautiful Changes* remains a remarkable achievement. It established at the outset a style that, however much a composite, was distinctly Wilbur's and which required from its author mainly finer tuning as the century unfolded. A Wilbur poem is often a perfectly controlled balancing of opposites by a poet enviably at home in the world, who knows his limits, even if, much later in "Mayflies," for instance, he admitted to the solitary aspect of life imposed by his calling.

A Summoning of Stones is a more typical first book—as is true, surprisingly, with Milton's *Poems* (1645). Its lyric variety is a feature of its initiating occasion: not by offering an annunciatory Nativity Ode, as Hecht recalled in his twenty-third birthday letter to his parents in

1946, or even a single sonnet, as Milton produced on the occasion of his twenty-third birthday, but a double sonnet, as we know, with the subsequent titles of poems in the volume often setting the stage for a rhetorical performance: "As Plato Said," "Discourse Concerning Temptation," "Fugue for One Voice," "A Deep Breath at Dawn," "Speech," "Harangue," "A Lesson from the Master." To tweak John Stuart Mill's formulation,[17] if Wilbur's poetry is overheard, much of Hecht's is designed to be heard, the attention to "eloquence" even figuring into the two stanzas of Hecht's attractive little poem "Speech."

> I have discouraged that in me
> Wherewith I most advance:
> Too easy eloquence of speech,
> A sailing present tense;
> Fearing that if the mind conspires
> Mainly to please the lip,
> Time will point out the flattery,
> The language will not grip.

The second stanza will favor a more spontaneous form of utterance, but what's interesting is not that Hecht shifts the rhetorical occasion from speech to silence, from what is heard to what is overheard, but to another mode of direct address.

> But when the talker's sleight of tongue
> Required us to laugh,
> Proving the agile, unrehearsed,
> Triumphantly pays off,
> Then praise was for a kind of art
> Whereof there is no school;
> There the unlettered instinct rides
> In all its bodily skill.

The conditions for dramatic address remain fully in place—a speaker, an audience, only the manner has changed, as if we shifted from Ciceronian euphony, as in Falstaff's great parody of it in *1 Henry IV*, to the agile wit of Touchstone in *As You Like It*.[18]

17. "Eloquence is *heard*, poetry is *overheard*," as quoted in *The Lyric Theory Reader*, 3.
18. Much later, in an illuminating and revealing discussion of poetic apprenticeship, Hecht cites "the great scene (2.4)" in which "Falstaff 'plays' the King" as an example of Shakespeare recycling Lyly's *Euphues: The Anatomy of Wit*. Letter, AH to Messrs Tigani and Wright, 3 November 1999 (*SL*, 305–6).

Overlapping in their interests, we might even imagine Wilbur and Hecht entering into a kind of garden poetry competition, if only to further particularize differences in their poetics at this stage in their careers. If a reader didn't know already, few would suspect, for instance, that the garden described in "Caserta Garden" in *The Beautiful Changes* belongs to one of the most elaborate estates in southern Italy. So Frost-like is the setting and the sound of the sentence, we might as well be in New England. It begins:

> Their garden has a silent tall stone-wall
> So overburst with drowsing trees and vines,
> None but a stranger would remark at all
> The barrier within the fractured lines.
>
> I doubt they know it's there, or what it's for—
> To keep the sun-impasted road apart,
> The beggar, soldier, renegade and whore,
> The dust, the sweating ox, the screeching cart.

Wilbur invites us at every turn to overhear colloquial speech while meditating on the meaning of a "silent tall stone-wall."

By contrast, here is Hecht at the beginning of "The Gardens of the Villa d'Este," already in full "bel canto" mode. He knows where he is, "*bella Italia,*" and what the magnificent local setting requires of him:

> This is Italian. Here
> Is cause for the undiminished bounce
> Of sex, cause for the lark, the animal spirit
> To rise, aerated, but not beyond our reach, to spread
> Friction upon the air, cause to sing loud for the bed
> Of jonquils, the linen bed, and established merit
> Of love, and grandly to pronounce
> Pleasure without peer.

Many years later, Hecht would praise Wilbur's skill at placing "pivotal and energetic verbs" in rhyming positions to give fluency, strength, and grace to his poetry, a practice Hecht would adapt to great effect in poems like "The Cost," the first poem in *Millions of Strange Shadows* (1977).[19] But here fluency is in the service of abundance, copiousness, spreading out, breadth, and breath: of pronouncing. It finds its figural

19. "Richard Wilbur," in *Obbligati*, 131.

source in the many-breasted goddesses of the water fountain, the
description of which spills out over three stanzas:

> The whole garden inclines
>   The flesh as water falls, to seek
> For depth. Consider the top balustrade,
> Where twinned stone harpies, with domed and virgin breasts,
> Spurt from their nipples that no pulse or hand has pressed
>   Clear liquid arcs of benefice and aid
>   To the chief purpose. They are Greek
>   Versions of valentines
>
>   And spend themselves to fill
>   The celebrated flumes that skirt
> The horseshoe stairs. Triumphant then to a sluice
> With Brownian movement down to the giggling water drops
> Past haunches, over ledges, out of mouths, and stops
>   In a still pool, but, by a plumber's ruse,
>   Rises again to laugh and squirt
>   At heaven, and is still
>
>   Busy descending. White
>   Ejaculations leap to teach
> How fertile are these nozzles; the streams run
> Góngora through the garden, channel themselves, and pass
> To lily-padded ease, where insubordinate lass
>   And lad can cool their better parts, where sun
>   Heats them again to furnace pitch
>   To prove his law is light.

"The Gardens of the Villa d'Este" appeared in *The Kenyon Review* in
the spring of 1953. In October 1955, *The New Yorker* published Wilbur's
"A Baroque Wall-Fountain in the Villa Sciarra." Wilbur has picked up
Hecht's flair for the baroque, immediately and gracefully at the outset
in the water's movement:

> Under the bronze crown
>   Too big for the head of the stone cherub whose feet
>   A serpent has begun to eat,
> Sweet water brims a cockle and braids down
>
>   Past spattered mosses, breaks
>   On the tipped edge of a second shell, and fills
>   The massive third below. It spills
> In threads then from the scalloped rim, and makes
>
>   A scrim or summary tent
> For a faun-ménage and their familiar goose.

The baroque fountain waterfall, in all its pagan sensuousness, serves to call to mind, as it so often does in Wilbur, the opposite, imposing a limit to excess in the figure of the struggling upward ascent of water in "the plain fountains that [Carlo] Maderna set / Before St. Peter's." Against Hecht's fertile ejaculations, Wilbur's poem is perfectly proportioned. It dedicates seven stanzas apiece to reflect the opposing values associated with each fountain: pagan pleasures versus Christian renunciation, sensuousness versus asceticism, body versus soul, intricate versus plain; and then concludes the whole on something of a balancing note, in which the figure of St. Francis enters the poem near the end and sees ("perhaps") earth as a shadow of heaven. The original magazine version perfectly captured the poem's balance: the poem was printed in double columns, with the last stanza, the fifteenth, placed in the middle underneath.

Enter W. H. Auden, not as judge for a competition that perhaps never was, nor as the source of inspiration he certainly proved to be for each, but as helpful commentator to a youthful Hecht seeking advice on some of his early poems. Auden and Hecht had become acquainted while living on Ischia in the early 1950s. On one important occasion that served as the subject of two separate letters written by Hecht in October 1951, one to his parents, the other to Allen Tate, Hecht reported in detail about a two-and-a-half hour "interview" with Auden, in which "he went over each one of my poems very carefully."[20] Auden's observations fell mainly into two related categories. He felt that Hecht had "been too much influenced by Ransom and Tate, not in style but in theory," and as a consequence Auden was critical of the overabundance of detail in the younger man's poetry. "He feels," wrote Hecht,

that details are an ornamental embellishment to verse and should never be allowed to distract the reader's attention from the main line of discourse, whereas I believe that the details should be made to subsume, to contain, to embody, to incarnate the point and meaning of the poem...He said of the "Aubade" for example (the one coming out in Kenyon [retitled in Stones as "A Deep Breath at Dawn"]) that there was too much detail, that the poem could have been written in the same number of stanzas, but with each stanza of four lines instead of ten.

Hecht went on to summarize:

And I think he may be right most of all in saying (as he said to the Rosenthals [mutual Ischian friends] but not to me) that my verse was perhaps too

20. The two letters can be found in SL, 93-6.

formal—not in the metrical sense, but in being somewhat impersonal in tone, disengaged from the central emotions of the poems. This is mainly what he has against Ransom and Tate, and with many qualifications, he's right.

I think, too, Auden was right, but Hecht also took away from their meeting some important words of encouragement. He reported Auden liking

> best of all the poem I sent to <u>Poetry</u> called "La Condition Botanique." And he told Ray and Elsa Rosenthal the next day, that he thought my poetry was better than most of the younger poets, specifically Wilbur's and Shapiro's—though I don't see how Shapiro gets into the "younger" category any more.

Auden's praise for "Botanique" was probably instrumental in Hecht's further experimentations in "The Gardens of the Villa d'Este," which bears the sign of Auden's influence not just in the speaker's greater emotional engagement with his subject but also in echoing the loose, essayistic devices from Auden's engagingly spacious poem "In Praise of Limestone," the focus of a later critical essay by Hecht.[21] And, no doubt Hecht must have been encouraged by the comparison with Wilbur.

Ornamentation would always remain an important part of Hecht's poetry, right down to his final poems, including the beautiful "Aubade" he wrote for his wife in 2004, the year of his death;[22] but even at this early stage in his career, he revealed reluctance to endorse completely Auden's strictures about detail. With regard to the early "Aubade" published in 1951 in *The Kenyon Review*, Hecht did not attempt to reduce each stanza to four lines apiece, needless to say. Auden was speaking only hypothetically about what "could have been written." But consistent with his thoughts about the function of detail, indeed perhaps spurred by his conversation with Auden, Hecht did make some important changes to this early war poem, including the change of title from "Aubade" to "A Deep Breath at Dawn." The revised title is better attuned to the action of the poem, the meaning incarnated in the details. It calls attention to the drama of the event being described, to the suspended, indrawn moment of time as perceived by the speaker, waiting for the possible reappearance for the spirit of a comrade slain in war at a similar time of day when the sun came up and—note the elocutionary moment—"the cocks cried brazenly against all ghosts."

21. "On W. H. Auden's 'In Praise of Limestone,'" in *Obbligati*, 27–50. The essay was originally published in *The New England Review* (Autumn, 1979).
22. The poem appeared in the 21 October 2004 issue of *The New York Review of Books*.

Moreover, the image of "breathing" is associated with life, "breath" with "death," and a deep breath drawn at dawn serves as a figure of speech that anticipates the hushed worries of their possible meeting:

> What if he came and stood beside my tree,
> A poor, transparent thing with nothing to do,
> His chest showing a jagged vacancy
> Through which I might admire the distant view?

The new title also justifies the decision to extend the descriptive moment to include a full, ten-line Yeatsian inhale:

> Morning has come at last. The rational light
> Discovers even the humblest thing that yearns
> For heaven; from its scaled and shadeless height,
> Figures its difficult way among the ferns,
> Nests in the trees, and is ambitious to warm
> The chilled vein, and to light the spider's thread
> With modulations hastening to a storm
> Of the full spectrum, rushing from red to red.
> I have watched its refinements since the dawn,
> When, at the birdcall, all the ghosts were gone.

Much later, in conversation with Philip Hoy, Hecht was to speak of this poem "as too fanciful and unreal, and almost embarrassing," especially with respect to the lines "about admiring a distant view through the shell-penetrated body of a dead soldier."[23] A strange image indeed: the problem, as Hecht realized, is not with too much detail here but simply a poor use of it in the rendering of violence, a problem that plagued the earlier war poems cut from *Stones*. In this poem, there is much to admire in the abundant descriptions, enough to warrant including the poem in the reduced version of *Stones* that reappeared, along with *The Hard Hours*, in 1967. But hypothetically admiring the distant view of a landscape through a hole in the chest is to make the violence of war an aesthetic event, one in keeping with the general artfulness of *Stones*. Hecht could improve the poem, as he did in rewriting the poem's ending—the earlier *Kenyon Review* version concludes with the image of Mars "drooling and gurgling like a child"—but he could not rewrite the underlying premise of the poem, which the new title only makes more melodramatically explicit.

23. *Anthony Hecht in conversation with Philip Hoy* (1999; rev. 3rd edn. London: BTL, 2004), 44.

Pace Auden, but at this stage in their careers I think Wilbur was a better, certainly a more comfortable, writer of war poems than Hecht, small in number though these poems were. But Wilbur was not a war poet in the sense Jarrell used that term.[24] Hecht was, and, if "A Deep Breath at Dawn" could not be fully improved along Auden's lines, the circumstances it recounted could not be forgotten. As was the case with the sestina described in Chapter 1, some twenty-five years later Hecht returned to the earlier poem, in a manner of speaking, and wrote the exquisitely detailed but dramatically powerful and finely situated "Still Life," the title artfully indicating the primary tensions to be explored. The poem appears in *The Venetian Vespers* (1979). It is also one of the poems representing Hecht's work in *The Norton Anthology of Poetry* and thus has a further claim on our attention.

As with the earlier war poem, "Still Life" fully reimagines a dawn scene, again from a soldier's perspective, replete with "a visitant ghost" and tautly managed spider webs, and again with attention paid to the undeniable beauty of the moment, but now—Auden's advice remembered too?—figured in five stanzas of only six lines apiece, a tautly managed web, compared to the seven stanzas of ten lines each of the earlier poem. Exactly half as long, here it is in full:

> Sleep-walking vapor, like a visitant ghost,
>   Hovers above a lake
> Of Tennysonian calm just before dawn.
> Inverted trees and boulders waver and coast
> In polished darkness. Glints of silver break
> Among the liquid leafage, and then are gone.
>
> Everything's doused and diamonded with wet.
>   A cobweb, woven taut
> On bending stanchion frames of tentpole grass,
> Sags like a trampoline or firemen's net
> With all the glitter and riches it has caught,
> Each drop a paperweight of Steuben glass.
>
> No birdsong yet, no cricket, nor does the trout
>   Explode in water-scrolls
> For a skimming fly. All that is yet to come.
> Things are as still and motionless throughout
> The universe as ancient Chinese bowls,
>   And nature is magnificently dumb.

24. See p. ix.

Why does this so much stir me, like a code
    Or muffled intimation
Of purposes and preordained events?
It knows me, and I recognize its mode
Of cautionary, spring-tight hesitation,
This silence so impacted and intense.
As in a water-surface I behold
    The first, soft, peach decree
Of light, its pale, inaudible commands.
I stand beneath a pine-tree in the cold,
Just before dawn, somewhere in Germany,
A cold, wet, Garand rifle in my hands.

The later poem is hardly less "poetic" than the earlier one, as the mention of "Tennysonian calm" at the outset makes clear, but it wears its effects differently. As the title "Still Life" suggests, it seems a deliberate reconceiving of the earlier poem but from an opposite angle. The emphasis falls on what is not said rather than on the drama of speech; not on the drama of a "deep breath" being drawn at dawn, but on the silence and stillness associated with the pictorial arts, an association that allows Hecht to maintain, without making explicit, the connection of the genre of "Still Life" paintings with death, the great unspoken subject of the poem, and great because unspoken. Everything, we might say, pivots on the pun in the title, "Still Life," in the sense of somebody still being alive, the image deftly pictured at the poem's end. This is a poem that chooses not to make a statement about the horror (or pity) of war through a grotesque image or by meeting with a dead other. And yet that possibility is just around the corner, just over the horizon, just beyond the poem's ending, embedded in the details. No birdsong yet, but also no battles either—for the moment. The cricket has stopped chirping.

To look more carefully into the momentous pause: the middle stanza is crucial to achieving this sense of taut suspension, not just with its images, but by shadowing those images with further ghostly portents, as if change is present as well, just below the surface. It's hard not to think of Yeats' "Long-Legged Fly" in the context of the great silence here and the image of the skimming fly still (yet) unmolested. And if we recall Yeats' refrain—"like a long-legged fly upon the stream / His mind moves on the silence"—we might remember several of the violent scenarios to which the refrain is juxtaposed: the first beginning,

"That civilization may not sink," and the second, "That the topless towers be burnt." It may be equally difficult not to hear in the stillness of "ancient Chinese bowls" a reference to Eliot's famous "Chinese jar" that "moves perpetually in its stillness" in "Burnt Norton," and the associated sense in that passage of words straining, almost cracking, under the weight of meaning—what Hecht will call in the next stanza, "this silence so impacted and intense." And finer still might be the recollection in the line "And nature is magnificently dumb" of the apocalyptic moment in Marvell's "Upon Appleton House" associated with the intense calm produced by the evening appearance of the modest halcyon: "And such an horror calm and dumb / Admiring nature does benumb." Hecht has simply cut the corner here with the rhyme.

None of these resonances or references "serve to distract the reader's attention from the main line of discourse"—to return to Auden's criticism—but, if gathered, they do add to the ripple of meaning here, the suggestion of apocalyptic momentum also captured in the image of "water-scrolls" carrying their hidden meaning. And in a specific sense it might even be suggested that meaning is "incarnated" through the details, including these embellishments, since the speaker's intense consciousness of them becomes their locus: "Why does this so much stir me, like a code / Or muffled intimation / Of purposes and preordained events?" Is he speaking of nature? Or nature as also interpreted and remembered through art? "It knows me." Auden worried that earlier Hecht was "too disengaged from the central emotions of the poems." Here, post-*Hard Hours*, Hecht is the quiet center of the poem's consciousness. He's back where he was in the army "somewhere in Germany," the general address he used in his letters in order not to give away the location, but used here to spell out his location, "just before dawn," with "a cold, wet, Garand rifle in my hand."

In many respects, *A Summoning of Stones* furnished subjects that would invite further work besides war. Hecht's interest in music and art was equally long-standing and helped to offset (as in the case of "The Venetian Vespers") or to focus (as in "The Deodand") the violence at the center of much of his poetry. The volume also introduces us to the organizing means of Hecht's poetry, indeed his habitually dialectic thinking through contraries—not just in the juxtaposition of forms and subjects that would expand and intensify down to the final collection in *The Darkness and the Light* but with the resources of language: from a baroque fascination with plenitude and the polysyllabic phrase to a classical emphasis on diction that is simple, direct, and immediate. Perhaps because of his European travels, early and late, Hecht would always maintain a connection to the continent through translation, a large concept in Hecht involving his own literary and linguistic past, glimpsed in works like "Spring for Thomas Hardy" and poems with a foreign, often Italianate location such as "A Roman Holiday," with its bloody imperial setting in sharp contrast to "the undiminished bounce / Of sex" in "Villa d'Este." Late in life, Hecht too would return to retranslating some favorites first explored in *Stones*, such as Charles d'Orléans' "Springtime." Lowell remarked in "Reading Myself"—and it is to Lowell we soon shall turn in this chapter—"[I]somehow never wrote something to go back to." Hardly true for Lowell: "*repeat, repeat, repeat; revise, revise, revise,*" said Bishop in her elegy to Lowell in "North Haven," attending to his manic habits of revision, and not true for Hecht either, who nearly always did improve what he had written earlier, whether in draft or published form.

But rather than continuing with seeing *Stones* as a blueprint for a career, I want to offer a wide-angle perspective of Hecht in the 1950s and early 1960s. My intention in doing so is to complicate the usual narratives given of American poetry after World War II. As the separate studies by James Breslin and Marjorie Perloff indicate, 1950s poetry is frequently constructed as a set of evolving oppositions and propositions about verse, usually pitting "closed" against "open" forms.[25] Wilbur is singled out as the epitome of the first, as is the early Lowell of *Lord Weary's Castle* (1946); but then the Lowell of *Life Studies* (1959) migrates, anticipates, parallels, and in some cases prepares the way for the second, in which "openness" finds multiple manifestations in the writings of Charles Olson, Robert Creeley, Allen Ginsberg, Frank O'Hara, and Sylvia Plath, among others. Hecht is often ignored in these larger discussions of the evolution of poetic history, in part because he is usually identified, *sotto voce*, with Wilbur, but his own

---

25. Breslin, *From Modern to Contemporary: American Poetry, 1945–1965* (Chicago: University of Chicago Press, 1983), 23–76; Perloff, *Poetry On and Off the Page: Essays for Emergent Occasions* (Evanston, IL: Northwestern University Press, 1998), 83–115 ("'A Step Away from Them': Poetry 1956").

familiarity with Lowell, dating back to the late 1940s and early 1950s, suggests a more anomalous configuration and complex journey, a journey that is crucial in further distinguishing his verse from that of Wilbur's and, in its distinctively darker engagements, making it still more his own.

Hecht's relationship to Lowell might be characterized as that of a distantly respectful and talented younger sibling or half-brother. The two poets were born six years apart, the one a New England Puritan, with a mysteriously German-Jewish ancestor, the other Jewish but with the ceremonial instincts of an Episcopalian, with each discovering, for a while, a surrogate poetic father in Allen Tate, a lineage that Lowell eventually and altogether repudiated with the publication of *Life Studies*, with its notoriously intimate revelations of the author's person and family as new subjects for poetry. Hecht never broke with Tate in the same abrupt manner. Indeed, the last poem in *Millions of Strange Shadows* (1977), "The Lull," is dedicated to his former mentor. But it is clear that immediately after finishing *A Summoning of Stones* in 1953–54, Hecht began branching out into new territory, slowly, it must be noted, but doing so with the aid of Lowell's example (and friendship) in a number of specific ways that encouraged Hecht to loosen up biographically as well as poetically.

Indeed, one of Hecht's more deeply private poems, "The Vow," about his first wife's miscarriage in 1954—the most personal poem Hecht had written at this stage in his career—was also among the first poems written and published after *Stones*. It appeared in 1957 in both *The Hudson Review* and *New Poets of England and America* (edited by Donald Hall, Robert Pack, and Louis Simpson), and it developed, Hecht remarked, in part from "a poem on this subject by Robert Lowell which appeared in his first book, 'Land of Unlikeness.'" (The unidentified poem is almost certainly "The Boston Nativity.") Hecht then hastened to add, in a note found among his papers at Emory but which serves as the draft for his comments accompanying the poem's inclusion in *Poet's Choice*, edited by Paul Engle and Joseph Langland (1962):

I decided not to look at his (and I only dimly remembered it) until I had finished mine, lest I be even unconsciously influenced by mood or tone. I did look at his after mine was done, and was glad to see how different they were, but I feel I still owe him a debt of gratitude for giving me by his example the courage to tackle a difficult and unpleasant subject.

That debt of gratitude noted here—Hecht's poem will be discussed in Chapter 3—would eventually be repaid publically in a richly detailed essay Hecht later published on Lowell, collected in *Obbligati* (1986). Based on a lecture delivered in 1983 while he was Consultant in Poetry at the Library of Congress, Hecht argued for a higher critical ground on which to evaluate Lowell's poetry—if not altogether apart, then at least at several removes from the notoriety surrounding the author, especially in light of his untimely death in 1977 and the rather quick publication in 1982 of Ian Hamilton's biography. At a crucial point in the argument, Hecht remarks,

Instead, I want to indicate what strikes me, and furthermore, I would like to claim, must have struck Lowell himself, as a remarkable, over-arching design to his poetry, a thematic recapitulation or recurrence that resonates from the early work to the very latest with hollow and mordant overtones. It expresses itself, early and late, as a domestic drama of a bitter and terrifying kind, and early exhibits itself in "Thanksgiving's Over."[26]

For my purposes, Hecht's choice of poems is illuminating, indeed perhaps more surprising than the familiar topic of domestic drama in Lowell itself, a subject that nonetheless still receives in Hecht's essay the pressure of urgency only a fellow traveler (and laborer) might give it. For as far back as 1951, "Thanksgiving's Over" was among those poems to which early Hecht was drawn. In fact, it is one of the few by a contemporary poet that actually filters into his early letters. "I saw that poem of Lowell's in <u>Partisan</u>," Hecht wrote to his brother Roger, from Ischia on 16 January, again his own birthday, but now actively in the thick of things even from afar:

It is part of a long narrative poem about his own life, which he started to write quite some time ago, before his breakdown. Tate had told me about it, or had at least told me that he was writing such a poem. This particular part is apparently about Jean Stafford's breakdown, with some of the imagery and ideas (especially the confusion between the plastic bird with bee bees in its tail and the Holy Ghost, usually represented by a bird, a dove) borrowed from Flaubert's story, "The Simple Heart," in which the protagonist, an old peasant woman, who has continually been deprived of affection and love throughout her whole life, comes to believe, in her senility, that her only possession, a stuffed parrot, is actually the Holy Ghost.[27]

The later Library of Congress essay builds on these initial observations, recalling not just the Flaubert story but, in a footnote, many of the

---

26. *Obbligati*, 282–3.
27. Remarks to Roger are included in Letter, AH to parents, 16 January 1951. Hecht Archive.

differences between the much longer *Partisan Review* version of the poem and the more abbreviated poem as it appears in Lowell's *Selected Poems*, but which, Hecht felt, still follows the basic outline of the original. True to his own interpretive convictions, Hecht also discreetly omits the biographical references. What is new in the essay is the attention Hecht pays to the drama of listening and the "complication of settings in time." "Michael as dreamer or meditator sets the scene," Hecht notes, "but even as he does so it is in retrospect, and chiefly in order to allow the remoter voice of his now dead wife to recall something still further in the past."[28] In this case her final words are interpreted by Hecht as a plea for Michael to "listen to the divine voice," but, as Hecht says, "divinity does not vouchsafe its voice to him, offers no mercy." And then he adds, with a view not possible in the early letter: "That muteness, that blank uncommunicative silence would reappear just as accusingly in poems Lowell wrote near the end of his career"—the sonnets, appearing side by side, bearing the Herbertian title "No Hearing," included in *For Lizzie and Harriet* (1973).

It would be foolish to attempt to fold one poet neatly into another on the basis of several poems, especially two writers as complex as Lowell and Hecht, but I think the exemplary "courage" Hecht evidently drew from Lowell in writing "The Vow" he also discovered in "Thanksgiving's Over," but with different consequences for his own poetic development. Here I mean to touch only on a nexus of general concerns (and not on prosodic particularities): an increasing interest, after *A Summoning of Stones*, with exploring the psychic attributes of the delusional, even using the same New York City locale in "Thanksgiving's Over" in "Third Avenue in Sunlight" (published in 1959), a direction that would continue and deepen in much of Hecht's later poetry (see, especially, his poem on John Clare, "Coming Home," in *Millions of Strange Shadows*); and a new emphasis on "domestic drama of a bitter and terrifying kind," different from Lowell's, but which also can mutate, in the course of a poem, into a "blank uncommunicative silence," as in the celebrated ending of "A Hill," the opening poem in *The Hard Hours*, to be considered in Chapter 3, in which Hecht describes himself "as a boy" standing "for hours in wintertime" before a hill "just to the left / Of the road north of Poughkeepsie."

28. *Obbligati*, 283.

But the most explicit, if not necessarily the fullest, working out of "Thanksgiving's Over," is "Behold the Lilies of the Field," published in *The Hudson Review* in Fall 1961. Ninety-five lines long, the poem is one of "enormous drama," along with "a complication of settings in time," in which the title, a quotation from Matthew 6:28 (Hecht chose the Tyndale translation, with its strong emphasis on transfixed surprise in the word "Behold," rather than the quieter more familiar "Consider" in the King James version), announces with grievous irony the plight of witnessing terrible cruelties ostensibly involving the Roman emperor Valerian but applicable to all war crimes. Lowell's couplets have been greatly loosened, turned into unrhymed lines of varying length, freighted with the methodical weight of biblical parataxis:

> They stripped him, and made an iron collar for his neck,
> And they made a cage out of our captured spears,
> And they put him inside, naked and collared,
> And exposed to the view of the whole enemy camp.
> And I was tied to a post and made to watch...

The projected setting here in a psychiatrist's office smacks of Lowell's "confessional" presence, no doubt made more immediate by the recent publication of *Life Studies* in 1959, which included "Three Months Away" and the line adapted from Matthew 6:28, "Recuperating, I neither spin nor toil," that furnished the title and scene of helpless voyeurism at the center of Hecht's poem. (Shortly after the appearance of his poem, in fact, Hecht would be in Gracie Square Hospital in New York City, suffering a breakdown of his own, and in touch with Lowell.) In this case, the remote voice called into being in Hecht's poem is that of a mentally shattered soldier, not a forlorn wife, who is, in a manner of speaking, "turned to stone," not by a bad marriage but from having witnessed horrific violence; and while the speaker is "ransomed" by an ambiguously presented mother (there is surely some domestic bitterness here), he has not spiritually or psychologically recovered at the poem's end, wanting instead the uncommunicative blankness of looking at flowers and wishing he "could be like them"—silent.

"Behold the Lilies of the Field" is one of several threshold poems for Hecht. War returns, but as if from afar; and yet its cruelties are held steadily in view: the pain of passively beholding undermines completely the emphasis on quiet faith in Matthew. The Gospel image of God as protectively clothing the faithful—"Wherefore if God so

clothe the grass, which is today in the field, and tomorrow shall be cast
into the furnace: shall he not much more do the same unto you, o ye
of little faith?"—is re-turned by Hecht in the image of Valerian's
skin being "tanned and stuffed and sewn":

And for what?
A hideous life-sized doll, filled out with straw,
In the skin of the Roman Emperor, Valerian,
With blanks of mother-of-pearl under the eyelids,
And painted shells that had been prepared beforehand
For the fingernails and toenails,
Roughly cross-stitched on the inseam of the legs
And up the back to the center of the head,
Swung in the wind on a rope from the palace flag-pole;
And young girls were brought there by their mothers
To be told about the male anatomy.

Discursive as the poem deliberately is, it is as tight as can be when it
comes to witnessing the inlaying of cruelty and its teachings. In this
regard, Hecht is miles away from Wilbur, who wrote a poem "On the
Eyes of an SS Officer" in *The Beautiful Changes*, but not about what
the eye sees. That is Hecht's territory and will be distinctly his from
The Hard Hours on.

Two further remarks by Hecht help to illuminate his thinking in
the later 1950s. Both are taken from *The Hudson Review*, for which he
served as poetry consultant and reviewer. The first helps to explain
his disenchantment with Wallace Stevens, not as a poet, who remains
in Hecht's thoughts as "one of the most gifted and distinguished
poets this nation has produced" and who will reappear significantly in
Hecht's later poetry, but as the potential model Stevens so conspicuously appeared to be at the end of *A Summoning of Stones* in the strange
poem, "A Lesson from the Master." Mulling over Stevens' idea of the
hero, in the context of William James' remarks that "thoughts are
things," Hecht notes that, in *Adagia*, Stevens "bears in common with
the exponents of this doctrine a steadfast confidence in and reliance
upon the constructs of the mind. And under the pressure of experience, such a confidence may certainly become heroic." He then
concludes:

But if thoughts are things, there are still plenty of things that are not thoughts,
and the world of Wallace Stevens is often thin for want of them. He certainly
realized that his poetry was a particular kind of poetry, and that there were

qualities of experience beyond or apart from his literary sensibilities. His knowing this adds pathos to the heroic loneliness of his most serious poems.[29]

The second remark, about the significance of facts in the form of history, appeared a year later while reviewing some books of translations, of which one, by Jerome Rothenberg, "offers the work of ten young German poets"—German being a language with which Hecht had some familiarity. "It is not surprising," writes Hecht, "that their tone should be grim, for the most part, and full of horror and bitterness. But it is surprising that they should have fallen back on the nightmare tricks of surrealism." He then continues:

I am not sure I know why this should be so. Perhaps it is because the accumulated horror of recent German history cannot be regarded in any way that seems straightforward and direct. But it is hard to keep an anonymous style of this sort from being an evasion or a mere excuse for violence.

I take these and the following remarks to form something of a credo for the remaining forty-plus years of his writing life:

The fantastic and hideous images from the unconscious certainly have their place in poetry, and they are no doubt universally available. The dear old gentleman who faithfully brings crumbs to the pigeons in winter may have nightmares as foul as the next man, and Bosch knew very well how monstrous and vivid these presences might become to a saint in the desert. They are demons, our secret evil longings, and they are very real. But these images exist outside of time, eternally, everywhere, and in their submerged and terrible domain we are pretty much alike. It is history that makes us, or lets us be, what we are uniquely, and gives to our lives their singular stamps and profiles.[30]

That last urgent sentence leads directly into *The Hard Hours*, with its deepened (and often demonic) emphasis on the singular pressures of history, but as this chapter has been largely grounded in Hecht's initial book of poems, I want to close by circling back to it from the curious perspective offered by a later poem, the marvelously funny "The Ghost in the Martini." The date is 1968, the scene, the American Academy in Rome. Fresh from having received the Pulitzer Prize in Poetry for *The Hard Hours*, the now established and single poet has returned for a third time to the Academy to work on his translation of Aeschylus' *Seven Against Thebes* (with the classical scholar, Helen

29. "Poets and Peasants," *The Hudson Review* 10 (1958–59), 608.
30. "To thy High Requiem Become a Clod," *The Hudson Review* 13 (1960), 132–3.

Bacon). Reminiscing a bit about his earlier visits, he visibly luxuriates in his present surroundings:

> I can look out over my immediate private terrace, with geraniums in terra cotta pots and a quite large bay tree trimmed into the shape of a perfect dome, out through the pines to a clear view of the Basilica of Maxentius in the Roman Forum which appears in the middle distance, and much of the rest of the city, littered, as it were, between green branches, to the Alban hills beyond.[31]

But at his back, it seems, another voice is heard, for the first poem Hecht wrote in Rome after the publication of *The Hard Hours* is "The Ghost in the Martini," the "ghost" in this case being none other than a repressed version of his earlier poetic self. "Well, summon me you did, / And I come unwillingly, like Samuel's Ghost." Just what prompted this "dialogue" with his past is open to interpretation. Much later Hecht offered, "as it were, two illegitimate parents" as literary sources of inspiration, in a 1992 letter to Sandra McPherson:

> One was Max Beerbohm, who wrote a Foreword to a reissue of his early novel, *Zuleika Dobson*, in which he announced that he had not ventured to make any changes in the book because he was keenly aware of how its young author would have resented the supervision of some elderly fogy breathing down his neck. The other parent was Mark Strand, whose poem, "The Man in the Tree," though it seems at first to have two characters, has actually, the more one studies it, only one.[32]

But a third possibility, nearer the occasion of composition, might well have been his own recent actions in the preparation of *The Hard Hours*—the self-maiming or, more exactly, the exhumation and maiming, the summoning of his earlier poetic self that occurred with the older poet's decision to include a portion of the long-out-of-print *Stones* to accompany the new volume. Hecht cut the earlier collection in half, and there the truncated volume has remained, one half still visible to the general reader of his collections, the other half lying in darkness. If Beerbohm reportedly refused to make any changes to an earlier work for fear of causing resentment in the young author, then imagine, as I think Hecht did, how the earlier maimed poet of *A Summoning of Stones* might feel.

---

31. Letter, AH to George Ford, 20 October 1968 (*SL*, 140–1).
32. Letter, AH to Sandra McPherson, 4 October 1992 (*SL*, 245–6).

The situation in both cases is preposterous, of course, but it also contains the germ of comedy, the double perspectives; and the ensuing dialogue in the poem builds off this basic disparity between the older poet-speaker, manifestly adept with wordplay and rhymes, now being lionized by a young lady, presumably after a successful poetry reading, and a resentful, angry version of his earlier self, suddenly released from below by a heady mix of memory, eros, and booze. "You arrogant, elderly letch, you broken-down / Brother of Apeneck Sweeney... You only got where you are / By standing upon my ectoplasmic shoulders." The whiny younger poet turns out to be nothing but a neurotic tissue of quotations, some italicized, some not, the boldest being from Milton (*Paradise Lost*) and Shakespeare (*Richard II*), as was earlier the case in his 1946 letter to his parents with which this chapter began. The earlier self declaims at length:

> Bloody monastic it was,
> A neurotic mixture of self-denial and fear;
> The verse halting, the cataleptic pause,
>   No sensible pain, no tear,
>
>   But an interior drip
> As from an ulcer, where, in the humid deep
> Center of myself, I would scratch and grip
>   The wet walls of the keep,
>
>   Or lie on my back and smell
> From the corners the sharp, ammoniac, urine stink.
> *"No light, but rather darkness visible."*
>   And plenty of time to think.
>
>   In that thick, fetid air
> I talked to myself in giddy recitative:
> *"I have been studying how I may compare*
>   *This prison where I live*
>
>   *Unto the world..."* I learned
> Little, and was awarded no degrees.
> Yet all that sunken hideousness earned
>   Your negligence and ease.

But for all his noise, the palm at the end of the poem goes to the older poet, the narrator who wants to see the past as over. "Still given to self-abuse!" he quips, getting in one final parting shot as he prepares to exit with the lady. "I touch her elbow, and, leaning toward her ear, / Tell her to find her purse."

The fun of the poem is surely its exaggerated postures all around, including the marked difference between the suave versus the sputtering use of quotations, a device perhaps owing to an appreciative reading at the time of some of Richard Howard's vividly impetuous dramatic monologues.[33] But the violent eruption from below is also, in one sense, true to circumstance, the memory stimulated perhaps by the recent abuse done to his earlier creation, but also responsive at another level to the real story of Hecht's largely disastrous, second year-long visit to the American Academy in 1954–55, rather than the tale of "happy delirium" alluded to in the 1968 letter previously quoted. Far more anguished than the first visit because of a troubled marriage, work on a second book had, in fact, slowed down to an ulcerous drip. As Hecht reported at length in a letter to his parents:

The work has been going forward with the greatest difficulty, chiefly because I cannot concentrate. I have no feeling about whether what I am writing is good or bad, and the whole business is totally without excitement and pleasure for me. And I am sure I know the reason. It's that I can't stand leaving unresolved my situation with Pat.[34]

A photo of Hecht from this period, sitting in his cell-like study, staring at the typewriter, ashtray nearby, fingers forming an upside-down "V," lends support to the Prufrockian view of this earlier self in "The Ghost in the Martini." "I have sat alone in the dark, accomplishing little, / And worth no more to myself, in pride and fee, / Than a cup of luke-warm spittle." Exaggerated perhaps, as the comedy requires and distance allows, but such grounded despair marks the psychic origins of *The Hard Hours* and its long, thirteen-year ascent into print.

33. See especially the poems in Howard's *Untitled Subject* (New York: Atheneum, 1969) and *Findings* (New York: Atheneum, 1971), published when the two were in active correspondence with each other. See *SL*, 137, 139, and 147–9. Much later, Hecht wrote a brief, illuminating essay on "The Browning-Howard Connection" for *The Wilson Quarterly* 23.1 (Winter 1999), 108–14. Although both poets shared in the common enterprise of expanding lyric to incorporate a sense of "story," their methods and means often took them in different directions: Howard more toward Browning in his desire to impersonate historical characters, often in syllabic stanzas, and Hecht toward Shakespeare in utilizing the resources of blank verse to explore the lives of fictional characters of a frequently mundane order, as in the case of the chamber maid in "The Grapes." Still, Stephen Edgar is right to notice the ghostly presence of Browning's "My Last Duchess" in Hecht's "A Brief Account of our City." Email, 22 September 2015.
34. Letter, AH to his parents, 9 November 1955 (*SL*, 112–13). A version of the photo referred to in the next sentence can be found in *SL*, 100, as well as on the book jacket.

3

About Suffering

History, Domesticity, and the Making of *The Hard Hours*

Now what do I recall of that interview. Well, chiefly, that Wystan felt that your poems were too detached from your personal life, good, even excellent as they were, that you should give yourself the task of writing poems that were more direct, more forthright. Why don't you, he said, write a poem that starts very simply with you sitting in a café, here in Ischia, and looking around and thinking of what you see. I remember that you were very struck by this advice and felt that Wystan had touched on something important for yourself...[1]

These comments are taken from a 1978 letter to Hecht written by Raymond Rosenthal, Hecht's traveling friend and journalist from his early days on Ischia in 1951 and, subsequently, a noted translator of works from Italian, including books by Pietro Aretino, Gabriele D'Annunzio, and Primo Levi. Hecht had been a guest at the Rosenthals for Thanksgiving and other occasions, sometimes leading to gatherings with Auden. The correspondence between the two men had been prompted by a possible collection of essays and memoirs in the making about Auden's time on Ischia. Although the project was never realized, it brought the two writers back in touch with each other, now almost thirty years after their time together on the island.

Rosenthal's recollection here is fascinating for a number of reasons. It affords, for one thing, a rare look into Hecht's past, in which, despite

1. Letter, Raymond Rosenthal to AH, 29 January 1978. Hecht Archive.

the wide gap in time, it vividly recalls Hecht's interview with Auden that Hecht had described in separate letters written in the fall of 1951 to his parents and to Allen Tate, discussed in Chapter 2. It also complicates and deepens the account reported in those letters. It repeats the general tenor of Auden's advice, in some regards as old as Sidney's admonition to "look into thy heart and write," a phrase also dear to later Hecht (it appears as an epigraph to "Murmur"). But it adds a new angle in the very specificity of its recollection:"Why don't you . . . write a poem that starts very simply with you sitting in a café, here in Ischia and looking around and thinking of what you see." A less thoughtful poet might have reacted differently, perhaps indifferently, but according to Rosenthal's recollection, Hecht seems to have sensed the special applicability of Auden's observations, a pertinence reflected in the very simplicity of Rosenthal's phrasing: "I remember that you were very struck by this advice and felt that Wystan had touched on something important for yourself…"

Something important for sure. Hecht's debts to Auden are many and too complicated to receive here more than a bald summary. They manifest themselves in a common interest in the challenge posed by complicated forms—Hecht's canzone "Terms" being perhaps the most elaborate of these single ventures, working its way back through Merrill's "Samos" to Auden's "Canzone" ("When shall we learn, what should be clear as day"), which ultimately derives from Dante ("Amore, tu vedi ben che questa donna")—and in mastering a multitude of complex forms, sometimes within a single suite of works (see Hecht's "A Love for Four Voices" and Auden's *The Sea and the Mirror*). We should add to this list the occasional appearance of Audenesque phrases and imagery in the younger poet's writings, an act of poetic counterpointing as Wyatt Prunty has suggested,[2] and note, too, a shared interest

2. Prunty,"Making and Taking," *The Kenyon Review* 31 (Winter 2009), 194–206, esp. 200–3. In singling out Auden's advice, I don't mean to suggest either its novelty or that Hecht couldn't have encountered a similar suggestion elsewhere. Hecht's earlier mentor John Crowe Ransom, for instance, voiced the comparable, although more severely phrased, observation: "It might be said that the occasion of a poem is a *moral* situation. But immediately it must be added as a correction that the occasion of a poem is a moral *situation*" (Ransom's italics). See *American Poetry at Mid-Century: Lectures Presented under the Auspices of the Gertrude Clarke Whittal Poetry and Literature Fund* (Washington, DC: The Library of Congress, 1958), 8. As a digest of Ransom's views on poetry, views he presumably held while Hecht was studying under him a decade earlier, the essay serves to illuminate major elements of continuity as well as differences between mentor and student. The differences are especially apparent in

in a variety of topics, theological and moral alike. That angle included revaluing Auden's bold critique of contemporary events in poems like "September 1, 1939" in the starker—and for the former soldier Hecht more psychologically immediate—light of post-World War II atrocities. Most of these concerns find a place, as well, in *The Hidden Law*, Hecht's 1993 book-length critical study of Auden's poetry. But it may be that the simple advice recounted by Rosenthal was the greatest gift Auden bestowed on Hecht, for it points to one of the signal differences, perhaps the signal difference, between *A Summoning of Stones* and *The Hard Hours* and the works that followed. It is the difference between writing poetry and writing poems, between verse that is largely and often exuberantly descriptive, in the manner, say, of "The Gardens of the Villa d'Este," and poems that are profoundly situated in a locale or landscape at once personal and dramatic. Beginning simply, a *Hard Hour*'s poem issues in something "more direct, more forthright," and, in the process, it risks nothing less than the discovery of an authentic voice.[3]

Think, for instance, of the dazzling display of artistry in "Double Sonnet" that inaugurates *Stones*, discussed in Chapter 2, an apparently timeless, indeed Orphean, summoning of poetic forms. Then

the Hecht emerging as the poet of *The Hard Hours*, in which there is little room for Ransom's warmly Wordsworthian view of the poet celebrating the triumph of good over evil (12). *The Hard Hours* poem best showing Ransom's influence, as Daniel Hoffman notes, is "Three Prompters from the Wings," reminiscent in its tripartite structure of Ransom's "Spiel of the Three Mountebanks" ("Poetry: Dissidents from Schools," in Daniel Hoffman, ed., *The Harvard Guide to Contemporary American Writing* (Cambridge, MA: Harvard University Press, 1979), 585. And indeed, the only surviving letter in the Hecht Archive from Ransom includes a carefully enthusiastic response to this poem, concentrating much on prosody, with Ransom wishing, as one might expect, Hecht's to be "a little tighter." Ransom's letter, dated 22 April 1959, also included the following remark: "I can see that you are at the height of your powers, and therefore it is very important for you to be thinking hard about the Next Step in your poetry." Thinking hard (or *Hard*) is exactly what Hecht was doing. Even as the context of Ransom's letter indicates that *The Kenyon Review* had turned down an earlier version of the poem, the tone of the teacher's response points to a continuing cordiality and fondness between the two, despite the fact the younger poet was moving off in a different direction. In a letter of his own to Allen Tate (October 1959), Hecht recounts, with considerable warmth and humor, Ransom's visit, alluded to in his 22 April letter.

3. Geoffrey Lindsay's fine essay, "'Laws that stand for other laws': Anthony Hecht's Dramatic Strategy," *Essays in Literature* 21.2 (1994), 285–300, anticipates the direction of this chapter and some of its points.

think of the poem that opens *The Hard Hours*, "A Hill," which
begins, quietly:

> In Italy, where this sort of thing can occur,
> I had a vision once—though you understand
> It was nothing at all like Dante's, or the visions of saints,
> And perhaps not a vision at all. I was with some friends,
> Picking my way through a warm sunlit piazza
> In the early morning. A clear fretwork of shadows
> From huge umbrellas littered the pavement and made
> A sort of lucent shallows in which was moored
> A small navy of carts. Books, coins, old maps,
> Cheap landscapes and ugly religious prints
> Were all on sale. The colors and noise
> Like the flying hands were gestures of exultation,
> So that even the bargaining
> Rose to the ear like a voluble godliness.

The imagined predicaments of these two inaugural poems could
hardly be more different. Here is Hecht now following Auden's advice
almost exactly: not sitting in a café and "looking around and thinking
of what you see" but telling a story as if he were sitting in a café,
reflecting on a remembered event in the company of others initially
stemming from a walk through a piazza. ("Piazza" was, in fact, a tenta-
tive early title for the poem.) The poem starts simply: "In Italy, where
this sort of thing can occur." He's already reduced the bel canto of
"Villa d'Este." It then quickly embarks on its own casual meandering.
The lines are variably measured and enjambed, the phrasing a bit
slovenly: "sort of" appears twice in seven lines. The opening section
possesses an easy familiarity of address ("though you understand"), as
the speaker picks his way through the details of his subject (the vision
was nothing like Dante's, indeed perhaps not a vision at all), rendering,
all the while, the feel of the specific place—its "lucent shallows." An
earlier draft of the poem, in fact, shows Hecht substituting "pavement"
for "brightness" to make the image of the "clear fretwork of shadows"
here literally more concrete and hence "brighter." Hecht also rewrote
the phrase "the colors and noise / *Kept a sustained crescendo* of exultation" as "the colors and noise / *Like the flying hands were gestures* of
exultation." The latter change animates the scene in a manner reminiscent of Wilbur's "Love Calls us to the Things of the World," a favorite
poem of Hecht's, as Hecht seems to have restitched Wilbur's "flying"
sheets and "rising" hands to make the "flying hands" of bargaining

rise to the level of "voluble godliness," itself a fine intensification of Auden's "voluble discourse" heard in "a square at midday" from "In Praise of Limestone." The echoing is allusive and enriching, the knitting tight.

This double heightening prepares for the poem's first major turn, beginning with "And then" and concluding in a "papery crash," and much in between, as memories of the past suddenly push their way forward:

> And then, when it happened, the noises suddenly stopped,
> And it got darker; pushcarts and people dissolved
> And even the great Farnese Palace itself
> Was gone, for all its marble; in its place
> Was a hill, mole-colored and bare. It was very cold,
> Close to freezing, with a promise of snow.
> The trees were like old ironwork gathered for scrap
> Outside a factory wall. There was no wind,
> And the only sound for a while was the little click
> Of ice as it broke in the mud under my feet.
> I saw a piece of ribbon snagged on a hedge,
> But no other sign of life. And then I heard
> What seemed the crack of a rifle. A hunter, I guessed;
> At least I was not alone. But just after that
> Came the soft and papery crash
> Of a great branch somewhere unseen falling to earth.

This is the first of Hecht's many "waste lands" in *The Hard Hours* serving as a "paysage interior." Smaller in scale, of course, than Eliot's and more evidently personal, the passage mixes, in symbolist fashion, visions of a bleak landscape initiated by thoughts of the hill with disconnected war memories. The details are exacting: the sound, for instance, of the "little click of ice" made by feet trudging through mud and the apparent "crack of a rifle"—to say nothing about the mysterious "piece of ribbon snagged on a hedge" or the false comfort contained in the rueful comment about having "at least" a hunter for a sole companion. And then the mysterious branch crashing somewhere—or is it a somebody?—casting a further shadow over the psyche like Stevens' "hemlock" in "Domination in Black."

Until the publication of *Millions of Strange Shadows* (1977), James Wright regarded "A Hill" as Hecht's "greatest poem"[4]—perhaps

4. Letter, James Wright to AH, 21 February 1977. Hecht Archive.

because of the suggestive depth of its imagery, the layered quality of its remembering. The description, moreover, is followed by a space on the page and then, in couplet fashion, apparent closure:

> And that was all, except for the cold and silence
> That promised to last forever, like the hill.

Separated as these lines are from the preceding passage and coming as they do at the bottom of the page in Hecht's *Selected Poems*, a reader might be forgiven for thinking the poem is finished at this point. The image of cold and silence feels utterly conclusive. Until, that is, we turn the page. As originally published, the couplet stands on its own, where, objectively, in its separateness it resembles more a stair, a place to pause, or prospectively a threshold marking a further descent from the "lucent shallows" into the remembered past, the poem's still darker psychic underworld, to continue in a different key the opening allusion to Dante:

> Then prices came through, and fingers, and I was restored
> To the sunlight and my friends. But for more than a week
> I was scared by the plain bitterness of what I had seen.
> All this happened about ten years ago,
> And it hasn't troubled me since, but at last, today,
> I remembered that hill; it lies just to the left
> Of the road north of Poughkeepsie; and as a boy
> I stood before it for hours in wintertime.

Here we do reach the poem's end, its bottom, but in the shift into the datable present, the writerly present tense—"but at last, today"—the cold and silence of that hill are resurrected to view, where they now seem to last forever, at least in this speaker's mind, now that he has recalled its original circumstance. Why, we must ask, is the boy alone for so long in this landscape?

"Part of the poem's beauty," writes an appreciative Mark Strand, "is that it resists, in its careful and cadenced disclosures, any reduction, any reading, in fact, of the hill."[5] Strand is describing the oblique ways American poets often approach the venerable and venerated subject of Mount Parnassus, and he locates the power of Hecht's poem in its

---

5. Strand, "Views of the Mysterious Hill: The Appearance of Parnassus in American Poetry," *The Gettysburg Review* 4 (1991), 677–8; also collected in *The Weather of Words: Poetic Invention* (New York: Alfred A. Knopf, 2000), 123–37.

careful ambivalence. "It resists interpretation, but perhaps it resists too much, perhaps in its plainness it is Parnassus after all; Parnassus wearing its American plain disguise." Perhaps, indeed: it was Howard Moss who first titled the poem "A Hill," but before that Hecht had called it "Poem"—a distinction, in other words, without much of a difference. There is little in this poem, or in Strand's account, to recall Lowell's exceptional mountainous climb and epochal clatter in "Beyond the Alps" to announce his crossing over into a new poetics in *Life Studies*, published in 1959, the year before Hecht's poem was written. Hecht's is only a hill, in the winter, mole colored and bare, but it is Hecht's alone to occupy, to make "the most of it," to use the title of the Frost poem that Strand rightly sees underlying the great branch's papery crash.

Nearly a half-century after being awarded the Pulitzer Prize in 1968, *The Hard Hours* remains a harrowing and moving reading experience, and Auden's advice helps us to understand in part why this is so. It illuminates the broader transformation of Hecht from primarily a descriptive to a dramatic poet, a process whereby the poet situates himself in a place or landscape, and, without writing confessional poetry per se, uses that space to reveal his thinking—often, as in the case of "A Hill," of a darkly Dantean order. "Behold the Lilies of the Field" would be another such test case—the situation not so much described as seen and narrated, but from where? Not a café but a psychiatrist's couch that somehow returns us to a brutal world coaxed into being from an incident in Gibbon's *Decline and Fall of the Roman Empire*. Although the couch, metaphorically speaking, was quickly becoming a convention in the 1960s, I am also reminded in this context of James Merrill's observation that

you hardly ever need to *state* your feelings. The point is to feel and keep the eyes open. Then what you feel is expressed, is mimed back at you by the scene. A room, a landscape. I'd go a step further. We don't *know* what we feel until we see it distanced by this kind of translation.[6]

A room, a landscape, or even—to go a step further—a Nazi concentration camp. *The Hard Hours* would not be so aptly titled, that is so

6. "On 'Yánnina': An Interview with David Kalstone" (1972), in J. D. McClatchy, *Recitative: Prose by James Merrill* (San Francisco: North Point Press, 1986), 22.

"hard" in almost every sense of the word (obdurate, painful, difficult, laborious, arduous, erotic, deeply etched, or cut—literally, in the case of Leonard Baskin's black-and-white wood engravings accompanying the sequence in the volume on "The Seven Deadly Sins"), indeed not quite the "breakthrough" volume it has rightly come to represent in the poet's career if it only introduced a way of seeing and thinking, both immediate and personal, as expressed in "A Hill."[7]

As it happens, in the same envelope containing "A Hill" sent to Howard Moss at *The New Yorker* in late 1960 was another poem.[8] Hecht was less sanguine about its prospects since he did not think it conformed to the subject matter generally favored by the magazine. It turns out he was right. While "A Hill" was accepted, the other poem was not. The title of the rejected poem was " 'More Light! More Light!' "— the quotation reputed to be Goethe's last words, now used ironically as a critique of German enlightenment more generally[9]—and often considered to be one of the great poems to come out of the devastation generated by World War II. Even readers not always drawn to Hecht's poetry find this poem exceptional.

Dedicated to Heinrich Blücher and Hannah Arendt, Hecht's colleagues at Bard, this first fully realized poem about Nazi atrocities involves more than the personal story of a young man's shocking encounter with the death camps. Randall Jarrell had already used that device in "A Camp in the Prussian Forest." In fact, at one level, " 'More Light!' " doesn't involve Hecht at all. He nowhere figures into the poem, the absence of a first-person speaker contributing to the careful objectification of ruthless suffering in a manner congruent with

---

7. Ted Hughes' ringing "breakthrough" endorsement for the English publication of *Hard Hours* in 1968 continues to appear on the back of the 1990 publication of Hecht's *Collected Earlier Poems*. It reads in part: "this most fastidious and elegant of poets shed every artifice and began to write with absolute raw simplicity and directness. Only a poet with an immense burden of something to say ever dreams of this course, and only an inspired artist can bring it off." On the significance of the "breakthrough narrative" as a distinct feature of mid-century modern poetry and the (rarely accurate) telling of its history, see James Longenbach, *Modern Poetry after Modernism* (New York: Oxford University Press, 1997), ch. 1 ("What was Postmodern Poetry"), esp. 5–10. Although Hughes is given to overstatement here, *The Hard Hours*, along with James Merrill's *Water Street* (1962), remain signal instances of "breakthrough" volumes by "formal" poets, both indebted in different ways to Lowell's example in *Life Studies*. See Timothy Materer, "Confession and Autobiography in James Merrill's Early Poetry," *Twentieth-Century Literature* 48 (2002), 150–73, esp. 168–9; and J. D. McClatchy, "On Water Street," in *White Paper: On Contemporary American Poetry* (New York: Columbia University Press, 1989), 247–89, esp. 252–3.

8. See *SL*, 119.   9. Letter, AH to Bill Read, 11 June 1969 (*SL*, 142–3).

Arendt's *Origins of Totalitarianism* (1951; 1958) and that exceeds Auden's famous but distant depiction of suffering in "Musée des Beaux Arts," especially as that poem might appear to a post-World War II audience.[10] But at another level, Hecht has engineered—the term is purposefully chosen—the poem to reveal two deeply circumstanced, historically contrasting situations: two versions of Hell on earth. One is drawn from the literature of English Protestant martyrdom in the examples of Nicholas Ridley and Hugh Latimer as reported by John Foxe in his *Acts and Monuments*. The other is borrowed from an incident in Eugen Kogon's *Theory and Practice of Hell*, one of the first and still most powerful investigations into the Nazi concentration camps, in this case Buchenwald, where Kogon himself had been imprisoned.[11]

In neither scenario are we situated in a café or a sunlit piazza, but in a memory bank of sorts, as Hecht uses one dark episode in the past to illuminate an even darker moment in more recent history—"darkness visible," as Milton said in a line Hecht made use of in "The Ghost in the Martini." Whatever barbarities exist in Foxe's story as recounted by Hecht, they still belong to a world where suffering has meaning, a world Hecht swiftly unfolds in the first stanza by recounting a single dramatic speech act.

> Composed in the Tower before his execution
> These moving verses, and being brought at that time
> Painfully to the stake, submitted, declaring thus:
> "I implore my God to witness that I have made no crime."
>
> Nor was he forsaken of courage, but the death was horrible,
> The sack of gunpowder failing to ignite.
> His legs were blistered sticks on which the black sap
> Bubbled and burst as he howled for the Kindly Light.
>
> And that was but one, and by no means one of the worst;
> Permitted at least his pitiful dignity;
> And such as were by made prayers in the name of Christ,
> That shall judge all men, for his soul's tranquility.

---

10. See the fascinating chapter "Talking back to Auden" in Diederik Oostdijk, *Among the Nightmare Fighters: American Poets of World War II* (Columbia: University of South Carolina Press, 2011), 57–71.

11. First published in German as *Der SS-Stat* (1946); translated and published in English as *The Theory and Practice of Hell* (New York: Farrar, Strauss, and Giroux, 1950). The episode Hecht recounts can be found on 89–90 of the revised edition, 2006.

The initiating verb "Composed" situates us immediately in the harsh world of Elizabethan England and its icon for punishment, the Tower of London. It also equates personal composure with the dignity of writing—the latter being Hecht's special invention for the occasion, since neither Latimer nor Ridley wrote verses at their death. It is the poet's way of leaving his mark on the page, an obdurate sign of his participating, at a radical remove, in the action of personal suffering in the first stanza. It also characterizes more generally Hecht's compositional practice. He serves as dispassionate but sympathetic witness of a horrible death, an ending only slightly ameliorated by the vision of the surrounding community of like believers praying on behalf of the victim and by the complex mix of "unmistakable anguish" and "wry irony" contained in the anachronistic reference to Cardinal Newman's famous hymn, "Lead Kindly Light."[12] To maintain a steady composure on events, Hecht's quatrains likewise possess a sturdy flexibility to them, as does the rhyme scheme. Only the second and fourth lines rhyme regularly—the last rightly connecting "dignity" with "tranquility." And the individual lines, of varying length, often stretch toward a prosy hexameter and sometimes beyond, perhaps reminding us that the polished pentameter favored by the great Elizabethan poets belonged to a different, slightly later, and more distantly courtly world.

" 'More Light! More Light!' " is an experiment in perspective, a diptych of sorts, as the doubling in the title intimates, and the first instance of a technique Hecht will return to frequently in his later poetry as a means of setting up often surprising and sometimes shocking contrasts. But before addressing the engineered turn to the second part, I want to widen the context a bit by way of an essay Donald Hall published in 1959 in the summer issue of *The American Scholar*.[13] Hall and Hecht had been in correspondence during the same year, and the Arnoldian title of Hall's essay, "Ah Love, Let Us Be True," a line from "Dover

12. Edward Hirsch, "Comedy and Hardship," in Sydney Lea, ed., *The Burdens of Formality: Essays on the Poetry of Anthony Hecht* (Athens: University of Georgia Press, 1989), 53.
13. Hall, " 'Ah Love, Let Us Be True': Domesticity and History in Contemporary Poetry," *American Scholar* 28 (Summer 1959), 310–19. Although Delmore Schwartz is never mentioned by name, Hall's self-critical essay seems to have been stung into being by Schwartz' "The Present State of Poetry," in *American Poetry at Mid-Century*, 15–30. *The New Poets of England and America* comes under fire precisely because of the limited scope of the subject matter: "One poem is about a toothache; and one poem is about a vacuum cleaner" (28).

Beach," reminds us that Hecht was shortly to publish "The Dover Bitch," his witty riff on Arnold's poem in the winter issue of *The Transatlantic Review* (1959–60). Hall, moreover, had become something of an authority on the contemporary scene as one of the editors of *New Poets of England and America* (1957, 1959, 1962). The first edition of the anthology printed four of Hecht's poems; several more would be added in subsequent editions, including, in fact, "The Dover Bitch" and " 'More Light! More Light!' " in 1962.

The subtitle of Hall's essay was "Domesticity and History in Contemporary Poetry," and from his unusual vantage point, Hall used this occasion to spell out emphatically what he saw as currently wrong with American poetry, choosing, as he says, to address the symptoms and "suggest remedies, but not to speculate on the origins of the disease." In Cold War America, Hall viewed domesticity and history in sharp opposition with each other: the latter being neglected at the expense of the former (hence the main title from Arnold): "I feel that I see a pattern among us of provinciality and evasion, which results in a reliance on the domestic at the expense of the historical" (p. 311).

To make the situation worse, in Hall's view, the insularity of American poetry put an already potentially anxious generation of poets at a significant disadvantage regarding their immediate predecessors: "When Eliot and Pound were our age, they wrote out of a sense of history which no one now seems to possess. They had no systematic theory of history, but they had an imagination of it, and they had sufficient knowledge to begin to discern connections and disconnections." "The truly historical imagination," Hall continued, "involves the copresence of the alien, not the domestication of the strange into the familiar" (pp. 315–16). A possible remedy to the present situation, Hall proffered, can be glimpsed in the writings of a few exemplary contemporary poets, who, in different ways, "seem to be nearest to what I am asking for" by managing to incorporate a version of history—architectural, religious, or political—into their verse: Geoffrey Hill, Robert Bly, and Louis Simpson. The essay concludes with Hall noting that "I leave out a number [of poets] who are very good, but about whom I have nothing special to say," and offers a final, rather dire, indeed Arnoldian, admonition "that none of us has yet attempted the universality of reference that greatness will manage to achieve" (p. 319).

There is much in this essay, especially its high-handed manner, that I can imagine Hecht resisting, and perhaps one of the sly signs of such resistance might simply be "The Dover Bitch" itself, with its splendidly comical quotation from the speaker of Arnold's poem, while "the cliffs of England [were] crumbling away" behind the lovers:" 'Try to be true to me / And I'll do the same for you, for things are bad / All over, etc., etc.' " There is more than one way to evade the apparent trap of domesticity. But on a number of points, there is enough convergence between the two to think that Hall's worries were also those of Hecht, who had fought in a war, had confronted the profound alienation of unwarranted suffering, had lived overseas, had read widely in history—Gibbon's *Decline and Fall of The Roman Empire* has already been mentioned—knew his Eliot and Pound, and whose own faltering marriage might have made him dubious about relying exclusively on the domestic as an escape from the historical.

Here is now the longer, second part of the poem, adapted from Kogon's *Theory and Practice of Hell*:

> We move now to outside a German wood.
> Three men are there commanded to dig a hole
> In which the two Jews are ordered to lie down
> And be buried alive by the third, who is a Pole.
>
> Not light from the shrine at Weimar beyond the hill
> Nor light from heaven appeared. But he did refuse.
> A Lüger settled back deeply in its glove.
> He was ordered to change places with the Jews.
>
> Much casual death had drained away their souls.
> The thick dirt mounted toward the quivering chin.
> When only the head was exposed the order came
> To dig him out again and to get back in.
>
> No light, no light in the blue Polish eye.
> When he finished a riding boot packed down the earth.
> The Lüger hovered lightly in its glove.
> He was shot in the belly and in three hours bled to death.
>
> No prayers or incense rose up in those hours
> Which grew to be years, and every day came mute
> Ghosts from the ovens, sifting through crisp air,
> And settled upon his eyes in a black soot.

Elegant as it is and perhaps because of its elegance, the shift into the present tense in the first stanza could hardly be more jarring or alienating, one of the points that Moss said led *The New Yorker* to reject the poem; but in light of Hall's comments, the rupture seems also highly purposeful, as if the camera were suddenly offering a panoramic view of history, with Hecht now assuming the impersonal voice of the newscaster: "We move now to outside a German wood." So much for the "moving verses" of the Elizabethan past permitting an element of "pitiful dignity" in death. We are now in the mid-twentieth century, where cruelty abounds, and Hecht's own experience as a reporter of sorts in World War II comes to the fore.[14]

Nonetheless, Hecht seems to have been drawn to this particular episode for the same reason as Kogon. It offers an instance, rare in the concentration camps, of resistance to authority, although, quite pointedly in Hecht's version, not dignity in death. The firmness of Hecht's, "But he did refuse," the shortest line in the poem, captures the element of surprise evident in Kogon's laudatory exclamation over the Pole's behavior, an action that cuts across the traditionally harsh ethnic divisions between Jews and Poles, and thus makes it unlikely, as has been sometimes suggested, that the refusal should be understood in the poem as an example of Polish scorn for Jews.[15] Hecht did adapt the account for his own purposes, however, by tampering "with the ending by having the Pole shot on the spot."[16] He also stripped away proper names. Buchenwald is only referred to indirectly through its proximity to Weimar; the name of the Pole (Strzaska) is excluded; and in revising the poem, Hecht even replaced a "German boot" with "a riding boot." All the changes are made with the intention of removing, as the concentration camps did, indeed as the military did, both German and American, any vestige of human identity. It is a Luger that does the killing. Indeed, not even a hand holding the Luger, but a Luger held in its glove, first one way, then another.

"The indoctrination process is very thorough," Hecht wrote upon his own arrival at boot camp.

We received our rifles the second day we arrived, and also our bayonets. We are always addressed as 'soldier' unless it is a personal conversation, and there

14. See *SL*, 22–3. On the subject of reporting and war poetry see Alan Marshall, "Quiet Americans: Responses to War in some British and American Poetry of the 1960s," in Tim Kendall, ed., *The Oxford Handbook of British and Irish War Poetry* (Oxford: Oxford University Press, 2007), 613–31.

15. Hoffman, "Poetry: Dissidents from Schools," 583. See also Ellen Miller Casey, "Hecht's 'More Light! More Light!,'" *Explicator* 54.2 (1996), 113–15, for a helpful survey of critical responses to the issue of heroism in this poem.

16. Letter, AH to Bill Read.

are an infinite number of little things that conspire to make us forget we were ever civilians. The most important one is—when you wake up in the morning it's too early to think, during the day you're too busy to think, and at night you're too tired to think.[17]

Something of this fatigue and resignation is registered in the poem, more extreme, of course, as were the circumstances, but perhaps not altogether beyond understanding, even if the Pole's motives remain on the outer edge of rational comprehension—almost a reflex to the harsh conditions. "Much casual death had drained away their souls," Hecht tells us, and we watch the process of mindless reduction, the sapping of whatever inner strength the Pole possessed, through the cruel routine of a mock burial, concluding in the riveting line: "No light, no light in the blue Polish eye." In marked counterpoint to the poem's title, the line sets up the shockingly indifferent real death (now the slow draining of the body), in preparation for the final stanza, whose strangely beautiful imagery offers no consolation whatsoever—"no prayers or incense," in sharp contradistinction to the martyrs in the Tower, but only the piling on of further ashes. The eyes covered in black soot see nothing, as was true for "years" with the eyes of the world more generally in regard to the Holocaust.[18]

"The psychological effects of the Second War are still largely repressed," wrote Charles Bernstein rather belatedly in 1992. "We are just beginning to come out of the shock enough to try to make sense of the experience."[19] This is true but only if one assumes, as Bernstein does, that the shock is real if it registers a crisis in representation through seeking "to dismantle the grammar of control and

17. Letter, AH to parents, 26 July 1943 (*SL*, 26).
18. I owe this last suggestion to a phone conversation with Jack Terry (24 March 2013), a survivor of the Flossenbürg Concentration Camp, whose experiences are described in Alicia Nitecki and Jack Terry's *Jakub's World: A Boy's Story of Loss and Survival in the Holocaust*, afterword by Jörg Skriebeleit (Albany: State University of New York Press, 2005). Strongly dissenting from Hannah Arendt's remark about the "banality of evil," which appeared as the subtitle to her *Eichmann in Jerusalem*, first published in book format in 1963, Terry also commented on the poem's accurate depiction of the brutal condition of concentrations camps captured by Hecht in the Pole's death and in the phrase, "Much casual death had drained away their souls." Hecht's poem, written before *Eichmann in Jerusalem* was published, is more in keeping with what Amos Elon calls Arendt's "Kantian notions of radical evil" found in *The Origins of Totalitarianism* (1951). See Elon's introduction to the Penguin reissue of *Eichmann* in 2006: xiii.
19. Bernstein, *A Poetics* (Cambridge, MA: Harvard University Press, 1992), 193, 202 ("The Second War and Postmodern Memory").

the syntax of command." But as the example of " 'More Light!' " attests in 1960, it's possible to represent violence—"to try to make sense of the experience"—by invoking just the opposite strategy: by using the precise control of grammar and syntax to unveil the barbaric cruelty of the concentration camps and not to make history into a game of language in the process. What is shocking can be, must be, represented, including, if need be, by borrowing from and adding to the historical record, as Hecht does by offering a comparative measure as a means to approximate the modern conditions of cruelty and a specific example (from an eyewitness, Eugen Kogon) to describe the effects. In choosing to represent this event in verse, moreover, Hecht was managing his own act of resistance, in this case, anticipating, *avant la lettre*, Theodor Adorno's now famous if sometimes misconstrued notion that after Auschwitz there can be no poetry. Hecht would later specifically address Adorno's remark,[20] but as his 1960 letter to Moss makes clear, he already saw himself challenging the idea that this sort of brutal topic could only be presented in prose.[21]

Not included in the envelope to Moss was a close relative of " 'More Light! More Light!,' " "Rites and Ceremonies," a poem that certainly did precipitate a crisis in representation for Hecht. A poet with a profound understanding of suffering could perhaps have written " 'More Light!' " but only a Jewish poet would have attempted "Rites and Ceremonies." The longest poem, at 306 lines, and the most ambitious work in *The Hard Hours*, it was among the first poems begun after *A Summoning of Stones*, and one of the last, if not the last, to be completed, thus spanning the creation of the collection. No poem in *The Hard Hours* was longer in the making. No poem was harder to finish, and none asked as much from Hecht with regard to both formal variety

---

20. Hecht, "Paralipomena to *The Hidden Law*," in *Melodies Unheard: Essays on the Mysteries of Poetry* (Baltimore: Johns Hopkins University Press, 2003), 135. See also Post, "Anthony Hecht's Exalted Manna," in Christopher Hodgkins, *George Herbert's Travels: International Print and Cultural Legacies* (Newark: University of Delaware Press, 2011), 234–5, and n.16.

21. As he noted in his 1960 letter to Moss (*SL*, 119): "I don't mean to accuse the exalted powers of squeamishness; after all, they put everything aside for [the 1946 publication of John] Hersey's 'Hiroshima.' But I have a feeling that they think this sort of brutally straightforward stuff is all very proper in reportage, and possibly even in a story, but that poetry is expected to exhibit the more fragile delicacies of the soul, etc."

and the meaning of form—and also of his own identity as a Jewish poet, someone who had served in the war and *seen* a concentration camp, an identification fully suppressed in *Stones*. As he remarked years later:

> In time I came to feel an awed reverence for what the Jews of Europe had undergone, a sense of marvel at the hideousness of what they have been forced to endure. I came to feel that it was important to be worthy of their sacrifices, to justify my survival in the face of their misery and extinction, and slowly I began to shed my shame at being Jewish.[22]

"Rites and Ceremonies" is a crucial document in Hecht's emerging identity as a poet profoundly rooted in his ethnic past. Divided into four sections, "The Room," "The Fire Sermon," "The Dream," and "Words for the Day of Atonement," the poem ranges from an opening Psalm-like personal confession to narrative pastiche borrowed from historical sources to a lyrical resounding of George Herbert to snippets of quotations from *King Lear* to passages selected verbatim from the Jewish Service for the Eve of the Day of Atonement to an elaborate use of Hebrew Scripture spun into stanzas of considerable complexity: all in the service of seeking an explanation for the suffering brought about by the Holocaust.

Hecht took his title, with some irony, from the Anglican *Book of Common Prayer*. The phrase, "Rites and Ceremonies," first appeared on the 1559 title page and in the prefatory "Act for the Uniformity of Common Prayer." Apart from this irony, "rites" draws attention to the notion of the poem as a "rite" of passage for the individual speaker and for the culture on whose behalf he speaks. ("The Room," Hecht tells us "is based on my own personal experience as an infantry rifleman in Germany...as well as on some written accounts by survivors of the German Concentration Camps.")[23] And in conjunction with "rites,"

---

22. Quoted from *Anthony Hecht in Conversation with Philip Hoy* (1999; rev. 3rd edn. London: BTL, 2004), 28.
23. The quotation is taken from Hecht's three-page typescript "Introduction" to a reading of "Rites and Ceremonies," given on Yom Kippur. n.d. Hecht Archive, Box 108. Along with Hecht's introduction, I am indebted to Peter Sacks, "Anthony Hecht's 'Rites and Ceremonies': Reading *The Hard Hours*," in *The Burdens of Formality*, 62–96; and especially to Helaine Smith, who let me read her manuscript, "Teaching Particulars: Conversations with My Students," which includes an extended discussion of this poem, with additional commentary and notes on Hecht's sources. Further quotations from Smith are to this work, which has now been published in slightly different form as *Teaching Particulars: Literary Conversations in Grades 6–12* (Philadelphia: Paul Dry Inc., 2015), 149–60.

the concept of "ceremonies" attends to the needful ways that cultures retain their identity through rituals, especially when confronted by threats. This is true, as the poem tells us, not just for the persecuted who pray in times of great need—"He is saying a prayer for all whom this room shall kill," the poet notes and quotes from Psalm 3: "*I cried unto the Lord God with my voice, / And He has heard me out [of] His holy hill*"—but also for the persecutors, whether the ceremony is of the trumped-up juridical kind reported in section II or, as recounted in section III, of the "annual event celebrated in Rome at Carnival time for some two hundred years, from 1468 to 1668,"[24] in which acts of cruelty against man and beast are the main entertainment. There is, of course, a great difference in the use to which rites and ceremonies are put, and one of the poem's burdens is to make this distinction emphatic.

But only part of the challenge involved the complex stitching together of different kinds of verse. Some ten years after completing the poem, Hecht still voiced uncertainty about the results in a 1979 letter to the poet and critic Daniel Hoffman, who had written an appreciative essay on Hecht for *The Harvard Guide to Contemporary American Writing* (1979):

> You are the only reader I have ever come across who has not stopped at noticing the debt to Eliot—Lowell remarked as much—but could see the "double-edged" nature of that allusion to him in a poem about the Holocaust. You were right in detecting the consequent complication of tone, involving homage but bitterness, and both overlaying the horror of historical fact. You are the first person to make me feel the poem is not a pretentious failure.[25]

Hecht was referring to the fact that not only does his poem employ, with the intention of updating, many of the devices of the modernist long poem initiated by *The Waste Land*—fragmentation, allusion, quotation, the employment of different voices, spiritual depletion, and so on—but that the second section of his poem, "The Fire Sermon," specifically begged to be compared to "The Waste Land." Eliot had used the same title for the third section of his poem, but Hecht's "Fire Sermon" has little to do with Eliot's concern with spiritual purification, whether Buddhist or Augustinian, except ironically, since the subject of Christian purification leads directly to Jewish punishment in "Rites

24. Hecht, "Introduction," 2.
25. Letter, AH to Daniel Hoffman, 14 November 1979 (*SL*, 184–5).

and Ceremonies" ("Gott mit uns" is "the motto of the German army, inscribed on the buttons and buckles of all their military uniforms"[26]) and has much to do with locating, in "historical fact," the European practice of Jewish persecution by Christians, dating back to the Black Death. Hecht recounts, in detail, an episode that comes to hideous fruition in the beautiful cathedral town of Strasbourg, its famous minster evidencing, says the poet, in a revealing phrase, "the perpendicular tendency / Peculiar to German cathedrals." His "Fire Sermon" comes to its dramatic point by describing not the soul's desired metaphorical "burning, burning, burning, burning" (Eliot's phrasing), but the burning of two Jews who, under torture, are made to confess to poisoning wells. The section then concludes on a more lyrical note, with a moving, complex, six-stanza adaptation of Herbert's "Denial," addressing the subject of God's abandonment of his people.

Hecht copied from Herbert the number of stanzas, the line patterning, the unusual rhyme scheme (ababx), indeed, even some of Herbert's phrases and spelling practices, as in the fourth stanza:

> O that thou shouldst give dust a tongue
> To crie to thee,
> And then not heare it crying! Who is strong
> When the flame eats his knee
> O hear my prayer...

In a strong countermove, however, Hecht's adaptation concludes not, as in Herbert, with an answering "chime" that signals a responsive God, but by turning back on itself, repeating nearly verbatim the first stanza and its troubling final line:

> It is barren hereabout
> And the wind is cold,
> And the crack of fire, melting of prayer and shout
> Is blown past the sheepfold
> Out of hearing.

As Mary Jo Salter has rightly observed, Hecht's "Out of hearing," a significant variant of Herbert's "No hearing," is a "brilliant stroke," and while, at one level, the repetition formally closes off this lyrical interlude, at another level, the closing phrase leaves the gap wide open between suppliant and auditor, speaker and God.

---

26. Hecht, "Introduction," 2.

Hecht, by saving his refrain "Out of hearing" for the initial and final stanzas—instead of the buried middle stanzas, as in Herbert—achieves a kind of formal closure. But the aural distance between Hecht's refrains is greater, a linkage almost "Out of hearing" itself, and any satisfaction we may have in the circular structure is undercut by the meaning of the words. No rhyme has been mended, the God–man relation remains "Out of hearing."[27]

To press further we might ask what wider purpose does this adaptation serve? As important as it was for Hecht—as well as poets of his generation—to come to terms with Eliot, I doubt that this anxiety alone is what created the long delay or gestation. The further challenge facing Hecht lay not in creating an alternative Hebraic narrative to Eliot's *Waste Land*—irony, after all, is one of modernism's great legacies—but to construct a narrative other than that of another gloomy wasteland, centering on spiritual depletion, for a people who have been through a horror far greater than what Eliot recounted in his poems. In this context, Allen Tate's "Ode to the Confederate Dead" must have formed an interesting object lesson for Hecht. Also long in the making, it wrestled with Eliot's ghost, eventually taking *The Waste Land* and its sense of cultural despair into the Deep South, as ironic commentary on, and moving elegy about, the disappearance of heroic values in a modern age. But it was hardly thinkable for Hecht to address his Jewish subjects in the same despairing elegiac manner, or simply to conclude with a variation on Eliot's "Shantih shantih shantih."

Hecht's solution was to continue in the ironic mode for one more section and then to dispense with irony altogether in the final section. In the first instance, to the artfully described ceremonial humiliations accompanying the Roman carnival, "The Dream" includes

a putative witness of this event…the French poet Joachim Du Bellay (1522–1560) who spent five years in Rome as steward to his relative, Cardinal Jean Du Bellay, to whose entourage his parents had attached him in the hope of getting him over a love affair they disapproved of. During his stay in Rome he wrote beautiful sonnets of heart-sick nostalgia for his home in Anjou.

Testifying to their attraction, Hecht, in fact, translated one of these "beautiful sonnets" in *The Hard Hours*, "Heureux Qui Comme Ulysse,

27. Salter, "But No Hearing: Hecht, Lowell, Moore, and their Responses to Herbert's Use of Rhyme." Quoted by permission of the author from her unpublished essay delivered at the University of North Carolina-Greensboro conference, "George Herbert's Travels: International Print and Cultural Legacies" (9–11 October 2008).

a Fait un Beau Voyage," but Du Bellay's appearance in "Rites and Ceremonies" is for a different reason. He is an example, tenderly ironized by Hecht, of a "putative witness" indifferent to, or who somehow overlooks, the scourging and buffeting of others: a poet who was "There, in the Corso," but thinking only of being elsewhere. As Hecht notes with a further touch of irony, remembering his major subject, but speaking now directly to Du Bellay, "And yet they too are exiles." He concludes:

> Think rather, if you must,
> Of Piranesian, elegiac woes,
> Rome's grand declensions, that all-but-speaking dust.
> Or think of the young gallants and their lust.
> Or wait for the next heat, the buffaloes.

We might be reminded of Allen Tate of the Ode, or, less immediately, of any poet who stands on the sidelines at the moment of crucial political events, and think too with sympathetic irony as Hecht does, because surely a part of him understands, with Du Bellay, the attraction to the themes and subjects he enumerates but relinquishes with the severe turn of thought in the final section of the poem.

"The Last Part is called 'Words for the Day of Atonement.' I will note about it only that it was written when this country was at war in Viet Nam."[28] This final section of the poem, honoring "the most solemn of all the holy days in the Jewish Liturgical calendar,"[29] is woven almost entirely out of the Hebrew Bible, especially Psalms and the prophets, but laden as it is with quotations, "like tesserae,"[30] it has its own logic: to balance humiliation against faith. The section begins with an often-quoted phrase: "Merely to have survived is not an index of excellence, / Nor, given the way things go, / Even of low cunning." To the recently persecuted, this sentiment might seem shocking, and Hecht, I think, imitates the swelling sound of righteous indignation in the Jeremiad-like quotation borrowed from Psalm 37:35: "Yet I have seen the wicked in great power / And spreading himself like a green bay tree. / And the good as if they had never been." But then, in the next stanza, recovering some balance, the biblical cadences, now taken directly from Isaiah 1:9, become quieter and

---

28. Hecht, "Introduction," 3.   29. Hecht, "Introduction," 1.
30. Letter, AH to Norman German, 16 September 1982.

their purpose more concentrated. Hecht's division of the scriptural quotation into verse highlights the natural rhythmic patterns of speech.

> Except the Lord of hosts had left unto us
> A very small remnant,
> We should have been as Sodom,
> We should have been like unto Gomorrah.
> And to what purpose, as the darkness closes about
> And the child screams in the jellied fire,
> Had best be our present concern,
> Here in this wilderness of comfort
> In which we dwell.

The concluding image of "this wilderness of comfort" captures much of the matter and tone of this final section, "comfort" being one of the ends of the poem but recognizing, too, that it must also include the concept of the wilderness, and that "the wilderness of comfort / In which we dwell" (as distinguished from a wasteland and "The Waste Land") begins at home, with "words for atonement," that is, with a recognition of sin's penetrating inclusiveness. "Shall we now consider the suspicious postures of our virtue / The deformed consequences of our love, / The painful issues of our mildest acts." Hecht will then hew this line of argument down to the finest point:

> Shall we ask
> Where is there one
> Mad, poor and betrayed enough to find
> Forgiveness for us, saying,
> "None does offend,
> None, I say,
> None."

The quotation, spoken by Lear,[31] "lays bare our guilt," as Peter Sacks notes.[32] Hecht's tripartite splitting of Shakespeare's single line, into smaller and smaller units, each further highlighting "None," makes ludicrous the possibility of even thinking that someone might be free of offense. As concerned as Hecht is with the idea of the "remnant," if there is a voice crying in the wilderness, it is fundamentally against exceptionalism.

---

31. *King Lear*, 4.6.168, in G. Blakemore Evans, general editor, *The Riverside Shakespeare* (Boston: Houghton Mifflin, 1974).
32. Sacks, "Anthony Hecht's 'Rites and Ceremonies,'" 87.

I understand Hecht's astringency here to be not only verbal and moral. It is also ethical and political, applicable to Jew and Gentile, conscious not only of the ancient religious occasion of Yom Kippur but of the present moment of writing, in which another "chosen nation" is exerting itself, this time in Vietnam. At the same time, the descent to "none" must be seen as also marking, indeed arriving at, a beginning. "And yet this light, / The work of thy fingers…"

For many years, I have looked longingly at the ellipses, hoping for something big to emerge on the part of the speaker, and it does, just not in the triumphal way that people like to hear—more along the lines of building a book of common prayer out of lines from the Hebrew Bible. In this case, it involves first carefully knitting the religious community together into a "we," in the name of God. As Helaine Smith notes, "these ten lines, with their powerful and lovely repetitions, begin the morning 'Selichos' ('forgiveness') service in the weeks preceding Yom Kippur. They are sung aloud by the person leading the service." The poem then shifts focus to include a lyrical, first-person, intimate rewriting of Job in Herbertian stanzas to sound the mystery of creation; and for the immediate Jewish community, Hecht reproduces in prose a prayer from the service of Yom Kippur, in the manner of sounding a general announcement of forgiveness to the "whole community." "These lines immediately follow the recitation of Kol Nidre ('All vows') in the evening prayer service that begins the Day of Atonement. It is recited three times by the cantor and then three times more by the congregation."

At which point, Hecht turns to address God, as he had done at the beginning of the poem, but now leaving no room for the earlier phrase, *"in whom we doubt."*

> Father, I also pray
> For those among us whom we know not, those
>   Dearest to thy grace,
> The saved and saving remnant, the promised third,
>   Who in a later day
> When we again are compassed about with foes,
> Shall be for us a nail in thy holy place
> There to abide according to thy word.
>
>   Neither shall the flame
> Kindle upon them, nor the fire burn
>   A hair of them, for they

> Shall be thy care when it shall come to pass,
>   And calling on thy name
> In the hot kilns and ovens, they shall turn
> To thee as it is prophesied, and say,
> *"He shall come down like rain upon mown grass."*

As Peter Sacks has remarked, "there is no sudden access of belief, and no miraculous escape from future pain. In the wake of the Holocaust we are not asked to believe in any actual rescue from the ovens."[33] But there is a heightening of a Miltonic register here: a note of prophetic assertion assumed by the poet as he imagines a future that is remarkably like the past and yet refuses to be swayed from his course. In such circumstances, we cannot help recalling, in the final italicized line also drawn from the Psalms (72:6), the hapless old man in "The Room" "saying a prayer for all"; but against that image of futility then, earlier in time, earlier in the poem, is one of remembrance now. The comfort in the wilderness Hecht finally offers is not from a false sense of triumphalism, let alone through expressing outrage or righteous indignation. It comes from the connecting line, the scriptural line, to be recalled here and remembered in the future, and the community that is recreated and sustained in the process. In the place of a wasteland is the promised "remnant."

Two poems in an envelope do not a book make, as the presence of a third poem, "Rites and Ceremonies" makes clear. "There will be / Many hard hours, / As an old poem says"—says father to son in "Adam," says the poet to the reader of *The Hard Hours*; and if one of the book's distinguishing and still much remembered features is to stretch in the direction of history, another, sometimes forgotten, is to produce poems of remarkable, often troubled intimacy:

> When you are crouched away
> In a strange clothes closet
> Hiding from one who's "It"
> And the dark crowds in,
> Do not be afraid—
> O, if you can, believe
> In a father's love
> That you shall know some day.

33. Sacks, "Anthony Hecht's 'Rites and Ceremonies,'" 89.

It's good to hear, at last, what a father can say. This is a stanza from "Adam," another poem about the place of belief when the "dark crowds in," in this case necessitated by parental divorce, leaving father and son on opposite sides of the Atlantic, the son where "men speak / A different mother tongue." What is immediately notable is the careful reduction in scale, appropriate to a child. Each stanza is a small room of regular proportion—eight lines of five or six syllables, each enclosed by a simple rhyme ("away"/"day"). The diction is mostly in monosyllables, the tonal range small but comforting, only swelling slightly with the apostrophe ("O"). This is a poet who knows about childhood fears (remember the boy in "A Hill"), and threatening games (the ominous "It" in caps and quotation marks looks forward, much later, to the game of "All Out" in "Presumptions of Death"), but seeks to offer paternal comfort. "O, if you can, believe / In a father's love." How strained if one recalls "Rites and Ceremonies." An earlier version read "In my unending love," but the change to "a father's love," along with continuing the poem's scriptural echoes on a smaller scale, invites us to think of its alien and painfully gendered opposite: that "Where you are men speak / A different mother tongue"—painful, that is, as well, to the person writing the poem. This is a father who knows all about loneliness.

　　"Adam" is one of many poems precipitated by Hecht's troubled marriage of five-and-a-half years to Patricia Harris. The two were married in February of 1954, separated in 1959, and finally divorced in 1961. The following year "Pat" remarried, this time a wealthy Belgian, Philippe Lambert, thus taking the two children (Jason, born 1956, and Adam, born 1958) abroad with her. It might be further noted that Pat, a one-time model for *Vogue*, came to move in the fast set, especially on Long Island, which temporarily at least included the Kennedys, and something of that "beautiful people" environment finds its way into "Clair de Lune." Much later Hecht remarked that "while the marriage had been an unhappy one virtually from the start, its failure was a terrible blow to my self-esteem, and it was not I who sought to terminate it."[34] There is little reason to question this description; evidence abounds in *The Hard Hours*. Not that Hecht followed Lowell in *Life Studies* and spoke of " 'Woe that is in Marriage,' " nor is Pat often the subject of the poems. She isn't. In fact, the only surviving poem

---

34. Letter, AH to J. D. McClatchy, 26 December 1984 (*SL*, 218–19).

directly addressed to her by name, "An Offering to Patricia,"[35] which reflects warmly, although at a distance, on their time together in Italy in 1954–55, never made it into the collection, but the wounds from what Hecht called "the terrible blow [done] to my self-esteem" ripple through *The Hard Hours* like the "sliding moonlit sea" described in "A Letter."

The major exception, and it is only partially an exception, is "The Vow." One of Hecht's celebrated early poems—as mentioned in Chapter 2, it was included in Donald Hall's anthology, selected by Hecht himself for *Poet's Choice*, edited by Paul Engle and Joseph Langland (1962), and it even appeared on the Advanced Placement exam in English given to college bound students—it too is based on an incident experienced during the turbulent first year of their marriage: a miscarriage.

The opening stanza makes it clear that this is a *Hard Hours* poem. The setting is quickly, indeed gravely, established with the first line, a truncated single sentence: "In the third month, a sudden flow of blood." We might catch an echo of the opening of Yeats' "Leda and the Swan," another abnormal "birth" poem, which begins with "A sudden blow," and furthers a sense of drama here, now figured on a domestic, not epochal, scale. (It also anticipates a classical concern by both poets with questions of knowledge.) Then follows some archaic biblical language to mark the occasion; the forthright presence of "blood," soon repeated with greater personal urgency as "blood of my blood, nearly my child"; and finally the haunting image of the speaker's wife, whose face is turned away to the window, its paleness reflected in the landscape beyond, like one of Hardy's wraiths:

> In the third month, a sudden flow of blood.
> The mirth of tabrets ceaseth, and the joy
> Also of the harp. The frail image of God
> Lay spilled and formless. Neither girl nor boy,
> But yet blood of my blood, nearly my child.
> All that long day
> Her pale face turned to the window's mild
> Featureless grey.

"Nearly my child," not "our child": mother and father are not a couple at this point in the poem.

Domestically speaking, the surprise here is how radically Hecht has rethought the actual events on which the poem is based as reported in

---

35. The poem is printed in *Poetry* 198 (September, 2011), 454.

several letters to his parents in late fall of 1954. What Hecht had called a "God-sent solution to our problems"[36]—the "problems" involving an unwanted pregnancy, including the possibility of an abortion, for reasons that remain obscure but seem to reflect on their marital difficulties and perhaps Pat's health—has been remade into something quite different in the poem: a later, further, more complex reflection about the after-effects of the miscarriage on wife and husband, as both struggle with the prospects of going forward. (The initial reference to the "third month" helps to sound the temporal alarm here.)

The poem also turns into one of Hecht's knottiest after the first stanza—no doubt justifying its placement on an exam, but also inviting some careful reading—in part because Hecht blends together classical, largely Sophoclean wisdom, drawn from *Oedipus at Colonus*, with a distant memory of Lowell's "The Boston Nativity" in *Land of Unlikeness* (1944), in which Lowell bitterly laments the stillborn birth of his own baby on Christmas Day, the same month of Pat's miscarriage. The choric Sophocles emerges abruptly as the subject of the second stanza, but put in the mouth of "the dead thing" as dreamt by the mother:

> And for some nights she whimpered as she dreamed
> The dead thing spoke, saying: "Do not recall
> Pleasure at my conception. I am redeemed
> From pain and sorrow. Mourn rather for all
> Who breathlessly issue from the bone gates,
>   The gates of horn,
>   For truly it is best of all the fates
>   Not to be born."

Best to forget me, the ghost child says, even the pleasure at my conception, since death has redeemed me from sorrow, and to mourn those rather issuing through "the gates of horn" (from Book 6 of Virgil's *Aeneid*), who come to experience the world as it is, which vision only serves to remind us that—looping back to Sophocles—it is better not to be born at all. This is consolation of a bleak order, to say the least, but one the poem seriously entertains, as did Hecht:

I like the idea of having a child so young as to be yet unborn speak with all the aged, bitter, Sophoclean wisdom of the great chorus in "Oedipus at Colonus." This is not just being tricky and paradoxical; you are meant to feel

36. Letter, AH to his parents, 2 December 1954 (*SL*, 109–10).

that the child, being somehow prior to life (in some Wordsworthian realm of glory, perhaps) and also dead, has a source of special knowledge that entitles it to make such formidable pronouncements. It is in a double sense separated from the world of the living. So there is something very cold-blooded about the way it talks.[37]

Not only would Hecht later publish a powerful translation of the chorus's full speech in *The Transparent Man* (1990), which includes the lines "Not to be born is, past all yearning, best. / And second best is, having seen the light, / To return at once to deep oblivion"; but some years later he would object to the Mezey/Barnes translation of Borges' sonnet, "Oedipus and the Riddle," precisely because it softens the prospects of oblivion as a necessary consolation for the woes of life.[38]

But the poem also works hard against these twin options of oblivion. Again through the continuing voice of the ghost child, the speaker offers advice of a more intimately urgent nature, with "the child" now taking on an even spookier role. Linked to Jesus by seasonal inference (with the joy of the nativity now inverted, and the Christmas lights associated with death), the unborn fetus reminds the mother that "she nearly died of an asphyxiating asthma on Christmas Eve,"[39] a memory, however, that she is urged to forget. In much the same manner, she must also separate herself emotionally from the flesh that was in her womb:

> "Mother, a child lay gasping for bare breath
> On Christmas Eve when Santa Claus had set
> Death in the stocking, and the lights of death
> Flamed in the tree. O, if you can, forget
> You were the child, turn to my father's lips
> Against the time
> When his cold hand puts forth its fingertips
> Of jointed lime."

After the apostrophe, the closing instructions are for her to turn to "my father's lips," turn away from the window, that is, and to embrace

37. Quoted from *Poet's Choice*, ed. Paul Engle and Joseph Langland (New York: The Dial Press, 1962), 201.
38. Letter, AH to Timothy Murphy, 3 July 2000. In turn, the Sophoclean line, "best of all the fates / Not to be born," becomes something of a signature phrase of Hecht's. Writes David Lehman to AH, 18 May 1980: "I was interested in the allusion to Oedipus at Colonus in your poem 'The Vow.' On page 112 of *Divine Comedies*, Merrill paraphrases the same Sophoclean line. That seems, for me, a matter worth pursuing." Hecht Archive. Hecht's relationship to Merrill will be pursued in Chapter 4.
39. Letter, AH to Norman German, 16 September 1982.

him before his hand becomes stone—the image of "jointed lime" hinting at the bond used to hold rocks together (in this case fingers), as well serving as a metonym for death. (Lime was used to dissolve dead bodies, as Hecht would have known only too well through his World War II experiences.)

But this is not a poem that moves forward easily. Having constructed this passionate plea for both forgetting the child and reuniting with the husband—and what could be more powerful than to have it issue from the mouth of the dead child itself?—the speaker still can't rid himself of the lure of Sophoclean oblivion (now phrased in italics) or thoughts about the troubled origins of the miscarriage itself: that this was a child created by a tempestuous couple, their combined mix too bold to inform (i.e. create, shape, compose) a child:

> Doctors of Science, what is man that he
> Should hope to come to a good end? *The best*
> *Is not to have been born.* And could it be
> That Jewish diligence and Irish jest
> The consent of flesh and a midwinter storm
>   Had reconciled,
> Was yet too bold a mixture to inform
>   A simple child?

If the first question is choric in nature, the last, more personal, is as much warning as a solution. To overcome this basic, indeed elemental, difference between "Jewish diligence and Irish jest" is the difficult work of the last stanza, the effort itself a sign of the challenge to be met. Hecht recasts the miscarriage as a trial for them both, recalling and adapting Zechariah 13:8. As gold is tried to find out if it is true, so are we, regardless of ethnic or religious differences. In conjunction with "gold" and trial, the additional reference to the inclusive Gentile *and* Jew by Hecht (as opposed to, say, the exclusive "Gentile *or* Jew," of Eliot's *The Waste Land*), might remind us of *The Merchant of Venice*, and, if so, of the work of bonding that lies ahead for both of them. To add further conviction to his argument, Hecht then concludes the poem with a triple series of oaths to the dead child, and in the process refashions the earlier image of the flames of death in the Christmas tree into the refining flames of an imaginary altar:

> Even as gold is tried, Gentile and Jew.
> If that ghost was a girl's, I swear to it:

> Your mother shall be far more blessed than you.
> And if a boy's, I swear: The flames are lit
> That shall refine us; they shall not destroy
>   A living hair.
> Your younger brothers shall confirm in joy
>   This that I swear.

"The Vow" is about the vows made to the ghost child, a vow that proved true as it happened since husband and wife were to produce two "younger brothers," but there is also more than a hint that the poem muses over the renewal of the couple's marriage vows: the hand mentioned in the third stanza now being retrieved as a symbol of their marriage by the reference to gold in the last—together suggesting the poet's desire for a renewed pledge of their fidelity to each other, the "us" mentioned near the end. "It was not I who sought to terminate" the marriage Hecht said much later, and "The Vow" indicates as much, the husband asking, through the dead child, for the wife to turn her face toward him and imagine, against many odds, including his own Sophoclean doubtings, a future together.

A far cry from the simple urgencies of "Adam," "The Vow" represents Hecht at his most Donnean in *The Hard Hours*: masculine in its persuasive force, complex in its imagery, startling in its shifts of thought, nervously walking the line between oblivion and assertion, except perhaps for one missing Donnean impulse: a pledge of love.[40] The word never appears in the poem, a telling omission perhaps, but its absence here is more than made up for by its presence elsewhere in *The Hard Hours*—"love" and its notable contrary "lust."

Into the latter group fall a number of poems, including "The End of the Weekend," based on an anecdote supplied by Ted Hughes,[41] which

40. For the general importance of Donne on Hecht's poetry see *Anthony Hecht in Conversation with Philip Hoy*, 71–2; and Post, "Donne, Discontinuity, and the Proto-Post Modern: The Case of Anthony Hecht," *John Donne Journal* 26 (2007), 283–94. To mention Donne is not to overlook the audible presence of Lowell here, especially apparent in the third stanza through the wrenched syntax and the alliterative pressure and marked stresses in the first and last syllables of the lines ("Death / death," "flamed / forget." I owe this point to my colleague, Stephen Yenser.

41. Letter, AH to Sandra McPherson, 4 October 1992 (*SL*, 245–6). Reflective of Hughes' primitivism, the poem also shows an interest in Frost's New England "gothic"—an interest to be developed more fully in Hecht's later dramatic monologues—as well as

begins as a teasingly proposed, sexually intense encounter ("the lariat /
Whirls into darkness"), only to be suddenly interrupted by the sound
of something in the attic. "The Dover Bitch," of course, Hecht's noto-
rious bad-boy poem, appeared in print about the time that he and his
wife were filing for separation ("But all the time he was talking she
had in mind / The notion of what his whiskers would feel like / On
the back of her neck"). His translation from Baudelaire, "To a Madonna,
ex voto in the Spanish Style," was also written about the same time,
but in pointed couplets. By the close, the torments of lust become
positively and grotesquely murderous:

> And like a circus knife-thrower, I'll aim
> At the pure center of your gentle frame,
> And plunge those blades into your beating heart,
> Your bleeding, suffering, palpitating heart.

And "The Man Who Married Magdalene," the seediest of the poems
in the volume, bore, as if for purposes of deflection, the subtitle a
"Variation on a Theme by Louis Simpson." In a note to Hecht, Simpson
took specific exception to Hecht's raunchy second stanza:

> And you can get a blow-job
> Where other men have pissed
> In the little room that's sacred
> To the Evangelist—

Rhyming "pissed" with "Evangelist"—the room sacred to him is a
John—provides something of a double shocker. We should keep these
poems in mind when Hecht is sometimes charged with belonging to
"a genteel tradition in American poetry."[42]

At the other end of the amatory spectrum are poems of a more
quietly meditative order. These are ruminative, not dramatic. Thinking
about the body in an era when people were reading and thinking
about Donne, Marvell, and Yeats—to say nothing of Plato—meant

---

bearing the stamp (again) of Yeats' "Leda and the Swan" in the image of "A great black
presence [that] beats its wings in wrath." And yet, for all its literary associations, the
poem is typical of Hecht at this point in his career in maintaining its composure and
pursuing its own "end."

42. Denis Donoghue, *New York Times*, 27 March 1977, 6–7, review of *Millions of Strange
Shadows*. Letter, Louis Simpson to AH, 17 April 1961. "Do I like the poem? Frankly,
I don't like stanza two. I know this makes me seem a prissy jerk; but I don't feel the
wit is really enough to offset the blow-job and the pissed. The rest of it seems lovely."
Hecht Archive.

considering, dialogically, the body's connection to the soul, not out of eschatological or redemptive yearnings but as a way of exploring the tension between the divided impulses of desire: the yearning to escape the body, by way of imagining its transcendence, or its extinction, as Hecht argues with considerable subtlety in an essay written in the early 1960s, "Shades of Keats and Marvell." The shades are, respectively, "Ode to a Nightingale" and "The Garden," the essay replete with an epigraph from Yeats: "One feels at moments as if one could with a touch convey a vision—that the mystic vision & sexual love use the same means—opposed yet parallel existence."[43] To put these competing claims between body and soul still more bluntly, in Lear's words: "But to the girdle do the gods inherit / Beneath is all the fiend's."[44]

The two most elaborate poems of this kind are "Ostia Antica" and "The Origin of Centaurs." The latter uses the lines quoted from *Lear* for its epigraph, although shorn of the misogynistic import of the full scene. (The line from Shakespeare preceding the quotation reads: "They're centaurs, though women all above.") Published alongside "The Vow" in 1957 in *The Hudson Review* and casting an odd shadow on it, "The Origin of Centaurs" is a poem of enticingly urbane indirection based on an obscure episode involving Ixion, king of the Lapiths, and utilizing, once again, "a beautifully articulated" stanza form reminiscent of the kind found in *A Summoning of Stones*.[45] Never mentioned by name in the poem, Ixion is more often remembered by readers as the tortured figure in Virgil's underworld, bound forever to a wheel of fire. (The image is recollected in Lear's famous utterance, "I am bound / Upon a wheel of fire, that mine own tears / Do scald like molten lead" (4.6.39–41).) But the part of the legend that fascinates Hecht is the story leading up to the punishment: a tale of eros (and potential adultery), in which Ixion attempts to seduce Hera at a banquet, but is thwarted by Zeus into coupling with a cloud created in Hera's image, "afterwards called Nephele."[46]

Genealogically speaking, it is from this act with the "false Hera" that the race of centaurs is said to spring, and where Hecht's poem

43. Hecht, "Shades of Keats and Marvell," *The Hudson Review* 15 (1962), 50–71; revised slightly in *Obbligati: Essays in Criticism* (New York: Atheneum, 1986), 230–63.
44. *King Lear*, 4.6.125–6.
45. See John Hollander, "On Anthony Hecht," *Raritan* 17 (1997), 140.
46. As described by Robert Graves, a likely source for Hecht's poem, in *The Greek Myths*, 2 vols (New York: George Braziller, 1955), I, 208–9.

eventually ends. But before arriving at this conclusion—the cloud barely hinted in the opening reference to "This mild September mist"—the languorously Marvellian poet seeks to imagine a world free of sensuality and the body's cravings, only to arrive at the recognition that "Sadly the soul must hear / Twitter and cricket where should be all hush." And from this recognition of the senses (teased into being by twittering memories of Keats in "To Autumn"), the poem widens to entertain a cruder truth, as if catching at something in flagrante delicto: that "from the belvedere / A muffled grunt survives in evidence / That love must sweat under the weight of sense." And from here it is only a short, but still delicate step, to the mythic origins of lust and human self-division associated with another moment of sensual "mist": not a season of "mellow fruitfulness" but the misty figure of the goddess Hera herself, as it seemed, at least, to the luxurious and ill-behaved Ixion. In Hecht's beautifully patterned, oblique retelling of the story:

> Or so once thought a man in a Greek mist—
> Who set aside
> The wine-cup and the wine,
> And that deep fissure he alone had kissed,
> All circumscribing line,
> Moved to the very edge in one swift stride
> And took those shawls of nothing for his bride.

Thus began, in a cloud of eros, the race of the centaurs, a myth or mystic vision called into being by sexual desire, but told without a sense of Pindaric outrage (as expressed in one of the sources, the Second Pythian Ode). Why not? The clue is perhaps in the final rhyme: Ixion (or the "Goddess herself"?) is hardly the only person to have suffered erotic marital delusions; and if the girdled poet of *The Hard Hours* is to be knowingly included within this "All circumscribing line"—and how can he not be?—he also charmingly shares, as he must, a further descent into his own centaur-like creation, leaving, in place of "hoofprints," a more delicately Parnassian imprint on the page:

> Was it the Goddess herself? Some dense embrace
> Closed like a bath
> Of love about his head;
> Perfectly silent and without a face.
> Blindfolded on her bed,

> He could see nothing but the aftermath:
> Those powerful, clear hoofprints on the path.

Nestled between "Adam" and "The Vow" in *The Hard Hours*, "The Origin of Centaurs" allows for a little playful Hellenistic breathing room between this pair of personal, urgently biblical poems.[47] (In its withholding of names, one is led to wonder if there is not another, more private story being withheld: not to name, as Hecht knew, invites speculation of this sort.[48]) "Ostia Antica," however, is an altogether more sober venture. As Hecht was to remark much later, in a 1968 letter to L. E. Sissman, about "Ostia Antica" and "Clair de Lune," "the writing of both, and even more, the prolonged thinking about them before writing, was a sort of therapy for me during a troubled time."[49]

"Ostia" was published in 1955, one of the few poems Hecht managed to complete during the difficult year he and Pat spent in Italy: for Pat not quite a year since she sailed home in June of that year, while Hecht continued on his own until returning in December. This is a poem that speaks of loneliness. Although connected to "The Origin of Centaurs" through a similar interest in the word "hush" or "hushed," but now as it appears in Augustine's *Confessions*, the setting for "Ostia" is more ominous. Despite beginning by announcing the sudden arrival of light after a storm and "the departing thunder head in its anger," the same stanza ends by raising the more difficult question: "Where is the spirit's part unwashed / Of all poor spite?" Nature (the body) can be reinvigorated by rain, but can the same be said of the soul, which tends to remember, especially when the matter involves spite?

The ancient Roman port of Ostia Antica was, for Hecht, a perfect site for prolonged thinking about the sexual body and the soul's aversion to the flesh. It included in its history equally rich strains of pagan and Christian culture: the former, in the artifacts testifying to a sexual freedom that Hecht explores with a sensuous naturalism befitting the

---

47. Breathing room perhaps aptly describes the strange coincidence in an undated letter to Richard Wilbur (but probably written around 1963), in which the following remark occurs: "First, thanks for the book and for letting me keep it so long. I'm not sure I really very much cared for it, and the portrait of Pat didn't seem to me very real. I enclose a poem Charlie [Wilbur's wife] asked for." The poem is "The Origin of Centaurs."

48. With regard to Hecht's comments about the identity of the person in "A Letter," see letter, AH to Howard Moss, 9 May 1961 (*SL*, 122).

49. Letter, AH to L. E. Sissman, 2 March 1968.

spaciously elaborate stanzas; the latter through its associations with St. Augustine, whose ninth chapter of the *Confessions* is set in Ostia, and from which chapter Hecht quotes Augustine's intense conversation with his dying mother, Monica, in a contemplative sequence that also owes something, at least initially, to Milton's "Nativity Ode" and the banishing of the pagan gods:

> But softly, beneath the flutesong and volatile shriek
> Of birds, are to be heard discourse
> Mother and son.
>
> "If there were hushed
> To us the images of earth, its poles
> Hushed, and the waters of it,
> And hushed the tumult of the flesh, even
> The voice intrinsic of our souls,
> Each tongue and token hushed and the long habit
> Of thought, if that first light, the given
> To us were hushed,
>
> So that the washed
> Object, fixed in the sun, were dumb,
> And to the mind its brilliance
> Were from beyond itself, and the mind were clear
> As the unclouded dome
> Wherein all things diminish, in that silence
> Might we not confidently hear
> God as he wished?"

This beautifully suspended quotation, ending with a question, has been rightly admired by the English poet Elizabeth Jennings for capturing "the intensity and the mystery of the prose translation" of Augustine's Latin;[50] and if Hecht exhibits greater freedom in the penultimate stanza in the poem, in exchanging "hushed" for "washed," it is in part to recall his earlier concern with the unwashed spirit and the matter of spite. Jennings is, in almost every respect, Hecht's ideal reader, as she climbs the rungs of religious mystery and the poetic imagination, but the

50. Elizabeth Jennings, *Every Changing Shape: Mystical Experience and the Making of Poems* (London: Andre Deutsch, 1961), 27–8. The prose translation is that of E. B. Pusey in the Everyman Edition of *The Confessions of St. Augustine* (London: Dent, 1907), ix. 24–5. Jennings writes of both Pusey and Hecht: "The precision of the Latin has been retained yet the uninflected English translations have provided a fluidity, a subtlety that are entirely faithful to the sense of wonder which informs Augustine's mystical experience" (p. 28).

answer Hecht gives to this carefully amplified question about hearing
"God as he wishes" is disconcerting:

> Then from the grove
> Suddenly falls a flight of bells.
> A figure moves from the wood,
> Darkly approaching at the hour of vespers
> Along the ruined walls.
> And bearing heavy articles of blood
> And symbols of endurance, whispers,
> "This is Love."

It's as if, in this Augustinian ascent, we have been led to hope for a
comforting whisper from Herbert but get Hardy instead, or if Herbert,
the austere Herbert of "The Sacrifice" in the reference to the "heavy
articles of blood," until we recall, as well, the flow of blood in "The
Vow." Endurance at this hard hour seems about all Hecht can muster
on Love's behalf. It is with some relief, no doubt calculated by the poet,
that we find the next poem to be "The Dover Bitch."

The palm for the loneliest of the "Pat" poems in *The Hard Hours*,
however, might well be awarded to the other verse Hecht mentioned
in his letter to Sissman, "Clair de Lune," which begins:

> Powder and scent and silence. The young dwarf
> Shoulders his lute. The moon is Levantine.
> It settles its pearl in every glass of wine.
> Harlequin is already at the wharf.

The poem, a magical work that should be better known,[51] appeared in
The New Yorker in August 1960, a year after the couple filed for separation—its title recalling Claude Debussy's serenely melancholic piano
rendition of Paul Verlaine's poem of the same title. "A reverie / Of light
chromatics" is how Hecht elsewhere refers to Debussy in conjunction
with Monet.[52] With the additional help of Watteau's painting, *The
Departure for Cythera*, and of a John Dowland lute song, Hecht managed to add a further level of symbolist mystery to the setting, which
is as exquisitely rendered as it is oblique. It is a mysteriousness that
continues even after Hecht, some thirty-five years later, offered a gloss
on the poem. In a brief essay entitled "Missing the Boat," about the

---

51. It is excluded from J. D. McClatchy's otherwise fine edition of *Anthony Hecht: Selected
Poems* (New York: Alfred A. Knopf, 2011).
52. "The Venetian Vespers," section II.

subject of dreams in poetry, his own included, he spoke again of this lyric being written during "a protracted interval of profound unhappiness, in which my first marriage was disintegrating."[53] As with the poem, the essay muses over, without quite revealing, the private circumstances underlying events, and yet in alluding to them, Hecht also courts our interest.

Without wishing either to repeat his helpful comments on some of the sources for the imagery or to turn this lyric into a realist narrative, I would suggest that the poem reflects (and like a recurring dream amplifies) the haunting moment of recognition whereby the speaker first comes to understand, finally but absolutely, that he has no place in the other person's heart and the accompanying sense of helplessness to be able to do anything about it: no further vows to make; no subjects to analyze; only to register the profound gulf of silence that now exists between two people after the party is over and the beautiful people, as in Watteau's painting, have gone elsewhere:

> Taffeta whispers. Someone is staring through
> The white ribs of the pergola. She stares
> At a small garnet pulse that disappears
> Steadily seaward. Ah, my dear, it is you.

The "garnet pulse" here (passed over by Hecht in his analysis of the poem) might be the light shed by the boat moving seaward or, more intimately, it might refer to the pulsating heart of someone on that boat, now longingly stared after by the woman—the original sense of "garnet," a gemstone, stems from the Middle English "garnet" meaning "dark red"—or it might even include the speaker's awareness ("Ah, my dear, it is you") that it is his beloved's heart that "disappears" over the horizon, leaving the now disembodied speaker ("But you are not alone"), like the gardener on the "dark estate," to tend to the "lunar ashes of a rose"—his own broken heart. Poems, like dreams, don't require that we chose only one meaning; but if this summary is at all on track, it's understandable that a poet of Hecht's guarded disposition

---

53. Hecht, "Missing the Boat," in Roderick Townley, ed., *Night Errands: How Poets Use Dreams* (Pittsburgh: University of Pittsburgh Press, 1995), 51–6. Hecht notes his ironic use of Dowland's last line in his poem ("Happy the heart that thinks of no removes"); other images in the song would seem to pertain as well, as does Dowland's concern for the superfluous trifles prized by "ladies" versus his own valuation of the true heart. "The moon-pearl" Hecht mentions from Pliny appears in Ben Jonson's *Volpone*, Act 3.6.190–1, not Act 5.

might wish to enwrap or enshroud this painful recognition at the heart of the poem in so many levels of mystery. "This is your nightmare," as he says to himself in the final stanza. The phrase might seem a little flat until we realize that, for all the nightmarish events depicted in *The Hard Hours*, this is the only time Hecht uses the word itself, as if reserving the word for this special but recurring occasion ("this is *your* nightmare").

> Those cold hands are yours.
> The pain in the drunken singing is your pain.
> Morning will taste of bitterness again.
> The heart turns to stone, but it endures.

"On the threshold of silence," "Clair de Lune" is the last of Hecht's poems about his failed marriage but not the last of Hecht's love poems in *The Hard Hours*.

By way of bringing this chapter to a close, I want to consider "A Letter" and "Message from the City" in light of the overall structure of the volume as Hecht came, I believe, to understand it. Both are epistolary poems linked together not only by their common genre but because the writing of them coincided with a period of intense friendship and epistolary exchanges with the poet Anne Sexton. The correspondence with a poet already celebrated for her confessional verse rubbed off on the making of these poems. They are remarkable for their directly stated, sensuous apprehension of feelings, even if Sexton was not the imagined recipient, as was the case with "A Letter":

> I have been wondering
> What you are thinking about, and by now suppose
> It is certainly not me.
> But the crocus is up, and the lark, and the blundering
> Blood knows what it knows.
> It talks to itself all night, like a sliding moonlit sea.
>
> Of course, it is talking of you.
> At dawn, where the ocean has netted its catch of lights,
> The sun plants one lithe foot
> On that spill of mirrors, but the blood goes worming through
> Its warm Arabian nights,
> Naming your pounding name again in the dark heart-root.

"Here is something hot off the typewriter," Hecht wrote to Howard Moss in May of 1961;[54] and indeed, the emotional impact, the "blundering / Blood," of these opening stanzas is both palpable and precise. The alternating lines, the one nearly double the length of the other, create in their rough regularity, a wave-like, restless ebb and flow of passion to match the major symbol of the sea that courses through poem and poet. Few Hecht poems get to their main point sooner. Denis Donoghue reports: "That poem makes me feel as if the top of my head were taken off."[55] The only remaining mystery, it might seem, is who could be the person causing such sleepless turmoil and gorgeously swelling and retracting lines, who inspired such a fabulous phrase as "Naming your pounding name again in the dark heart-root"? Hecht noted to Moss that he preferred to keep the identity a secret in order "to lend a curious excitement by indicating that there are some things that cannot safely be said." True enough, but Hecht was also still officially married at the time of writing the poem, and along with protecting the recipient's identity, I suspect that anonymity allowed him to write with greater emotional freedom: indeed to approach the kind of direct emotional urgency associated with confessional poetry but without quite crossing over into the immediate familiarity that Sexton was exploring in the poems that would comprise *All My Pretty Ones* (1962). After all, it's not simply the name of his lover that is discreetly kept under cover. "Others are bound to us, the gentle and blameless / Whose names are not confessed / In the ceaseless palaver." Even for epistolary Hecht, the expression of passion didn't mean there weren't limits to what you should say in poetry when the subject involves other people.

"Message from the City" benefited directly from Sexton's advice. "As you see, I have used your discovery about how to end it," Hecht wrote to her, probably in September of 1961.

But I had to put other things in. I know you were trying to pare it down, and I have not stuck things in to make it longer or out of attachment to any lines or details. But I have never tried before, by shifting the order of the parts of a poem, to discover a new emotional sequence for them, and I found it very difficult. The problem was to arrive at the last lines with clarity and restraint, and still have an emotional logic to the little shifts in tone.[56]

54. Letter, AH to Howard Moss, 9 May 1961 (*SL*, 122).
55. Donoghue, review of *Millions of Strange Shadows*.
56. Letter, AH to Anne Sexton, September? 1961 (*SL*, 123). Many years later, in *On The Laws of the Poetic Art* (Princeton: Princeton University Press, 1995), 115–16, Hecht can be found objecting to Sexton's poem, "Her Kind," from *To Bedlam and Back* (1960),

"Little shifts in tone," paring it down: "Message," as the title suggests, is deliberately smaller in scale than "A Letter." The speaker's sense of solitude is measured with raindrops rather than the swelling ocean (until we get to the ending); the verse is loose trimeter, utilizing occasional slant rhymes and generally smaller units of thought, reflecting, as well, the speaker's sense of himself as a small boy hoping to grow. The poem's appeal is along the lines of a familiar letter, in much the same way that letters and poetry were becoming intricately entwined in Sexton's work at the time. "Message" mixes bits of local description and personal details with tender thoughts about the other (the unusual outpouring of "Oh my dear, my dear" is in keeping with Sexton's many private addresses and expostulation).[57] But a named identity is no longer a matter of registered concern, only her distance from the speaker. The careful rendering of small details even suggests Hecht might have begun reading Elizabeth Bishop with profit; her *Poems: North and South* had received the Pulitzer Prize in 1956. Sexton is never as patient with description as Hecht is when he sets the scene in a manner that has now become second nature to his art:

> It is raining here.
> On my neighbor's fire escape
> geraniums are set out
> in their brick-clay pots,
> along with the mop,
> old dishrags, and a cracked
> enamel bowl for the dog.
>
> I think of you out there
> On the sandy edge of things,
> Rain strafing the beach,
> The white maturity
> Of bones and broken shells,
> And little tin shovels and cars
> Rusting under the house.

precisely because of its tonal disjunctions, for which he, in turn, was criticized by Helen Vendler (*NYRB* 43.8 (9 May 1996), 39–42. This difference of opinion then led to an illuminating epistolary exchange, described more fully at the end of Chapter 5. AH to Helen Vendler, 15 June 1996; HV to AH, 28 July 1996. Hecht Archive.

57. See especially Sexton's "Letter Written on a Ferry While Crossing Long Island Sound," in *Anne Sexton: The Complete Poems* (Boston: Houghton Mifflin, 1981), 81. The poem shares a number of features in common with "Message." The event reported occurs before the two knew each other, which doesn't preclude it, however, as a possible "source" for Hecht's poem.

Beautifully pared down as this is—think of Auden's earlier criticisms brought up in Chapter 2—if all *The Hard Hours* were in this mode, we could see Hecht succumbing to the kind of domestic critique Hall was making of American poetry; but as a single snapshot of Hecht struggling with being a lonely, not-yet-divorced parent—"And between us there is—What? / Love and constraint, / conditions, conditions, / and several hundred miles of / of billboards, filling-stations, / and little dripping gardens"—the poem offers some relief from the larger, more intense pains recorded elsewhere in the collection. I haven't been able to determine the "discovery" Sexton offered Hecht about how to end the poem, but the closing segment possesses a finely graded emotional intensity to it—the lines expanding from six to seven syllables until arriving at the end "with clarity and restraint," the pause signaled by a diminuendo shift to short lines that encourages us to ruminate over the meaning of "the faint, fresh / smell of iodine."

> O my dear, my dear,
> today the rain pummels
> the sour geraniums
> and darkens the grey pilings
> of your house, built upon sand.
> And both of us, full grown,
> have weathered a long year.
> Perhaps your casual glance
> will settle from time to time
> on the sea's travelling muscles
> that flex and roll their strength
> under its rain-pocked skin.
> And you'll see where the salt winds
> have blown bare the seaward side
> of the berry bushes,
> and will notice
> the faint, fresh
> smell of iodine.

I like to think, but probably only sentimentality warrants the suggestion, that Sexton contributed the final image—"iodine" being not only what seawater is thought to contain in a high concentration, letting in a little fresh air in the process, but what someone, especially a small boy, might put on a wound. As Randall Jarrell said in another context: "The deepest feeling always shows itself in scratches; / not in scratches, but in iodine."[58] For all the muscularity associated with the sea in both these poems, the image of their maker here, and in "Clair de Lune," speaks powerfully of his powerlessness in matters of love.

When it came time for Hecht to assemble the poems into a single volume, the task must have seemed daunting, composed as the verses were over a thirteen-year period. How might such a book best be organized? What poems, if any, should be excluded? Hecht clearly mused over this matter, and among the papers in his archives is a draft version of the Table of Contents, which differs significantly from what finally emerged, but is of interest nonetheless for shedding some light on the process itself. This earlier draft Table of Contents is divided into five sections, each with its own Roman numeral, some bearing subtitles, with the poems selected and placed in each more or less according to genre or topic or common subject matter. Thus the first section, although untitled, brought together a number of personal or domestic poems. These included, in order of appearance, "A Letter," "Message from the City," "The Vow," "Jason," "Adam," "The End of a Weekend," and "A Hill." The second, in a lighter mode, was designated "Animal" and included under one heading: "The Origin of Centaurs," "Pig," "The Song of the Flea," "Birdwatchers of America," "Giant Tortoise," and "Tarantula." The third section was dedicated simply to "Three Prompters from the Wings," Hecht's "exceedingly disillusioned" foray into the Oedipus story from the perspective of the three fates, Atropos, Clotho, and Lachesis, in which Ransom finely noted, "You have boldly impoverished your poetic diction."[59] The fourth was then devoted to "Religious Poems," in the following order, "Ostia Antica," "The Seven Deadly Sins" (his emblem poems accompanied by Leonard Baskin's drawings), "'More Light! More Light!,'" "The Man Who Married Magdalene," and "Behold the Lilies of the Field." The fifth section, again untitled, was given over to a medley of poems: "'And Ye Can Sing Baluloo When the Bairn Greets,'" "Upon the Death of George Santayana," "Third Avenue in Sunlight," "Egypt, The Floating Lover," and "The Dover Bitch." The last section, marked "Translations," represented nine poems, of which the

58. Jarrell, "Her Shield," review of Marianne Moore's *Collected Poems*, in *Poetry and the Age* (1955; rpt. Faber and Faber Ltd., 1996), 161.

59. Both quotations are taken from Ransom's letter mentioned in note 2.

only translation to survive from this list was "To a Madonna." There are also some poems not represented in this earlier Table of Contents, the most noteworthy omissions being "Clair de Lune," "Lizards and Snakes," "Rites and Ceremonies," and the concluding poem, " 'It Out-Herods Herod. Pray You, Avoid It.' "

The most obvious difference between this draft version of the Table of Contents and the final version of *The Hard Hours* is the decision to do away with the section divisions. Hecht must have felt that these were, at best, too artificial, and at worst, a falsification of the vision of the whole. Indeed, why "Pig," for instance, would be placed under "Animal" rather than "Religious Poems," is to begin to raise questions about the usefulness of the categories. That poem focuses on an episode reported in Mark 5:1–13, "on Christ's exorcism of a persecuted man whose devils were cast into a herd of Gadarene Swine."[60] A similar over-restrictiveness pertains to "Birdwatchers of America," which has far less to do with birds than madness. By the time we arrive at the medley of poems in the fifth section, we can begin to see the problem Hecht was up against with this system of classification. The problem wasn't getting the poems into the right compartments. Rather, to compartmentalize at all was itself the problem, especially if the practice resulted, as it did in the draft version, in separating out the domestic and personal poems in section I from the religious and historical poems in section IV, placing them in divided and distinguished worlds, as if one category of experience bore little or only a distant relation to the other.

In light of this problem, we might look more closely at Hecht's initial desire to begin the volume with three poems on intensely personal subjects ("A Letter," "Message," and "The Vow"), and see that his decision to rearrange drastically the opening sequence of poems in *The Hard Hours* by replacing "A Letter" with "A Hill" was a crucial first step in rethinking the order of the whole; for if he now began with an appropriately Parnassian poem to establish a bleak vision distinctly his own, he was also, in this new arrangement, in a position to see that the domestic should not be privileged over the religious or the historical, and that "A Letter" and "The Vow" could be placed not only later in the volume but also no longer next to each other, as they represented different experiences addressed to different people. In fact, "A Letter"

60. Sacks, "Anthony Hecht's 'Rites and Ceremonies,' " 78.

ends up coming right after "Rites and Ceremonies." And if establishing the right tone with the first poem was important, so was achieving a proper conclusion. Unmentioned in the draft Table of Contents was "'It Out-Herods Herod. Pray You, Avoid It,'" as if waiting for its proper location in the volume. Here was a poem that brought together, in a single, brief, powerful lyric, the domestic with the religious and the historical; that symbol of American 1950s comfort, the television, with Hecht's memories of the concentration camp, along with a single, slightly tipsy parent's concern for "others [who] are bound to us, the gentle and blameless." What bound *The Hard Hours* together wasn't the collective sum of a number of separate parts, nor the deliberate eclecticism of *A Summoning of Stones*, but a single overwhelming vision, a modern-day book of hours, capable of endless gradations and refinements, as are the forms themselves,[61] at times lightened through wit, but all part of the poet Hecht's brooding, shaping consciousness.

61. As with *A Summoning of Stones*, every poem in *The Hard Hours* is in a different form (including "The Seven Deadly Sins" sequence), with only one exception: rhyming quatrains are used for both "Third Avenue in Sunlight" and "Clair de Lune."

4

Stretching Out, Looking Within

In Medias Res, with James Merrill

Thanking Hecht for a copy of *Millions of Strange Shadows*, James
Merrill remarked in a brief letter dated 27 December 1976:

Between cooking my goose + packing my bags for a month in Athens, I've
not had as much time with your new book as I should need before saying
much else than that it is a marvel: entirely yours—no trace of pains taken,
yet everywhere the print of experience [and] thought. Is it presumption to
say—who else is there to say it to?—that, different as we are, surely in this
respect, I feel in complete <u>technical</u> sympathy with you; and am not at all
sure that this isn't by far the deepest sympathy <u>to</u> feel in our trade—not
unlike 'compatibility' in the erotic sphere. This beautiful purified skill of
course comes to underline what the poems have to say—far more than has
met the eye in these few hours.[1]

Merrill's is the warm response of a fellow traveler, perhaps a slightly
beleaguered traveler, to be sure, during the free-verse swagger of the
1970s, when both poets were occasional targets of attack and yet also
at the top of their game. Seizing on their mutual interest in technique,
Merrill sees it as a reflection—no, that's not quite right—an underlining, rather, of what the poems have to say. Underlining lines is a fine
redundancy here, but also a fruitful way to highlight the "beautiful
purified skill" of Hecht's art by another shared lover of craft ("who else
is there to say it to?").

No doubt Hecht was gratified by the remark. The opening poem of
that volume, "The Cost," speaks plenty about the discipline of art, both
ancient and modern—the interlacing ribs of a Calder design versus the

<hr/>

1. Letter, James Merrill to AH, 27 December 1976. Hecht Archive.

spiraling narrative of Trajan's column—and of the relationship between art and life, the turn of verse and the acrobatic turn of the body in the image of a young couple skillfully banking a Vespa motor scooter around the Roman monument, "Forever aslant in their moment and the mind's eye"; and about poetry, especially Hecht's poetry, to raise pointed questions about the moral consequences of action, which, for Hecht, always includes the potential for violence. The poem's title, a variation on Othello's famous line, "It is the cause, it is the cause" (5.2), finds its apt target, as Othello's does not, in the endless spiral of military campaigns, whether those of Trajan "accounted 'the most just,'" or by the United States in Vietnam. Hecht's poem was composed in 1970, at the height of the Vietnam War, and with little hope of an end in sight. Eleanor Cook makes a fine point about the enjambment in the opening line, "'Think how some excellent, lean torso hugs...' Hugs? Hugs a friend or child or lover?"[2] We are reminded immediately of the cost of human life.

About the same time as Merrill's letter, Harold Bloom was reviewing *Millions of Strange Shadows* (1977) as part of a survey of what he called "the middle generation of American poets":

> Hecht's distinction, like Richard Wilbur's, demonstrates that "development" may be only a critical trope, since neither Hecht nor Wilbur has "developed," and yet this is a strength rather than a lack in both poets. Emotional intensity and formal power were combined in Hecht from his beginnings; if there has been a deepening in so elegant and grave an art, it has been in the release of a humor gentler than the initial ironies of apprehension that Hecht once cultivated. The 30 poems in Hecht's new book are all fully *written*, but several truly are the best he has published and are very likely to endure. The very best is "Green: An Epistle," which is a lesson in profound, controlled subjectivity and self-revelation, an exact antithesis to the opaque squalors of "confessional" poets. Almost equally remarkable are "Coming Home," in which the poet John Clare receives a deeper interpretation than any critic has afforded him, and "Apprehensions," again a masterwork of dramatic introspection.[3]

What is interesting about the juxtaposition of quotations is how Bloom's generous comment leaves out an important influence on Hecht surfacing at this point in his career, the emergence of Merrill. And yet it is the presence, the example, of Merrill, I think, that illuminates a shift

---

2. Cook, *A Reader's Guide to Wallace Stevens* (Princeton: Princeton University Press, 2007), 325.

3. Bloom, *The New Republic* (26 November 1977), 24–5.

in Hecht's direction that might also be said to constitute a "development" in the usual critical sense—most explicitly in "Apprehensions," "a masterwork of dramatic introspection," as Bloom notes—and continued into Hecht's next volume of poetry published only two years later, *The Venetian Vespers* (1979).

To be fair, Bloom came to recognize as much in response to "The Venetian Vespers," Hecht's explicit venture at writing a "long poem." In a 1978 letter to Harry Ford, he remarked: on the basis of "repeated readings" of "Vespers," "Hecht has achieved a long poem that rivals Merrill's *Ephraim* and *Mirabell*, and Ashbery's *Self-Portrait*," and then proceeded to "repeal" his earlier statement.

> "Development" indeed may be only a critical trope, but unlike Wilbur and like Merrill, Hecht certainly *has* altered with this poem, and truly into what is rich + strange...I don't know what to praise more: the authentic Jacobean Shakespeare richness of language (as sumptuous as *Othello*) or the remarkably subtle balance between dramatic monologue and a kind of discursive bitterness, too finely grained to be called "bitterness."[4]

And to be fair to Wilbur, he too had experimented in the late 1960s and early 70s with writing psychologically searching, blank verse dramatic monologues, most notably in "Walking to Sleep" and "The Mind Reader," poems highly valued by Hecht, and the commentary Wilbur offered on the difference between the "ironic meditative lyric," popular in the 1950s, and his own emerging interest in the dramatic monologue has a wider relevance applicable to the transition Hecht was undergoing as well:

> The virtue of the ironic meditative poem is that the poet speaks out of his whole nature, acknowledging the contradictions that inhere in life. The limitation of such a poem is that the atmosphere of contradiction can stifle passion and conduce to a bland evasiveness. The virtue of the dramatic poem is that, while it may not represent the whole self of the poet, it can (like the love song, hymn, or curse) give free expression to some one compelling mood or attitude. The fact is that we are not always divided in spirit and that we sometimes yield utterly to a feeling or idea.[5]

Wilbur's astute remarks might serve as a blueprint for Hecht's own thoughts; but Hecht would yield himself more completely to the ventriloquizing allurements of the dramatic poem, especially in his further

---

4. Letter, Bloom to Harry Ford, 7 January 1978. Hecht Archive.
5. Wilbur, "On My Own Work," in *Responses: Prose Pieces, 1953–1976* (New York: Harcourt, Brace, Jovanovich, Inc., 1976), 121–2. The essay was originally published in 1966.

experimentations in *The Venetian Vespers* and beyond, whereas the two poems by Wilbur represent the outer extreme of his ventures in this direction.

As for Merrill, his is an easy voice to miss among the many actively summoned in *Millions of Strange Shadows*, either in titles (the title of the volume itself represents a double borrowing: from a poem of his own ("A Birthday Poem") that makes resonant use of the opening of Shakespeare's Sonnet 53: "What is your substance, whereof are you made, / That millions of strange shadows on you tend?"), or further sounded in echo or epigraph. Indeed, to my knowledge, with but a single exception, the only person to remark on the Merrill connection is Lachlan Mackinnon, and then only in passing and much later. In a 1991 review of Hecht's *Collected Earlier Poems*, Mackinnon rightly observed that "Apprehensions"

> is as brilliantly turned as another piece centred on a governess, James Merrill's "Lost in Translation." Merrill ends with the possibility of all being "Lost... / Or found" in a world where "waste" can become "shade and fiber, milk and memory." Beautiful and unarguable as Merrill's vision is, the playfulness seems whimsical beside Hecht's apparently looser, more associative structure, because Hecht resists the drive to explanation or symbolic closure.[6]

The single exception is Merrill himself. In 1976, he wrote to Stephen Yenser: "I've just read a splendid vol. (bound galleys) by Tony Hecht. He's written a poem about <u>his</u> governess, a terrible Fräulein—but the poem is glorious."[7] The underlining belongs again to Merrill. The letter was written exactly a week before he wrote to Hecht, complimenting him on *Millions of Strange Shadows*, in which Merrill modestly omits any reference to his own poem and the role it might have played as a source for Hecht's.

I will want to look more closely at this pair of governess poems, this productive connection for Hecht in the 1970s, and to glance beyond these two poems as well; but for the moment, as Bloom recognized, the way to "Apprehensions," Hecht's governess poem, is through "Green: An Epistle." In the aftermath of *The Hard Hours*, both poems represent powerful "beginnings," in Edward Said's sense, in which "the mind finds it necessary at certain times to retrospectively locate a point of origin for itself as to how things begin in the most elementary sense

---

6. Mackinnon, *Times Literary Supplement* (26 July 1991), 4.
7. Letter, James Merrill to Stephen Yenser, 20 December 1976. Beinecke Library.

with birth."[8] Whether "Green" is "the very best" poem in *Millions of Strange Shadows*—Allen Tate confided to Hecht it was "one of the great 20th Century poems"[9]—it indicates a new direction in Hecht's thinking, and does so with marvelous certainty. "The Cost," although written just about the same time as "Green," could have been a *Hard Hours* poem, I think, so carefully edged is Hecht's art, even putting into service Wilbur's practice of placing "pivotal and energetic verbs" in rhyming positions.[10] But "Green" operates on a different scale altogether. The poem gives "free expression to some one compelling mood or attitude." More markedly improvisational (like Wilbur's "Walking to Sleep"), it approaches the sublime in its epical and epochal investigation into the all-consuming subject of rage, a search for origins that includes a widening of vision that will (with the further inspiration of Merrill) continue magnificently in "Apprehensions" and on through "The Venetian Vespers," a vision set down here not in rhyme but in blank verse. This break with rhyme alone might remind us of Milton, as does the opening line in its ominous use of the word "forbidden," and the subsequent exploration of the genesis of rage as a Satanic or Blakean creation myth.

What differentiates "Green: An Epistle" from either a straightforward exploration of pastoral in, say, the Marvellian vein of "The Gardens of the Villa d'Este" or a Romantic revision of Milton, is not simply the darkly ironic reading of nature inspired by ideas of Darwinian survivalism. Green, for Hecht, is associated not with the innocent or recuperative powers of nature—hence he was eager to avoid Tate's suggestion that the poem should possess "a quasi-17th Century title"[11]—but its deceptive opposite: apparent innocence, or what Hecht calls, at one point, "The primal wash, heraldic hue of envy." The distance from these potential forebears is also a consequence of the decision to cast this mythic inquiry into the origins of evil in the form of a *familiar* epistle, with startling shifts in tone and address, written to another, who also turns out to be a version, perhaps the essential version, of himself. The

8. Said, characterizing his earlier book, *Beginnings*, in *On Late Style: Music and Literature against the Grain* (New York: Pantheon Books, 2006), 4.

9. Tate, quoted by Hecht in letter to Harry Ford, 20 September 1970. Hecht Archive.

10. See Hecht, "Richard Wilbur," in *Obbligati: Essays in Criticism* (New York: Atheneum, 1986), 130–1.

11. Letter, AH to Harry Ford, 20 September 1970: "As for the title, I am eager to avoid associations with Andrew Marvell, and took conscious pains to keep him out of the poem in the course of writing."

imagined setting for this 150-line epistle-cum-meditation is, Hecht tells us early on, some "grubby little border town / With its one cheap hotel," in which the speaker, writing on a desk that "wobbles unless propped with matchbooks," feels safe enough to unburden himself. So finely and firmly nuanced are these personal revelations that Tate reported that the closing paragraph, in which self-admission swims suddenly to the surface, "gives me a frisson—so simple and so strange it is." Hecht is seemingly writing to someone else ("us" vs. "you"), seemingly at rest with himself, but someone the speaker also appears to know better than the person knows himself.

> These days, with most of us at a safe distance,
> You scarcely know yourself. Whole weeks go by
> Without your remembering that enormous effort,
> Ages of disappointment, the long ache
> Of motives twisted out of recognition,
> The doubt and hesitation all submerged
> In those first clear waters, that untroubled pool.
> Who could have hoped for this eventual peace?
> Moreover, there are moments almost of bliss,
> A sort of recompense, in which your mood
> Sorts with the peach endowments of late sunlight
> On a snowfield or on the breaker's froth
> Or the white steeple of the local church.
> Or, like a sunbather, whose lids retain
> A greenish, gemmed impression of the sun
> In lively, fluctuant geometries,
> You sometimes contemplate a single image,
> Utterly silent, utterly at rest.
> It is of someone, a stranger, quite unknown,
> Sitting alone in a foreign-looking room,
> Gravely intent at a table propped with matchbooks,
> Writing this very poem—about me.

Where, one wants to ask, does a poem like "Green: An Epistle," come from, one that can enlist the admiration of two critics as far apart from one another as the visionary Romantic Bloom and the Eliotic southerner Tate? The poem has a genesis, of course, in Hecht's earlier verse, as Kenneth Gross has thoughtfully explored,[12] but

12. Gross, "Anthony Hecht and the Imagination of Rage," in Sydney Lea, ed., *The Burdens of Formality: Essays on the Poetry of Anthony Hecht* (Athens: University of Georgia Press, 1989), 159–73.

nothing that can quite explain the depths sounded in phrases like "the long ache / Of motives twisted out of recognition." This possesses the wisdom of years, the kind of authority, indeed, sounded in late Shakespearean tragedy or by Eliot at the end of "Little Gidding" II ("the shame / Of motives late revealed"); and while Hecht was initially reluctant to do more than touch on the biographical and psychological circumstances underlying the poem—"It was a consuming paranoia that I had chiefly in mind (and, though this is scarcely relevant, and certainly not meant to be legible in the poem, I had in mind three different people only one of whom is a woman")[13]—he later came to admit that "in some ways it may be one of the most personal I've written." Coming from the poet of *The Hard Hours*, this is saying something. "The way we disguise our deepest truths from ourselves is the subject of 'Green: An Epistle,' which was prompted by, first, an insight into symbiotic family ties, and later into myself." Hecht made these subsequent revelations to his friend, the Roman architectural historian, William MacDonald, some twelve years after he wrote the poem, in the context of reporting the shock he felt over his brother Roger's apparently careless disposal of some books, heirlooms of a kind that Hecht deeply valued.

I knew at once that the loss was almost entirely symbolic, though the knowledge did not in the least diminish my Gordian knot of rage, guilt, and other violent emotions that I had thought pretty well buried for good. In fact, the chief shock was to find myself experiencing feelings that had blissfully been banished for so long, but which had once festered in ulcerous silence for years.[14]

Those "symbiotic family ties," as we will see, form the visible narrative of "Apprehensions." In "Green," they are submerged, indeed repressed in the classic Freudian sense, and distilled into parable or myth or even epigraph, as in the example of the one chosen from Roethke:

> This urge, wrestle, resurrection of dry sticks,
> Cut stems struggling to put down feet,
> What saint strained so much,
> Rose on such lopped limbs to a new life?

13. Letter, AH to L. E. Sissman, 14 August 1970 (*SL*, 146–7).
14. Letter, AH to William MacDonald, 24 June 1982 (*SL*, 199–200).

Roethke means these lines to honor the stubborn nature of horticultural life, but the emphasis in Hecht, in light of what follows in the poem, falls on "lopped limbs" and questions, rather than asserts, the relationship between suffering and sanctification.

The quotation, moreover, comes from "Cuttings" in Roethke's *Lost Son* sequence, aptly named for Hecht, for it raises the further question of who is the lost son in Hecht's poem: the speaker or his reflection? And if the latter, who would that person be? "Green" refuses to name that other person, although Hecht's younger brother Roger is an obvious possibility, and not just because of the incident Hecht described above to MacDonald. A poet of sorts, with several published volumes, Roger was, in many regards, a reflection of his older brother, one of the many strange shadows that make up the volume. The brothers were close when younger: Roger visited his older brother on Ischia, attended Kenyon, and even studied under Tate, but as "Apprehensions" points out in considerable and climactic detail, Roger suffered from a variety of physical infirmities, including epilepsy, which left him less able to function independently, and perhaps too from envy and resentment at his older brother's success. But did he suffer more than his older brother? Or just suffer differently? And which of the brothers, or did they both, put on a good face so "that almost all of us were taken in"? The poem invites these questions but offers no explicit answer.

If "Green" is a dark parable about growing up, as Gross has suggested,[15] the speaker looks through a world of "prelapsarian disguise" to lay out a "Gordian knot of rage" at its center:

> I write at last of the one forbidden topic
> We, by a truce, have never touched upon:
> Resentment, malice, hatred so inwrought
> With moral inhibitions, so at odds with
> The home-movie of yourself as patience, kindness,
> And Charlton Heston playing Socrates,
> That almost all of us were taken in. (lines 1–7)

And it includes, as the Edenic expulsion must, a hint of the Cain–Abel story, but only as partly disguised in the form of self-reflection. The powerful circularity of the poem prevents any firm identification of the other to emerge, or a final release from these emotions, either—only

15. Gross, "Anthony Hecht and the Imagination of Rage," 181.

a further and deeper inquiry into its effects. As the speaker observes
early on in the poem, in the fourth paragraph:

> Here is the microscope one had as a child,
> The Christmas gift of some forgotten uncle.
> Here is the slide with a drop of cider vinegar
> As clear as gin, clear as your early mind.
> Look down, being most careful not to see
> Your own eye in the mirror underneath,
> Which will appear, unless your view is right,
> As a darkness on the face of the first waters.
> When all is silvery and brilliant, look:
> The long, thin, darting shapes, the flagellates,
> Rat-tailed, ambitious, lash themselves along—
> Those humble, floating ones, those simple cells
> Content to be borne on whatever tide,
> Trustful, the very image of consent—
> These are the frail, unlikely origins,
> Scarcely perceived, of all you shall become.
> Scarcely perceived? But at this early age
> (What are you, one or two?) you have no knowledge,
> Nor do your folks, nor could the gravest doctors
> Suspect that anything was really wrong.
> Nor see the pale beginnings, lace endeavors
> That with advancing ages shall mature
> Into sea lettuce, beard the rocky shore
> With a light green of soft and tidal hair.

The question this passage and the poem keep raising, but without
answering, is who is being addressed, who is this "you" who is "one or
two" (a neatly charged ambiguity)? And the fact that, at one level, this
is a letter to and about the speaker ("about me") means, at another
level, the poet is free to explore these "cuttings" in all their mounting
significance and maximal concentration, as happens in the poem's
penultimate paragraph:

> Consider, as one must, what was to come.
> Great towering conifers, deciduous,
> Rib-vaulted elms, the banyan, oak, and palm,
> Sequoia forests of vindictiveness
> That also would go down on the death list
> And, buried deep beneath alluvial shifts,
> Would slowly darken into lakes of coal
> And then under exquisite pressure turn
> Into the tiny diamonds of pure hate.

In that exquisite final image, one might think the poem is done, has arrived at a point of resolution, but the passage continues, with ever widening ingenuity:

> The delicate fingers of the clematis
> Feeling their way along a face of shale
> With all the ingenuity of spite.
> The indigestible thistle of revenge.
> And your most late accomplishment, the rose.
> Until at last, what we might designate
> As your Third Day, behold a world of green:
> Color of hope, of the Church's springtide vestments,
> The primal wash, heraldic hue of envy.
> But in what prelapsarian disguise!
> Strangers and those who do not know you well
> (Yourself not least) are quickly taken in
> By a summery prospect, shades of innocence.
> Like that young girl, a sort of chance acquaintance,
> Seven or eight she was, on the New York Central,
> Who, with a blue-eyed, beatific smile,
> Shouted with joy, "Look, Mommy, quick. Look. Daisies!"

Poetry is rarely as terrifying in its Satanic delicacies of expression, its deviant phrasings and apparent intimacies and insinuations, including the final image of the young girl (a shadowy vestige of his first wife? In his letter to Sissman, Hecht mentioned having in mind a woman.) It has a simple innocence to it, but only if one overlooks, or is ignorant of, the Daisy Girl context: a 1964 political advertisement, one of the most controversial ever, which aired only once, but was credited with helping Lyndon Johnson defeat Barry Goldwater for the presidency.[16] A camera shows a young girl innocently counting the petals she is plucking from a daisy, starting from one and then moving, in slightly meandering fashion, numerically higher. As she approaches the number ten, however, another voice, this time male and sounding like Truman's, begins a strict countdown. As the zero moment approaches, with the camera closing tightly on the girl's face, then her eyes, the scene suddenly changes and morphs into the shocking image of an atomic bomb exploding. "Look. Daisies!" The exclamation mark might even be seen to suggest, in point and image, the bomb itself. If this seems a circuitous allusion even by Hecht's standards, the voice-over

16. I want to thank Callie Siskel of the Johns Hopkins Writing Seminars for pointing out this allusion.

by Johnson should remove any doubt regarding Hecht's intentions: "We must either love each other or we must die." Auden said as much in the (in)famous line from "September 1, 1939," a line Hecht surely knew by heart: "we must love one another or die."

The imagined explosion does mark the end of this great descant on "prelapsarian disguise" (consider the ramifications of that phrase in conjunction with the advertisement) and not with a whimper but a bang. But reverberations continue into the finale that so moved Tate. Reread the transitional phrase, "These days, with most of us at a safe distance," in light of the atomic bomb, and then think again about the closing image of "matchbooks" propping up the writing table. Not only does the image echo ("match") the initial description of the poet's workplace—"and my desk wobbles unless propped with matchbooks," an echo Hecht wished to preserve in the process of composition[17]—but together the matches serve as bookends that affirm the precarious, inflammatory condition of existence: the burning rage for disorder that underlies the appearance of order, even the family order, in which two brothers might be seen to—how else can it be phrased?—match books.

The Roethke epigraph also looks in another direction. "Green: An Epistle" surely anticipates "Apprehensions," but at the time of its composition, "this urge, wrestle, resurrection of dry sticks / Cut stems struggling to put down feet," reflects the radical effort by Hecht to write this poem, to put down feet in new territory. He was no longer only the boy abandoned at the end of "A Hill," but a "lost son" seeking to explore and explain his part in "the strange mutations life requires."

"Apprehensions" is born out of this struggle, the wrestling now given greater narrative shape in the context of his increasing admiration for Merrill's poetry in the 1970s. Hecht wrote to Merrill in April 1974:

Evan [Hecht's two-year-old son] has been allowed to tear up any copies of *The New Yorker* he has a mind to, except the one in which "Lost in Translation" appeared. I can't tell you how glad I am at last to see it before me and read it at leisure. It is every bit as stunning as when I first heard it, full of tact, splendor and perfectly controlled emotion. It seems to me, more and more, one of the finest poems of our time. I can't think of a poet alive who wouldn't be lucky to have written it.[18]

17. See letter to Sissman in note 13.
18. AH to James Merrill, 17 April 1974 (*SL*, 155).

Merrill's poem clearly opened up a new, or rather an old, vein in Hecht. The last sentence, especially, sounds a note somewhere between heartfelt praise and wishful desire. Hecht certainly knew, as did Merrill, that fine poems weren't made by "luck" alone; they also required inspiration and discipline. But "luck" carries with it notions of special selection, or election, in the sense of one poem inspiring a response or answer by another. "Hence with denial vain, and coy excuse; / So may some gentle muse / With lucky words favor my destined urn," wrote Milton as part of his justification for writing "Lycidas." The word also includes a sense of local epiphany, of something discovered, which is the sense Merrill assigned to it in his poem, a piece of the puzzle lying on the floor ("lucky finds / in the last minutes before bed"), ready to complete a larger picture, and now perhaps recollected by Hecht for this purpose of completion as well.

Merrill's poem has since acquired a fabled place in the criticism of his poetry, but in 1974 it possessed a refreshingly new light. It was a mark to shoot at for sure, one that had the further advantage, in the aftermath of Lowell's *Life Studies* and in the era of "confessional poetry," to sponsor an exemplary form of highly crafted autobiography, "full of tact, splendor and perfectly controlled emotion," terms that might remind us of Bloom's praise of Hecht. Not that Merrill was everyman or anyone. Just the opposite, in fact, and if one reads Merrill's "story" from Hecht's perspective, knowing what we know about Hecht's development, it must have seemed an invitation to follow. There it was, the shaping of an autobiography: the boy abandoned by the parents; the French-speaking governess but of German descent and accent ("Mademoiselle was only French by marriage"); a portentously Audenesque setting, "With 1939 about to shake / this world where 'each was the enemy, each the friend'"; a Manhattan address—the puzzle shop is located "in the mid-Sixties"; a poem of domestic and interna- tional scope, reveling in a fascination with puzzles and colors, especially green, and foreign phrases: a poem about losing and finding.

"Different as we are" wrote Merrill to Hecht in 1976, stating the case accurately. Both poets were in mid-career flight. Differences could be readily calculated, the parallels a sign of independence and strength. The same is true with these two masterful poems. Overlapping in nar- rative details, they are remarkably different in the telling and the stories they report. Merrill's employs a dazzling array of forms and phrases, a complex time frame stemming from "three different autobiographical situations," and a series of intricately related parts, five in all—the combined density of reference tempting the poem's subtlest explicator to exclaim that "it begins to seem that there is no subject 'Lost in Translation' cannot handle as it shifts among home and world, world and page, often by virtue of the manifold richness of its particulars."[19] A slight exaggeration, of course, knowingly sown by the critic: there are some topics that don't receive much of an airing in Merrill's poem, most notably cruelty, Hecht's special territory. Merrill's governess kindly whispers a hybrid prayer at bedtime to the young boy," 'Schlaf wohl, cheri.' Her kiss. Her thumb / Crossing my brow against the dreams to come." Hecht's is pure sadist,"a Teutonic governess / Replete with the curious thumbprint of her race, / That special relish for inflicted pain."

A "glorious" poem with "a terrible Fräulein," as Merrill remarked, "Apprehensions" is a less complicated narrative than "Lost in Translation," and deliberately so. Hecht was exploring the capacity of story-telling in verse to reclaim some of the ground he saw its having ceded to the novel. In this regard, the most telling point of contact with Merrill's poem involves, notably, the word "reverberation" itself. Merrill uses it near the end of his poem: "And after rain / A deep reverberation fills with stars," and inspires the following bright trail of commentary:

And what is such a "reverberation" if not at once an emptiness and a plenishing? "Reverberation": the word means a redounding of sound or repeated reflecting of light (or heat), a re-echoing, as of Merrill's echoing of Rilke's echoing of Valery (echoing his own sources). "Reverberation" might almost be a translation of "translation," and even though *verberare* is unrelated to *verbum*, Merrill wants us to catch a Cratylean glimpse of "rewording" behind the term, much as Stevens, for instance, means us to see "luminous" shining through his phrase "Voluminous master folded in his fire."[20]

Hecht uses the word, also after a rainstorm, but his definition can only seem stringently pointed by comparison: "Reverberations (from the Latin, *verber*, / Meaning a whip or lash) rang down the alley / Of Lower Manhattan." Even in a poem as bookish as "Apprehensions"—at this point in the poem, the narrator, stepping into the child's psyche, has

19. The two quotations in this sentence are from Stephen Yenser, *The Consuming Myth: The Work of James Merrill* (Cambridge, MA: Harvard University Press, 1987), 12 and 25, respectively.
20. Yenser, *The Consuming Myth*, 29.

already cited both "The Book of Knowledge" and Auden's "Vision of Dame Kind"—this insertion of a scholarly footnote into a poem is still striking. I can't think of another such occasion in Hecht's verse; for the moment it invites us to concentrate absolutely on the point of contact and the difference between the two poems. Merrill's is a soundboard of doublings; Hecht's poem, a reverberation of Merrill, renders a different meaning to the word, charts a different course, one in which the proliferation of doubling is compressed into a single story told largely in the past tense about an unhappy home and an even more horrendous "homecoming."

Although utilizing the simple past tense, Hecht's narrative has something of the stripped-down, plain-style flavor of George Herbert's autobiographical "Affliction [I]"—the stripped-down aspects focusing on shameful expositions of voyeurism his creepy governess forced him to endure. Like Herbert's childish speaker, Hecht's suffers from a lack of love from his parents—"benign neglect"—as he puts it in quotation marks to wring a drop of irony from the cliché. He also endures physical punishment from his governess: "I moved in a cloudy world of inference / Where the most solid object was a toy / Rake that my governess used to beat me." For a brief instant, the hesitation involving the enjambed "toy" suggests the possibility of child's play before it is joined with "Rake" and turned into an instrument of abuse in the hands of the governess.

Nonetheless, in this narrative of purposeful pacing, benign neglect has its momentary rewards and the seven-year-old child his wish and way. His first refuge is reading—in particular "The Book of Knowledge," in which there "were puzzles and, magnificently, their answers." No Merrill there; or rather Merrill but with a difference. His second gift, "more peculiar, / Rare, unexpected, harder to assess," comes from looking out the window of "the sixth floor of an apartment house," where Hecht recalls an extended epiphany of sorts, which at its most intense concludes:

> The streetcar tracks gleamed like the path of snails.
> And all of this made me superbly happy,
> But most of all a yellow Checker Cab
> Parked at the corner. Something in the light
> Was making this the yellowest thing on earth.
> It was as if Adam, having completed
> Naming the animals, had started in

On colors, and had found his primary pigment
Here, in a taxi cab, on Eighty-ninth Street.
It was the absolute, parental yellow.

Definitely more Merrill here in the dazzle of colors, and some
Vaughan or Traherne in the Edenic celebration of visionary innocence, but the primary color of "parental yellow" is all Hecht—the
adjective reminding us also of what is missing in his life. And as a toy
can become a rake, so a Checker Cab can vanish in a thunderstorm.
"Someone or other / Called me away from there, and closed the
window." The use of the impersonal here is a perfect, if painful touch,
as is the finality of the window coming down on his dreams. No
father calls "my child," nor mother either. Only a stark gap between
stanzas appears as we navigate this empty space and find "Reverberations"
to be the first word on the other side. The closed window creates
whiplash all around.

Hecht is a gifted story teller, and "Apprehensions" possesses a number of calculated pauses and false epiphanies or pseudo-endings, lav-
ishly and intricately described. The most extreme instance involves the
extraordinary series of revelations about his family: the discovery of his
father's attempted suicide, his brother's epilepsy, the silence of the
mother in all of these collapses set off by the stock market crash of
1929. These would appear to be the climax of the family narrative
anticipated in the very first lines of the poem: "A grave and secret
malady of my brother's, / The stock exchanges, various grown-up
shames;" and much later answered by the poet: "How dark and Cabbalistic
the mysteries. / Messages all in cipher, enthymemes / Grossly suggestive, keeping their own counsel, / Vivid and unintelligible dreams,"
sentiments ultimately moralized as we might expect: that the world the
speaker has come to understand is not (if it ever was) a child's world
but ominous, complex, and nasty. The penultimate stanza concludes
even with a reference to "holy text."

Then another pause, another gap in Hecht's not-so-holy text. As
with the ending of *King Lear*—to summon a favorite play of Hecht's—
the poet has had us looking the wrong way. The "frisson" produced by
the twenty-line conclusion to "Apprehensions" is, I would wager, at
least on a par with what Allen Tate reported to having felt at the end
of "Green." "Just when it was that Fräulein disappeared / I don't recall"
Hecht begins. The casual tone noting her reappearance in the story
(now recounting her disappearance) is precisely measured. "Great thing of

us forgot."[21] It's been 135 lines since she was last mentioned. I recall the gasp from the audience at a Silliman College reading given by Hecht at Yale in 1977—sensing now suddenly the turn and that the real ending has begun. All the work done earlier to introduce the Teutonic governess in the particular—the sleazy magazines, the young boy's eroticized and disgusted sense of what he was also viewing—comes home to roost in this strange mutation of a Wagnerian liebestod. The speaker's earlier shames, his apprehensions, are now magnified, because of history, beyond all comprehension. Again, the management of tone is everything:

> Just when it was that Fräulein disappeared
> I don't recall. We continued to meet each other
> By secret assignations in my dreams
> In which, by stages, our relationship
> Grew into international proportions
> As the ghettos of Europe emptied, the box cars
> Rolled toward enclosures terminal and obscene,
> The ovens blazed away like Pittsburgh steel mills,
> Chain-smoking through the night, and no one spoke.
> We two would meet in a darkened living room
> Between the lines of advancing allied troops
> In the Wagnerian twilight of the *Reich.*
> She would be seated by a table, reading
> Under a lamp-shade of the finest parchment.
> She would look up and say, "I always knew
> That you would come to me, that you'd come home."
> I would read over her shoulder, "*in der Heimat,*
> *Im Heimatland, da gibts ein Wiedersehen.*"
> An old song of comparative innocence,
> Until one learns to read between the lines.

At this terminal point in the poem, deep reverberations fill the night, including perhaps a glancing echo of Merrill's "Mademoiselle": "Tu as l'accent allemande." The accent is now given its special voice in the original German quoted by Hecht from "an old song of comparative innocence," a sound, moreover, whose distinctive accent reverberates, pierces the sky, like a whip or lash, against the ominous silence of the night "when no one spoke." There is also the terrifying image of the ovens blazing "away like Pittsburgh steel mills, / Chain-smoking

21. *King Lear*, 5.3.237, the Duke of Albany speaking, in G. Blakemore Evans, general editor, *The Riverside Shakespeare* (Boston: Houghton Mifflin, 1974).

through the night." Earlier in the poem Hecht had pointed to the different smoking preferences of the Fräulein and his mother: "she chain-smoked Camels as she scanned the pages, / Whereas my mother's brand was Chesterfield." Those apparent distinctions and their social markers, if remembered, simply collapse in light of this later reference, as well they should. And born out of the collapse is the figure of Fräulein, transformed or translated into a mythic personification of Germany fit for Wagnerian opera: a seductive mix of gypsy cunning and German high culture, reading, as she does, "Under a lamp-shade of the finest parchment"—the shade further reminding us of those made of human skin in the Nazi factories, and of the vast distance between Hecht's poem and Merrill's in the different meanings to which "shade" is put, the word appearing as a verb in the last line of "Lost in Translation."

As for Hecht's final line, about learning to read between the lines, the author risks a cliché unless we remember (with Mackinnon) that reading between the lines recollects the dark readings that are a consequence of their meeting "Between the lines of advancing allied troops." The experience of war, kept out of this "autobiography" until the very end, changes our or, more to the point, changes Hecht's reading habits permanently. It insists on the "whip" or "lash" being discovered at the root. "Such tricks hath strong imagination," remarked Theseus in his famous speech in *A Midsummer Night's Dream* on the "lunatic, the lover, and the poet," "That if it would but apprehend some joy / It would comprehend some bringer of that joy" (5.1.7, 18–20). "Apprehensions" comprehends that idea and turns it into a bad dream that is neither bush nor bear but a Fräulein, a dysfunctional family, and a twilight of wartime terror.

About the same time that "Apprehensions" was happening, Hecht wrote another letter to Merrill, this one in March 1976, to congratulate him on his recently published book of poems, *Divine Comedies*. In fact, he wrote not one but two letters about the book. The second, to their Atheneum editor, Harry Ford, was sent the following day. The letter to Merrill begins: "I've been reading *Divine Comedies*, and while I am no longer absolutely speechless, it has taken me several days to find my voice among the keys I write with." It concludes on a similar note:

[Your book] arrived when I was in the midst of time-off from teaching and set aside to do my own work. But reading it, I confess, has stopped me dead in my tracks. I expect gradually to recover my self-esteem, and to go on; but for the moment I'm dazzled, and choose to do nothing but admire.[22]

High praise indeed, but the letter to Ford is even more exuberant and more revealing:

I wrote a letter recently to Richard Howard, expressing my great admiration for FELLOW FEELINGS. Then, a few days ago, Jimmy Merrill's book arrived. I have been overwhelmed by it. I'm scarcely able to express how extraordinary it is. I've written a brief note to Jimmy, which I fear sounds clumsy and fulsome, and possibly insincere, but the truth is that, Stevens's HARMONIUM apart, (which I read first at the age of sixteen as a freshman) I can think of no single volume of poetry that has impressed me so much.

Its virtues are so rich and so complex, its formal intricacies so vivid and without ostentation, its comedy, its wit and its sadness so compellingly managed, that it does what it incredibly set out to do—it controls and assembles the poet's entire life and work. If the book is only half as good as I think it is, it's the most important book of poetry, the most accomplished, the most enduring, of the last—what?—fifteen or twenty years. He makes all of us, including the Big Names, into Tin-Pan-Alley hacks. I am filled with the most uncomfortable mixture of envy and admiration. And I hope the admiration will win out, since I am trying to do my own writing, and don't like being stopped dead in my tracks. This book deserves to win every literary prize that exists, and a few special, unprecedented commendations. I hope you'll forgive what must seem like raving, but I'm still dazzled.[23]

So frank a letter—now joining envy to admiration—requires little further interpretation, except to note the irony of its timing. In the mid-1970s, the current rage among literary critics and theorists was Harold Bloom's influential and learnedly melodramatic *Anxiety of Influence* (1973), which analyzes the often formidable, crippling pressures put on poets by their parents, the dead authors of the past. For practicing poets, however, things could look different, as they clearly did for Hecht. Sometimes, it is a concern with the present and not the past that threatens to produce anxiety, a concern raised in both letters, just as sometimes it is the past that allows the poet to fend off the present (Eliot's legacy to modernism). This was also clearly the case with Hecht and perhaps too for the Merrill Hecht valued.

22. AH to James Merrill, 10 March 1976 (*SL*, 157).
23. AH to Harry Ford, 11 March 1976.

Exaggeration aside, Hecht, of course, did gather his wits, recover his self-esteem, and return to writing. *Divine Comedies* couldn't have taken him completely by surprise. The second poem is "Lost in Translation," the volume thus offering in this poem the belief that what had stopped him dead in his tracks at one point might also quicken the pulse and pace at another. And so it did, but this time in the form of what would eventually become the longest poem Hecht would ever write, and certainly one of his most celebrated, "The Venetian Vespers." "Vespers," it will be recalled, was the poem that caused Bloom to "repeal" his earlier views of Hecht's career and to place him in the company of Merrill, and, as these letters suggest, it is difficult to think that Merrill was not himself partly responsible for this transformation, in this case through "The Book of Ephraim."

Merrill's long poem constitutes about two-thirds of the entire *Divine Comedies*, and it would be hard to understand Hecht's dazzled response to the volume or the terms of Hecht's praise —"it controls and assembles the poet's entire life and work"—were "The Book of Ephraim" not in the forefront of his thoughts. Indeed, the phrase "controls and assembles" recalls the image of the Ouija board in Merrill's poem. The mechanism serves as muse and conduit for controlling the masque-like assembly of persons, places, and ideas in that poem. And of the many places summoned, the city that is most fully realized is Venice: "A whole heavenly city / Sinking, titanic ego mussel-blue / Abulge in gleaming nets of nerve, of pressures / Unregistered by the barometer / Stuck between Show and Showers."[24] Between rain and vivid imagery, Merrill's "Venice"

24. Quotations from "The Book of Ephraim" are taken from Merrill, *The Changing Light at Sandover* (New York: Alfred A. Knopf, 1996), 75–83. The sections in "Ephraim" follow the alphabet; references to Venice begin with "V" and continue through "W" and "X." My chapter is written largely from the perspective of the inspiration Hecht found in Merrill, but in conjunction with the emerging subject of Venice linking the two, it is worth touching on the reciprocal nature of their relationship. Responding to Hecht's letter of 10 March 1976, Merrill wrote, beginning with praise of his own for someone "whom I've admired so long and so deeply," but then turned with startling particularity to the Venetian sections of "The Book of Ephraim":

This may seem ingenuous; but, rather than go on about what your poems have meant to me over the years, let me refer you first to lines 3–5 on p. 126 of DC [*Divine Comedies*, section W], and then to some lines of your own from The Hard Hours where something precious and submerged in the past is rendered in terms of blocks from a deep azure quarry. That book's in Stonington, I can't be exact, and may indeed be giving the image back to you distorted. But that's my point: those lines (like so many others by the same author) have [been] kept alive within me, and been therefore subject to change—yet when I came to what I felt was the 'high

shimmers with glassy reflections: the famous wooden Accademia Bridge creakily thinks about the disappearance of the select few, replaced by the tread of many feet; the poet reflects on Giorgione's famous painting in the Accademia, "*Tempesta*—on the surface nothing less / Than earthly life in all its mystery." Such reflections, the city's mirroring essence, are also, as they always are in Merrill, subjected to further self-reflection: "I thanked my stars / When I lost the Leica at Longchamps. Never again / To overlook a subject for its image, / To labor images till they yield a subject— / Dram of essence from the flowering field."

Admiration mixed with envy may not be the only, nor necessarily the worst, recipe for writing. The following summer, the summer of 1977, that is, some sixteen months after writing to and about Merrill, Hecht and family would spend time in Europe including two weeks in Venice. Hecht would return home with a "Dram of essence" of his own: the conviction to write a lengthy poem using "the flowering field" of Venice as setting. As he remarked to W. D. Snodgrass in August, with characteristic frankness, "Our trip was not only a success in itself but has excited me into assembling notes for what will be, if I can write it, a poem that will be distinctly ambitious, even if it has no other merit."[25] And then again to Harry Ford, in September:

Right now I am at work on a long narrative poem (God save the mark!)—not long by Hollander's or Merrill's book-length standards, but still, ... I've got about 500 lines down and estimate I may be half-way through. It is set in Venice, and its efficient cause was our very happy and successful sojourn in Europe this summer.[26]

If the efficient cause was the recent visit, the formal cause—to continue Hecht's Aristotelian logic—was the desire to write a long narrative poem. The example of Merrill and now Hollander (both Atheneum poets) still lingers a bit anxiously in the background. But the subject of Venice

---

point' of my Ephraim poem I knew no better, literally, than to turn to you, to something of yours, for encouragement and inspiration. (23 March 1976, Hecht Archive)

The lines Merrill had in mind were surely those from "A Letter" ("My dearest, the clear unquarried blue / Of those depths is all but blinding"). They are much changed, incorporating other images from Hecht's poem in the process of arriving at their own special purpose, which included, as Hecht must have liked, Merrill's closing, witty, obstinate refusal in this section, "in these sunset years," to mend his ways and break with rhyme in order "to speak to multitudes and make it matter."

25. AH to W. D. Snodgrass, 2 August 1977.
26. AH to Harry Ford, 28 September 1977.

was also too deeply ingrained in Hecht's past for the poem that eventually emerged to be indebted to a single source of inspiration. Although his poem was not to equal Merrill's in length, its concentrated focus on this one place endows it with special depths that deserve a chapter of its own.

As for his debts to Merrill, Hecht repaid them in kind some two decades later as one of a number of poets who offered tributes, in verse and prose alike, to memorialize the significance of Merrill's passing in February of 1995. The poem is included in *Flight Among the Tombs* (1996). As we might expect, Hecht's elegy is a dignified remembrance, as the title suggests: "James Merrill: An Adieu." No attempt is made stylistically to imitate Merrill, although it's just possible Hecht's focus on a wished-for farewell performance by Merrill alludes to Merrill's own elegy bearing the title "Farewell Performance," written in Sapphics for "DK" or David Kalstone, the literary critic also remembered by Hecht in an elegy that appeared in *The Transparent Man* (1990).

Hecht's "Adieu" is also further dignified by a single-line epigraph from "A Palinode" by the little-known but artful Elizabethan poet, Edmund Bolton: "As fadeth Sommers-sunne from gliding fountains." The sentiment is appropriately conventional in Bolton's elegant double sonnet on life's transience and applicable to the commemorative occasion at hand, even preparing us distantly for the reference to "Sandover's sunlit end." But it also serves as something of a link, a shared line, borrowed from an earlier poet of considerable technical virtuosity bequeathed to a later poet of the same. As Merrill said two decades earlier to Hecht, we might recall, "I feel in complete <u>technical</u> sympathy with you; and am not at all sure that this isn't by far the deepest sympathy <u>to</u> feel in our trade—not unlike 'compatibility' in the erotic sphere."

Hecht hews perfectly to this line. He wasn't part of Merrill's "erotic sphere," but no matter. The tribute is poet to poet, but Hecht's major point is not Bolton's—that all life is evanescent. It's that Merrill's leaving is so much like his living: one more surprise, which, like his poetry, keeps everyone guessing what might be his next turn.

> The daily press keeps up-to-date obits
> Cooling in morgues and is piously prepared
> For the claim that any day may be one's last.
> Dictators, famous short-stops, felons, wits
> Intimately recline in darkly shared
> Beds of fine print, their leaden, predestined past.

But you, dear friend, managed to slip away,
Actually disappear in the dead of winter
More perfectly than Yeats. As at a show,
While we were savoring all your skills, the play
Of your words, your elegant, serious banter,
You cloaked yourself, vanished like Prospero

Or Houdini, escaping from cold padlocked fact,
Manacles, blindfolds, all our earthly ties,
And there we sat, the master illusionist
Leaving us stunned in the middle of his act,
The stage vacant, expecting some surprise
Reentry from the wings to a rousing Liszt

Fanfare, tumultuous applause, a bow
And a gentle, pleased, self-deprecating smile.
There comes no manager hither to explain.
Words fail us, from the weak and fatuous "ciao,
Bello," to the bellowing grand style,
As we shuffle out to the shabby street and the rain.

You are now one of that chosen band and choice
Fellowship gathered at Sandover's sunlit end,
Fit audience though few, where, at their ease,
Dante, Rilke, Mallarmé, Proust rejoice
In the rich polyphony of their latest friend,
Scored in his sweetly noted higher keys.

Even in his absence, Merrill holds center stage, making his appearance in the central part of the elegy, the continuing middle framed by two end-stopped stanzas: the first conspicuous by its weight, the last by its lightness, and as different from one another as night is from day, leaden print from "rich polyphony"—and, we might continue, bearing down on the celebrated subject at hand, dictators from Dante, short stops from show-stoppers, felons from magicians, wits from "master illusionists." And, of course, the allusion to both Yeats and Auden, in Auden's elegy on Yeats, even allows Merrill the rarer virtue of having outdone—perfected—Yeats in his Prospero or Houdini-like disappearance. The poem is not overtly showy; indeed by the standards of both poets, the rhyme scheme is sedate, the stanzas customary, indeed a bit old-fashioned. "No trace of pains taken, yet everywhere the print of experience [and] thought," Merrill might have said—did say. This is not about the poet writing; it commemorates the poet leaving, and, of course, arriving, and in this regard it is about poetic tradition—"fit audience though few," the familiar phrase from Milton perhaps constituting a private recollection about the "lucky words" connecting these two poets in life.[27] Modern elegies, we are often told, are about mourning and the failure of consolation: "There comes no manager hither to explain," Hecht duly observes. But this is only a single line, the shortest sentence, abrupt in context, bringing us suddenly down to earth, but also one to be passed through, not words on which to end. In this generous, moving, summary poem, in which a twig from the Elizabethan past in the form of a line from Edmund Bolton can become part of a new laurel crown, the final note belongs to none other than Merrill. Hecht didn't believe in an afterlife, at least of a theological order, but tracing out, indeed sweetly noting, a new poet's place in Parnassus was nothing to sniff at.

27. Robyn Creswell, "Painting and Privacy: On Anthony Hecht," *Raritan* 21 (Winter 2002), 34–6, makes the good point that, even after his elegy, Merrill continues to live on in Hecht's imagination in "Mirror," in *The Darkness and the Light* (2001). This chapter was written before the appearance of Langdon Hammer's glorious biography, *James Merrill: Life and Art* (New York: Alfred A. Knopf, 2015), in which Hecht makes only an occasional appearance.

5

"The Venetian Vespers"

"Full of the splendor of the insubstantial"

I like elements which are hybrid rather than "pure," compromising
rather than "clean," distorted rather than "straightforward," ambiguous
rather than "articulated," perverse as well as impersonal, boring as
well as "interesting," conventional rather than "designed," accommo-
dating rather than exclusive, redundant rather than simple, vestigial
as well as innovative, inconsistent and equivocal rather than direct
and clear. I am for messy vitality over obvious unity. I include the
non-sequitur and proclaim the duality.[1]

This passage, with its cascading series of contrasts, almost sounds as
if it could be by Whitman, but it is taken from "a gentle manifesto" found in Robert Venturi's landmark study, *Complexity and
Contradiction in Architecture*. First published in 1966, the book is an exuberantly written, many-headed, detailed refutation of mid-century
orthodox architectural modernism, epitomized in the writings and
works of Le Corbusier and Frank Lloyd Wright, and studded with
aphorisms, the most popular being "less is a bore."

One of Venturi's resonant phrases, "the obligation toward the difficult whole,"[2] has been recently revived by the literary theorist Brian
McHale in his fine study of postmodernist long poems, but, as McHale
notes, before it could be applied, the phrase required dusting off
because of "its residual modernist connotations."

1. Robert Venturi, *Complexity and Contradiction in Modern Architecture*, with an introduction
   by Vincent Scully (New York: The Museum of Modern Art, 1966), 22.
2. Venturi, *Complexity and Contradiction in Modern Architecture*, 89.

"Obligation" retains more than a trace of modernist architecture's high-minded purism and absolutism; "difficulty" evokes the modernist conviction that difficult times call for difficult forms ("poetry in our civilization, as it exists at present, must be *difficult*," wrote Eliot in 1921); while "whole" sounds hopelessly dated, a relic of New Critical organicism.[3]

But its utility continues for McHale because Venturi's study initiates a vocabulary that anticipates, even defines, areas of major concern found in postmodern aesthetics in general and the long poems McHale chooses to explore, albeit from a more explicitly deconstructivist perspective.

No dusting off is necessary when it comes to Hecht and his masterful long poem, "The Venetian Vespers." Hecht and Venturi are cut from similar modernist cloth, tailored in the same era, indeed from practically the same shop. The two men first met at the American Academy in Rome in 1954–55, during Hecht's second visit. Both shared an enthusiasm for the baroque environment that would have been part of daily life in Rome with its Berninis and Borrominis, to say nothing about their mannerist predecessor in Michelangelo and their later rococo refinement in Tiepolo; and if Venturi looked to some of Hecht's literary models, like Eliot and Empson, to help delineate important principles of architecture, Hecht willingly trespassed into the field of architecture to identify and define values central to poetry—the earliest example being drawn, in fact, from the Gardens of the Villa d'Este, just outside of Rome, in his poem of that title.

And it is to Venturi, among others, Hecht would turn many years later. In his 1992 Mellon Lectures he highlighted what he termed "The Contrariety of Impulses" as a defining feature of the "richest, most eloquent and durable of the arts in general and poetry in particular"—presumably the same values he aspired to in his own poetry. "This quality of what Venturi called 'complexity and contradiction' is intrinsic not only to the art of poetry itself, to its created artifacts, but to the experience of poetry as a psychological event on the part of the reader." Hecht had already introduced his discussion with a lengthy quotation from Venturi's "gentle manifesto," which included the remarks: "I like complexity and contradiction in architecture. I do not like the incoherence or arbitrariness of incompetent architecture nor

---

3. McHale, *The Obligation toward the Difficult Whole: Postmodernist Long Poems* (Tuscaloosa: The University of Alabama Press, 2004), 12–13.

the precious intricacies of picturesqueness or expressionism."[4] Here is the Architect (in caps) speaking, and the equally high-minded Poet quoting, both banishing in one fell swoop incoherence, arbitrariness, incompetence, the precious and the picturesque, while retaining complexity and contrariety.

It may be only a happy coincidence, but one worth observing, that Hecht was drawing his quotations from the 1977 edition of Venturi's book—the same year he undertook "The Venetian Vespers," a period that also included not simply the example of Merrill's experimentation with longer poems but coincided with Hecht's restlessness over what he perceived to be the current limitations of lyric poetry in general. He would soon write, in an essay on Robert Lowell:

[I]t is true that lyric poetry in our days has conceded vast territories to the writers of fiction, of which the impelling narrative drive is merely the most obvious advantage to the novelists. By its concentration, its narrowly focused point of view, its determined elimination of anything but the absolutely pertinent, its inviolably single tone, the lyric has elected to exclude all the contingent, chancy shifts of event, character, atmospherics, the alternations of time and consciousness that are the chief textures of our lives, and the vital substances of our very sense of reality. Novels are omnivorous, capable of assimilating everything, whereas the lyric has, since the Victorians, become more and more emaciated.[5]

If Merrill provided an example and Venturi a method, here was a wide-angle rationale, or apologia, for embarking on a long poem, or a series of long poems as it would turn out. Nothing less than truthfulness to life was at stake, in all its contingencies and complexities.

---

4. Hecht, *On the Laws of the Poetic Art* (Princeton, NJ: Princeton University Press, 1995), 130 and 125, respectively.

5. "Robert Lowell," in *Obbligati: Essays in Criticism* (New York: Atheneum, 1986), 275–6, based on a lecture given at the Library of Congress, 2 May 1983. Hecht's contrast between the omnivorous habits of the novel and the emaciated lyric not only reflects worries he shared with his friend and fellow poet, Richard Howard; it also anticipates a number of concerns involving the return to the "story" characteristic of the movement known as New Narrative or Expansive Poetry, whose origins generally date to the early 1980s. See R. S. Gwynn, ed., *New Expansive Poetry: Theory, Criticism, History* (Ashland, OR: Story Line Press, 1999), and Steven P. Schneider, ed., *The Contemporary Narrative Poem: Critical Crosscurrents* (Iowa: University of Iowa Press, 2012). However much Hecht might have valued some of its practitioners and the narrative poets they admire, including Frost, Hecht's modernist inheritance was too immediate and deep to participate in the populist statements associated with this "movement."

What differentiates "The Venetian Vespers" from everything else Hecht had written up to this point is simply scale and scope—two words, however, of considerable purpose in this poem, in which so much depends on upwards looking. Not that writing a long poem in blank verse is simple, but length—in this case of more than eight hundred lines—allows for many other opportunities and obligations to emerge; and while further quotations from Venturi could be produced (and some will be) to illuminate individual aspects of Hecht's poem, none better encapsulates the underlying challenge he faced than his sense of "the obligation toward the difficult whole." Nor does any phrase better capture the possible solution than Hecht's corresponding belief: " 'complexity and contradiction' is intrinsic not only to poetry itself, to its created artifacts, but to the experience of poetry as a psychological event on the part of the reader." Hecht's aim, in other words, was to construct an artful edifice out of opposites, but have those opposites express the contradictions as "events" experienced in time by the reader through the speaker's roiled musings, and in the process to give a fuller representation of life than lyric, both perceived and practiced by Hecht, had so far allowed.

And what better setting was there for these contradictory and complex musings than Venice? Paris wouldn't do for Hecht—that other city especially dear to artists and writers of the early twentieth century. Paris has "a heavy, sometimes even lugubrious quality to it," Hecht observed as far back as 1949: "the buildings are consistently grey, and all the principal landmarks are massive in their impressiveness."[6] But Venice, even as it appeared to Hecht in 1949, "est quelque chôse d'autre." Developing a list of parallels between the two cities, he notes, or implies, mainly differences, mostly to Venice's advantage.

The buildings are all in delicate pastel colors...and the large palaces, like the Doge's, are light in feeling and color. [...] There is a greater variety of architectural style, including Byzantine (as in St. Mark's Cathedral), Romanesque, Moorish, Gothic and Baroque. [...] Both the streets and canals are devious, and therefore, because one sees much less of it at a glance, it has a much more intimate feeling.

Varied, colorful, devious, and intimate, Venice, even in 1949, offered a potentially ideal setting for a long dramatic monologue, especially for a poet who rejoiced in color and ornamentation.

6. Letter, AH to his parents, 18 August 1949 (*SL*, 81–4).

Much later, reflecting on the poem's origins, Hecht made the connection between setting and subject, city and psyche even tighter, as hindsight will often do.

It wasn't until I'd gotten well into the poem...that I hit upon who the speaker should be. But even before I found him I knew that he must be American, that his past must be befouled in a way from which he was trying to escape, and that if the decay of the city was an analogue of his sickness, so were its beauties an image of his dreams of redemption. And his concentrated attempt to see things clearly in the famous clarity of Venetian light would be a metaphor for his virtually hopeless attempt to fathom and understand the mystery of his own anguish.[7]

Here, in a nutshell, was the city in relation to the self, the self in the city. "...Where's that palace whereinto foul things / Sometimes intrude not? Who has a breast so pure / But some uncleanly apprehensions / Keep leets and law days, and in session sit / With meditations lawful?" The first epigraph to the poem, a question from *Othello* uttered by Iago, perfectly captures the reciprocal mirroring between person and place—the palace, with its elaborate defenses, and the heart's simple wish for protection. The second epigraph, from Ruskin's *The Stones of Venice*, responds in vesper-like kind: "We cannot all have our gardens now, nor our pleasant fields to meditate in at eventide." And neither can Hecht's speaker, however much he yearns for stasis.

Long drawn to Venice, Hecht had become, in the meantime, well practiced in that baroque specialty, the art of chiaroscuro and the thematic contrarieties and "atmospheric depth"[8] associated with darkness and light ("'More Light! More Light!'"), and in the peculiar sensitivity, or drama, between sight and suffering, as explored in excruciating detail in "Behold the Lilies of the Field." He had also become increasingly interested, as exemplified by "Green: An Epistle" and "Apprehensions," in the longer dramatic monologue as a vehicle for exploring aberrant psyches—"sick souls," either in the present or in the making, and the events of both a historical and family kind that helped give them unique shape.[9] But so far he had not attempted

7. AH, unpublished note. Hecht Archive, Box 100.
8. Quoted from Hecht, *On the Laws of the Poetic Art*, 7.
9. The phrase "sick souls" comes from William James and is quoted by Hecht to explain part of his "metabolic make-up" in his letter to John Van Doren, 16 February 2002 (*SL*, 331–2).

anything on quite the same scale. The imagined scope required the poem to be divided into six sections, with each movement, in turn, containing a countermovement or movements of its own, as Hecht adhered to the principles of contrarieties at a structural level to admit the many contingencies, the ebb and flow of memory and desire, "the alternations of time and consciousness," that he saw as constituting "the chief textures of our lives," and born out in explicit detail in this poem.

Nor had he been as vested in a single setting in which contrary impulses could be so fully developed: from cathedral to canal, from high art to low, from the fragility of Murano glass to "the ochre pastes and puddings of dogshit" on the pavement. And here I mean to underscore not just the visual variety and atmospherics offered by the sinking city itself—"The world's most louche and artificial city, / (In which my tale some time will peter out)"—but the rich, varied verbal history associated with its grand decline. Although Venice has produced few great writers of its own, it has authored numerous famous reflections, a good many of which Hecht had read in advance of writing his poem: from Shakespeare to Jonson to Byron, Ruskin, and Thomas Mann— to mention some of the familiar names or their works alluded to in "Vespers"—to which Hecht would add a few of his own, mainly associated with madness.[10]

Both the city's visual and verbal associations, in other words, encouraged a many-sided baroque amplitude of expression, a wooly and at times wildly eccentric strain of reflection:

> Wagner died here, Stravinsky's buried here,
> They say that Cimarosa's enemies
> Poisoned him here. The mind at four AM
> Is a poor, blotched, vermiculated thing.
> I've seen it spilled like sweetbreads, and I've dreamed
> Of Byron writing, "Many a fine day
> I should have blown my brains out but for the thought
> Of the pleasure it would give my mother-in-law."
> Thus virtues, it is said, are forced upon us
> By our own impudent crimes. I think of him
> With his consorts of whores and countesses
> Smelling of animal musk, lilac and garlic,

---

10. For some additional sources beyond the familiar ones, see Hecht's letter to Dimitri Hadzi, 31 March 1979 (*SL*, 179).

A *ménage* that was in fact a menagerie,
A fox, a wolf, a mastiff, birds and monkeys,
Corbaccios and corvinos, *spintriae*,
The lees of the Venetian underworld,
A plague of iridescent flies. Spilled out.
O lights and livers. Deader than dead weight.
In a casket lined with tufted tea-rose silk.
O that the soul should tie its shoes, the mind
Should wash its hands in a sink, that a small grain
Of immortality should fit itself
With dentures.

In a line Hecht added to an earlier draft of the poem, the speaker refers to this passage as "an invented litany of my own." And indeed the only other place in Hecht where we might find such a bizarre mix, an inspired mélange of garbled quotes and striking allusions, is in some of his more deliberately ludic letters, especially those to his brother Roger, written during the war.[11] In the case of the poem, one can track each of the references to a specific source. Some Hecht gives; others pour out, indeed are "spilled out" in often corrupted form: from *Lear*, from *Volpone*, issuing in some desperate apostrophes—metaphysical wit, we might say, gone astray, as both sign and symbol of the madness the speaker fears. It's not so much the individual references but their totality that is impressive. The blank verse, like the mind, bursts at the seams, hinting at some underlying wound, one, in fact, that can be glimpsed here in the image of "sweetbreads," out of which grows the bad dream by Byron. But at this point we mainly want to know: Who is this strange, brilliantly wayward talker?

The question is not easily answered since the poem begins by situating us *in medias res*, in the graveled psyche of an unnamed or otherwise identified speaker, which strategy lends a detective-story mystery to the poem, as Gregory Dowling has suggested.[12] Piece by piece, phrase by phrase, we become his familiar, we assemble a psyche, a consciousness from the inside out, as it were, and while he is never explicitly named, we come to know him intimately: through his distinct voice and perverse reflections at first, and then only later through biographical

11. See, for instance, Letters, AH to parents, 28 October 1944 and 25 March 1945 (*SL*, 33–4, 39–41).
12. Gregory Dowling, " 'Bewildered Tourists': Anthony Hecht's 'See Naples and Die,' " *New Walk* 5 (2012–13), 18–25. See also the same author's earlier essay, " 'Pearly Vacancies': The Venice of Anthony Hecht's 'Vespers,' " in *Il Bianco e il Nero*, 4 (2000), 51–66.

tidbits that cast a retrospective light on the strange habits of thoughts—
his macabre "humor" in the Jacobean sense of the word. Literarily, he
is a descendent of all who seek release from suffering: Dante's infernal
inhabitants, Milton's Satan, and more immediately Eliot's spiritually
depleted Gerontion (quoted by the speaker: "thus virtues, it is said, are
forced upon us / By our own impudent crimes"), and the limbo-like
Prufrock, whose remark, "No. I am not Prince Hamlet, nor was meant
to be," is, in fact, an ironic reflection of the speaker's Hamlet-like biographical circumstances as they gradually emerge in the second half
of the poem. Hecht's speaker knows the byways of religious doubt
but none of the relief that comes from faith, and it is this complex act
of teetering and twisting, of knowingly wandering between these psychic extremes, that animates the poem's fundamental set of contrasts
between darkness and light and earns our sympathies.[13]

Unnamed though he may be, he nonetheless suffers depravities of
his own, indeed of a particular Hechtian order. (The point is made
slyly by the poet when he inserts "own" into the quotation from
"Gerontion.")[14] Haunted by recollections of World War II (even more
so than the speaker of "Apprehensions") and of a dysfunctional family,
incestuously sullied, it seems, like Hamlet's—and part of his suffering
is that he is never, down to his last words in the poem, certain about his
lineage—he seeks repeatedly to empty the self, with its accumulated
burdens, into the immediacy of a deeply realized visual presence of
which Venice offers so many opportunities.

Here is one such example, taken from the poem's third section.
It is a moment that every visitor to Venice has experienced—when,

13. On the subject of sympathy for Hecht's protagonist, see especially, J. D. McClatchy,
"Summaries and Evidence," *Partisan Review* 47.4 (1980), 643–4.
14. I owe this fine point to Christopher Ricks, *True Friendship: Geoffrey Hill, Anthony
Hecht, and Robert Lowell under the Sign of Eliot and Pound* (New Haven: Yale University
Press, 2010), 75–6, although I see the quotation more as an assertion of ownership and
differentiation by Hecht's speaker, who shares a number of characteristics with Hecht
the poet. As Ricks goes on to note, quoting Hecht, "'The Venetian Vespers' is about an
invented character, largely a man I knew in Ischia, partly my brother, and necessarily
something of myself. But for the most part the character is invented." Since critics
have occasionally read "Vespers" as if it were transparent autobiography, it is worth
emphasizing the matter of "invention" here as well as Hecht's wish to differentiate
"Vespers" from "Green: An Epistle" on precisely this issue of self-involvement. In
"Vespers," there is a deliciously willful indulgence in the ludic—"I wander these
by-paths and little squares, / A singular Tyrannosauros Rex, / Sauntering towards
extinction, an obsolete / Left-over from a weak ancien régime"—that ought to prevent any simple identification between Hecht and his speaker.

upon entering St. Mark's Cathedral, the eye begins to adjust to the dim surroundings—though few have phrased it better or with greater intensity, a feature attributable in part to Hecht's use of the present tense here (and elsewhere in the poem) "as a way of conveying the speaker's attempt to escape from past and future by concentrating on the immediate present":[15]

> Gradually
> Glories reveal themselves, grave mysteries
> Of the faith cast off their shadows, assume their forms
> Against a heaven of coined and sequined light,
> A splatter of gilt cobblestones, flung grains
> Or crumbs of brilliance, the vast open fields
> Of the sky turned intimate and friendly. Patines
> And laminae, a vermeil shimmering
> Of fish-scaled, cataphracted golden plates.
> Here are the saints and angels brought together
> In studied reveries of happiness.
> Enormous wings of seraphim uphold
> The crowning domes where the convened apostles
> Receive their fiery tongues from the Godhead
> Descended to them as a floating dove,
> Patriarch and collateral ancestor
> Of the pigeons out in the Square. Into those choirs
> Of lacquered Thrones, enameled Archangels
> And medaled Principalities rise up
> A cool plantation of columns, marble shafts
> Bearing their lifted pathways, viaducts
> And catwalks through the middle realms of heaven.
> Even as God descended into the mass
> And thick of us, so is He borne aloft
> As promise and precursor to us all,
> Ascending in the central dome's vast hive
> Of honeyed luminosity.

15. Letter, AH to Norman Williams, 14 September 2003. Even more pertinent to the Venetian narrative at hand is Hecht's observation in *On the Laws of the Poetic Art*, 26, that J. M. W. Turner's "Mother died insane when he was in his twenties, and it is possible that he sought the refuge in painting that can be provided by acute attention to the visible world, which is, in the very nature of things, a constant obsession with *the present tense*, and a purposeful disregard of past and future" (Hecht's italics). Explicit reference to Turner appears in Section VI of "Vespers," in conjunction with the speaker's praise of "the blessèd stasis of painting."

This is deliberately grand verse, in keeping with its setting—"A splatter of gilt cobblestones, flung grains / Or crumbs of brilliance, the vast open fields / Of the sky turned intimate and friendly." How many poets today can carry blank verse as far as Hecht and with so little apparent effort? Or can come up with a phrase like the last: "Ascending in the central dome's vast hive / Of honeyed luminosity." For all his copious attention to description, Ruskin—Hecht's immediate source here—never gets close to the final image. This is a poet who thinks through light, and all the sweetness it might afford.

Still, grandly Miltonic as it is—and it's hard not to think of Milton in the reference to "Thrones...Archangels...Principalities"—it's easy to fault this kind of poetry for appearing to be static, enameled in mosaic in precisely the same way as the cathedral itself, the marmoreal effects of the original artifact reduplicated in the Latinate phrasing of "Patines /And laminae, a vermeil shimmering / Of fish-scaled, cataphracted golden plates." One can argue, of course, that's part of the point, but not for long, as Hecht understood. A better argument can be made—and Hecht makes it—if we respect the poem's amplitude and widen the narrative lens a bit, as we do when we're reading and not just quoting selectively. We might see this passage as an expression of the speaker's desire, unfolding in time, one carefully positioned by the poet and calculated in a larger arc of meaning that respects pace and variety, contrary movements and complex effects.

For all the passage's grandeur, indeed because of its grandeur, Hecht has taken care to frame the St. Mark's ekphrasis by stories or allusions of the plainest sort delivered in the vernacular. "I am a person of inflexible habits / And comforting rigidities," is how Section III begins, with a brief, down-to-earth, humorously irreverent account of the "spiriting away of the dead saint" from his original location in Alexandria by one "Buono and his side-kick Rustico." (The irony of "spiriting away" is obvious but to the point in commercial Venice.) The movement then concludes with a casual reference to, of all odd people, the Miller of Dee, who is allowed a footnote for his famous ballad, which concludes, in Hecht's version, with a slight variant:

> And this the burden of his song
> Forever used to be—
> I care for nobody, no, not I,
> And nobody cares for me.

The variant involves the purposeful substitution in the final line of "And" for "If" to underscore the speaker's further misanthropy; but the waywardness with the original text, like the embellished version of the solemn legend of the Evangelist's body, also dovetails with, and highlights by contrast, the greater spiritual waywardness that is the poem's larger subject, and is deftly explored in the first-person narrative introducing the ekphrasis.

As such, although the speaker might visit the cathedral twice a week, he does so as a self-described "twentieth-century infidel." This dark groping with the obscure informs his entrance into the cathedral and establishes the frame of mind in which he—and the reader—will experience the interior:

> I enter the obscure aquarium dimness,
> The movie-palace dark, through which incline
> Smoky diagonals and radiant bars
> Of sunlight from the high southeastern crescents
> Of windowed drums above. Like slow blind fingers
> Finding their patient and unvarying way
> Across the braille of pavement, edging along
> The pavonine and lapidary walls,
> Inching through silence as the earth revolves
> To huge compulsions, as the turning spheres
> Drift in their milky pale galactic light
> Through endless quiet, gigantic vacancy,
> Unpitying, inhuman, terrible.

We—he—might begin in a familiar place (an aquarium or movie-palace), but we end up in some altogether other, alien, space, and the vehicle that carries us slowly and waywardly upward is a simile seemingly detached from an immediate referent. It refers, apparently, to the movement of the shadows, but it also tracks the speaker's shadowy thoughts inching vertically upward until reaching the "gigantic vacancy" of the macrocosm: "Unpitying, inhuman, terrible." Perhaps for no other reason than its threefold repetition of terror, and the later references to *Hamlet*, it's difficult not to think of the ghost of Hamlet's father wandering in purgatory: "unhouseled, dis-appointed, unaneled." But the major point is that this view into emptiness immediately precedes and prepares, by contrast, the viewing eye as it opens to the full, indeed overflowing, splendor of the cathedral's heavenly interior. It is splendid not just because it is filled with beautiful mosaics but because, included in these mosaics, is a depiction of a lost community that expands in significance as a sign of the speaker's longing. Initially perceived at a distance—"Here are the saints and angels brought together / In studied reveries of happiness"—it grows in immediacy to include the priestly intonations of the speaker himself:

> And we are gathered here below the saints,
> Virtues and martyrs, sheltered in their glow,
> Soothed by the punk and incense, to rejoice
> In the warm light of Gabrieli's horns,
> And for a moment of unwonted grace,
> We are so blessed as to forget ourselves.

This is one of many moments in "Vespers" where lyric and narrative, a spot in time and linear time, briefly coalesce to produce a moment outside of time—of "unwonted" but deeply "wanted" grace. But as the references to "punk and incense" and the Venetian baroque musician Giovanni Gabrieli (not the angel Gabriel) hint, this is an exquisitely reflective aesthete whose pathos is to know that he will not remain part of the flock for long. Indeed, the bubble is punctured with a one-word sentence of doubt: "Perhaps." And we (and he) begin the long thirty-two-line decline downward to the lonely Miller of Dee, traversing, in the process, through a myriad of images of sufferings, including a vertiginous vision of the mind that suffers over the world's sufferings. If Venice, with its secret byways, is also a hall of mirrors, so is the reflecting mind. The speaker might want a drink at Florian's, the famous café in St. Mark's Square, but what he really needs, but cannot get, is a drop of water from the river Lethe.

"The obligation towards the difficult whole" requires calculating the poem's narrative scale, its tonal gradations and contrasts, well beyond what lyric generally insists. "In the validly complex building or cityscape, the eye does not want to be too easily or too quickly satisfied in its search for unity within a whole."[16] This process of necessarily slow reading includes navigating our way through some strange words, such as "pavonine," "cataphracted," and "mucid," Latinisms calculated to send us to dictionaries, often threatening to turn the poem into a Tower of Babel. Of course, they enhance our experience of difficulty—and are lamented or criticized by some for doing so. But as Venturi remarked more generally about the past intruding into the present: "the vestigial element discourages clarity of meaning; it promotes richness of meaning

16. Venturi, *Complexity and Contradiction in Modern Architecture*, 103.

instead."[17] True, and to the point about a city with so much evidence of the vestigial and a poem intent on recapturing much of it; but Hecht was also too careful with language just to send his readers on errands into the deep. His archaisms more often draw attention to meaning in the manner Venturi accorded to the concept of "inflection": as a way of "distinguishing diverse parts while implying continuity."[18] They also anticipate and underline, we discover later, the distinctive emphasis placed on "*elocution*" as a feature further delineating the speaker's eccentric, isolated, anti-social identity as a first-generation immigrant. At the same time, Hecht hints at the peculiar alliance between poetry and architecture at the heart of this wayward poem, captured in quotations in the familiar phrase " 'building a vocabulary,' " which the poet then extends to include the idea of "A project that seemed allied to architecture, / The unbuttressed balancing of wooden blocks / Into a Tower of Babel."

"Nor can we dignify confusion by calling it baroque." Hecht might have had Marianne Moore's warning in mind, a warning she admitted often ignoring in her desire to be "complete as I like to be."[19] Here, teetering on the edge, perhaps, but not collapsing into nonsense, the apparently obscure "pavonine," for instance, means "of, relating to, resembling, or characteristic of a peacock": related, therefore, to the physical material of the cathedral ("pavement"); suggestive of the symbolic value of the peacock in religious art, often found on church walls; and finally, in its showy iridescence, anticipating the rich play with color that marks the poem's glorious, final evocation of a Venetian sunset. The word's location in the poem distinguishes and connects.

Much the same can be said of "cataphracted," from the Latin meaning "an ancient coat of armor," with a more specialized zoological association with fish. It is used by Hecht to describe the shimmering surface quality of the cathedral walls as golden plated, but the reference to armor also recollects the nightmarish image of the modern Nazi helmet in Section I, and the more poignant reference to the helmet at the end of Section III, to be discussed more fully later in this chapter. As for "mucid," used in the first section, also from the Latin meaning

---

17. Venturi, *Complexity and Contradiction in Modern Architecture*, 44.
18. Venturi, *Complexity and Contradiction in Modern Architecture*, 91.
19. *The Complete Prose of Marianne Moore* (New York: Viking, 1986), 420.

snotty or moldy, and appearing in the phrase "the mucid glitter of an eye," it may not be a sufficient defense of the word to cite its appearance in the *OED*, but it is surely not "picturesque" and represents an improvement over "Reptilian heavy-lidded eye," found in an earlier draft, on the basis of both sound and sense. Small beer perhaps, but this is a poem about self-loathing and disgust, indeed about the deep wish for clarity of vision, and "mucid" is one of many bodily reminders about why this condition is so difficult for the speaker to achieve. The word, rightly, stops us in our tracks.

To follow our speaker further though, as indeed we must, is to wend our way through the palpable obscure to arrive at moments of intense illumination, and here I am referring not to the famous Venetian light or even the reflected light from ekphrasis but to the manner of the poem's exposition at crucial junctures. Nearly halfway through the poem, the contingencies, the glancing phrases and odd diction, the many descriptive flights and descents need grounding if the narrative is to have psychological truth. It needs to be lodged, that is, in the world of incident, which is also the world of chance and accident, reported by the speaker with Hemingway-like matter-of-factness at the end of the third section:

> It wasn't always so. I was an Aid Man,
> A Medic with an infantry company,
> Who because of my refusal to bear arms
> Was constrained to bear the wounded and the dead
> From under enemy fire, and to bear witness
> To inconceivable pain, usually shot at
> Though banded with Red Crosses and unarmed.

The triple repetition of "bearing" carries the burden here, with the last usage—"to bear witness"—surely the crucial one, as this "autobiographical" insert will make clear. But in order to grasp the full weight of this passage near the poem's center, it needs quoting in full:

> There was a corporal I knew in Heavy Weapons
> Someone who carried with him into combat
> A book of etiquette by Emily Post.
> Most brought with them some token of the past,
> Some emblem of attachment or affection
> Or coddled childhood—bibles and baby booties,
> Harmonicas, love letters, photographs—
> But this was different. I discovered later

That he had been brought up in an orphanage,
So the book was his fiction of kindliness,
A novel in which personages of wealth
Firmly secure domestic tranquility.
He'd cite me instances. It seems a boy
Will not put "Mr." on his calling cards
Till he leaves school, and may omit the "Mr."
Even while at college. Bread and butter plates
Are never placed on a formal dinner table.
At a simple dinner party one may serve
Claret instead of champagne with the meat.
The satin facings on a butler's lapels
Are narrower than a gentleman's, and he wears
Black waistcoat with white tie, whereas the gentleman's
White waistcoat goes with both black tie and white.
When a lady lunches alone at her own home
In a formally kept house the table is set
For four. As if three Elijahs were expected.
This was to him a sort of *Corpus Juris,*
An ancient piety and governance
Worthy of constant dream and meditation.
He haunts me here, that seeker after law
In a lawless world, in rainsoaked combat boots,
Oil-stained fatigues and heavy bandoleers.
He was killed by enemy machine-gun fire.
His helmet had fallen off. They had sheared away
The top of his cranium like a soft-boiled egg,
And there he crouched, huddled over his weapon,
His brains wet in the chalice of his skull.

Here, we should note, the poem is at its most novelistic—admittedly so, in fact, as Emily Post's book of etiquette is even converted into a work of fiction, "A novel in which personages of wealth / Firmly secure domestic tranquility." And if domesticity is the purview of the novel, there is also, and for the only time in the poem, a strange intimacy that emerges between the speaker and another person: the latter a lonely kin of a kind brought up in an orphanage, and a shadow of the speaker's own past "kindliness." He chose not to "bear arms," we recall, but only the "wounded and the dead." The irony of that burden hardly needs comment in light of the poem we have been reading and what immediately follows, but for the moment there is relief in the revelation of incidental detail, what "Mr." might and might not do, how to set a dinner table, but also false hope in what such manners might signify in a lawless world. Again, it's hard to miss the further irony in labeling a book of etiquette a "fiction of kindliness" in these circumstances.

This brief episode is told with both appealing tenderness and appalling clarity, but whatever personal wartime memories underlie this episode, its significance in the poem is better understood through recourse to a passage from the "Lowell" essay, indeed from the same paragraph quoted earlier in this chapter. Hecht recounts an episode (from Frank Bidart) in which

> One day in Robert Lowell's class, someone brought in a poem about a particularly painful and ugly subject. A student, who was shocked, said that some subjects simply couldn't be dealt with in poems. I've never forgotten Lowell's reply. He said, "You can say anything in a poem—if you place it properly."

Nor obviously did Hecht forget Lowell's comment, even passing it down to a student of his own.[20]

The most profound redaction of Lowell's advice might well be at the end of this most novelistic section of the poem. Few who have read "Vespers" have ever forgotten the closing brutal four lines. The helmet is as useless as the "cataphracted golden plates" of armor on the walls of St. Mark's, the chalice of the skull now a grotesque redetermination of the sacred—all described with lucid equanimity and a sense that domesticity has gone luridly awry in the shocking image of the soft-boiled egg. Nor, of course, can Hecht's speaker forget the image, so maimed by it that it keeps reappearing in distorted form throughout "Vespers." It is this image he keeps trying to erase, whether in St. Mark's Cathedral or by looking across the "lagoon's waters in mid-morning" to "the great church of Health," Santa Maria della Salute, in one of the poem's more luminous passages beginning: "Lights. I have chosen Venice for its light, / Its lightness, buoyancy, its calm suspension / In time and water." Or by honoring "San Pantaleone, heavenly buffoon" for the film that could be played backwards.

So well placed is the image, in fact, that it almost stands as a fully sufficient explanation for the speaker's perilous mental condition. But like much else in reflective Venice, Hecht's poem is double plotted, a twice-told tale, complex at the level of story line. "Where to begin?" The question, first encountered in the poem's opening paragraph,

---

20. Along with the passage in "Robert Lowell," 276, see Hecht's letter to Charles Tung, 2 February 1994 (*SL*, 263–4).

where it might properly be seen to inaugurate action, is repeated at the beginning of Section IV, where the subject of beginnings, of origins, his own included, explicitly surfaces and haunts the speaker down to the poem's final line with its allusion to the proverb that "It is a wise child that knows its own father." If, as Hecht asserts in his "Lowell" essay, "the impelling narrative drive is merely the most obvious advantage" that lyric poets have ceded "to the novelists," this is a poem that doubly seeks to make up for this loss.

The second plot widens the search for identity—ours with regard to the speaker, his with respect to his parents—with accumulating urgency but without ever resolving the question. The force of the narrative, however, lies in a different direction: not in the story it tells, a variation on the American immigrant tale laced with a touch of *Hamlet*, but in the images that it contains and which contribute to our sense of the poem as a whole. Years later, Hecht might have been thinking of "Vespers" when he wrote to his screenwriter friend Al Sapinsley about the value of description over dialogue in the novel:

> To be sure, there is wonderful dialogue in Dickens, as there is in Dostoyevski; but this is not what we remember about them. I taught Crime and Punishment for years, made notes and outlines, read the critical commentaries (some of which were wonderfully illuminating) and I came to see how many descriptive elements and symbolic devices, operating subliminally, work so effectively in that wonderful book. The color yellow all by itself plays a major role in the story.[21]

Hecht then goes on to quote from *Madame Bovary*—Flaubert and Joyce being his "heroes as fiction writers"—in order to focus on the descriptive elements in that novel. In the process of doing so, he also distinguishes prose narrative from film precisely because of the former's considered attention to the selective, sequential handling of detail. Tracing through the imagery, Hecht concludes:

> Finally, Emma's awkward, amused, slightly clumsy attempt to get a taste of the liquor from the almost empty glass is a touching symbol of the insatiable craving for experiences that were never hers because they were unreal and belong entirely to the realms of her imagination.

21. Letter, AH to Al Sapinsley, 11 December 1998 (*SL*, 297–9). The same passage from Flaubert is quoted for slightly different purposes by Hecht in *On the Laws of the Poetic Art*, 21–2.

With regard to "Vespers," beginning again allows the poet to fulfill an obligation toward the difficult whole primarily through further intensity of description, an intensity that allows the elevation of image to symbol: the discovery, for instance, of the ramifying significance of rain in the poem. Not only is it associated with the "rainsoaked combat boots" of the dead soldier and more subtly with the metaphorical prayer at the end of this first section for mercy à la Portia of *The Merchant of Venice*; it is also retrospectively backdated to the death of his mother and further personalized: "Next day they told me that my mother was dead. / I didn't go to school. I watched the rain / From the bedroom window." Window, glass, rain, watching: this cluster of images in turn touches on a variety of themes in the poem, the suddenly imposed sense of isolation on the speaker, for example, and his movingly rueful and punning admission, made *sotto voce*, that he is a failure and as frangible as glass: "*Ho fatto un fiasco*, which is to say, / I've made a sort of bottle of my life, / A frangible and a transparent failure." (*Fiasco*, in Italian, means "flask or bottle.")

One can see why Hecht was drawn to the symbol of "the almost empty glass" in Flaubert. In anticipation of his use of it here in Section VI as a symbol of his speaker's fragility, at the end of Section II he presents an elaborate turn on the image though his description of glass-making in a Murano workshop, the makers possessing all the artistry of little gods:

> They take the first crude bulb of thickened glass,
> Glowing and taffy-soft on the blow tube,
> And sink it in a mold, a metal cup
> Spiked on its inner surface like a pineapple.
> Half the glass now is regularly dimpled,
> And when these dimples are covered with a glaze
> Of molten glass they are prisoned air-bubbles,
> Breathless, enameled pearly vacancies.

As Emma Bovary's half-empty glass represents her unfulfilled desire, Hecht's delightfully detailed fashioning of glass represents the temptation presented to his burdened speaker's wish to be self-translated into one of those air-bubbles imprisoned in a beautiful, breathless globe of "enameled pearly vacancies."

Where Hecht's speaker differs from Madame Bovary is in his ability to reckon the symbolic value, the significance, of the image, and that recognition in turn allows description itself—and the act of looking—to acquire a level of pressured importance unrivalled elsewhere in Hecht and in the poetry of his contemporaries:

> Perhaps because of those days of constant rain
> I am always touched by it now, touched and assuaged.
> Perhaps that early vigilance at windows
> Explains why I have come to regard
> Life as a spectator sport.

This is logical enough, if uninspiring as a prelude, but then comes the turn, gradual at the outset, and then gathering energy as the eye turns upward:

> But I find peace
> In the arcaded dark of the piazza
> When a thunderstorm comes up. I watch the sky
> Cloud into tarnished zinc, to Quaker gray
> Drabness, its shrouded vaults, fog-bound crevasses
> Blinking with huddled lightning, and await
> The vast *son et lumière*. The city's lamps
> Faintly ignite in the gathered winter gloom.
> The rumbled thunder starts—an avalanche
> Rolling down polished corridors of sound,
> Rickety tumbrels blundering across
> A stone and empty cellarage. And then,
> Like a whisper of dry leaves, the rain begins.
> It stains the paving stones, forms a light mist
> Of brilliant crystals dulled with tones of lead
> Three inches off the ground. Blown shawls of rain
> Quiver and luff, veil the cathedral front
> In flailing laces while the street lamps hold
> Fixed globes of sparkled haze high in the air
> And the black pavement runs with wrinkled gold
> In pools and wet dispersions, fiery spills
> Of liquid copper, of squirming, molten brass.
> To give one's whole attention to such a sight
> Is a sort of blessedness. No room is left
> For antecedence, inference, nuance.
> One escapes from all the anguish of this world
> Into the refuge of the present tense.
> The past is mercifully dissolved, and in
> Easy obedience to the gospel's word,
> One takes no thought whatever of tomorrow,
> The soul being drenched in fine particulars.

In so finely nuanced a passage, "drenched in fine particulars," how right it is that one of the few changes Hecht made in the final draft involved replacing the line "No room is left / For longings or memory, for past or future," with "No room is left / For antecedence, inference, nuance." The new line closes perfectly in on itself, metrically and sonically. There is nothing left to say—or think. At least that is the speaker's hope. And how right, too, for the poet to substitute the deeper "shrouded vaults" for the more superficial "deep" as a way to way to hint again at the skull beneath the surface in this poem.

In these intensely concentrated visual moments, we can't help thinking of one of the contemporaries Hecht most admired, Elizabeth Bishop, but mainly to note the different pressure placed on seeing in each. Bishop writes in "Poem," "Heavens, I recognize the place"—a sign of surprise, a small epiphany in response to what she has seen, and goes on to discriminate between the grander concept of "vision" in favor of the more modest "looks." For all his concentration on particulars, Hecht's speaker, by contrast, is a visionary manqué. Although knowing he won't succeed, he nonetheless seeks transcendence—in fact, nothing less than salvation—through the act of "looking." Indeed, one of the most striking contrasts developed in "Vespers" springs from the speaker's desire to see and the radical critique of sight at the beginning of Section V, a passage that seems simultaneously, if oddly (for Hecht), steeped in Bishop's "The Fish" and Ashbery's "Self-Portrait in a Convex Mirror." The speaker states flatly at the outset that "Seeing is misbelieving":

> All lenses—the corneal tunic of the eye
> Fine scopes and glazier's filaments—mislead us
> With insubstantial visions, like objects viewed
> Through crizzled and quarrelled panes of Bull's Eye Glass.

We might think of this as Hecht's gaze into postmodernism's hall of mirrors, but one quickly averted, in much the same way that Hecht's Venice avers from Merrill's. Doublings and contradictions are deeply unsettling for Hecht's speaker, who seeks, but doesn't receive, an explanation for his identity. "Seeing is misbelieving," whereas "blindness," paradoxically, is illuminating, is "merciful." For all his endearingly outlandish talk of being a sauntering Tyrannosaurus Rex, Hecht's speaker is, rather, a lineal descendent of Adam and Eve. The eyes are truly opened only with, and because of, the Fall, the expulsion from Paradise.

He quotes Genesis: " '*And the eyes of them both were opened, and they knew...*' " But what do they glimpse? Hecht's is a self-portrait that cannot be scrubbed clean.

It is in the context of these visual misgivings, this radical critique of the eye, that the final passage of the poem must be read. Beginning again means creating another ending, the poet setting another challenge for himself; and while it's hard to believe that the lengthy passage about rainy Venice quoted earlier in this chapter could be topped for sheer visual splendor, here is Hecht at work once more, in a different key, with his speaker now looking skyward, putting yet greater pressure on the act of seeing, or rather, "looking," to use a near-synonym. The meanings are so close and yet so far. Seeing is associated with the moment of perception itself (or misperception) and understanding—Bishop's small epiphany ("Heavens," I see, I understand); looking with the action of directing the eye or one's sight at an object at a distance in the hope of illumination, of seeing something:

> In these late days
> I find myself frequently at the window,
> Its glass a cooling comfort to my temple.
> And I lift up mine eyes, not to the hills
> Of which there are not any, but to the clouds.
> Here is a sky determined to maintain
> The reputation of Tiepolo,
> A moving vision of a shapely mist,
> Full of the splendor of the insubstantial.
> Against a diorama of palest blue
> Cloud-curds, cloud-stacks, cloud-bushes sun themselves.
> Giant confections, impossible meringues,
> Soft coral reefs and powdery tumuli
> Pass in august processions and calm herds.
> Great stadiums, grandstands and amphitheaters,
> The tufted, opulent litters of the gods
> They seem; or laundered bunting, well-dressed wigs,
> Harvests of milk-white, Chinese peonies
> That visibly rebuke our stinginess.
> For all their ghostly presences, they take on
> A colorful nobility at evening.
> Off to the east the sky begins to turn
> Lilac so pale it seems a mood of gray,
> Gradually, like the death of virtuous men.
> Streaks of electrum richly underline

> The slow, flat-bottomed hulls, those floated lobes
> Between which quills and spokes of light fan out
> Into carnelian reds and nectarines,
> Nearing a citron brilliance at the center,
> The searing furnace of the glory hole
> That fires and fuses clouds of muscatel
> With pencilings of gold. I look and look,
> As though I could be saved simply by looking—
> I, who have never earned my way, who am
> No better than a viral parasite,
> Or the lees of the Venetian underworld,
> Foolish and muddled in my later years,
> Who was never even at one time a wise child.

This is surely one of the most richly polyphonic of Hecht's endings, with its long crescendo into the clouds, then its decrescendo into "the lees of the Venetian underworld," for a second time, his tale now evidently petering out. Thematically, the final lines round off the plot of the second half of the poem by underscoring the speaker's predicament as the proverbially ignorant child as well as his recognition of his fruitless dependence on others. "Foolish and muddled in [his] later years," he reminds us of Lear but without the latter's tragic grandeur. So, too, but broader still, the setting at the window arcs back to the poem's opening reference to the wished-for "clean coolness at the temple," with the temple now sounding, through the echo of Psalm 121, a firmer devotional note, carried on through the echo of Herbert's "Prayer" [I], to accompany the speaker's final extravagant wish for salvation on the basis of sight alone. And temporally, the shaded, prolonged, evening moment serves as an antiphonal response to the Canaletto-like bright clarity of the speaker's earlier celebration of mid-morning festivities in the lagoon at the close of Section II. There he had remarked, "I am for the moment cured of everything." Here, though, the difference is sounded, and we are left with him, looking at the image of a gorgeous Venetian sunset, now quietly amplified by the opening line of Donne's "Valediction: Forbidding Morning" ("As virtuous men pass mildly away")—in his loneliness, a complex mix of pathos and nobility, subliminally wishing for the good death in Donne to replace his present condition as Gerontion. (The association is made through the different uses of "virtue" by each.) Taking his cue from Hecht's speaker perhaps, Howard Nemerov remarked that the closing passage refutes the view that "among the many things language didn't and perhaps couldn't deal with were clouds."[22] Surely not the case here: their heroic shapes, as Hecht's speaker says, "visibly rebuke our stinginess. For all their ghostly presences, they take on / A colorful nobility at evening." And so does Hecht's verse.

Curiously, Hecht was himself rather late at arriving at the poem's title. He had tried out a variety of possibilities including "A Passage," "A Passenger," "The Forfeit," "Clouds," and "Vacancies"—all relevant to a specific theme or image but none especially memorable. Then last, in pencil, he wrote "Venetian Vespers," the title rising to the level of a symbol in all its visual and acoustical inclusiveness, perhaps even reminding us of the polyphonic composer of the 1610 *Vespro della Beata Vergine*, Monteverdi, who lies buried in the Frari Church. As symbol, it reminds us, too, of Hecht's obligation toward the difficult whole in this poem and of the larger role the contrariety of impulses holds for him as a distinctively modernist aesthetic. Such contrarieties include the plainest of speech amid the most colorful, as this passage shows: baroque extravagance in the service of the heart's simple wish to know the whole shebang.

But rounding off a poem, it needs to be stressed, is not quite the same thing as reconciling its diverse meanings. Helen Vendler raised the latter concept in a critique of Hecht, about whom, she observed, "the aesthetic of the deliberately imperfect or incomplete is foreign, I think, to Hecht, for whom beauty is harmony, wholeness, order and unity."[23] I don't think this is a mischaracterization of either Hecht's ideal version of beauty, nor of an aesthetic preference or impulse often at work in his poetry, although it is often the gap between the ideal and the real that he seeks to explore in his verse. But in so far as her comment includes a sidelong glance at his poetry, it seems insufficiently responsive to questions often raised but not resolved, and perhaps nowhere more so than at the end of "Vespers." Among those questions, the most haunting is contained in the phrase, "I look and look, / As though I could be saved simply by looking—" The dash at the end of the line is hardly the radical break we encounter at the end of

---

22. Letter, Nemerov to AH, 29 November 1979. Hecht Archive.
23. Vendler, "Worth a Thousand Words?," *New York Review of Books* 43.8 (9 May 1996), 41.
    Vendler was reviewing *On the Laws of the Poetic Art*, and John Hollander, *The Gazer's Spirit: Poems Speaking to Silent Works of Art* (Chicago: University of Chicago Press, 1995).

"Home Burial," one of Vendler's examples of "presentation-without-reconciliation,"[24] but it leaves the door slightly ajar, the meaning open: not the matter of the speaker's identity, which also remains unresolved but is of lesser consequence than the matter of looking more generally and its role in reconstituting a sense of the self's wholeness. Is looking at a sky that looks like a painting potentially redemptive? Or is it purely escapist—the soul's last refuge? And what further questions do these questions, in turn, raise about the role of art and poetry in the world more generally?

These are important but not readily decidable issues, especially for someone who has dedicated a life to the making of art, and we should not be surprised that Hecht, in his comments about the poem's ending, leaves the door somewhat ajar as well. Although agreeing with Philip Hoy about "the absence of epiphanies" from his work generally, he goes on, nonetheless, to say of the ending of "Vespers," "I think there may be some connection with the idea of 'looking' as a crucially important act."[25] And, in seeming support of this point, he cites remarks by Simone Weil that "looking is what saves us," and by John Ruskin that

The greatest thing a human soul ever does in this world is to see something, and tell what it saw in a plain way. Hundreds of people can talk for one who can think, but thousands can think for one who can see. To see clearly is poetry, prophecy, and religion all in one.

How "crucially important" is the question that won't quite go away at the end of this poem—or with this chapter, as we shall see.

24. Letter, Vendler to AH, 28 July 1996. Hecht Archive.
25. *Anthony Hecht in Conversation with Philip Hoy* (1999; rev. 3rd edn. London: BTL, 2004), 64.

6

"A shutter angles out"

Hecht's Ekphrastic Verse

In 1987, Hecht published a modest essay on two poems by Elizabeth Bishop. These weren't the first words he had published on Bishop, but they include patient, brilliant explications of two Bishop poems: "Wading at Wellfleet" and "The Man-Moth."[1] The first section focuses, by way of Herbert's "Affliction [IV]," on the physical and psychological torment suggested by the comparison of waves to the blades of an Assyrian charioteer, and it includes praise for how Bishop's simple, colloquial language touches, from time to time, on "such terrifying matters in the same chilling and cheerful way" (p. 162). The second, longer section addresses Bishop's "The Man-Moth" in light of a single pictorial analogue: that strange, mysterious painting by Hieronymus Bosch—part of a sequence— "to be seen in the Ducal Palace in Venice," which portrays "the ascent to the Heavenly Paradise" (p. 165). Once viewed, it is rarely forgotten. Luminously cleansed bodies are escorted, like children, delicately upward by ministering angels toward a tunnel of light. Hecht uses the image to delve perceptively into the Man-Moth's subterranean existence.

Bishop's relationship to Herbert has received much commentary, Hecht's less so, although Herbert remains a potent influence in his poetry.[2] But it is the second section of his Bishop essay with its focus

---

1. "Two Poems by Elizabeth Bishop," in Hecht, *Melodies Unheard: Essays on the Mysteries of Poetry* (Baltimore: The Johns Hopkins University Press, 2003), 159–71. Hecht had earlier reviewed Bishop's *Poems: North and South—A Cold Spring* in *The Hudson Review* 9 (1956), 456, and *Geography III* in the *Times Literary Supplement* (26 August 1977).
2. See the essay by Stephen Kampa noted on page 146. I have also written on this topic in "Anthony Hecht's 'Exalted Manna,'" in Christopher Hodgkin, ed., *George Herbert's Travels: International Print and Cultural Legacies* (Newark: University of Delaware Press, 2011), 225–41.

on painting that anticipates the concerns of this chapter: the place of ekphrastic verse in Hecht's poetry. This is a large topic in Hecht, as it has become so in modern and contemporary poetry,[3] and in using the term "ekphrasis," I am thinking of it primarily in the more restrictive sense often employed in literary criticism to indicate a poem about a painting. (Ekphrasis means "to speak," from which a variety of applications derive as one adds the preposition "to," "about," or "for.") As with many examples of a genre that certainly came of age in the twentieth century, Hecht's ekphrastic verse might well have remained merely humdrum, a studious exercise in description or dilettantism (one can readily find examples of both in his early poetry), but it became, instead, a major creative force in his middle and later years. Initially touched on in *A Summoning of Stones* (1954), ekphrasis lay largely dormant in *The Hard Hours*; the pleasure he habitually discovered in visual art finds little place in this rarely relenting anatomy of sorrow. (The main exceptions are the references in "Rites and Ceremonies" to the façade in the Cathedral at Strasbourg and to a few paintings of martyrs.) It re-emerged selectively as a topic in *Millions of Strange Shadows* (1977), then flourished triumphantly in "The Venetian Vespers," as we have seen in Chapter 5, and in other poems included in that 1979 volume. And it continued into the later collections, where not only is the subject of painting responsible for some of his most memorable

---

3. Important critical works on this subject include John Hollander, *The Gazer's Spirit: Poems Speaking to Silent Works of Art* (Chicago: University of Chicago Press, 1995), and Willard Spiegelman, *How Poets See the World: The Art of Description in Contemporary Poetry* (Oxford: Oxford University Press, 2005). In reviewing Hollander's book, in conjunction with Hecht's *On the Laws of the Poetic Art* (Princeton: Princeton University Press, 1995), Helen Vendler remarks that "there are two chief reasons why poets love the stimulus to description offered by a work of art. First, description is *par excellence* a means of multiplying words. Any verbal description is potentially unlimited, and the more slender the *point d'appui* on which the fantasy-construct of words is raised, the more magnificent and self-sustaining (as in Ashbery's 'Self Portrait') is the effect created. On the other hand, a visual image can also be a challenge to the usual concision of lyric. The richer the original art work, the greater praise accrues to the author who can convey its power with compression and point." ("Worth a Thousand Words?," *New York Review of Books* 43.8 (9 May 1996), 39). This helpfully distinguishes between the motivations for writing longer or shorter poems, but the desire to write about art, in the first place, would seem to spring, as it does with Hecht, from a prior experience of deep admiration or love for what the artist has accomplished and the poet seeks, in some way, to convey. That sense of admiration for the work also comes into play in the different treatment Hecht affords paintings and photographs. Photos are of interest to Hecht primarily for their thought-provoking subject matter.

poems but his poetic sequence, "The Presumptions of Death," done in connection with Leonard Baskin's woodcuts, constitutes an extended exploration into the ancient idea attributed to Simonides of poetry as a "speaking picture."

That Hecht blossomed so fully in this field is partly owing to his having greater leisure, but also partly to the inspiring example, if not direct influence, of Bishop. By the time of his death in 2004, Hecht had as deep a knowledge of the classical fields of art as any poet in the twentieth century, but by his own admission, his poetic eye had required schooling. "It was not a faculty with which I was endowed," he remarked in 1999. In contrast to his musical aptitude, "it took conscious pains to acquire." Hecht was perhaps being a bit modest on this score, given the child's intense visionary response recalled in the autobiographical "Apprehensions." Nonetheless, if he went on to credit Hardy and Frost with generally teaching him the importance of seeing with "particularity and clarity," it is to Bishop he keeps returning when it came to citing actual poems. "Again and again in her poems she holds things up 'close to the eye.' "[4]

Like painters (and it is no accident that Bishop writes about painting, admired painters, and was herself a painter), Bishop often focuses her poems on ocular and empirical knowledge, on the actuality of the visible world. Even when painting itself is not her subject, her poems often concern themselves with the act of inspection.[5]

"Close to the eye" is a crucial phrase: it distinguishes her methods from those of Hardy in Hecht. And the specific Bishop poem that keeps coming to Hecht's mind is "Sandpiper." What Hecht especially admired was the poem's "fidelity" to "a visible aspect of experience" and the humility that accompanies such "straightforward inspection."[6] But he was also drawn to the sandpiper itself. As "a student of Blake," in Bishop's phrase, the bird offered a kind of defense or apologia for artful looking, seeking, as Blake said in "Auguries of Innocence," "To see a world in a Grain of Sand" and, Hecht crucially adds, "the horrors that compass [innocence] about." At the same time, the bird's obsessive concern with "looking, looking, looking," again Bishop's words in

---

4. *Anthony Hecht in Conversation with Philip Hoy* (1999; rev. 3rd edn. London: BTL, 2004), 64.
5. "Two Poems by Elizabeth Bishop," 170.
6. This and the subsequent quotations are taken from Hecht, *On the Laws of the Poetic Art*, 25–6.

"Sandpiper," served as a figure, Hecht emphasized, for the artistic process itself, "threatened by regular seismographic shocks that need deliberately to be ignored. Indeed, such conscious, active 'ignoring' is nothing less than a strategy to maintain sanity in a world of constant upheaval." Bishop's sandpiper, indeed Bishop herself, it would seem, could have been understudies for the speaker in "The Venetian Vespers"; and although Hecht was always cautious about drawing simple causal connections between artistic practice and individual biography, he saw in Bishop's broken home—the early death of her father, "followed almost immediately by her mother's collapse into insanity, which required her permanent institutionalization"—an explanation of a kind for the habitual practice of careful looking in her poems.

Hecht was not a painter, in contrast to Bishop, although he briefly entertained majoring in studio art in his first year at Bard. But his growing interest in art can be readily reckoned in his writings: from the casually witty asides in some of the war letters ("If I pick up any cheap Daumiers or Matisses over here, I'll ship 'em right home for that big bald spot between the bookcases in the living room") to the more sustained enthusiasms of his postwar travels, which included purchasing "2 Rouaults and a Braque. The Braque was an original signed wood-cut in three colors, limited to 50 copies, of which I had the 40th."[7] Some of these remained in his possession throughout his life and formed part of a modest core of original artwork in his home, occasionally supplemented by gifts from artist friends. (His poem "Black Boy in the Dark" was part of a gift exchange with Thomas Cornell, a student of Leonard Baskin's, in return for the artist's proof for a fine engraving of Frederick Douglas.) Indeed, Hecht's repeated trips to Italy from the 1950s on, often with extended stays, further sharpened his knowledge of Renaissance Italian art and architecture, sparking a liking for Venetian art and the paintings of Bellini, Carpaccio, and Tiepolo in particular. During these middle years, too, he formed important friendships with artists and art historians. Both the Harvard-based sculptor Dimitri Hadzi (to whom "The Origin of Centaurs" is dedicated) and the Roman architectural historian William MacDonald were valued friends, the latter an especially important sounding board for ideas; while Hecht's collaboration with the celebrated woodcut artist and engraver Leonard Baskin framed much of his creative life.

7. Letters, AH to his parents, 25 March 1945 and 1 September [1949], respectively.

But it wasn't just the masters and masterpieces of high culture that caught Hecht's eye. Film, photographs, magazines, advertisements, billboards, the now omnipresent bric-à-brac of modern, mid-twentieth-century visual life filter into his poetry, forming something of a variable, prosy counterpoint to the Renaissance Hecht, and appearing some-times at surprising moments, like the "parental yellow" Checker-Cab in "Apprehensions," as if on loan from Andy Warhol. In something of the same Pop Art manner, the speaker in "Vesper's" recounts his youthful fascination with labels like "The Great Atlantic & Pacific Tea Co.," elevating the commercial script to the status of high art: "Formed into formal Caslon capitals / And graced with a pretzeled, sinuous ampersand / Against a sanded ground of fire-truck red, / ... The period alone appeared to me / An eighteen-karat doorknob beyond price." He also used ekphrasis as a source and symbol of desire, as in the case of Shirley's fatal attraction in "The Short End" to a famous Drambuie advertisement in *The New Yorker*.[8] And if ekphrasis can promote and enchant, it can also demote and ridicule. Among Hecht's uncollected poems is his wickedly funny "Instructions to a Painter for the Capital Dome," composed after the manner of Andrew Marvell's political satire but in an appropriately foreshortened sonnet of thirteen lines, which gives an added snap to the end.[9]

Hecht's writings are peppered with perceptive references and allu-sions to art, but the culmination of his critical ventures in this direction is the chapter on "Poetry and Painting" in his *On the Laws of the Poetic Art* (1995), which was originally presented as part of his 1992 Mellon Lectures in the Fine Arts. In this work he ranges over a wide variety of statements and examples from Aristotle to Mark Rothko and describes a number of practices that apply to his own work. The most embracing is a general Horatian understanding ("ut pictura poesis": as in painting so in poetry) of the mutually informing rather than the intensely agonistic relationship between the arts. The latter was made famous through Leonardo and the Renaissance concept of the paragon or rivalry among the arts, where it continues in the excerpt quoted by Hecht from Ben Jonson: that "the Pen [writing] is more noble, then the Pencill [drawing]. For the one can speak to the Understanding, the

8. For the significance of this poem as "sleazy contrast" to the opulent world of "The Venetian Vespers," see Hecht's letter to Harry Ford, 10 June 1978 (*SL*, 173–4).

9. The poem is quoted in Hecht's letter to Timothy Murphy, 15 January 1999 (*SL*, 300).

other, but to the senses." Although certainly alert to the different aesthetic domains of each, the one temporal, the other spatial, on this occasion Hecht smoothed over the Jonsonian edges by pointing out parenthetically that in many European languages " 'see' is a synonym for 'understand.' "[10]

From this basic Horatian assumption of the commonality of the arts, a number of other preferences follow in somewhat random but revealing fashion. These include Hecht's interest in one art evoking or reflecting the stylistic manner or mood of another (as in the association, in his own case, of "Vespers" with the baroque, or the dreamy world of "Clair de Lune" with Watteau's "Fêtes Galantes"); a concern with the genre of "still life" paintings to be explored in radically different ways in several of his own poems, including the poem called "Still Life" looked at in Chapter 2; the recognition that painting (like poetry) is not "always inspired by what is conventionally called beauty," a view most interesting for the support it derives from a quotation by John Constable: "The sound of water escaping from mill-dams... willows, old rotten planks, slimy posts, and brickwork, I love such things.... Those scenes made me a painter, and I am grateful" (the sentiment underlies Hecht's "Devotions of a Painter" and his poetic career); a fascination, as we might expect in so formal a poet, with the idea of the frame, which Hecht develops to great effect in "Matisse: Blue Interior with Two Girls—1947"; the exemplary place of Elizabeth Bishop touched on earlier in this chapter; political satire in the cartoons by the German Dadaist George Grosz; and, in the "brief word" allotted to "nonrepresentational art," serious attention paid to the devotional content of the work of the Abstract Expressionist, Mark Rothko, of Russian Jewish descent. The chapter on "Poetry and Painting" develops a number of other points, but these suggest the main direction of Hecht's profoundly humanistic thinking on the subject. There is always a person in his ekphrases.

As much as Hecht admired Bishop, I don't think it is possible to pinpoint the moment in his work when her acute emphasis on the ocular took hold and began to bear fruit—perhaps in *The Hard Hours*, with

---

10. Hecht, *On the Laws of the Poetic Art*, 5–6. All the references in the next paragraph are taken from Hecht's opening chapter, "Poetry and Painting," 5–38.

the tense act of "looking" in "Behold the Lilies of the Field" and the "straightforward inspection" of the "hideous life-sized doll...with blanks of mother-of-pearl under the eyelids / And painted shells that had been prepared beforehand / For the fingernails and toenails." The disjunction described earlier by Hecht between Bishop's manner and matter in his analysis of "Wading at Wellfleet" is certainly at work in this poem and at other moments in *The Hard Hours*—but usually in more floridly gruesome ways than in Bishop, although her own "Florida" combines the ornamental and sea-life detritus in ways that might have caught Hecht's attention. But Hecht's nascent descriptive attributes were, in a sense, always ripe for further focusing, as Auden recognized,[11] and by the time of *Millions of Strange Shadows*, Hecht shows a keen interest in the practice of holding "things up 'close to the eye,'" including domestic objects of a sort found around the home, as in "'Auguries of Innocence,'" the title from Blake perhaps hinting at a subliminal link with Bishop. It begins:

> A small, unsmiling child,
> Held upon her shoulder,
> Stares from a photograph
> Slightly out of kilter.
> It slipped from a loaded folder
> Where the income tax was filed.
> The light seems cut in half
> By a glum, October filter.

The poem is too pronounced in its rhythms and rhymes to be confused with Bishop, but the appearance of an everyday object, prompting attention and description, is certainly reminiscent of her visual habits. In this case, the object of focus is not a small painting by an uncle ("Poem") or a simple bit of domestic art like a "doily" found in "Filling Station," but a photograph "slightly out of kilter"—the weak rhyme auguring further instabilities to be explored. The photo's seemingly

11. See Hecht's several letters on this topic involving his first meeting with Auden, discussed in Chapter 2: AH to his parents, 4 October 1951 and to Allen Tate, 16 October 1951. Both acknowledge Auden's criticism of too much detail in the young Hecht's poetry. Although Auden wrote one of the most influential ekphrastic poems of the century in "Musée des Beaux Arts," indeed echoed by Hecht in one of his earliest attempts at ekphrasis, "At the Frick," Auden didn't serve Hecht as an important model for concentrating on visual detail. See Hecht's comments on Auden's poor eyesight and general indifference to painting in *The Hidden Law: The Poetry of W. H. Auden* (Cambridge, MA: Harvard University Press, 1993), 98.

accidental arrival joins a long list of mysterious objects found in
Bishop's poetry. In Hecht the found object becomes a source for
intense concentration: "It slipped from a loaded folder." Loaded with
what we wonder? And what is the photo doing with the income tax?
A recollection of payment for child support? Or is the unhappiness of
the child somehow the tax paid for an earlier relationship now grown
cold? Or is this detail simply, accidently, part of the poem's "naturalistic" setting and not part of some larger narrative?

As the eye moves from child to mother, other mysteries, bespeaking
further estrangements, unfold:

> Of course, the child is right.
> The unleafed branches knot
> Into hopeless riddles behind him
> And the air is clearly cold.
> Given the stinted light
> To which fate and film consigned him,
> Who'd smile at his own lot
> Even at one year old?
>
> And yet his mother smiles.
> Is it grown-up make-believe,
> As when anyone takes your picture
> Or some nobler, Roman virtue?
> Vanity? Folly? The wiles
> That some have up their sleeve?
> A proud and flinty stricture
> Against showing that things can hurt you,
>
> Or a dark, Medean smile?
> I'd be the last to know.
> A speechless child of one
> Could better construe the omens,
> Unriddle our gifts for guile.
> There's no sign from my son.
> But it needs no Greeks or Romans
> To foresee the ice and snow.

Searching for answers, we might begin to allegorize the poem in the
manner, say, of a "Madonna and Child" painting by Bellini, in which
the mother tries to hide the Christ child's earthly future from him by
adopting the guise of a mysterious smile. But the final lines render that
higher accommodation impossible. The scale is wrong, the color lacking.
The child belongs to the speaker ("my son"), and if the one-year-old

can somehow "unriddle" a relationship between mother and father that is more than just out of kilter, he is helpless to make it better. That much the speaker-poet does know, speaking over the speechless child, giving voice to the silent photo. The poem also plays out its own obsession with looking. Although it reveals a number of sight lines— the child staring out of the photo, the speaker (and reader) at the photo, and the mother smiling (at the child? the viewer?)—none of these lines intersect. Nor do their lives. Momentarily brought together, they inhabit different spaces or universes—now, in the poem, for as long as there are readers.

Heavy as these memories are, the poem wears its literary debts lightly. What attracted Hecht to this aspect of Bishop's verse was a process, an angle, a means of earnest and intent looking, not a list of subjects or objects, although one can readily spot here a shared interest in an estranged family. In choosing a faded photograph for inspection, the poet has also deliberately selected a seasonally appropriate medium. In the half-light of October, fate and film are bound together in their mutual dimness, as are, in this case, family relationships.

Suggestive too of the wider tonal significance is the visual connection the photo, as a form of representation, forges with the book's title, *Millions of Strange Shadows*, hinting that the prevailing mode of ekphrasis in this volume is the monochromatic black-and-white photograph, what Hecht designates as "mere light and shade" in "A Birthday Poem." That poem includes the resonant query from Shakespeare's Sonnet 53, which supplies the title of the collection: "*What is your substance, whereof are you made, / That millions of strange shadows on you tend?*" The poem is also an "answer poem" in kind to " 'Auguries of Innocence.' " The two are linked through the intimate world of an old family snapshot but are otherwise studies in contrasts: one a meditation on the riddling estrangements surrounding a failed first marriage, the other a moving celebration of the birthday of the poet's second wife, each finding in the smile a marked archetypical difference—one shaded in the direction of Medea, the other toward a Madonna, whose look of gratitude inspires from the poet a closing prayer for worthiness.

Not that Hecht's interest in light and shadow erased all signs of color from *Shadows*, as we will recall from the presence of the "parental yellow" taxi in "Apprehensions." "Gladness of the Best" begins, as the public occasion requires, with a fanfare response to the Duc de Berry's

polychromatic *Très Riches Heures*, and in "Black Boy in the Dark," at
the center of the poem, Hecht situates his political subject in small
town America in an

> all-night service station,
> Where Andy Warhol's primary colors shine
> In simple commercial glory, the Esso sign
> Revolving like a funland lighthouse, where
> An eighteen-year-old black boy clocks the nation,
> Reading a comic book in a busted chair.

The "Esso sign" will recall for many readers the famous repeating
logo of "Esso" at the end of Bishop's "Filling Station," but it is put to
a completely different use here as part of a wider, gloomier portrait
of commercial and military exploitation in America, of which Andy
Warhol serves as prophet and symbol and the black boy its unsuspecting victim.[12]

But these colorful excursions are largely exceptions that prove the
shadow's enigmatic rule in this collection. In the first part of " 'Dichtung
und Wahrheit' "—after Goethe's work of the same title, meaning
"Poetry and Truth"—both "The Discus Thrower's marble heave" "and
the clumsy snapshot of / An infantry platoon" are equal in posing the
same challenging question to the poet: "How can such fixture speak to
us" who are "all aswim in time"? This is the question underlying all
ekphrasis—how to make the silent, still object speak. But though
sculpture and photo pose the same question, it is the latter that increasingly occupies the poet's attention:

> The chisel and the lens
> Deal in a taxidermy
> Of our arrested fights,
> And by their brute translation we
> Turn into Benthamites.
> Those soldiers, like some senior class,
> Were they prepared to dye
> In silver nitrate images
> Behind the camera's eye?

12. For a detailed analysis of "Black Boy in the Dark" see Peter Steele, *Expatriates: Reflections
on Modern Poetry* (Melbourne: Melbourne University Press, 1985), 81–99, esp. 95–6. For
a fine discussion of George Herbert's poem see Stephen Kampa, "Anthony Hecht's
'Raddling Eye': 'Gladness of the Best' and the Ghost of George Herbert," *Sewanee
Theological Review*, 52 (2009), 377–95.

The jarring pun on "dye," activated by the comparison between camera and gun, student and soldier, is surprisingly jaunty for Hecht, given the military context, but that is part of the point when we see only the fixed image and especially from afar, an idea Hecht airs in "The Birthday Poem" and elsewhere ("An Overview"). The proximity of being translated brutally into Benthamites, moreover, in conjunction with being killed by the camera's eye, suggests that even though Hecht resisted reading Michel Foucault,[13] he understood the dehumanizing element of the penitential gaze. The next stanza "speaks" to this dilemma as only poetry can do:

> It needs a Faust to animate
>   The wan homunculus,
> Construe the stark, unchanging text,
>   Winkle the likes of us
> Out of a bleak geology
>   That art has put to rest,
> And by a sacred discipline
>   Give breath back to the past.
> How, for example, shall I read
>   The expression on my face
> Among that company of men
>   In that unlikely place?

The "wan homunculus," alluding to Goethe's fantastic creation in his *Faust* in need of animation, is a fitting reference given the poem's title, but the palm for the unusual word goes to "winkle," which sounds like "wrinkle" but is military slang meaning to extract, draw forth, find out, or elicit (*OED* v.2), in effect to give life or breath, as the poem states, as part of poetry's "sacred discipline." And it does so by revealing, by drawing forth, the questioning speaker at the same time as insisting on the deadness of the photographic image. As the subject of both the photograph and the poem, Hecht puzzles over what even he, the creator of the poem, might have been thinking "Among that company of men / In that unlikely place," so alien has the past and his earlier identity become.

"Strictly speaking," writes Susan Sontag, "there is never any understanding in a photograph, but only an invitation to fantasy and speculation." She then adds, for good measure, "only that which narrates can

---

13. From his letter to Richard Howard, 27 July 1968.

make us understand,"[14] a distinction that anticipates Hecht's more extensive use of ekphrasis in his later poetry. For Hecht, strictly speaking, the old photograph represented an opportunity to evoke or summon, genii-like, the image of another from the past (including the "other" that was or is himself), for purposes of speculation, of wondering, and also for wonder.

The most gripping instance of this latter effect occurs near the end of "A Birthday Poem," an "answer" poem of a sort, as I mentioned earlier in this chapter, to "'Auguries of Innocence.'" The more elaborate and grander of the two, it is also the riskier. The grandeur is a feature of the complicated stanzaic pattern created for the birthday occasion, a gift in its own right. The pattern allows Hecht room to exercise at the outset his aptitude for poetic flights as a means to establish what will be the poem's guiding axis: the difference between long and close views and the burden of meaning associated with each, and also to consider the "hocus-pocus," the tricky effects of perspective itself: how distance is represented spatially in the work of the early Renaissance painters, Andrea Mantegna and Hans Holbein, and Flemish art to "disclose / A clarity that never was," and temporally in the writings of scholars, who dispassionately recount terrible battles "without batting an eye / As if all history were deciduous," that is, without *seeing* the human consequences of their subject matter. (Hecht did, of course, more than bat an eye, although not in this poem.)

The risk comes from the poem's elongated, cerebral, seven-stanza staging of the "background" to highlight the shift to the immediate foreground, at which point, however, the photograph of his second wife, Helen, comes into view. Hecht carefully cues the turn:

> It's when we come to shift the gears of tense
>   That suddenly we note
> A curious excitement of the heart
>   And slight catch in the throat:—
> When, for example, from the confluence
> That bears all things away I set apart

14. Sontag, *New York Review of Books* (18 October 1973), near the end of the article. This is the first of a series of important essays by Sontag on photography running through 23 June 1977, collected and published with some revisions in *On Photography* (New York: Farrar, Straus and Giroux, 1977). Although Hecht owned a copy of Sontag's book and his "photo" poems were written during the period when Sontag was publishing her essays, the essays are most interesting as a gloss on ideas the two held in common rather than as a source for any particular poem: the photo as enigma, the camera as a surrogate gun held at a (deadly) distance from the subject, the appropriation of life into a "still life," and so forth.

> The inexpressible lineaments of your face,
>   Both as I know it now,
> By heart, by sight, by reverent touch and study,
>   And as it once was years ago,
> Back in some inaccessible time and place,
>   Fixed in the vanished camera of somebody.

"The most powerful human forces are found in the meeting of the face and the gaze. Only there do we exist for one another. In the gaze of the other, we become, and in our own gaze others become."[15] Hecht's poem, indeed Hecht's poetry, and not just his ekphrastic verse, forms an extended meditation on this important imperative. Here, exquisitely managed, the shift into the present tense accompanies the waking heart, but we only arrive at the poem's true subject as it is "set apart" in the next stanza—rather as "I set apart" (enjambment: a pause for focusing) "the inexpressible lineaments of your face." The speaker emerges from the shadows as if striding across a room (which he is doing, metaphorically, in moving from one stanza to another), acquiring in the process an "I" for the first time in the poem.

Now, in her presence, he is more than the disembodied, cerebral "eye" of the poem's first part. He is able to study and appreciate the object of his devotion. "On Helen's cheek all art of beauty set," remarked Shakespeare in Sonnet 53, the source text for this part of the poem. For all the attention given to the "fine diminishings" in Mantegna (Hecht had in mind "The Crucifixion" in the Louvre), nothing compares with the real thing, an imagined (let us remember), three-dimensional, intimate close-up, in which appreciation involves "the heart," the crucial first word in a series of responses that quickly stretches to incorporate sight, touch, contemplation—and memory, in the form of a faded photo. The image in the photograph is "fixed," as in the case of " 'Dichtung und Wahrheit,' " but access to it is not blocked by the alienating eye of another. The camera has vanished, leaving a space for *pure* description:

> You are four years old here in this photograph.
>   You are turned out in style,
> In a pair of bright red sneakers, a birthday gift.

15. Karl Ove Knausgaard, "The Inexplicable: Inside the mind of a mass killer," *The New Yorker*, 25 May 2015, 28–32. The quote appears on p. 32. Like Hannah Arendt, whom Knausgaard cites, the author seeks to understand and explain the presence of evil in light of the disintegration of the civilizing structures that value human life.

> You are looking down at them with a smile
> Of pride and admiration, half
> Wonder and half joy, at the right and the left.
> The picture is black and white, mere light and shade.
> Even the sneakers' red
> Has washed away in acids. A voice is spent,
> Echoing down the ages in my head:
> *What is your substance, whereof are you made,*
> *That millions of strange shadows on you tend?*

Remembering " 'Auguries of Innocence,' " we might ask where did the photo come from? We can only say that it certainly did not slip "from a loaded folder." It simply appears on the scene, miraculously transported from "some inaccessible time and place," although loaded with meaning in the present. It is a small epiphany, "half / Wonder and half joy," registered in part through the recognition of the "bright red sneakers," the color somehow visible to the speaker, even though the photograph has faded into "mere light and shade," but prompting a further, deeper reflection about the mystery of the person's identity simultaneously distilled and amplified in the italicized quotation from Shakespeare.

I take the quotation to be a supplement to the photo in the Horatian manner of one art, pictorial, stimulating a connection with another, poetry. But it is also the case that neither of these, even together, is quite adequate as a lasting mode of representation, as framed by Hecht. One has faded and the other is "spent," their partial evaporation leaving a space for the heart's final outpouring—no "slight catch in the throat" here—in a succession of concluding apostrophes that effect, in their repetition, an attempt to escape time, "the confluence / That bears all things away."

> O my most dear, I know the live imprint
> Of that smile of gratitude,
> Know it more perfectly than any book.
> It brims upon the world, a mood
> Of love, a mode of gladness without stint.
> O that I may be worthy of that look.

More than a quarter of a century later this passage, privileging "look" over "book," would continue to exercise its mysterious, paradoxical power in the form of the epigraph to the author's *Collected Later Poems* (2003).

Whether this poem or " 'Dichtung und Wahrheit' " is the later of the two, both came near the end of the composition of *Millions of Strange Shadows* and seem to have altogether exhausted Hecht's interest in the family photo ekphrasis.[16] Its intimate subject matter and faded form is tonally in keeping with the many shadows depicted in this collection, but the concentration it exacted was also restricting, as restricting as the snow in Rochester in his "Sestina D'Inverno," and, except on a few occasions by way of reference to magazines, in which photos serve the larger purposes of narration, Hecht never returned to this mode of ekphrasis in later works.

Instead of Rochester, there was Venice in all its color and light, paintings and architecture, and a bold new appreciation for the potential of the visual in his poetry. Along with its magnificent title poem, *The Venetian Vespers*, published only two years after *Millions of Strange Shadows*, included Hecht's first—and his longest—poem dedicated to a single painting, "The Deodand," based on Renoir's *Parisians Dressed in Algerian Costume*, and the few years on the other side of the collection's publication in 1979 saw Hecht at his most ekphrastically exuberant and inventive, everywhere alert to the lure of the eye and a wider canvass for expression.

An important catalyst in this shift in emphasis was the Victorian sage John Ruskin, as important as Bishop, but pointing in a different direction. As recounted in a 1978 letter to MacDonald, Hecht had been reading *The Stones of Venice* in conjunction with "The Venetian Vespers," and after inquiring into some small points about terminology and worrying over what he calls Ruskin's "rank evangelism, a sort of shrill and even hectoring high moral tone," he waxes at length about "the vast variety of things that are brilliant and good and sane about him":

Not least of these is that sound moral sense which condemns that aesthetic and moralistic purist who, finding an unsullied spiritual simplicity in Fra Angelico, is unable to stomach the worldly exuberance and vigor of, in his

16. " 'Auguries of Innocence' " is the earliest of the photo poems, published in *The Harvard Advocate* in the Fall 1973; followed by " 'Dichtung und Wahrheit' " in *The American Scholar* in December, 1976. "A Birthday Poem," bears the date "June 22, 1976," and appears for the first time in *Millions of Strange Shadows*. "Exile," which I've not discussed because it includes only a brief reference to Walker Evans, first appeared in *The Times Literary Supplement* (30 July 1976). For dates, I have relied on Hecht's letter to Harry Ford (2 May 1977).

example, Rubens…But even this sound, well-founded amplitude and catholicity of taste, is not in itself what impresses. What I find so striking on virtually every page is a vast knowledge—including the geological and topographical conditions that antedate all building—together with a deeply felt (I suppose there is no other word for it) "Moral" sense of the ways we live, or ought to live, or have failed to live, and the ways that these modes of living, healthy and unhealthy, worldly and spiritual, exalted or debauched, reflect themselves in works of art, and especially of architecture.[17]

Much of this commentary is directly applicable to "The Venetian Vespers" and its deeply divided speaker, but the sentiments also anticipate, in their fusion of knowledge, exuberance, and moral sense—the last a term to which Hecht repeatedly returns—key elements in Hecht's further experimentation with ekphrasis in that trinity of great poems in his middle years, "The Deodand," "Devotions of a Painter," and "Meditation." Out of date as Ruskin was in some circles, he served as an unexpected release from what Hecht humorously termed "the Dominations and Powers of art criticism in this century," Erwin Panofsky and Edgar Wind, and their detective-like pursuit of iconography. Although Hecht admitted to reading them with "fascination and delight, and of course with improvement," he also found, with some irony, that "their approach to art is often a narrowly literary one," and that Ruskin, by contrast, "is simply far more philosophic, immediate, and direct, risking more and not showing off as much."

Hecht was skeptical enough to realize that "perhaps I'm just being carried away by a current enthusiasm," but the enthusiasm was a liberating one and blended with a number of other poetic impulses in the late 1970s, including extending the descriptive range of blank verse in the service of middle-length dramatic monologues. (*The Venetian Vespers* begins with one of his most notable, "The Grapes.") Written soon after "The Venetian Vespers," "The Deodand" (more on the title later) assumes a number of Ruskinian risks, some of which have put off Hecht's readers. The poem is moral and philosophical, as Hecht found Ruskin to be, although on a topic Ruskin seems to have thought not fitting for high art.[18] The emerging narrative pivots thematically on a well-known

17. Letter, AH to William MacDonald, 25 July 1978 (*SL*, 175–6).
18. See Joan DelPlato, *Multiple Wives, Multiple Pleasures: Representing the Harem, 1800–1875* (Madison: Fairleigh Dickinson University Press, 2002), 66–7. Given that Hecht is responding to a painting made in 1872, in turn influenced by Eugene Delacroix's 1834 painting on the same subject, it is hardly surprising that the first part of his poem recounts a number of conventional European attitudes about harems. There is nothing conventional about the poem's language, however, nor about the anti-colonialist moral

observation by the philosopher, George Santayana (eulogized by Hecht in *The Hard Hours*), that "those who cannot remember the past are condemned to repeat it." Hecht's variation is: "Those that will not be taught by history / Have as their curse the office to repeat it." Its subject, the poem's that is, deals with modes of behavior, especially debauchery, or more specifically, the careful preparation for it as a sign of "cruel imperial pride," and, as we shockingly discover, its "answer."

Hecht's lines patiently, surely, trace out the central action of the painting: the application of make-up and costuming going on in a Parisian harem (Figure 6.1). And as an ekphrasis, as a response to an oil painting saturated in color, character, and action, it delves directly into its subject matter, immediately raising questions about what the speaker is looking at and, eventually, what it signifies:

> What are these women up to? They've gone and strung
> Drapes over the windows, cutting out light
> And the slightest hope of a breeze here in mid-August.
> Can this be simply to avoid being seen
> By some prying *femme-de-chambre* across the boulevard
> Who has stepped out on a balcony to disburse
> Her dustmop gleanings on the summer air?

Only, in fact, when the curious eye ceases with its queries and observations do we learn the identity of the painter, almost as a parenthetical afterthought as the speaker disengages himself from the painting's now highly charged erotic atmosphere with the urbane transition, "And for this little spiritual debauch." Until that moment, the sensuousness of Renoir's paint (and painting) finds its parallel in the poet's sensuously ample diction, and the presumed stuffiness of the Parisian atmosphere has its linguistic coordinates in the sudden proliferation of French terms:

he draws from the painting. See Ali Behdad, "The Eroticized Orient: Images of the Harem in Montesquieu and his Precursors," *Stanford French Review* 13 (1989), 109–26.

Hecht seems to have first encountered Renoir's painting in Mario Praz, *Mnemosyne: The Parallel between Literature and the Visual Arts* (Princeton: Princeton University Press, 1970), 20. See letter to MacDonald, note 17. But it is possible he viewed it earlier. The painting is housed in the National Museum of Western Art in Tokyo, but it had been sequestered by the French government in 1944, thus making it impossible for Hecht to have seen while on duty in Japan in 1945–46. It was later widely exhibited, including in Florence in 1955, when Hecht was in Italy.

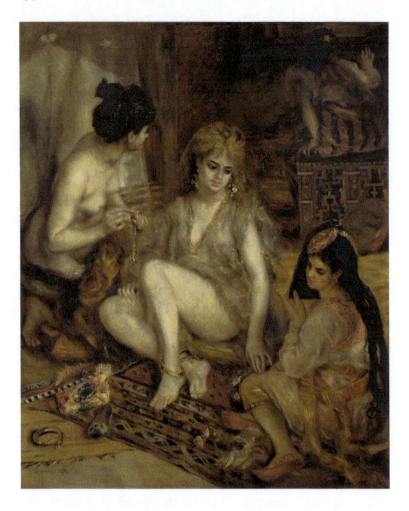

Figure 6.1. Pierre-Auguste Renoir, *Parisians Dressed in Algerian Costume (Harem)*, 1872. Found in the collection of the National Museum of Western Art, Tokyo. (Photo credit: HIP/Art Resource, NY)

What would their fathers, husbands, *fiancés*,
Those pillars of the old *haute-bourgeoisie*,
Think of the strange charade now in the making?
Swathed in exotic finery, in loose silks,
Gauzy organzas with metallic threads,
Intricate Arab vests, brass ornaments
At wrist and ankle, those small sexual fetters,
Tight little silver chains, and bangled gold

Suspended like a coarse barbarian treasure
From soft earlobes pierced through symbolically,
They are preparing some *tableau vivant*.

"Gauzy organzas" is, well, intricately orgasmic—suggestively thick
enough with sound to seem almost redundant, but the phrase refers to
the vibrant effect created by the sheer dress, as the eye, in the manner of
a blazon, proceeds to slide down to wrist and ankle before returning to
the earlobe with its "bangled gold." The adjective is an archaism meaning to beat about, flutter aimlessly (*OED* 1), but not, as we discover,
harmlessly, linked as it is by sound and sense to "barbarian." And to what
might be loosely described as already "in" the painting, the viewer-poet
adds another level of fantasy by entering into the women's thoughts
and, in the process, transforms this indolent, bordello-in-the-making,
the harem, into an arena teeming with sexual violence: "leather thongs,
hinting of violations, / Swooning lubricities and lassitudes."

The countermovement to this overcharged *tableau vivant* is the
emerging *tableau moralisé* that is not part of Renoir's painting but
does come to dominate the later part of Hecht's poem. We—painter,
poet, speaker, and reader—are rightly, if uncomfortably, acknowl-
edged confederates, "invisible" voyeurs of the harem, but what Renoir
could not know in 1872, could not *see* at that time, is the full working
out of the consequences of his painting's subject matter. Indeed, the
mirroring in Renoir that captures Hecht's attention (the painting is
indebted to Ingres or Delacroix, the naked girl is painting the eyes of
the blond favorite with kohl, the clothed girl is holding up a mirror
for the favorite to view herself) points to the intense insularity of the
hot-house subject and its time-bound manner of representation. But
the poet—to state the matter in the language of the rival arts—sees
into the dark, hideous, ironic consequences of this "strange charade":
the ironic parallel between the French women dressing up in erotic,
"exotic finery," and the Legionnaire being dressed up by his captors
as a French whore. "Though it takes ninety years, / All the retributive
iron of Racine / Shall answer from the raging heat of the desert."

The reference to Racine gives a measure of authority to the poet—
indeed to verse. Breaking the poem at this point, as Hecht does, also
gives the closing lines something of the force of a couplet, with the last
line, an alexandrine, perhaps paying homage to Racine's measure, and
the reference to "iron" in that measure hinting further of the tragic
"irony" of Racine's high art now being put to the service of the colony
striking back against the former empire; and though Hecht may not

have been thinking specifically of Racine's *Phèdre*, the plot of Phèdre's illicit desire for her stepson, Hippolytus, and his subsequent death by a horned sea-monster, gives a sexual basis in ancient myth to the historical "answer" Hecht will recount, with searing objectivity:

> In the final months of the Algerian war
> They captured a very young French Legionnaire.
> They shaved his head, decked him in a blonde wig,
> Carmined his lips grotesquely, fitted him out
> With long, theatrical false eyelashes
> And a bright, loose-fitting skirt of calico,
> And cut off all the fingers of both hands.
> He had to eat from a fork held by his captors.
> Thus costumed, he was taken from town to town,
> Encampment to encampment, on a leash,
> And forced to beg for his food with a special verse
> Sung to a popular show tune of those days.

As calmly delivered as a Bishop description, Hecht's includes the ostentatiously high-tone "Carmined."With its long vowel, as if the line were now being redrawn across the lips (the word is derived from the French, instead of, say, "crimsoned," from the Arabic), the word is an especially grotesque mockery of the costuming seductively practiced in the painting and so carefully described by the poet.And the reduction—"the most excruciatingly violent in poetry I know," writes Brad Leithauser[19]—continues into the "popular show tune," given in the poem only in its demotic French (no remnants of the "old *haute-bourgeoisie*" here):

> "*Donnez moi à manger de vos mains*
> *Car c'est pour vous que je fais ma petite danse;*
> *Car je suis Madeleine, la putain,*
> *Et je m'en vais le lendemain matin,*
> *Car je suis La Belle France.*"

I am reminded here of Marjorie Garber's point that "a quotation is a ghost: a revenant taken out of context, making an unexpected, often disconcerting appearance—the return of the expressed."[20] More disconcerting still: when it appears in a foreign tongue, untranslated, as the poem's last word.

19. Leithauser, "Anthony Hecht (1923–2004)," *New York Review of Books* (2 December 2004), 57.
20. Garber, *Shakespeare's Ghost Writers: Literature as Uncanny Causality* (New York and London: Routledge, 1987), 52.

Hecht had occasionally associated sexual desire and violence, most notably in "The Feast of Stephen," a harrowing four-sonnet sequence. With two poems each on facing pages, the individual sonnets form a narrative panel of sorts about the four stages of masculinity leading up to the martyrdom of St. Stephen: from the initial "cap-gun snapping of wet towels" in the boy's locker room to the eventual bullying of the unnamed victim by "burly youths" who "Strip to the waist for the hot work ahead." With ominous prescience (it's difficult not to think of the Matthew Shepherd story), the sequence speaks to age-old rites of male passage and the role of sexuality in the social production of violence. But as a sequence, it differs fundamentally from "The Deodand." It offers separate views of these stages as a kind of transhistorical explanation for male aggression toward other men and a perverse, even queer, account of the first Christian martyr, whose murder Paul glimpses askant.

"The Deodand" pushes the logic of sexual retribution further and in a more alien direction still—"alien" being a key word here. The behavior depicted in a Parisian apartment is offered as an explanation for a peculiar kind of victimization in a raging desert inferno that is Dantesque in its cruelty, as the disfigured French legionnaire is imagined singing his daily fate into eternity. This is to ask a lot from a poem about a painting and of the women in it, who, we're told, have forgotten what happened to Marie Antoinette; but if the poem daringly stretches credulity at one level (had they remembered Marie Antoinette, the Algerian outcome would hardly have been different), it's hard to think that Hecht's central critique of imperialism and the decadent behavior of the dominant culture as represented in both the poem and the painting—but especially as the poem interprets the painting—is not right on target. One way to measure its significance is simply to note that, in the same year he composed his poem, in 1978 that is, appeared a work he could not have read: Edward Said's *Orientalism*, a foundational text for postcolonial studies, in which Hecht's poem surely deserves a place.

Another way to think about the matter of retribution is to reckon the meaning of the arcane title, surely one of the strangest in all of Hecht and the only one for which he supplied a gloss in a footnote: "Deodand" is defined as "A thing forfeited or to be given to God; *spec.* in *Eng. Law*, a personal chattel which, having been the immediate occasion of the death of a human being, was given as an expiatory offering, i.e., forfeited to the Crown to be applied to pious uses." The

thing forfeited in the poem as an expiatory offering is, of course, the French Legionnaire; but to whom? The legal usage as quoted by Hecht presumes the dead animal to be given to the Crown (as the earthly representation of God). Hecht retains something of the feudal language in the poem with regard to the women's slavish sexuality. But quite clearly there is no God in this poem to whom to make immediate expiatory offerings, and no Crown or State represented as a worthy intermediary. In the most memorable use of "deodand" in English poetry, Andrew Marvell's nymph in the "Nymph Complaining for the Death of Her Faun" wishfully notes: "Even beasts must be with justice slain, / Else men are made their deodands." That is, in the absence of justice for the faun's death, men will have to perform the function of the expiatory offering. Hecht's poem adds a further twist to Marvell's irony. The working out of the beastly in his poem, of the Algerian hatred of the French, like Hardy's "Convergence of the Twain" (but without the "Spinner of Years" machinery), seems merely the law of an inhumane universe, set in motion by human vanity, and operating at its own leisurely, retaliatory pace, "though it takes some ninety years."

After the torrid heat of "The Deodand," it is with pronounced relief to come upon several of Hecht's quieter ekphrases: "Devotions of a Painter" and "Meditation." "Devotions" even begins with the welcoming phrase, "Cool sinuosities, waved banners of light," in response to the movement of water. Although not published in a collection until 1990, when the two poems appeared in *The Transparent Man*, both were composed in the summer of 1981 while Hecht was on holiday in the Italian Veneto, and something of their relaxed manner is surely a feature of the favorable circumstances of their creation. As reported in a letter to his Oxford editor, Jacqueline Simms, the first poem was conceived while traveling along the Brenta Canal, on whose bank is also located the famous Palladian Villa, the Malcontenta. (The building is referred to in "Eclogue of the Shepherd and the Townie.") The second was based on a "synthesis of recollected paintings (by Bellini, Carpaccio and Cima) in the Accademia of Venice. Recollected, I may add, in the superb tranquility and comfort of the Hotel Cipriani in Asolo."[21] Both might be characterized as among Hecht's more religious poems, although not in any simple doctrinal sense; and both represent departures from his

---

21. Letter, AH to Jacqueline Simms, 17 September 1981 (*SL*, 190–1).

earlier use of ekphrases, neither taking off from a specific work of art but inventively fabricating their own.

About "Meditation," Hecht remarked, quoting the art historian Kenneth Clark, "facts become art through love." That sentiment seems equally true for "Devotions," a thirty-four-line tribute to both the French Impressionist Claude Monet and the English painter John Constable, a tribute that turns into something of a defense of art and therefore an *ars poetica*. The poem also affords some of the smooth pleasures of a canal boat ride. (All the early usages of "sinuosity" in the *OED*, in fact, are associated with water and rivers especially.) Among the beautifully rendered effects viewed in passing—"Weeds flatten with the current. Dragonflies / Poise like blue needles, steady in mid-air, / For some decisive, swift inoculation"—only a few eddies catch the attention, the turmoil of "benign / Cross-purposes," as Hecht calls the movement of the light on the water, as the reader reflects on a scene that seems out of a Monet painting, with its footbridge and lily-pads, but is the poet's creation. Understatement is everything, and we arrive quietly at the end of the first movement, a carefully measured still point, almost exactly halfway through the poem:

> It's midday in midsummer. Pitiless heat.
> Not so much air in motion as to flutter
> The frail, bright onion tissue of a poppy.

The only surprise is to discover, in the second movement, that the speaker, linked by his frailty to the image of the poppy, is not the poet. He is a painter—another instance of "benign / Cross-purposes"— who resembles Monet:

> I am an elderly man in a straw hat
> Who has set himself the task of praising God
> For all this welter by setting out my paints
> And getting as much truth as can be managed
> Onto a small flat canvas.

He also quotes Constable—the phrase springing to mind because of the riverbank setting—in support of the belief that there is nothing ugly in nature. Modesty is not simply a matter of a painting's size, we discover, but of the kind and the quality of materials that go into the making of art:

> Constable
> Claimed he had never seen anything ugly,
> And would have known each crushed jewel in the pigments

> Of these oily golds and greens, enamelled browns
> That recall the glittering eyes and backs of frogs.

This simple but hardly narrow philosophy then reinforms the subject
of devotion itself, and the poem arrives at its final destination point
with a sense of gusto that belies the speaker's advanced years. The sun,
associated with the pitiless noon heat a moment earlier, now suddenly
opens its rich coffers indiscriminately:

> The sun dispenses its immense loose change,
> Squandered on blossoms, ripples, mud, wet stones.
> I am enamored of the pale chalk dust
> Of the moth's wing, and the dark moldering gold
> Of rust, the corrupted treasures of this world.
> Against the Gospel let my brush declare:
> "These are the anaglyphs and gleams of love."

Without being able to prove it, I've long thought these lines about
the sun—and indeed the whole rhetorical situation of "Devotions" as
an act of prayer—is more indebted to Bellini's *St. Francis in Ecstasy*
than to any other specific painter or painting. Bellini's great painting
captures St. Francis at the moment of singing his celebrated canticle
to the sun, and it formed, in all its "holiness," the subject of Hecht's
early ekphrasis, "At the Frick." In the later poem, however, the devotional celebration of the natural world, for all its stated modesty, is a
vision of art worthy of being placed "Against the Gospel"—holy writ,
in praise of this life, not the next. An earlier draft of the poem read
even more pointedly, "Counter to Matthew," probably because the
immediately preceding lines about the "corrupted treasures" represent a strong revision of Christ's words in the Sermon on the Mount
in Matthew 6:19–20:

> Lay not up for yourselves treasures upon earth, where moth
> and rust doth corrupt, and where thieves break through and steal:
> But lay up for yourselves treasures in heaven, where neither moth nor
> rust doth corrupt, and where thieves do not break through nor steal.

But the alteration to "Gospel" is a good one. It widens the boundaries
of the poem's claim, and along with sounding a note of alliteration
("Against the Gospel), it anticipates sonically its replacement by "anaglyphs and gleams of love" (my italics).

It is also possible in this poem of many reflections and cross-currents,
of "cool sinuosities," in which "enamelled" winds up as "enamored"

and "the glittering eyes and backs of frogs" recall (but in better detail) Marianne Moore's famous definition of poetry as "imaginary gardens with real toads in them," we also hear something of an *ars poetica*, especially in the final two lines: "let my brush declare"—"declare" being associated with speech and hence poesis, with the poet's signature, as it were, appearing at the bottom of the work in the characteristic use of an unusual word, "anaglyphs." No doubt in part inspired by its harmonic association with "gleams," "glyph" is from the Greek meaning "to carve," carrying with it a rare association with "symbol." (The *OED* cites Coleridge's *Aids to Reflection*: "They were originally symbolical Glyphs or Sculptures, and afterwards translated into words"—a translation that is itself illuminating in the context of a poem about a painting.) And in a more technical sense, "anaglyph" is associated in architectural usage with ornamentation in low relief. "Glyph" in this context is even associated with "canal."

How deeply we are invited to delve into the mystery of these associated meanings is left open. Our immediate pleasure in the poem hardly depends on this sort of digging, and therefore, at one level, it's probably enough to see that the fusion of the two (ornamentation and low relief) is what the poem seeks in turning the "corrupted treasures of this world"—weeds, dragonflies, as well as moths—into the subject of art and professing gleams of love in the process. And yet to conclude with a word that invites us to think about the depth of words in a poem celebrating painting is to encourage us also to see the depths in surfaces, the depths underlying surfaces, as if on a bridge looking down into water, and to consider the symbiotic relationship between word and image, between the arts, especially when joined together by love. Painting helps us to think about poetry, poetry helps us to see into creation from the eyes of the painter, and both help us to understand the world in which we live. In reclaiming the corrupt through art "Devotions of a Painter," a generous moving poem, with a touch of declamatory resistance to it, owes more, in Ruskin's sense, to Rubens than Fra Angelico.

"Meditation," nearly three times longer than "Devotions" and divided into three parts of unequal length, is one of Hecht's very finest poems, and perhaps Hecht thought so as well. It was the poem he chose for David Lehman's anthology, *Ecstatic Occasions, Expedient Forms* (1987), with brief explanatory comments by each of the sixty-five contributors. But even more unusual, at the bottom of the finished draft, Hecht uncharacteristically wrote "Asolo, July 21, 5:10 p.m."

I can't think of any other instance where Hecht commemorates the occasion of composition so precisely: in time for either cocktails or even song or both. The poem grew out of a visit to the Accademia Galleries in Venice, in which Hecht recalls being again

struck by the stunning beauty and serenity of those great altarpieces by Bellini and Carpaccio and Cima da Conegliano that are crowded into one astonishing room. One is more breathtaking than the next, and most center upon a throned Madonna, and whether or not any one of them is actually entitled 'Sacred Conversation,' they closely resemble others that are so titled.[22]

Hecht then transposed that memory on to the Italian landscape as viewed from the garden of the Hotel Cipriani in Asolo, the place of the poem's composition, which is perhaps also obliquely alluded to in the famous lines from Yeats' "Under Ben Bulben," which serve as the poem's epigraph:

> Quattrocento put in paint,
> On backgrounds for a God or Saint,
> Gardens where the soul's at ease;
> Where everything that meets the eye
> Flowers and grass and cloudless sky
> Resemble forms that are, or seem
> When sleepers wake and yet still dream,
> And when it's vanished still declare,
> With only bed and bedstead there,
> That Heavens had opened.

"Meditation" raises some immediate questions, posed most notably by Philip Hoy. Whether the description of the painting in the poem's third part is based on an actual painting? And what is the relationship of the three parts to the whole? Hecht's answer to the first question is straightforward: it is a "painting of my own making, with details borrowed from great altarpieces by the likes of Giovanni Bellini and Cima da Conegliano."[23] As to the second, Hecht quotes selectively from his comments in *Ecstatic Occasions, Expedient Forms*, which I am quoting even more selectively from Hoy. The poem

is based on a set of metaphors or figures that are acoustical or auditory in character, and that move from music and its opposite, cacophony, to an articulate

22. David Lehman, ed., *Ecstatic Occasions, Expedient Forms: 65 Leading Contemporary Poets Select and Comment on their Poems* (New York: Macmillan, 1987), 81–2.
23. *Anthony Hecht in Conversation with Philip Hoy*, 91.

silence; that is, from a perilous oscillation between the real world and an imagined one; or rather, not oscillation but interpenetration. The imagined world is art, whether as music or painting. But it is a world in which we enter, and even seem to inhabit, however briefly. The poem in its three parts is about the strange way we negotiate our entrance into this world, and the strangeness of that world in which all disharmonies are somehow reconciled.[24]

"Meditation" is the most complex and beautiful intertwining of the visual and musical arts in all of Hecht, and both responses serve as excellent starting points for understanding this poem. By a kind of backformation, thinking about the silence encoded in painting encourages the poet to think about the acoustical significance of sound, as he suggests, and the relationship between the two informs the poem's division into three parts. Although Hecht doesn't say so, it's difficult not to think of Dante's *Commedia*—we're in Italy after all—and its tripartite structure; and, in fact, "Meditation" corresponds roughly to the different imaginative locales of Dante's poem. The first part is distinctly reminiscent of Hell in its attention to cacophony and the obviously fallen and prideful nature of the individually personified instruments. (Like Dante's damned, their actions are precisely rendered: "The flute fingers its priceless strand of pearls / Nasal disdain is eructed by the horn.") The second part is more obliquely purgatorial in the image of repeated prayers amid coughs and whispers, and of the tunnel, borrowed perhaps from the Bosch painting noted at the beginning of this chapter, and leading in "perfect circles" heavenward. The third and longest part is focused on "This perfect company... here engaged / In what is called a sacred conversation."

As might be expected, we also travel upwards from profane to increasingly sacred spaces: from an imagined cocktail party, in which three martinis disable the senses—Hecht is always interesting when it comes to drinking—and sets the mind reeling, to the closing of cathedral doors, leaving us alone inside with "grottoed sounds / Below the threshold of the audible," to the luminous world of a richly described painting where, as Eliot might say, it is always "eight o'clock / On a sunny April morning." These separate locales, in turn, give rise to further differences and resemblances as Hecht weaves the parts into a whole. His silent St. Sebastian, for instance, "relaxed but powerful," is notable for attending "to everything except himself," in sharp contrast

---

24. *Anthony Hecht in Conversation with Philip Hoy*, 92.

to "each instrument" in the orchestra, "in lunatic monologue putting on its airs." Indeed, wordplay, of even a sort indulged in the purgatorial second part, annoying to some readers ("whirled without end"), is thinned out in the altitudinous quiet of the sacred conversation. "No one in the group seems to be speaking. / The Baptist, in a rude garment of hides, / Vaguely unkempt, is looking straight at the viewer / With serious interest, patient and unblinking." "A small seraphic consort of viols and lutes / Prepares to play or actually is playing." The qualifying "or" helps to draw attention to the silence that accompanies the ineffable.

Here, in the third section, Hecht is at his most serene. In the garden at the Cipriani, "where the soul's at ease," as Yeats said, the mind's eye lovingly traces out the memory of a painting interfused with a view of the pastoral landscape across the valley:

> A landscape of extraordinary beauty
> Leads out behind the personages to where
> A shepherd tends his flock. Far off a ship
> Sets sail for the world of commerce. Travelers
> Kneel at a wayside shrine near a stone wall.
> Game-birds or song-birds strut or take the air
> In gliding vectors among cypress spires
> By contoured vineyards or groves of olive trees.
> A belfry crowns a little knoll behind which
> The world recedes into a cobalt blue
> Horizon of remote, fine mountain peaks.

The diction here ("personages," "gliding vectors") is slightly old-fashioned in the manner of a connoisseur viewing a Bellini or Carpaccio painting, and the prospect, carefully and minutely described, takes us into the distance as far as the mind's eye can see, especially Hecht's mind with all its past cargo. At the vanishing point, the paragraph ends, the break on the page signaling a transition, as we move from description to meditation, from images of concentrated silence to those of acutely rendered sound in the final twenty-seven lines:

> The company, though they have turned their backs
> To all of this, are aware of everything.
> Beneath their words, but audible, the silver
> Liquidities of stream and song-bird fall
> In cleansing passages, and the water-wheel
> Turns out its measured, periodic creak.

They hear the coughs, the raised voices of children
Joyful in the dark tunnel, everything.
Observe with care their tranquil pensiveness.
They hear all the petitions, all the cries
Reverberating over marble floors,
Floating above still water in dark wells.
All the world's woes, all the world's woven woes,
The warp of ages, they hear and understand,
To which is added a final bitterness:
That their own torments, deaths, renunciations,
Made in the name of love, have served as warrant,
Serve to this very morning as fresh warrant
For the infliction of new atrocities.
All this they know. Nothing is ever lost.
It is the condition of their blessedness
To hear and recall the recurrent cries of pain
And parse them into a discourse that consorts
In strange agreement with the viols and lutes,
Which, with the water and the meadow bells,
And every gathered voice, every *amen*,
Join to compose the sacred conversation.

If the poem's division into three parts has reminded us of Dante, the vision that remains is pure Hecht. Dante's poem insists on absolute separations and distinctions, as no other poem ever has. If one is among the elect, the beauty of being a saint in the *Paradiso* is not just that you're close to God. You are also far from Hell and don't have to hear the sounds of suffering. Milton is less absolute on this point since his guardian angels—no Catholic saints for this most Protestant of poets—attend on Adam and Eve knowing full well the couple's painful future. In the last portion of the poem, Hecht disavows Dante and takes Milton several steps further, indeed deep into the twentieth century in the double irony that suffering in faith has been a warrant for new atrocities, and that it is the condition of their blessedness "to hear and recall the recurrent cries of pain."

Hecht had spoken eloquently of the poem being about "the strange way we negotiate our entrance into this world [of art], and the strangeness of that world in which all disharmonies are somehow reconciled." But the poem is "strange" in another sense as well: if disharmonies are reconciled, they are done so in the poem in the manner, say, of Bach's *St. John Passion*, where great pain remains resonantly articulated or, in the case of Hecht's poem, even amplified in the knowledge of the "new atrocities" they've helped to produce.[25] I take the amplification here as an oblique reference to the many killed—and still being killed—in the name of religion. In the same splendid room in the Accademia housing the three "great altarpieces" is a fourth painting, also by Carpaccio: *The Crucifixion and Apotheosis of Ten Thousand Martyrs of Mount Ararat*. But, if one is counting, ten thousand is a small number when it comes to the twentieth century. The painting doesn't bear mentioning.

It is at this point we might note a strange detail of Hecht's own making, not in any of the three great altarpieces, nor visible from the Cipriani garden: the view "far off" of a ship setting sail "for the world of commerce." Might that detail be a remnant not of a painting but of a poem? Of the conclusion of Auden's "Musée des Beaux Arts," in which "the expensive delicate ship," having seen something amazing, nonetheless "sailed calmly on," its journey symbolic in that poem for "how everything turns away / Quite leisurely from the disaster" of Icarus' fall?

"Everything," of course, in Hecht's poem, is exactly what the saints cannot turn away from, indeed is what "the sacred conversation" represents in its inclusive, endlessly circulating vision of suffering, "whirled without end." Hecht's pun is not a throwaway.[26] It's a shy or sly corrective reminding us that only in art might we imagine, momentarily, all harmonies resolved—as Yeats says, a dreamer's moment in the garden when the "Heavens had opened." Which is also to say that in this poem of interpenetrations, Hecht incorporates the pastoral sentiment, indeed as epigraph, something on the edge of his poem; but the body of the poem widens to include the "world," "whirled without end," and that when he closes off the poem on the richly solemn note by pairing

---

25. The analogy with Bach, and in particular the *St. John Passion* (as distinguished from the more harmonious *St. Matthew Passion*), is supported by Hecht's comment to Harry Ford that the German epigraph to "The Book of Yolek" "comes from a chorus in the St. John's Passion." AH to Harry Ford, 17 September 1981. The letter to Ford was written on the same day he wrote to Jacqueline Simms, announcing the completion of the sestina plus the two ekphrastic poems.

26. Expressing irritation over Hecht's addiction to "wretched puns," William Logan adds "Whirled without end" to a list included in his *New York Times Book Review* of *The Transparent Man* and *The Collected Earlier Poems* (22 July 1990), 26–7. Two years later "In Reply to Eleanor Cook, 'From Etymology to Paranomasia,'" *Connotations* 2.2 (1992), 201–4, Hecht offers a brief defense of word riddling and the pleasure he finds in witty compression, with examples of puns taken from Richard Wilbur to William Shakespeare, and a double dactyl of his own making on T. S. Eliot for secretly relishing "Paronomasias, / Zeugmas and rhymes he de- /Plored in his prose."

"*amen*," with "conversation," not only does the rhyme remain slightly ajar, the note of dissonance audible, so we can hear the world, but the final word heard is "conversation" and not the liturgical "*amen*." Hecht would never go so far as to say, with Stevens in "The Poems of Our Climate," that the "imperfect is our paradise"—let alone follow that credo with the statement: "Note that, in this bitterness, delight." Delight, so right for Stevens, is simply too joyous for the complex tonal registers emanating from a "sacred conversation," which by its very phrasing recollects the pain encoded in "sacrifice." In this most artful of poems, however, Hecht did make sure that paradise included the imperfect.

The final ekphrasis I want to consider is Hecht's enchanting triumph of introspection, "Matisse: Blue Interior with Two Girls—1947" (Figure 6.2). It was written some years later at the invitation of the poet Jorie Graham who was contemplating an anthology of poems based on paintings at the University of Iowa's Museum of Art. (The project was never brought to fruition, although Hecht's poem appeared in a 1995 issue of *The Colorado Review*, a year before its inclusion in the publication of *Flight Among the Tombs*.) Not that Hecht was on perma-nent holiday from the visual arts after his highly productive trip to the Veneto in 1981. In "See Naples and Die" (1990) he turned to Bellini's great *Transfiguration*, now in the Museo di Capodimonte. But as an imaginative resource Italy was thinning. Nor did the Matisse poem represent Hecht's sole venture in his later years with poems about art, a subject that will be further explored in Chapters 8 and 9.

But the Matisse poem (and the accompanying painting) is one Hecht cared about a great deal, judging by the length and sensitivity of his own commentary in his *Conversation with Philip Hoy*, and by the title, which declares unequivocally—and the only time in his verse—his visual source. It may be of some personal significance as well that he chose a painting from the Iowa collection with the date 1947. This was the year he spent as a graduate student at the University of Iowa, a year disrupted in part by a nervous breakdown, the cause of which would now be identified as post-traumatic stress syndrome, following his mil-itary service. But the poem is not a mulling over of the past and its demons, in contrast to "The Book of Yolek." It is manifestly a work of the present, although a sense of the war, as well as obvious temperamental

Figure 6.2. Henri Matisse, *Blue Interior with Two Girls*, 1947. (Reproduced courtesy of the University of Iowa Museum of Art. Gift of Owen and Leone Elliott)

differences in response to trauma, was on Hecht's mind in providing a frame for the poem. Appended to the poem is a lengthy epigraph, indeed the longest in all his poetry, about Matisse from *The Shock of the New* by the art critic Robert Hughes:

[H]e lived through some of the most traumatic political events of recorded history, the worst wars, the greatest slaughters, the most demented rivalries of ideology, without, it seems, turning a hair... Perhaps Matisse did suffer from fear and loathing like the rest of us, but there is no trace of them in his work. His studio was a world within a world: a place of equilibrium that, for sixty continuous years, produced images of comfort, refuge, and balanced satisfaction.

Hughes was no doubt recalling Matisse's famous remark: "What I dream of is an art of balance, of purity and serenity devoid of troubling or disturbing subject-matter... like a comforting influence, a mental balm—something like a good armchair in which one rests from physical fatigue."[27]

Hecht's own comments on the painting make it clear that this tranquil view of Matisse is one he shared, indeed found "full of feeling" and deeply attractive, feelings that carry over into the mood of his own poem: a tone poem in a single voice attuned to the painting. And yet when pressed about the "something extra" that a poem adds to a painting, Hecht also noted, after offering a complicating analogy to Hardy's poem, "A Light Snowfall After Frost," that:

I could well imagine an art critic feeling that all this commentary of mine was utterly irrelevant; that Matisse was intent on painting a tranquil and harmonious picture, and that he felt his green (outside) worked harmoniously with his blue (inside) and that nothing else was of concern to him. That's perfectly okay with me. I was busy making a poem, and took my occasion from a painting and what it suggested to me.[28]

Hecht was speaking not just about Matisse's colors and the significance attached to them in the poem. He was also addressing the radical liberties he took in sharply dividing the poem between outside and inside. The first fifteen lines are his response to what in the painting is "outside," the next eighteen to what is "within." Achieving a sense of tranquility and harmony, in other words, wasn't his goal or his only goal. Rather, as the example of Hardy's poem suggests, and his commentary indicates, Hecht was thinking about the two colored spaces in the painting as representing two separate places connected by a window and yet in another sense quite far apart from each other: "two worlds, one seen through the aperture of a window from the point of view of another." If not quite riven or bifurcated, the vision inspired

27. Quoted from *The Oxford Dictionary of Art*, 2nd edn., ed. Ian Chilvers and Harold Osborne (Oxford: Oxford University Press, 1997), 359.
28. *Anthony Hecht in Conversation with Philip Hoy*, 115–17. Subsequent quotations from Hecht are to remarks found in these pages.

by the painting oscillates. Depending on your focus, the viewing impulse tends toward irreconcilable opposites. How close the poem seems to being balanced, to achieving an art of balance, performing in something of the manner of "a good armchair in which one rests from physical fatigue." And yet, when examined carefully, also how far.

To look out through the window is to observe, comfortably, that:

> Outside is variable. May, a lawn of immediate green,
> The tree as blue as its shadow,
> A shutter angles out in charitable shade.

This is as leisurely a beginning as Hecht ever wrote. But, descriptively responsible as these lines are to Matisse's painting, variability also encourages laxity, as Hecht's initially prosy lines intimate, and soon the mind begins to wander, even as the iambic meter takes hold. "It is a world of yearning," Hecht tells us (not, say, a world of color or beauty). He's already left description for feeling—for a world of "luxe, calme, et volupté," as Hecht suggests, alluding to the famous Matisse painting of that title. And now the erotic imagination begins to swell:

> we yearn for it,
> Its youthful natives yearn for one another.
> Their flesh is firm as a plum, their smooth tanned waists,
> Lit through the fluttered leaves above their heads,
> Are rubbed and cinctured with this morning's bangles.

With "bangles," as in "ring-bracelets," not its sound-alike "spangles," we've reached one of the poem's outer "angles." (Hecht interrupts his discussion of Hardy's poem to talk subtly and acutely about the importance of belatedly "mated" rhymes.) This one ("angles") variably signals the turn ("Yet") after the eighth line, in the manner of a fifteen-line Petrarchan sonnet:

> Yet each, if we but take thought, is a lean gnomon,
> A bone finger with its moral point:
> The hour, the minute, the dissolving pleasure.
> (Light fails, the shadows pool themselves in hollows.)
> Here, in the stifling fragrance of mock orange,
> In the casual glance, the bright lust of the eye,
> Lies the hot spring of inevitable tears.

We've been here before in Hecht, most recently in "The Deodand," but never with such elegantly cascading deliquescence. The crucial phrase is "if we but take thought." And as soon as we do, the "lean gnomon" (or the homophonic "no man"?) of reflection reduces the body's once firm erotic presence to a shadow, to a moral point, with Herbertian perspicuity. There is a clock in this forest, and also, handily, parentheses to cradle the failing light and pooled shadows. By the time we arrive at "the hot spring of inevitable tears" produced by the flesh, "inevitable" seems almost a veritable anagram for "variable," and what is hot and "variable" at one moment, can be perceived as remarkably cool at the next:

> Within is the cool blue perfect cube of thought.
>   The branched spirea carefully arranged
>   Is no longer random growth: it now becomes
> The object of our thought, it becomes our thought.
>   The room is a retreat in which the drone
>   Of the electric fan is modest, unassertive,
> Faithful, as with a promise of lemonade
>   And other gentle solaces of summer,
>   Among which, for the two serene young girls
> In this cool tank of blue is an open book
>   Where they behold the pure unchanging text
>   Of manifold, reverberating depth,
> Quiet and tearless in its permanence.
>   Deep in their contemplation the two girls,
>   Regarding art, have become art themselves.
> Once out of nature, they have settled here
>   In this blue room of thought, beyond the reach
>   Of the small brief sad ambitions of the flesh.

"Within," by contrast, is exactly where we remain in this remarkable stanza of concentrated description—contained in this "cool blue perfect cube of thought," to quote from a line as sonically minimalist as the line introducing the first stanza is metrically "variable." Not only does the stanza stay tightly focused on the painting throughout (only a few incidental details are added) but we also end where we began: "in this blue room of thought." And, in between, we're told, that "the object of our thought...becomes our thought" in the Stevensesque manner of transferring subject and object. Then in a further act of compression, the transfer is realized when we are asked to concentrate on "the two serene young girls / In this cool tank of blue" and the "open book / Where they behold the pure unchanging text." The image of the "branched spirea" in Matisse's painting has become a symbol of these two worlds, framed by the window. Now "carefully arranged" in a vase on the table, it no longer signifies "random growth." But as the second stanza evolves in the direction of pure thought and object, the pleasures of isolation acquire a weight of their own, as Hecht remolds the erotic yearning in the first stanza associated with Keats' "Ode on a Grecian Urn" into Yeats' wish, in the second, to be translated out of nature into an "artifice of eternity" in "Sailing to Byzantium." Hecht doesn't need to disrupt the mood of concentration and moralize the point in the manner of the first stanza. He simply tightens the spiral of thought to exclude the spirea of nature in favor of art: "Deep in their contemplation the two girls, / Regarding art, have become art themselves." Two girls now doubling as art: this "blue room of thought," it needs to be noted, is also no longer described as "perfect," nor is it a "cube," leaving open the possibility that blue characterizes a state of mind. To be "beyond the reach / Of the small brief sad ambitions of the flesh" seems slightly less than a triumph and more like a consolation prize. We're not quite sure where pity should best be bestowed.

Yes, the poem, like the painting, is something of a balancing act, but of a different kind. Attentive to the comforts of domestic design and yet not exclusively so, poetry, at least Hecht's poetry, is rarely devoid of troubling or disturbing subject matter, and perhaps neither is Matisse's art, now that we've read this poem. We might have thought, too, that Hecht as a poet would valorize the object of the book in the painting, but he doesn't. Matisse's painting remains remarkable in his eyes and perhaps now in ours as well, if it wasn't before, since one of the great attractions of ekphrastic verse is the pleasurable opportunity it offers readers of the written text to study art: to learn to think with their eyes by comparing one art form with another and expanding their vision of knowledge in the process. The sanity of Hecht's commentary, deeply sympathetic to both body and mind, but not completely enthralled by either, might also remind us of something further in the context of the Hughes remark framing the poem: that both painter and poet survived the traumas of World War II, albeit in different ways. What matters, though, is not just surviving. As Hecht said in "Rites and Ceremonies," "merely to have survived is not an index of excellence." What you do with that opportunity also counts, as both painting and poem quietly declare—the latter an example of the schooling of the eye, on which this chapter has been a commentary.

7

S*hecht*speare

Odd that a thing is most itself when likened.

Richard Wilbur, "Lying"

This chapter begins with a simple observation: that Anthony Hecht belongs to a line of poet-critics, who first appeared in English in the time of Shakespeare and who made Shakespeare their subject, sometimes in verse, sometimes in prose. The line might be said to begin with Shakespeare's contemporary, Ben Jonson, run through Dryden, Pope, and the other Johnson (Samuel), move on to Keats and Arnold and include in our own time, the recent twentieth century, that is, Yeats, Eliot, Auden, and Ted Hughes. As with the community of poets he imagines at the end of his elegy to James Merrill, Hecht would, I suspect, be pleased to be numbered among these authors.

This last mentioned quaternion, in fact, forms the subject of Neil Corcoran's astute book, *Shakespeare and the Modern Poet*—astute in part because, among many other perceptions, he anticipates in a small way the direction of this chapter: "Of other modern American poetic engagements with Shakespeare," Corcoran remarks in his opening survey, "one of the most notable is Anthony Hecht's [poetic] sequence 'A Love for Four Voices.'"[1] And the two paragraphs Corcoran devotes to this sequence are richly responsive to the complexities of Hecht's fifteen-page poem, a poem that dazzles by turns, paying triple homage to Shakespeare (*A Midsummer Night's Dream*), to Auden's commentary

---

1. Neil Corcoran, *Shakespeare and the Modern Poet* (Cambridge: Cambridge University Press, 2010), 14–15.

on *The Tempest, The Sea and the Mirror,* and to Franz Joseph Haydn's Quartets. Included in Corcoran's roll call of American poets are Robert Lowell, who uncharacteristically seems always to have held Shakespeare at arm's length, and John Berryman, who didn't, and spent much of his life wrestling, mostly in manuscript, with a variety of Shakespearean problems, *King Lear* being the largest of them.[2]

The interest we have in these authors is special. We value them not only for their criticism but for how their critical judgments play across and potentially infuse, enliven, and illuminate their own creative efforts. As a critic, I confess a natural aversion to the time-honored, often-invoked distinction between critical and creative writings, as if criticism weren't at all a creative act, or writing poetry weren't a critical one, and to some degree this chapter, while assuming these different activities in practice, presumes to diminish their distance in the process. In doing so, I am reminded of Wallace Stevens' remark that "poetry is the scholar's art"[3]—surely applicable to Hecht—as well as the fact that underlying Milton's famous image that prose is written with the left hand and poetry by the right is the possibility of discovering a single two-handed engine.

Still, it would be foolish to pretend that important distinctions don't exist between these two forms. "When we read poetry we are either won by it or not," Hecht observed in a letter to his friend, also a poet-critic, John Frederick Nims. "When we read critical prose we are inclined to wonder whether or not we want to argue with it."[4] Simple as it is, the difference is useful to keep in mind when reading Hecht in either format. In observance of the old Horatian formula, poems for Hecht use all the art they can muster to instruct and delight in an attempt to win over the reader. Criticism, springing from a disagreement with another or a representative other, seeks to argue for a new understanding of the truth of the work itself. Hecht's solemnity in both capacities has been occasionally noted, but it is a solemnity that manifests itself differently in each case. Hecht writes criticism from the point of view of how a poet would like to be read: with intelligence and seriousness, perhaps even Arnoldian "high seriousness." As

---

2. Corcoran, *Shakespeare and the Modern Poet,* 10–14.
3. Stevens, from "Adagia," in *Opus Posthumous,* ed. Milton J. Bates (New York: Alfred A. Knopf, 1989), 193.
4. Letter, AH to John Frederick Nims, 3 April 1985.

he remarks in the "Preface" to *Obbligati*, published in 1986, at once elevating and subordinating the critic's task:

> I also mean to affirm what I conceive to be the proper role of criticism as a musical obbligato: that is, a counterpart that must constantly strive to move in strict harmony with and intellectual counterpoint to its subject, and remain always subordinate to the text upon which it presumes to comment.[5]

He writes poetry, though, more from the point of view of how an educated reader, who is not necessarily a poet, might best be wooed and won. There is more latitude for fun in the second category. Witness his riff on Arnoldian "high seriousness," "The Dover Bitch." And much else, as this chapter hopes to show.

In the case of Hecht and Shakespeare, our interest in the ambidextrous, bicameral poet-critic becomes even more acute because his lifelong involvement with Shakespeare not only aligns him with a past from which he sought both inspiration and differentiation; it also helps to distinguish him from some of his immediate contemporaries. Neither Bishop nor Merrill, for example, engaged extensively with Shakespeare in their writings: Bishop obliquely with *Twelfth Night* in "Varick Street" and "Twelfth Morning; or What You Will," and Merrill, charmingly, in "The School Play," with its humorously rueful reminiscence about being assigned "a small part" in *Richard II* and more generally with the figure of Prospero as an artist magician. Wilbur, by comparison, found in "Up, Jack," a brief means to write obliquely about war in *The Beautiful Changes* (1947). He also wrote a distantly appreciative introduction to Shakespeare's Poems (not the Sonnets) for the 1966 Pelican edition of Shakespeare's works under the general editorship of Alfred Harbage, but his theater interests took him in the direction of France, where he translated Molière and Racine with great facility and success. Only John Hollander, like Hecht, was active as a poet-critic of Shakespeare's writings, although Hollander more often in his criticism than his verse. But for Hecht Shakespeare was not just a recurrent subject in his writings, both formal and informal; he also (and here is the crucial point) fed into the creation of some of Hecht's finest poems.

Since most of this chapter will focus on Hecht's poetry and will feature both long views and some detailed close-ups, I might indicate

---

5. *Obbligati: Essays in Criticism* (New York: Atheneum, 1986), vii.

here his most prominent critical engagements with Shakespeare. These include, among a rich harvest of critical essays and reviews written over a lifetime, a lengthy essay on *The Merchant of Venice* of nearly ninety pages, bearing the subtitle, "A Venture in Hermeneutics," and another shorter one simply titled *Othello*—both appearing in *Obbligati*. Somewhat surprisingly, given Hecht's enthusiasm for Venice, the two Shakespeare essays turn out to be not Venetian twins inspired by a common setting, but separate reflections on subjects of long-standing interest to Hecht: military and religious matters. Hecht also wrote about *The Tempest* on several different occasions; played, while teaching at Bard in the early 1960s, the role of Don Adriano de Armado, "a fantastical Spaniard," across from the romantic leads Blythe Danner and Chevy Chase in *Love's Labours Lost*. And, much later, he wrote a substantial introduction for the Cambridge edition of Shakespeare's Sonnets in 1996: substantial in part because of a single long paragraph, the third, which includes one of the most profound (and painful) digests of the "intimate emotional experience" of love that can be found any-where in the criticism of the Sonnets.[6] It could only have been written by a fellow traveler—whoever Shakespeare is or was—and author of a volume of poems called *The Hard Hours*.

As we might expect from a direct descendent of New Criticism— John Crowe Ransom, let us remember, was one of Hecht's teachers, and William Empson one of his heroes—the Shakespeare essays, as with Hecht's criticism generally, are attentive to the works them-selves, with a further eye toward viewing the plays as artistic wholes. The essay on *Othello*, for instance, while taking issue with Eliot's famous characterization of Othello as "*cheering himself up*" in his final speech, does so only in the context of having established a broad and detailed understanding of the rhetorical world in which Othello functions, or fails to function; a world, it turns out, that takes account of Othello's doubly divided psyche as "Christianized Moor" and "'Roman' General."

Even more elaborate in this regard is *The Merchant of Venice* essay, Hecht's first scholarly foray into the crowded field of Shakespeare studies and a bit overwritten perhaps because of this. The essay is a

6. *The Sonnets*, ed. G. Blakemore Evans (Cambridge: Cambridge University Press, 1996),
     1. Hecht's introduction is structured around detailed readings of seven Sonnets in the
     following order: 35, 73, 18, 57, 151, 87, and 138.

zealously expansive "search for the play's hidden architecture, its secret skeletal structure," an attempt "to discover and to display such design as integrates and unifies the play."[7] But it is also no ordinary New Critical venture. If the attention to "design" suggests spatial affinities with, say, the exemplary criticism of Robert Heilman (among other works, the co-author with Cleanth Brooks of *Understanding Drama* (1945)), its concern with the play's "hidden architecture" takes us in the direction of biblical hermeneutics, of much interest in literature departments at the time. Frank Kermode's *The Genesis of Secrecy* (1979) and Northrop Frye's *The Great Code* (1982), as well as the iconographical practices of art historians, are relevant to Hecht's quest here.

The *Merchant* essay seeks to unravel the many threads connecting the play to the widespread habit in Shakespeare's England of reading the Bible typologically, in which the Old Testament finds its fulfillment in the New, a cultural exploration into a method of reading that Hecht displays with considerable, if not always persuasive, ingenuity and also with some profound misgivings of his own. In a brief afterword, he "confesses" finding "distasteful" or "abhorrent" the "conventional view of the Bible" that he has been at pains to elucidate. This resuscitated "view" Hecht nonetheless intends as a corrective to the often modern reading of the play as "a fairy-tale" romance, and it leads the author inevitably and inexorably to associate Shylock with the Old Law and Bassanio and Portia with the New, with the character of Bassanio undergoing a conversion of sorts, a reversal or "peripeteia,"[8] and Portia in the trial scene being associated with the young Jesus in the Temple, and later with the Epiphany. It is, to say the least, a reading that runs against the grain of most post-Holocaust studies or performances of the play, which in one way or another seek to finesse the play's anti-Semitism and the matter of the blood-libel that Hecht sees as the motive for Shylock's revenge. The Program Notes for a recent production, in fact, usefully quotes Hecht on this matter:

It must be clear that the goal of obtaining his pound of flesh is more important to Shylock than any financial considerations, and he makes that goal nothing less than a religious obsession, swearing an oath to heaven in regard to it. The solemnity with which he takes that oath is the more awful in that it respects one of the Ten Commandments. And it is the more devout in its conspicuous

---

7. *Obbligati*, 142 and 219–20, respectively.   8. *Obbligati*, 164.

contrast to virtually all the other oaths in the play, which are made with ease and broken with impunity. Indeed, Shylock's fealty to his oath has a dark and lonely courage about it, a kind of inverted nobility that would be heroic if it were not perverse, and pious if it were God-inspired instead of engendered by the insatiable appetite for the destruction of innocence that I have indicated.[9]

Neither essay, however, has had a measurable impact on the world of professional Shakespeare scholarship. Their failure in this regard is no doubt in part attributable to their already dated appearance in the 1980s, a decade that witnessed the rise of New Historicism, the continued vitality of feminism, branching out to include gender studies, the demise of Paul de Man, and a renewed emphasis on performance studies.[10] But for a reader of Hecht's poetry, the two essays play across, indeed highlight and illuminate a number of important themes and practices beyond their obvious, albeit still important concern with military and religious matters. Hecht's determination to argue on behalf of a noble ending for Othello, for example—"the judgment he passes upon himself is absolute and remorseless"—points not just to the central place the dramatic monologue was coming to occupy in his middle years but to the considerable attention given to dramatized endings and the often moving recognitions and self-revelations they contain, sometimes even spoken by characters at the end of their lives,

9. Program Notes for the Theatre for a New Audience's *The Merchant of Venice* (14–24 April 2011), with F. Murray Abraham as Shylock. I have restored the slightly abbreviated version of the quotation as it is found in *Obbligati*, 157–8.

10. In an otherwise sympathetic 1986 review of *Obbligati*, Louis Menand called attention to the book's datedness—its "solemn attitude toward canonical works and values that were a feature of the [Eliotic] critical school to which [the essays] belonged." "A Metaphor is a Terrible Thing to Waste," *New York Times Book Review* 91 (7 September 1986), 19. As for Hecht's later thoughts about *Obbligati*, in a 10 May 1991 letter to Harry Ford, he recounts a crumb of comfort passed on to him by David Lehman, found in a remark made by the great scholar of Japanese literature, Donald Keene: "A couple of years ago," Keene comments, "I read an essay by Anthony Hecht on Othello that stunned me by its insights into a work that I thought I knew well. I thought that as long as even a few critics were writing so incandescently I had models to follow." Grateful for small favors, Hecht still wasn't fooled about the essay's fortunes, and he concluded his letter on a note of plangent realism: "It's heartening to be sent tidbits of praise like this, since, on the whole, Obbligati may be said to have been received with stifled yawns. I still think there is much good in it, but I feel more and more lonely about this as time goes on. [...]" One reviewer who found much good in the book was William Pritchard ("Formal Measures," *The New Republic* (15 December 1986), 37–9). Another was Anthony Thwaite, "Anthony Hecht: Criticism as Counterpoint to Literature," *Washington Post Book World* (31 August 1986), 9.

as in "The Transparent Man." So, too, Hecht's fascination with typology marks some of his strongest poems in unexpected ways. And the kind of careful attention given to the Sonnets vouchsafes a poet-critic of remarkable subtlety, everywhere responsive to diction, form, and argument: an example, no doubt, of how Hecht—indeed any serious poet—would like to be read.

To turn to Hecht's poetry more generally: his earliest published book of poems, *A Summoning of Stones* (1954), already hints at a habit of thinking that would be highly hospitable to the practice of imitation and allusion that characterizes much of his poetry.[11] As the title of this volume suggests, echoes of the past reverberate everywhere. A young Orpheus summons. What changes in Hecht over time is not the presence of echo, but its place and placement in creating moments of maximal urgency, comic as well as tragic, as he matured as both person and poet. But even as far back as his war letters, Hecht had shown a special knack for the Shakespearean phrase. These were plucked most often from *Hamlet*, as the times were certainly out of joint for a soldier either bored, depressed, and often both, or on the front in Germany.

"How weary, flat, stale and unprofitable / Seem to me all the uses of this world," Hecht concludes one letter to his parents, signed "Gloomily, Tony"—for good measure.[12] In another letter, in a more resolute mood, he simultaneously reveals and shrouds a portion of his identity: "I have that within me which passeth show / These but the trappings [and] the suits of woe." The familiar quotation hovers oddly and proleptically—indeed prophetically in light of his later war poetry—if we remember that the person writing the letter is a soldier in uniform wearing "suits of woe," and wonder further to what degree he was aware of this concern himself or of signaling this concern to his immediate readers, his worried parents. And then in the same letter, but in an altogether different mood he addresses his younger brother, Roger: "Dear old goat— How's the old petty pace coming along? From day to day?" Here's the witty wiseacre coming suddenly into view with his parody of Macbeth's famous speech. And then, in another letter, simply: "I am translated!" Exclamation point. Bottom, from *A Midsummer Night's Dream*, makes a

---

11. See Christopher Ricks, *True Friendship: Geoffrey Hill, Anthony Hecht, and Robert Lowell under the Sign of Eliot and Pound* (New Haven: Yale University Press, 2010).

12. Letter, AH to his parents, 12 June 1944 (*SL*, 28–9); quotations from other letters to his parents are, respectively, 28 October 1944 (*SL*, 33–4) and 9 October 1945 (*SL*, 52–3).

brief cameo appearance in a letter to announce a change in Hecht's wartime fortunes while stationed in Japan. Actually, not quite simply, since the quotation from *A Midsummer Night's Dream* is followed quickly by a quotation from Isaiah, followed by one (again) from *Hamlet*: "I am bound in a nutshell, but count myself king of infinite space."

Among other gifts, Shakespeare gave Hecht in the war letters a vocabulary of pitch-and-stress, a way to fathom, negotiate, and artic-ulate the emotional extremities of military life, to provide and continue a civilian identity within drab olive fatigues; and, given this heightened charge, it is perhaps not surprising, in retrospect, that Shakespeare played little part in *A Summoning of Stones*. In the immediate after-math of World War II, many poets, indeed many people, were looking for relief from the omnipresence of war, and perhaps no one more so than Hecht in this first collection of what is often beautifully shaped topiary verse.

The transition from *Stones* to *Hard Hours* is one of the more radical and memorable shifts of its era, as I have mentioned in earlier chapters— right up there with, though different from, and yet influenced by, Robert Lowell's famous break with fixed forms in his inaugurating turn toward "confessional" poetry with the publication of *Life Studies* in 1959. The shift in *Hard Hours* is, in some regards, more harrowing because of the presence of the Holocaust. It is also marked, no less, by a return to Shakespeare. Lear's great query, "is there any cause in nature that makes these hard hearts"[13] hovers everywhere around the edges of *The Hard Hours*, but especially "Rites and Ceremonies." As Hecht made clear in a 1978 letter to Ashley Brown, *Lear* was the Shakespeare play that he knew best, a sentiment he would repeat much later in a 2002 letter to John Van Doren. "Of all Shakespeare's plays *King Lear* is the one I have been and continue to be most moved by. It is probably the bleakest of the plays, the most unconsoling."[14] And at the climactic moment in "Rites and Ceremonies," we will remember, it is the voice of Lear, on the heath, in the wilderness, a sort of Christ figure-cum-scapegoat, offering to speak on behalf of the innocent if only it could be found that "None does offend, none, I say none."

13. *King Lear* 3.6.77–8. Quotations from Shakespeare are from *The Riverside Shakespeare*, ed. G. Blakemore Evans, general editor (Boston: Houghton Mifflin, 1974).
14. Letters, AH to Ashley Brown, 18 April 1978; AH to John Van Doren, 16 February 2002 (*SL*, 170–2, 331–2, respectively).

If *Lear* is, and remains, at the epicenter of Hecht's holocaustic and post-holocaustic sense of suffering from *The Hard Hours* on—Lear's "Thou must be patient. We came crying hither" is part of an epigraph for *The Venetian Vespers*, published in 1979—Hecht still hadn't altogether forgotten the *Hamlet* of his war years; and it is the final poem in *The Hard Hours* that makes perhaps the most surprising use of Shakespeare in the quotation from *Hamlet* that serves as the poem's memorable mouthful of a title:"It Out-Herods Herod. Pray You, Avoid It."

The poem, short enough to be quoted in full, is appropriately Audenesque in its ballad-like simplicity of plot and stanza, swift movement of thought, and nearly allegorical habits of naming. But the details, domestic and personal, are not. The speaker is a parent, alone, with his children, making himself a drink (of which Auden would certainly have approved); and in concert with his increasing inebriation come nightmarish hallucinations about the spread of wickedness.

> Tonight my children hunch
> Toward their Western, and are glad
> As, with a Sunday punch,
> The Good casts out the Bad.
>
> And in their fairy tales
> The warty giant and witch
> Get sealed in doorless jails
> And the match-girl strikes it rich.
>
> I've made myself a drink.
> The giant and witch are set
> To bust out of the clink
> When my children have gone to bed.
>
> All frequencies are loud
> With signals of despair;
> In flash and morse they crowd
> The rondure of the air.
>
> For the wicked have grown strong,
> Their numbers mock at death,
> Their cow brings forth its young,
> Their bull engendereth.
>
> Their very fund of strength,
> Satan, bestrides the globe;
> He stalks its breadth and length
> And finds out even Job.

> Yet by quite other laws
> My children make their case;
> Half God, half Santa Claus,
> But with my voice and face,
>
> A hero comes to save
> The poorman, beggarman, thief,
> And make the world behave
> And put an end to grief.
>
> And that their sleep be sound
> I say this childermas
> Who could not, at one time,
> Have saved them from the gas.

Although there's much to say about the poem's restraint—the "signals of despair / In flash and morse" hint at the sudden, terrifying intrusion of World War II memories, quickly expanded in the next two stanzas—it is the poem's tender, prayerful conclusion that is so quietly disarming. The final rhyme is part of the muted surprise, as Hecht finds a mate for the archaic but vocally uplifting "childermas," the festal date on 28 December commemorating Herod's slaughter of the innocents, in the ever modern but blandly lethal "gas." The word is almost but not quite an afterthought. One is reminded here, as was not the case with "'More Light! More Light!,'" of Hannah Arendt's famous remark about the "banality of evil"—as the Jewish father speculates over what would have been his and his children's fate had his own history been different, had he been born, that is, in Germany, his ancestral home, rather than in the United States. It is the last word in the volume.

But the poem's further "rondure," to borrow another momentarily distancing archaism in the poem, this used in Shakespeare's Sonnet 21, meaning a circular or gracefully rounded object, is the paradoxical rounding off supplied by the ungainly title that functions like morse code to signal a new level of anxiety. Imagine it flashing mysteriously across a screen as a kind of warning: "It Out-Herods Herod. Pray You, Avoid It." As many will recognize, the title is a quotation from Hamlet's advice to the players in Act III, but arrived at, by Hecht, rather late in the poem's composition. Readers will recall how testy Hamlet can be about overacting, and he concludes his remarks to the players by calling attention to the noisy and violent acting in medieval mystery plays: "I would have such a fellow whipt for o'erdoing Termagant, it out-Herods Herod, pray you avoid it."[15] OK. But how are we to understand the meaning encrypted in Hecht's title? An earlier title of the poem, I should note, was simply "Dirty Work." Not bad, but perhaps too limited to the domestic scene. The new Shakespearean title (now including, in its dark irony, what I would call the dirty work of literary allusion) is, by comparison, of the typologically widening, historicizing sort. It reads like a newspaper headline, all in caps. Herod's massacre of the innocent, recollected in the reference to "childermas," anticipates, but is outdone by, the gassing of the Jews under Hitler, and the laconic, "Pray You, Avoid It," speaks miles—as if choice were possible for the victims—and then some, since further reflection reminds us that Hamlet is objecting to those who will tear a speech to tatters. The poem becomes at once both a harrowing personal parable about evil, a fitting conclusion to *The Hard Hours*, and a notable comment on how to find a language suitable for expressing horrific truths without tearing a speech to tatters in the highly theatrical manner, say, of Sylvia Plath's "Daddy," a poem that Hecht viewed with deep suspicion because of the "raving" carried on through the insistently employed "oo" rhyme.[16] These are concerns that engaged Hecht for a lifetime and, as in this case, Shakespeare helped him to articulate.

While *The Hard Hours* was on its way to multiple reprintings—twenty thousand copies were sold over the next two decades—Hecht's engagement with Shakespeare was also expanding and deepening. From, roughly, 1968 to 1981, the latter date the year "Love for Four Voices" appeared in *Poetry* magazine, Hecht was busy assimilating an array of Shakespearean situations and effects into his poetry as well as writing on *Othello* and *Merchant of Venice*. The most notable and pervasive influence with regard to his poetry is probably the rich patterning of Shakespearean blank verse. As George Wright observes in *Shakespeare's Metrical Art*, Hecht, along with Yeats, Stevens, Eliot, Berryman, Lowell, Larkin, Merrill, and Wilbur, are among "a dwindling remnant of superb practitioners" in the twentieth century, "for some of whom, as for the poets of the Renaissance, the regular meter once again seems a figure

15. *Hamlet* 3.2.13–14.
16. Letter, AH to Richard Wilbur, 7 October 1989 (*SL*, 233–4).

for normal life, departure from it a trope for individual eccentricity, manner, or mania."[17]

Prosodically speaking, Hecht could hew blank verse in the manner Wright describes, but he was probably most influenced by late Shakespeare—*The Tempest*, in particular—where the hypermetrical line almost becomes the norm, the extra syllable giving license to explore a greater variety of rhythm and sentiment to underscore individual eccentricity rather than mania, for which, in *The Winter's Tale*, "Leontes' jealousy /in Shakespeare's broken syntax" afforded a better example for the likes of Berryman, as Lowell understood.[18] This metrical preference in Hecht is especially true of the extended dramatic monologues that emerge in *Millions of Strange Shadows* (1977), and which are further developed in *The Venetian Vespers* (1979), both in the celebrated poem bearing that title and in the inaugural poem for that volume, "The Grapes," in which an aging chambermaid recognizes, in the context of her slowly revealing passion for a younger "Marc-Antoine," that "my little life had somehow crested."

But the presence of Shakespeare is not just a metrical matter. Nor is it even a question of establishing a subtle network of allusions, especially from *Othello*, that begins to proliferate in the poetry from this period.

> Where's that palace whereinto foul things
> Sometimes intrude not? Who has a breast so pure
> But some uncleanly apprehensions
> Keeps leets and law days, and in session sit
> With meditations lawful?

Iago's insinuating query serves as an epigraph to "The Venetian Vespers," in which the quotation invites the reader to view the sinking city's architecture as a richly complicated metaphor for the speaker's sullied conscience. In this fertile middle period, the Bard is everywhere: from the pointed variation on Othello's benighted quest for justice, "It is the cause, it is the cause,"[19] in "The Cost," to the echoing pathos of Portia's "mercy" speech at the end of the first movement in "The Venetian

---

17. Wright, *Shakespeare's Metrical Art* (Berkeley: University of California Press, 1988), 263. Many of these authors, including Hecht, are given sensitive treatment by Robert B. Shaw, *Blank Verse: A Guide to its History and Use* (Athens: Ohio University Press, 2007).

18. Quotation is from Lowell's poem "For John Berryman," in *Robert Lowell: Selected Poems* (expanded edn. New York: Farrar, Straus, and Giroux, 2006), 304–5.

19. *Othello* 5.2.1.

Vespers," to little comical one-offs.[20] Indeed, the experience of watching a Shakespeare play forms the subject of one of Hecht's most admired and deeply personal poems, "Peripeteia." First published in *The New Yorker* in 1974, "Peripeteia" is to the theater what Auden's "Musée des Beaux Arts" is to the picture gallery: a poem fully situated in its social and artistic milieu. But in sharp contrast to Auden, it is not about a general indifference to personal suffering witnessed in the work of old masters. It is a poem, rather, about change brought about by and through art, in this case a transformation of a wondrous kind and, as the title further suggests, the poem is clearly, even ostentatiously, dramatic, with its scholarly nod to Aristotle.

I don't think Hecht is being simply pedantic here. Hecht greatly admired and learned from Auden, at least as much as he did from Eliot; but one of the areas where he differed most vividly from Auden was in his interpretation of Shakespeare and in the consequent difference this spelled for his art. In his book-length study of Auden, *The Hidden Law*, published in 1993, and in a later review of Auden's lectures on Shakespeare published in 2001, Hecht noted Auden's essentially allegorical habits of thought as manifested in both his poetry and criticism, a habit largely indifferent to dramatic values, whether in his own poetry or operas or in his lectures on Shakespeare's plays. As Hecht observed about Auden's most Shakespearean poem, *The Sea and the Mirror*, the commentary only begins once the final curtain on the play has already dropped. "The poem, for all its beauties," writes Hecht, "has no action, no plot, and is made up of eloquent meditations in a variety of verse forms."[21]

"Peripeteia" alerts us to this fundamental difference between these two poets. In Hecht, the dramatic transformation, or turn, is everything, reminding us further of Browning's dictum regarding the

---

20. Letter, James Merrill to Stephen Yenser, 2 June 1973: "Last night Wm Meredith passed on to me something called 'The Great American Poem'—itself (whenever completed) to consist of 100 lines by 100 different practitioners. It's about half done and sounds like a trip through Tiffany's. My favorite bit so far is the following by Robert Sward & Tony Hecht in that order: 'The Great American Hockey Team / Plays with an emerald puck, like Oberon.'" Hecht's playful line about characters from *A Midsummer Night's Dream*, it bears noting in light of Wright's remark, is perfect pentameter, with a trochaic substitution in the first foot, and anticipates, in its playfulness, "A Love for Four Voices." For Hecht's refractions of Portia's speech in "Venetian Vespers" see Ricks, *True Friendship*, 109–10.
21. Hecht, "Bard on Bard," *Yale Review* 89 (July 2001), 142.

Shakespearean-inspired dramatic monologue more generally: that its focus is on "Action in Character, rather than Character in Action."[22] And, as the poem is about change, we need to view it from its carefully realized, casual beginning, the moment when the slightly fussy, solitary "I" first sinks into his seat in the theater:

> Of course, the familiar rustling of programs,
> My hair mussed from behind by a grand gesture
> Of mink. A little craning about to see
> If anyone I know is in the audience,
> And, as the house fills up,
> A mild relief that no one there knows me.
> A certain amount of getting up and down
> From my aisle seat to let the others in.
> Then my eyes wander briefly over the cast,
> Management, stand-ins, make-up men, designers,
> Perfume and liquor ads, and rise prayerlike
> To the false heaven of rosetted lights,
> The stucco lyres and emblems of high art
> That promise, with crude Broadway honesty,
> Something less than perfection:
> Two bulbs are missing and Apollo's bored.

It's hard to know what to admire most: the initial grand gesture of mink mussing up the hair in our mildly annoyed speaker? Or the wandering eyes moving about and eventually upward, toward a false Broadway heaven, prayerlike (in anticipation of a later miracle)? Or the pun on lyres to be reactivated later ("Can it be that poems lie")? Or the concluding joke, properly sized in perfect pentameter, about Apollo's being bored, in conjunction with two "missing bulbs"—a reflection of the less than fine conditions of the Broadway theater and a comment as well on the uninspired speaker-poet himself.

"Peripeteia" works as a poem because over the course of its ninety-three lines it goes from a fully realized "some place"—we have all been in this person's seat—to a romantic somewhere we all hope to enjoy. But it wouldn't work so well were the speaker any less of a "connoisseur of loneliness." The middle portion of the poem makes a case for a delicious solitude that is excelled in English perhaps only by Andrew

---

22. Browning, Preface to *Strafford: An Historical Tragedy* (1837), in *The Complete Works of Robert Browning*, ed. Roma King, general editor, Morse Peckham, Park Honan, and Gordon Pitts., 17 vols (Athens: Ohio University Press, 1969–2011), vol. 2 (1970), 9.

Marvell in "The Garden." In the brief interval between the lights
going down and the curtain rising, the speaker, having temporarily
sloughed off his fallen identity as one among the "Foul-breathed,
gum-chewing" crowd, happily retreats into a green world of the imagination. Controlled and populated by his own thoughts, savoring "all
the sweet and sour of loneliness," he finds,

> In an endless umber landscape, a stubble field
> Under a lilac, electric, storm-flushed sky,
> Where, in companionship with worthless stones,
> Mica-flecked, or at best some rusty quartz,
> I stood in childhood, waiting for things to mend.

Readers of *The Hard Hours*, especially of "A Hill," or of "Apprehensions"
in this volume, will discover the memories here comfortable by comparison—the only discontent surfacing in the note of perhaps too
much solitude. Like Adam before the creation of Eve, the speaker can,
however, turn,

> To solitary, self-denying work
> That issues in something harmless, like a poem,
> Governed by laws that stand for other laws,
> Both of which aim, through kindred disciplines,
> At the soul's knowledge and habiliment.
> In any case, in a self-granted freedom,
> The mind, lone regent of itself, prolongs
> The dark and silence; mirrors itself, delights
> In consciousness of consciousness, alone,
> Sufficient, nimble, touched with a small grace.

The beginning of this passage is often quoted out of context, as if it
were Hecht's *ars poetica*, but there is an element of exaggeration in this
finely rendered depiction of the potentially narcissistic poet, and by the
time we arrive at the overly self-absorbed second sentence—three
"selfs" in two lines—the whole passage begins to seem a bit over the
top. We, he, and also, though we're not there yet, she, hang in the balance; but the moment, the dramatic moment, that is, has been perfectly
calculated by our poet at the close of this stanza; for at the opening of
the next the curtain does rise on the wider vista of the stage.

Still, the speaker isn't going to give himself up readily to thoughts of
another even if the other is, in the first instance, no less than "Something
by Shakespeare." Nor would we want him to, since it seems only right

that he reserve himself for a someone *really* worthwhile: a Miranda who, like Hermione in *The Winter's Tale*, can suddenly come to life. That act, or action, of the speaker's increasingly discombobulated involvement and resistance is the matter and point of the grand finale. Stirred out of himself by the near catastrophe at the end of *The Tempest*, a no longer bored speaker is led out of the theater by a coup de théâtre more surprising than Shakespeare's:

> Something is happening. Some consternation.
> Are the knives out? Is someone's life in danger?
> And can the magic cloak and book protect?
> One has, of course, real confidence in Shakespeare.
> And I relax in my plush seat, convinced
> That prompt as dawn and genuine as a toothache
> The dream will be accomplished, provisionally true
> As anything else one cares to think about.
> The players are aghast. Can it be the villain,
> The outrageous drunks, plotting the coup d'état,
> Are slyer than we thought? Or we more innocent?
> Can it be that poems lie? As in a dream,
> Leaving a stunned and gap-mouthed Ferdinand,
> Father and faery pageant, she, even she,
> Miraculous Miranda, steps from the stage,
> Moves up the aisle to my seat, where she stops,
> Smiles gently, seriously, and takes my hand
> And leads me out of the theatre, into a night
> As luminous as noon, more deeply real,
> Simply because of her hand, than any dream
> Shakespeare or I or anyone ever dreamed.

In casually demoting Shakespeare as well as himself, the closing lines form an elegant compliment: a bit of hyperbole in keeping with the comic ending, with its hints of a marriage in the image of the hand. And yet, at the same time, we should recognize that in this modern-day romantic revision of a Renaissance play, there is truth in this feigning, for it is the lady who breaks out of her appointed theatrical role. She takes the "hand" of her unsuspecting male admirer and leads him into the night. Together, the two leave behind the gum-chewing audience and the poet's earlier self, the narcissistic connoisseur of loneliness. I don't think either Shakespeare or earlier Hecht ever did quite dream this reality. So if reality trumps art in the figure of the hand, art would seem to trump reality in imagining this ending. Of course, Shakespeare, too, said as much in the late plays; and in this comparable spiraling between art and nature, the two bards together seem on equal footing.

Not all Hecht's dramatic monologues are as perfectly plotted as "Peripeteia." The five paragraphs, or stanzas, correspond to the five-act structure of the usual Shakespearean play, with the Prosperian poet even calculating the peripety, or turn, to begin at what would be the equivalent of the fifth act of the play. But the process of dramatic action is crucial to most of Hecht's monologues, with the drama relying not simply on the evolution of thought, on "Character in Action," often signaled by variations in metrical emphases, but on those lexical properties heightened by verse: puns, echoes, allusions, contrasts in vocabulary, shifts in imagery—what we think of as a talented poet's necessary stock-in-trade—and also on "the hidden architecture" associated with typology. Miranda is another merciful Portia-figure; the isolated speaker/poet is a bored Bassanio in need of a new life, but it is art that enacts the miraculous transformation of the old into the new, not (for Hecht) the divisive Pauline Gospels, with the insistence on separating people out on the basis of religious faith.

In a revealing note, Joseph Brodsky recounted a conversation with Hecht, in which he recalled Hecht saying "something to the effect that all [t]hat we do in our profession is essentially a commentary to—'making sense out of' you've said—the Holy Book," a sentiment with which Brodsky was in agreement.[23] We might think of Shakespeare here as performing a thankful intervention: the biblical elements of miracle and salvation are within human reach in this poem, are realized through Shakespeare in "Peripeteia," in a manner that also throws an odd typological light in the opposite direction: on another dramatic monologue, "The Grapes," and the articulated plight of its speaker.

An isolate from the outset—the speaker is not identified until we're deep into the poem—the chambermaid dwells initially in a beautifully described, shadowy darkness, and while she too has an epiphany of sorts, produced, in this case, by observing "a crystal bowl of grapes / In ice-water," the vision only deepens her sense of isolation and the mysterious recognition on her part that "there was nothing left for me now, nothing but years," that "My destiny was cast and Marc-Antoine / Would

---

23. Letter, Brodsky to AH, 18 April 1990. Hecht Archive.

not be called to play a part in it." Without carrying over the heavy biblical freight associated with hermeneutics, the poem maintains, amid its Shakespearean echoes and confessional circumstance, an underlying typological structure in its reliance on the antinomies of darkness and light, old world and new, the shadowed valley (of death) where she works and the "bright green fields across the valley / Where, at the *Beau Rivage*, patrons are laved / In generous tides of gold," and a younger "Marc-Antoine" is "One of the bellboys." But it is not within her powers to halt time and cross over into the light, and the judgment she passes upon herself, while hardly intended to match the heightened measure of Othello's final speech, is absolute if not quite remorseless, with a pathos distinctly its own. Her destiny is not to commit suicide but to be a "sole survivor":

> And I knew at last, with a faint, visceral twitch,
> A flood of weakness that comes to the resigned,
> What it must have felt like in that rubber boat
> In mid-Pacific, to be the sole survivor
> Of a crash, idly dandled on that blank
> Untroubled waste, and see the light decline,
> Taper and fade in graduated shades
> Behind the International Date Line—
> An accident I read about in *Time*.

Othello would never speak of having "a faint, visceral twitch," but what can we say about a chambermaid who uses phrases like "idly dandled on that blank / Untroubled waste" or "laved / In generous tides of gold"? Hecht's elevated diction here and elsewhere in his dramatic monologues (most notably, again, with a female voice in "The Transparent Man") has been criticized, causing some readers to distrust the voice in the poem. Hecht's response is illuminating on a number of levels, even if, by his own admission, it will not be entirely satisfying for all.[24] Arguing on behalf of a greater flexibility in poetry than might be found, say, in realistic fiction, he understood the central challenge in the longer monologues to be one of maintaining the

---

24. Quotations from Hecht are taken from two letters to Ira Sadoff, 22 October 1981 (*SL*, 191–3) and 10 November 1981. I take Sadoff's criticism of the "diction" in "The Grapes" as representative, and Hecht's two responses as the most extensive defense of his use of heightened language in the longer dramatic monologues, but with important implications for many of his poems. As Hecht notes, the distinction between "shorter" and "longer" monologues is itself imprecise.

reader's interest. "As a poem lengthens, I would claim that the poet has an obligation to his reader, whose interest must continuously be courted, to rise above what might dangerously become the pedestrian limitations of insight and vocabulary that might conventionally be assigned to a particular character." This freedom includes the belief that "virtually any character, if given the chance, would rise to rather remarkable pitches of eloquence," and he found the greatest support for this classically inflected, rhetorical view of language in Shakespeare—not only in the examples of Bottom and Caliban, whose social status would, on the surface, hardly seem to justify their separate poetic flights, but in "a splendid quotation from Othello [:]"

> ... do but stand upon the foaming shore,
> The chidden billows seem to pelt the clouds;
> The wind-shaked surge, with high and monstrous mane,
> Seems to cast water on the burning Bear
> And quench the Guards of th'ever-fixed pole.
> I never did like molestation view
> On the enchafed flood.

About which Hecht continues:

> It is a speech of extraordinary strength, hyperbole, and majesty, and Shakespeare assigns it, not to a major character in the play, nor even to one designated for howsoever small a role in the list of dramatis personae, but to a nameless "second gentleman," who has virtually nothing else to say or do in the play.[25]

Whether a memory of this particular visionary moment underlies, or is a source for, the "nameless" chambermaid's revelation in

---

25. See letter, AH to Sadoff, 10 November 1981. The quotation from *Othello* is from 2.1.12–17. The reference to Bottom is to his "dream" (*A Midsummer Night's Dream* 4.1.200–19) and to Caliban, to his speech beginning "The isle is full of noises" (*The Tempest* 3.2.135–43). Hecht also cites as a precedent Frost's "The Witch of Coös," but Frost is generally more relevant to Hecht's further development of the dramatic monologue, as in "The Transparent Man." To Hecht's own defense, one might add the following observation made by Langdon Hammer with regard to "The Grapes": "the effect is not naturalistic (only a rare chambermaid would speak of 'the meaning of sidereal time'). But verisimilitude is not the point. The poet doesn't presume to speak for the chambermaid; he is asking her to speak for him—or, to give voice to a condition, a primal loneliness, they each feel. The pentameter that he creates for her links her to great blank verse speakers of the past, from Shakespeare to Frost" ("Two Formalists: Remembering Thom Gunn and Anthony Hecht," *American Scholar* 74.1 (Winter 2005), 51–2.

"The Grapes" is perhaps impossible to say for certain, but she enjoys a similar license of expression and imagery to accompany her moment of "discovery":

> They were green grapes, or, rather,
> They were a sort of pure, unblemished jade,
> Like turbulent ocean water, with misted skins,
> Their own pale, smoky sweat, or tiny frost.
> I leaned over the table, letting the sun
> Fall on my forearm, contemplating them.
> Reflections of the water dodged and swam
> In nervous incandescent filaments
> Over my blouse and up along the ceiling.
> And all those little bags of glassiness,
> Those clustered planets, leaned their eastern cheeks
> Into the sunlight, each one showing a soft
> Meridian swelling where the thinning light
> Mysteriously tapered into shadow,
> To cool recesses, to the tranquil blues
> That then were pillowing the *Beau Rivage*.
> And watching I could almost see the light
> Edge slowly over their simple surfaces,
> And feel the sunlight moving on my skin
> Like a warm glacier. And I seemed to know
> In my blood the meaning of sidereal time
> And know my little life had somehow crested.

Little here can be definitively attributed to Shakespeare: Hecht's blank verse phrasing is leisurely—the oceanic and planetary imagery stretching out for eleven lines—especially when compared to the syntactically compacted, muscular personification of the storm in the second gentleman's description, although the Latinate swell of Hecht's "nervous incandescent filaments" sounds Shakespearean enough (as in Macbeth's "murderous seas incarnadine"), as does the concluding use of "crested" (as in its appearance in Cleopatra's eulogy to Antony: "his legs bestrid the Ocean his rear'd arm / Crested the world"), but now scaled down, or rounded, to fit the present circumstances, with the phrase "my little life," calling up, with fetching irony, Prospero's famous lines, "We are such stuff / As dreams are made on, and *our little life* / Is rounded with a sleep" (*The Tempest* 4.1.157–8; my italics).

All of these possibilities enrich the poetic texture, amplify and contextualize the chambermaid's circumstances, for the reader's benefit and pleasure; but for the author, what is significant is the Shakespearean stamp—a liberating one—authorizing Hecht's belief that the needs of the dramatic situation, not an absolute fidelity to a character's social station, determine the scope and shape of the poem's language. The expansive syntax and brilliant imagery account for the impact of the incandescent recognition of aging, common to all, but unique to her situation and psyche. Sensuous in every respect, her monologue is a valediction to the sensual life, a quiet, even heroic reckoning of a life alone, "idly dandled on that blank / Untroubled waste."

There are dangers, of course, with an overreliance on the pentameter line. Auden rather bizarrely noted that "it is a commonplace that Shakespeare's characters are all rather like each other at emotional climaxes." A commonplace that won't stand much scrutiny, but Auden then went on to observe, less controversially: "Blank verse is a medium suitable to a certain type of character, the heroic: when the emotional tension is relaxed it tends to become flat."[26] Hecht was certainly aware of this danger (as he was of the line's potentially ennobling strength), and he has been occasionally accused of succumbing to both. As part of the exchange quoted earlier in this chapter, Brodsky, who called Hecht, in 1981, "without question, the best poet writing in English today," in 1990 expressed impatience for what he perceived to be long stretches of soft, meandering pentameter verse in "See Naples and Die"; and while Hecht rallied to a defense on this occasion, as we will see in Chapter 8, on an earlier, different one, involving his collaboration with George Dimock on a translation of Sophocles' *Oedipus at Colonus*, he recognized his faulty rendering of,

the play in blank verse, which has had, in more places than I can care to think of now, the effect of very inferior Shakespearean rhythms and diction, and a certain amount of detectable padding. There are places where an elaborate and complex syntax, no doubt parallel to the Greek, but very "Shakespearean" for all that, is too much at odds with modern, or at least less stylized, rhetorical modes of address; and which would require such concentrated attention for the audience to follow as to become a serious irritation and an impediment to clarity and enjoyment.[27]

26. Corcoran, *Shakespeare and the Modern Poet*, 177, quoting from Auden's 1932 review of John Skelton's *Complete Poems*.
27. Letter, AH to George Dimock, 2 May 1975 (*SL*, 155–6); for his response to Brodsky see the draft letter which I've tentatively dated April 1990 (*SL*, 234–5).

"A serious irritation and an impediment to clarity and enjoyment": Hecht could be as severe on himself as he sometimes was on others. He eventually disbanded the project. All that remains are two stanzaic fragments: "Praise for Kolonos" in *Millions of Strange Shadows*, a trophy of sorts as his only surviving attempt at what he took "to be a legitimately free and licensed English version of Sapphics";[28] and "The Chorus from *Oedipus at Colonos*" in *The Transparent Man*, partially excavated in "The Vow," is now given fuller amplitude of address.

But in 1981, in full mid-career flight and unfettered by the requirements of translating from the Greek, Hecht was at the height of his Shakespearean inventiveness in "Love for Four Voices." "Here we have fallen transposingly in love." The opening hypermetrical line of the poem belongs to Hermia, but it is Hecht's, too, commenting on the happy prospect of rewriting—of transposing in a different key—the plight of Shakespeare's youthful lovers as originally presented in *A Midsummer Night's Dream* and of composing a work in homage, as the subtitle notes, to Franz Joseph Haydn.[29] And as Auden did for *The Sea and the Mirror*, Hecht invents a variety of forms for the occasion. Each speaker is accorded his or her own metrical and stanzaic pattern, as well as instrumental association: Hermia as First Violin; Helena as Second; Lysander with the Viola; and Demetrius as Cello. Accompanying the leads are some pleasant choric groupings marked "Tutti," and rounding off the four movements is the return of Hermia in a twenty-one-line epilogue that serves as the poet's apologia or defense, much as Caliban's had served Auden. And to this variety of verse forms Hecht adds a plot, tonally keyed to the four movements of the Quartet's different musical markers but hinging on the oldest of stories: the fundamental change that happens to individuals, and individual expression—the sound of their voice—with the realization of sex; and in the process of orchestrating this machine-less mask, Hecht manages what neither Auden

28. Letter, AH to W. D. Snodgrass, 27 March 1977.
29. Hecht's use of "transpose" was not, to my knowledge, influenced by Julia Kristeva's concept of "transposition" in *La Revolution du langue poétique* (1974; English version New York: Columbia University Press, 1984) to designate "the passage from one sign system to another," although her version of "intertextuality," as opposed to source study, is a useful way to regard the matter of "semantic polyvalence" prevalent in this poem, especially as Hecht moves with great fluidity between musical and dramatic texts. *The Kristeva Reader*, ed. Toril Moi (New York: Columbia University Press, 1986), 111. I want to thank Kim Hedlin for initially raising this possibility.

nor Shakespeare did or sought: a fuller differentiation of the four lovers as characters.

Hecht's own comments about the poem's origins are too illuminating (and charming) not to be quoted in full. They appear in the context of preparing the poem for publication in a fine press edition:

I'm glad you like the idea of doing the quartet, but I question, just as you do, whether a portrait of Haydn would be sufficiently relevant. The association of his name with the poem is a highly personal one and very subjective. I became enamored of his Opus 77, # 2, and wondered to myself for quite a while about how it might be possible to capture its extraordinary varieties of mood and tone, of gaiety and seriousness, and total coherence in a poem. Then it occurred to me that the moods of love offered just such variety; and suddenly the four young lovers of *A Midsummer Night's Dream* presented themselves as the fitting cast or instrumentalists for my purpose. The poem, therefore, is neither purely Haydn nor Shakespeare, though I think it is closer to the latter in that, like his play, it is about love, and employs his characters, though they are entirely altered and modernized to suit my purposes. And I have had fun dealing with them because they are paid so little attention in general when the play is thought of or talked about—everyone turning first to Puck or Bottom or Titania and Oberon or even Theseus and Hippolyta, while the four young lovers seem to remain blank, conventionalized, stereotypic. So how about something sexy instead of an eighteenth-century bewigged portrait?[30]

Something sexy indeed: the "fun" Hecht enjoyed in composing the poem flows over into both the happy play with language and the situation itself, into a kind of Shakespearean revelry with puns as well as in the opportunity to invent a new reality for the lovers. As with much else, we might take the poem's title, for instance, in a double sense. "A Love for Four Voices" signals the distribution of a topic (love) among its four voices, and it hints too of the author's love for the four voices he has created. To "fall transposingly in love," moreover, not only hints at the underlying motive that generates the poem; it also describes several other features central to the sequence. Each character—each lyric, in fact—gives individual voice to the transforming power or effect of falling in love while the sequence as a whole is structured around the concept of temporality or change, the "fall," that is, that occurs with the act of seduction. The decussation at the center of this sequence, furthermore, is the cross-over, the transposition, from pre- to post-coital love. To indicate as much, Hecht's headings (*Allegro Moderato, Minuetto:*

30. Letter, AH to Michael McCurdy, publisher of the Penmaen Press, 2 May 1982.

Presto ma non troppo) follow, with slight variations, Haydn's until the poet gets to the third movement, the *Andante*, to which he adds *"post-coitum triste."* Needless to say, there is no such designation in Haydn, just as in *A Midsummer Night's Dream*, although chastity is sometimes threatened, there is no sex. Shakespeare's youthful lovers arrive at court in the fifth act unsullied, even if the play, as Hecht understood it to be, is often couched in shadows and otherwise "cunningly hedged about with peripheral omens and reminders of the imperfection of life."[31]

In "Love for Four Voices," the much sought-after intercourse between couples is realized off-stage, as it were, between the second and third movements. *"Post-coitum triste,"* or as Demetrius says: "Between post oak and propter oak / Falls the inevitable shade." Hecht's play with the logical fallacy, *post hoc ergo propter hoc* ("after this, therefore because of this"), forms a complex allusion to Eliot, as Christopher Ricks has explored,[32] but we don't want to miss the forest for the trees and ignore the full frontal, before-and-after, phallic joke as part of the fallacy, in keeping with Demetrius' humor, and the larger puzzlement about the will of desire toward which it points and the poem unveils. "Before, a joy propos'd, behind, a dream," as Shakespeare remarks in Sonnet 129.

If the division of the poem into four parts pays homage to Haydn and the characters to Shakespeare, the lyrics are pure Hecht. Or better yet, impure Hecht, given the range of situations and jokes that keeps this shadowy comedy happily afloat. Diminutive Hermia, as first violin, rightly establishes the theme and tone, from which the rest of the work descends:

> Here we have fallen transposingly in love,
> And the fireflies, the Japanese lanterns, flare
> With little conjugate passions, images of
> The cordial, chambered ignitions of the heart.

"Cordial" points to the civility of address in this miniature garden-like setting, to the civility underlying the concept of transposing nature into art, "fireflies" into "Japanese lanterns"; but "cordial" also puns on the Latin (*cor*) for heart, just as the reference to the "chambered ignitions" reminds us of the intimacy associated with chamber music, while the phrase "little conjugate passions" points in a different direction. The

---

31. Letter, AH to Joseph Summers, 11 October 1990 (*SL*, 236–7).
32. Ricks, *True Friendship*, 84–5.

shorter of the two female leads in Shakespeare, Hermia is distinguished from the taller but more emotionally fragile Helena by her height and her expressed marital loyalty toward Lysander.

Precious as it is, the heady, delicate, politely circumscribed world of passion associated with the first violin's airy "Here" also hints at a beyond "below," indeed "far down below," that will be developed more firmly into a fundamental ground note by the masculine viola and cello. (We will reach rock bottom in Lysander's prose disquisition on man's "mere fundament," saved for the last of the lovers' soliloquies.) For the moment, though, whatever slippery sexual suggestions surface in the stock image of the pleasure craft wandering in the cove (as in Thomas Carew's "A Rapture"), they are quickly transposed by the poet-composer into a *mise en abŷme*, a complex set of reflections on the poem's art—nature's "broad-loomed duplicate" being woven before our eyes:

> Far down below, the lilting, debonair
> Pleasure craft blink and wander in the cove
> Like slippery constellations, as if man's art
> Had made a prayer rug of the firmament,
> A broad-loomed duplicate night wherein to trace
> Patterns of happy prospect, drawn from the blent,
> Breath-taking features of a cherished face.

As the reference to the "cherished face" suggests, we're still in the distant realm of Petrarchan worship, although there is, as yet, no direct first-person address. But Hermia is also warming to her role in the beautiful closing aria, in "smooth ascending thirds," now spoken from the point of view of a couple ("our whispered words") and concluding with her signature pun on "husband":

> Lemon verbena blooms in the tufa wall,
> And the mild night air, warm as our whispered words,
> Circulates like a bloodstream, invisible
> Yet parallel as smooth ascending thirds
> To our most inward workings. Warmth and youth,
> All the clear promptings of this clement weather,
> Invest our bodies with a looming truth
> To be pursued and husbanded together.

Even the old "weather"/"together" rhyme is nicely chummy, as if Hermia is about to become a Broadway star, a role a bit more fitting for Hecht's Helena, as we'll see.

With the mention of "husband," Lysander arrives right on cue but in a different key. As the poet teases out a darker strand of meaning associated with Hermia's "looming truth," this one tied to the loom of Fate, he introduces a different stanza to accent the change, a modular descent toward "another night" than the one Hermia had in mind: "the fixed future, where neither glance shall linger / Nor pulse nor god prevail." Lysander's is the melancholy viola's drawn-out somber note. The "warning finger" alluded to in the first stanza introduces more than just a body part, as we work our way downward in the second stanza:

> Diminished sevenths, modular descents
> Full of alarming jumps
> And sudden accidentals strike a note,
> Brief as a lovers' quarrel,
> That shakes us with an obscure significance.
> Like a whiff of creosote
> Tainting the garden, they proclaim in trumps
> The *carpe noctem* moral.

Hecht is not trying to mimic, in the manner of Dryden's "Alexander's Feast," the different sounds associated with each instrument. Rather, he is using the language of musical notation to alert us to the startling, fractious movement in this section and to imagine the dissonance that is their moralized subject here and in the third stanza:

> These dissonances but serve to underscore
> The score nobody knows
> Except the taciturn composer, Fate.
> Sensing at the deep base
> Of our being the ultimate cadences before
> They gather to their close,
> We feel the fickle fingering and confess
> It's already getting late.

The pun on "score" is surely, deliberately, heavy-handed. Slightly more modulated is the "ultimate cadence" produced by having the long suspended rhyme that mates "Fate," the concluding word of one sentence, with the expected "late," the concluding word of the poem. We arrive at the end, "the *carpe noctem* moral," almost ahead of time.

Fortunately, there is Helena to liven things up with her blowsy speech and loose lines. "You think you know who you are, when all at once / You stand amazed." She is the husky alto, the second violin to Hermia's first. Hecht's lines capitalize on Helena's association in Shakespeare

with long legs and poor self-image, as well as more generally on the
pun on "amazed" with the maze into which Shakespeare's lovers enter
when they run off into the woods outside of the city of Athens—the
play's symbol of rational order. In Helena's case, looking into the mirror produces a surprising image of her new sexy self:

> But who's that nymph the cheval glass now discloses?
> This calls for thought.
> It seems to you you've seen her. Couched on roses?
> Attended by a little, wingèd brood?
> Somewhere. Perhaps in Kenneth Clark's "The Nude,"
>   Bearing the alias
> Of *Miss O'Murphy*, or superbly wrought
> In ravishing undress
>
> By Renoir or Correggio or Lachaise.

"Things base and vile, holding no quantity, / Love can transpose to form
and dignity": Helena's couplet in *A Midsummer Night's Dream* (1.2.231–2)
has sometimes been seen as a motivating gloss for Hecht's poem, in part
because his poem activates the musical puns on "base and vile." (It is in
other ways an imperfect gloss, the transposition failing to capture the
lovers' comical and undignified downward plight.) But the lines fit
Hecht's Helena better than anyone else, although in a comically ironic
way ("you know, you know"). She is transported by "the upright ways /
Of a lad," Cupid, or Boss Cupid, as Thom Gunn would call him, into
a pornographic movie star, a climactic figure of desire:

> And then you know: you are the latest find
>   Of Hollywood
> Featured in private screenings of the mind
> In an inventory of post-Freudian sex
> Called "Civilization and its Discothèques."
>   In a lingua franca phrase
> Of body language at last you've understood
> What gauds and gilds your days.

At which point, in this drama of entrances and exits, appears
Demetrius. With him, we can descend no further down the scale in
more than one sense. His opening line tells us all we need to know
about his character at this point:

> Mine is the firm bass clef that shall unlock
> A world of passions in our *théâtre à clef*

> Which is all about the ways of human clay
> When freed from the simple props of summer stock.
> Enter, Myself, for a turn about the stage.
> I muse on the causes of my ecstasy,
> Displayed well-stacked in billowing deshabille,
> Yielding in levantine concubinage.

A buffoon, priapic and narcissistic, he speaks in blunt quatrains (although Hecht still can't resist some fanciful out-of-character rhymes). His puns hardly require glossing: his French, while connecting him with Helena, has made post-Freudian sex coarse and earthy, as eye and ear wrestle over whether to pronounce "*clef*" as "clef" (with an intimation of "cleft" for vagina) or "clay" as in "lay."

Hecht has always been good at satirizing a certain kind of masculine stance: "I am the singular thing on which she dotes," Demetrius notes. "Singular," maybe; single certainly: the reductions worth both ways. The pool she is said to represent but he looks into shows "Intoxicating images of Me, / Classical, isolate, withdrawn and cool." "Withdrawn" hints at a lack, alack, and "cool" the absence of its opposite: being *cool*, meaning hot. As with Shakespeare, there seems little that will bring Hollywood Helena and narcissistic Demetrius together except "the taciturn composer, Fate," or Time, and the imperious pressure of form. The sonnet that concludes the first movement works to bring all the lovers under one roof in a choric straitjacket "that binds in ligatures beloved and lover." But now that they are pressed together into a single "Tutti," each "seeking the counterpart for which it longs," the question for the composer-poet and for us is what will he do with them?

In Shakespeare, the woods allow for confusion and mix-ups. Under the mistaken activities of Puck, sprinkling his magical potion of "love-in-idleness," the two men who had initially wooed Hermia, Lysander and Demetrius, come to pursue a disbelieving and increasingly paranoid Helena. Hecht's variation on this transposition begins with the second movement, the "*Minuetto: Presto ma non troppo*" (quickly but not too quickly), in which a dialogue on the theme of time allows time for each to talk to his opposite number. Lysander, punningly, to the group:

> Question: Isn't to fall in love to fall
> Away from Time or out of it, to break
> Tempo in a sort of contretemps,

Flouting the linear ways of chronicle?
Only in fantasies and tales of love
Can we imagine the "terminally well."

But it is Helena, not Hermia, who responds, suavely, as if espoused:
"Agreed, my dear…," just as it is Demetrius, not Lysander, who fin-
ishes off Hermia's thoughts comparing lovers to tourists:

And so it is, as you were going to say,
With lovers. They pass through familiar sordors,
Worn curbstones foul with uncollected garbage,
Which they translate into the Côte d'Azur.
Noting the gleam on the lip of a coffee mug,
They remember all the ricochets of light
That return from darkened corners in Vermeer,
Reflective, upon a beautiful young servant.

Admittedly, Hecht can't flout the "linear ways of chronicle" with quite
as many zigzags as Shakespeare. He's limited to four lovers and the
two-dimensional page; but he can suggest through imagery "ricochets of
light" coming from corners of darkness, and swift, sudden shifts in language as if characters were changing or exchanging roles on the spot.
Demetrius now appears in different dress, speaking about Vermeer, as
if magically transformed by Puck's "love-in-idleness," or, rather, by a
modern equivalent as suggested by this passage: "eros-in-tourism."
Translating the erotic in Hecht, as it is in Shakespeare, involves updating,
transposing: from Ovid to Shakespeare, from Shakespeare to Hecht; from
classical to Renaissance to modern. As Corcoran remarked of "Love for
Four Voices," "this is poetry as delighted repossession and self-possession,"
but its rambunctious vulgarities, its ever looming Id, make further comparisons of the poem with Russian dolls a little iffy.[33]

As with updating the idiom, so with modernizing the dating situation: the confusion only intensifies, as I've already suggested, in the
transition into the third movement, the "*Andante: post-coitum triste.*"
We don't really know who slept with whom, only the individual
post-coital responses of each. (Hermia humorously identifies her mysterious, her "hermetic," bedmate as one Fred Trismegistus, the fabled
hermeticist intimating her name but who otherwise has little connection with wisdom.) Eros, tightly bound in the sonnet closing the

33. Corcoran, *Shakespeare and the Modern Poet*, 15.

first movement, is released in the unrhymed group hymn to Venus
Anadyomene ("Venus Rising out of the Sea") that concludes the second. The final lines read:

> Anadyomene, restless, of the waters,
> Powerful, rash and salty, hear our prayer.
> Make glad our passage with your ritornello;
> Furnish each humble thing that greets our sight
> With pure ipseity; transpose the world
> With augmentations of your major theme.

Their request is heard, returned, and augmented. Transposing the
world—in the sense of being turned upside down—is exactly what we
and the lovers get in the post-coital third movement, as the adjectives,
"powerful, rash and salty," serve perfectly to characterize, in that order,
the speeches of Demetrius, Hermia, and Helena. Demetrius is simply
exhausted, overwhelmed by the power of love. His previous sturdy bass
clef and confident touring measures have been reduced by a foot, into
a languid, elegiac, tetrametric, post-coital, pastoral dreaminess. Pre-
eminently a mood piece, it's hard not to quote it all, so easily does it
slide down the page, until the allusive "post oak" bump at the bottom:

> Late afternoon. The canted light
> Sieves down through elevated glooms
> Of linden, sycamore and beech
> As lengthening shadows stripe the grass.
> The cricket concertmaster's A
> Is taken up through the dense fields,
> Heavy with scent and irony,
> Dotted with common everlasting,
> Bitter dock and cocklebur.
> From the cool shadows of this rock,
> These crowding blues and heliotropes,
> As from some attic of my youth
> I gaze out at the distances
> That contrast renders almost white,
> Like frocks of garden-party girls
> I once knew or desired to know,
> Speckled and flecked by shadow-leaves
> Like missing jigsaw puzzle parts.
> And whether those yearnings were stillborn
> Or were met with kindness, now they lie
> Like quilts of sunlight spread to dry,

Scattered and thin and dimly gold
And permanently out of reach—
Small flags of failure, or, at best,
Triumphs with all their glory lost.
Between post oak and propter oak
Falls the inevitable shade.

By contrast, Hermia wakes up embarrassed over her rash behavior with Fred. Her vocal difference with Demetrius—and her earlier self—could hardly be greater. In a mode of Whitmanian cradle-rocking, too long to quote in full but expressive in its phrasing, she somehow finds a rhyme for "rockabye" in "where am I" to underscore her confusion:

Out of the cotton batting clouds, the scentless gauze
Of sleep, out of the pendulous rockabye
Of dreamt treetops, one floats down leaf-like to be received
Without resistance by the sustaining bed
As, one by one, the faculties grab their discarded
Clothing and make themselves decent, the five
Little senses answer the rollcall roster of school
And that ten o'clock scholar, the mind, late
As always, shows up confused, asking, "Where am I?"

In the *Quartet in F Major*, Haydn's "Andante" is a movement of great simplicity and serene beauty in passing around its theme from instrument to instrument, from cello to violin, major to minor. Early Beethoven was impressed by it. Inflect it with post-coital *tristesse* and these two melancholic low points by Hecht's lovers may well be the poetic highlights in the sequence. Knowingly errant, the lonely lovers evince an inviting pathos, rueful humor, and pity from their composer-maker, who, like Shakespeare, cares about his creations:

But meanwhile your own clothes,
strewn here and
There, begin to recall your imbecilities
Of last night. What will your hostess, a friend since
grade school, say?
Better get dressed as quietly as possible
And slip out for a cold, long, sobering walk.

Amid the strewn clothes and phrases, we recall that in Shakespeare Hermia and Helena had once been friends from schooldays before they went off to the forest.

It remains only for Salty Helena to break the spell with an abrupt allusion:

> Take Waller's stoic, gladiatorial rose,
> Saluting you as it prepares to die
> On orders, simply to make a vulgar point:
> That Time and the poet's nose are out of joint,
> That flesh is grass, and he's a blade who grows
> Green till he has what you can best supply.

And for Lysander, sounding like Bottom sounding like the earlier Demetrius, to transpose the prayer to Venus for "pure ipseity"—divine selfhood—into prose stripped of romantic illusions:

Man, that with the heated imagination of a poet lies down in the finest linens to caresses, must rise in due course *from the sack* in all the frosty solitude of a philosopher. "How came this spell upon me," he inquires, "that made my very flesh to stand on end? made me, who am otherwise all head, vision and mind, become mere fundament, pure Bottom, someone's ass?" It is sheer fantasy confers such power: I vote her beautiful out of my need. Her grace is in the gland of the beholder. This is plain masturbation, thinly disguised, in which I dub her my sea-born Galatea, and she brightly replies, "Baby, you're aces." Bodies themselves in plain truth are no more shapely than potatoes; they are as pallid of flesh and take up their residence under the same brown sod. Let him who can be aroused by a potato plight his true oath and purchase wedding bands. I, divested of illusions, must now inhabit among essences.

Racy, colloquial, earthy, but perhaps not "pure Bottom" either, since, like Theseus, he speaks against fancy but in a crazed humor that undoes logic and finds what? A kind of strange poetics or erotics in a potato? But like all the lovers, he—whoever he is—also cannot answer the central question of what happened: "How came this spell upon me"?

In Shakespeare, it is Theseus' spouse-to-be, Hippolyta, who hears overtones of agreement among the lovers, which "grow to something of great constancy" (5.1.26). In Hecht, it is the imprint of form that once again brings them together. For the first and only time in the poem, the lovers speak individually using the same stanza, but saying roughly (although in smoothly composed verse) the same thing in their individual arias. It's difficult to know whom to quote: Helena leads the way, followed by Lysander, then Hermia and Demetrius; but

the order hardly matters. They're all climactically witty, so best to quote
the combined, harmonic finale marked "Tutti":

> And shall not humble humankind
> Aspire to godly ways,
> Utter the disembodied mind
> In fleshly paraphrase?
> Therefore come all ye neophytes,
> Observe the Rule of Thumb;
> With ever more intense delights
> And mounting pleasures, come!

This is the author, we need remind ourselves, of a great many painful
poems: "Rites and Ceremonies," "'More Light! More Light!'" "The
Deodand," and "The Book of Yolek," to name only a few of the more
obvious possibilities. I have always felt a little let down—how could it
be otherwise, given the triumph sounded in the "Tutti"?—that Hecht
didn't end the poem right here, where the musical score stopped, and
we could all leave the theater humming some imagined tune. But perhaps the instinct to follow Shakespeare encouraged a "coda." In any
event, Hermia's apology in Hecht is finely written, a proper closing as
early dramatic custom would have encouraged when there was no
curtain to signal the end of the play; but a little too defensive for so
wonderfully exhilarating and inventive a poem. Along with "Peripeteia,"
another Shakespearean-inspired poem about love, it is Hecht's happiest
and most entertaining, a poem that invites pleasurable reading and
re-reading, especially in relation to its twin "sources." Perhaps the best
ending had already been deployed when Helena responded to Lysander's
observation that "Only in fantasies and tales of love / Can we imagine
the 'terminally well.'"

> Agreed, my dear. Love is in fact the nostrum
> Compounded of plain meum/tuum simples,
> That takes its crabbed critic by the throat
> And renders him a tender Juvenal.

Now to risk a coda to this chapter: after "A Love for Four Voices,"
Shakespeare continued to feed into Hecht's poetry, but not quite with
the same nourishing force or comic flavor. We find echoes, allusions, or
quotations from an array of plays: Banquo from *Macbeth* in "Curriculum

Vitae"; Rosalind from *As You Like It* in "In Memory of David Kalstone"; *Julius Caesar* in "Murmur"; Richard, Duke of Gloucester, from 3 *Henry VI*, in "Death the Punchinello," in conjunction with an epigraph from Kent and the Fool in *King Lear*. No doubt there are other references, each adding something of value, but only one poem might be said to be constructed out of a single reference: the hilariously mean "Lapidary Inscription with Explanatory Note," which begins (deep inhale): "There was for him no more perfect epitaph / Than this from Shakespeare: 'Nothing in his life / Became him like the leaving it'" (*Macbeth* 1.2.7–8). Then the exhale, the imprecation. But even at the height of his Shakespearean infatuation and invention, Hecht rarely was influenced by a single Shakespeare work or by Shakespeare in isolation from other texts; and perhaps one reason why he didn't feel anxiously burdened by the Bard had to do with the fact that Shakespeare also had to share space with a great many other voices and sounds in Hecht's poetry, indeed even with an old photo in "A Birthday Poem."

Christopher Ricks gets it exactly right when he remarks:

Anthony Hecht did not think of himself as being—or yet more liberatingly, did not feel himself to be—the heir to anyone in particular. Great though his respect was for W. H. Auden, he was expansively free from all that can make heirdom a frictive matter. In this fretlessness as to whether he is an heir, Hecht resembles both Eliot and Pound and differs from both [Geoffrey] Hill and [Robert] Lowell.[34]

Just why this is so is probably impossible to determine. The best peek into Hecht's thoughts on this matter can be found in a 1980 letter to the poet David Lehman, also quoted by Ricks. Addressing the topic of literary monuments of the past, Hecht speaks of the

[m]atter of coming to terms with the Ruins of Rome, as in Ronsard and Du Bellay and Piranesi. It is, or seems to be, a choice of whether to consider ourselves the ghosts of ghosts, or the immensely favored beneficiaries of priceless heirlooms. And the final truth is that we have no choice but to become comfortable with the past.[35]

Not every poet, of course, will accept Hecht's view of the "final truth," nor perhaps would early Hecht, even the Hecht of "Rites and

34. Ricks (2010), 143.
35. Letter, AH to David Lehman, 15 December 1980 (*SL*, 187–8).

Ceremonies," in which there are plentiful signs of a poet struggling with the past. But by 1980, with "Peripeteia," "The Venetian Vespers," and "The Grapes" behind him, and "A Love for Four Voices" soon to be on the horizon, and much Shakespeare to be studied and feel right about, it is surely reasonable for Hecht to think of himself not as a ghost of ghosts but as an "immensely favored beneficiar[y] of priceless heirlooms."

We can see this sense of expansive, favored freedom with "sources" still at work in his later poetry, and perhaps nowhere more movingly than in his celebrated "Sarabande on Attaining the Age of Seventy-Seven," the final poem I want to consider in this chapter, and chosen by Robert Hass for inclusion in *The Best American Poetry* for 2001, the same year it appeared in Hecht's last collection of poems, *The Darkness and the Light*:

> Long gone the smoke-and-pepper childhood smell
> Of the smoldering immolation of the year,
> Leaf-strewn in scattered grandeur where it fell,
> Golden and poxed with frost, tarnished and sere.
>
> And I myself have whitened in the weathers
> Of heaped-up Januarys as they bequeath
> The annual rings and wrongs that wring my withers,
> Sober my thoughts and undermine my teeth.
>
> The dramatis personae of our lives
> Dwindle and wizen; familiar boyhood shames,
> The tribulations one somehow survives,
> Rise smokily from propitiatory flames
>
> Of our forgetfulness until we find
> It becomes strangely easy to forgive
> Even ourselves with this clouding of the mind,
> This cinerous blur and smudge in which we live.
>
> A turn, a glide, a quarter-turn and bow,
> The stately dance advances; these are airs
> Bone-deep and numbing as I should know by now,
> Diminishing the cast, like musical chairs.

Reading this late poem is a bit like listening to Handel (who, like many baroque composers, did write a stately Sarabande), in which strands of the past, Monteverdi in particular but Handel's own as well, keep making their way to the surface to create a tonal complexity that can only be called, despite its subject matter, musical and harmonious. George

Herbert is there at the outset, in the epigraph from "The Forerunners": "The harbingers are come. See, see their mark; / White is their colour, and behold my head." Thomas Hardy and (still not to be forgotten) Hamlet are present in the poem as well, now blended together into a new mix in that utterly fantastic eruption, "The annual rings and wrongs that wring my withers." ("Neutral Tones": "wrings with wrongs"; and Hamlet: "Let the gall'd jades winch, our withers are unwrung"—3.2.241) So much rhetorical fancy, youthful wringing and ringing, helps to set off the grave dignity of the line that follows. And we might catch a smoldering whiff of smoke from Shakespeare's Sonnets in the emphasis on seasonal change, especially Sonnet 73, which begins, "That time of year thou may'st in me behold," a poem Hecht had explicated in his Introduction to the Sonnets.

But there is another figure in the shadows here. Whatever other sounds that went into the making of Hecht's late verse, Lear forms a resonant ground note, the ultimate and continuous ritornello. To recall Hecht's letter of 2002 to John Van Doren, in which the poet seeks to explain the metabolic make-up that might have contributed to the timbre of near "despair" in many of his poems:

> It might also be that my experience and reading have contributed to this. It occurs to me that of all Shakespeare's plays *King Lear* is the one I have been and continue to be most moved by. It is probably the bleakest of the plays, the most unconsoling.[36]

Lear's age is "fourscore and upward"; Hecht's is seventy-seven in "Sarabande." This is a case of resemblance, not identity or even direct influence, but a commonality of vision seeping up from below and put into play by Hecht's reference to "the dramatis personae of our lives" and by the bleak but chastening vision, in which this connoisseur of loneliness, this Archduke of Darkness, unflinchingly contemplates the diminishing cast of characters everywhere around him, in diction at once archaic and familiar, stately and striking. The surprise in Hecht, as with Lear, comes with the thought of renunciation: that one is leaving childhood behind, in the beginning, only to discover it is there in the end, in Hecht's case in the game of musical chairs. But the "air" has changed in the meantime: from smoke-and-pepper atmospherics to "bone-deep" clarity, and includes the strangely consoling irony (not

---

36. Letter, AH to John Van Doren, 16 February 2002 (*SL*, 331–2).

consoling for Lear, but for Hecht, now pulling on the Herbertian epigraph) that with "forgetfulness," "this clouding of the mind," comes forgiveness—of "even ourselves." The Shakespearean shadow of Lear seems only a quarter of a turn away, but also, in this case, something to turn away from as "the stately dance advances."

Hecht's is a birthday poem. The poet has another few years ahead of him before arriving at Lear's age, and though he won't sing now like Hardy in "The Darkling Thrush" of "some blessed Hope," Hecht's glide into the new century—his seventy-seventh birthday fell on 16 January 2000—allows for a muted sense of quiescence for having survived past tribulations and endured "this cinerous blur and smudge in which we live." The line in draft read simply, blandly, "a pale necessity by which we live." A quarter-turn of a stanza admits just enough holocaustic and penitential depth to earmark the dance as characteristically Hecht's.

8

Later Flourishings

The Transparent Man and *Flight Among the Tombs*

Although there is a certain truth to the legend that Hecht wrote slowly and published carefully—"he never littered the scene with throwaways," remarked John Hollander in 1997[1]—the publication of Hecht's *Collected Later Poems* in 2003 should give one pause about viewing the total corpus of Hecht's poetry as slender. Published in the poet's eightieth year, the volume included all of the poems from *The Transparent Man* (1990), *Flight Among the Tombs* (1996), and *The Darkness and the Light* (2001). It alone is hefty enough to belie occasional numerical comparisons made of Hecht with Elizabeth Bishop and Philip Larkin. Kindred in other ways perhaps, they were not perfect matches in this.

In the long period represented by the *Collected Later Poems*, I take one sign among many of his continuing creativity the decision by poets as diverse as John Ashbery, Jorie Graham, John Hollander, and Robert Hass to choose a Hecht poem for inclusion in their respective editions for their year of *The Best American Poetry*.[2] "Sarabande" has

1. Hollander, "On Anthony Hecht," *Raritan* 17 (1997), 141.
2. The poems, in order of appearance in *The Best American Poetry* are: "Envoi" (Ashbery, 1988); "Eclogue of the Shepherd and the Townie" (Graham, 1990), both included in *The Transparent Man*; and "Rara Avis in Terris" (Hollander, 1998), and "Sarabande on Attaining the Age of Seventy-Seven" (Hass, 2001), both included in *The Darkness and the Light*. Hecht's uncollected poem, "Motes," was chosen posthumously by Paul Muldoon for inclusion in *The Best American Poetry* (2005). Other signs of general recognition coinciding with the period covered by the *Collected Later Poems* include receiving The Bollingen Prize for Poetry (1983, shared with John Hollander), the Ruth B. Lilly Poetry Prize (1988), the Wallace Stevens Award by the Academy of American Poets (1997), and the Robert Frost Medal by the Poetry Society of America (2000). Hecht was awarded posthumously the National Medal for the Arts in 2005.

been discussed in Chapter 7, and much could be said about the other three. The wordplay in "Envoi" shows Hecht at his most light-fingered and syntactically slippery—one can understand why the poem appealed to Ashbery. The "Eclogue of the Townie and the Shepherd" is a sumptuous, perfectly appointed, descriptively beautiful, funny update on the sometimes dry classic theme of art versus nature, and as out of place as a poem can be in the landscape of American poetry in the 1990s. And equally out of date, although for different reasons, is "Rara Avis in Terris." Hecht borrows a topic and stanzaic form from Richard Wilbur's "All These Birds" and sets off on a wild, satirical ride through the "shady groves of academe," in full attack mode, before arriving at his goal of celebrating "a quarter-century of faultless love" with his wife.

To look for a moment at the shortest of these, "Envoi" is not a poem, I think, that could have appeared in *The Collected Earlier Poems*. Its playfulness is almost entirely a creation of the poet's perception of himself as aging—"A dodderer among these dancing lads," as he parenthetically singles himself out, the slightly archaic idiom in the manner of Housman here drawing attention to his outdated place among a younger generation of poets. (The author of a shrewd essay on "Technique in Housman," Hecht liked to remind his friends that you could spot "A.E. Housman lurking in my initials."[3]) But the poem's soundscape has more than one idiom to it, just as the overall view suggests a poet still holding on to a place in a wider universe.

> A voice that seems to come from outer space,
> Small, Japanese (perhaps the pilot of
> One of these frisbee saucer flights that trace
> Piss-elegant trajectories above
>
> Sharp eyes and index finger landing pads),
> Speaks to me only with its one-watt tweeter
> (A dodderer among these dancing lads)
> And firmly orders: "Take me to your reader."
>
> My Muse. I'd know her anywhere. It's true
> I'm no Bob Dylan, but I've more than one

3. Letter, AH to Richard Wilbur, 5 November 1994, in which Hecht also whimsically notes finding Hilda Doolittle in his wife's name (Helen D'Alessandro) and Robert Penn Warren in Richard P. Wilbur. The essay on Housman is included in Hecht, *Melodies Unheard: Essays on the Mysteries of Poetry* (Baltimore: Johns Hopkins University Press, 2003), 95–105.

Electric fan who likes the things I do:
Putting some English on the words I've spun

And sent careening over stands of birch
To beat the local birds at their own game
Of taking off and coasting in to perch,
Even, perhaps, in pigeon-cotes of fame.

They are my chosen envoys to the vast
Black Forests of Orion and The Bear,
Posterity's faint echo of its past,
And payload lifted into haloed air.

This is a poet who could almost appear trendy if he tried just a bit harder: frisbees, tweeters, Bob Dylan, sci-fi; but it's the spin on words that marks him out as entirely, endearingly, old-fashioned: "'Take me to your reader.'" Reader? Not your leader? Does this poet really care about me? Apparently so, since, small as the voice is, it is known immediately by its firm address (Hecht insisted on a colon after "firmly orders"),[4] which brings together reader, poet, and muse, "My Muse," in caps. And for the benefit of us, his "fans," the poet likes to play games to keep us amused, not just with things arriving from outer space, but with the space on the page to highlight his skill with words, as in the case of the opening line's arrival from white space itself—I'm reminded of Glyn Maxwell's recent remark that "the white is everything but me"[5]—followed by the vertiginous pivot on the word "above" to mark out the line's descent across the enjambment, and then, further along, more dramatically and triumphantly, the gulf across which the poet sends "the words I've spun"—huge space—"careening over stands of birch." Attuned as it is to hearing a small voice, my ear picks up an echo of "stanza" in "stands of," to keep the visual and the aural in play here, even as we nod in agreement over, or rather cheer, the winning run the poet has apparently hit—and on the other team's field, no less. (In this regard, "stands of" is a felicitous replacement for "oaks and" in an earlier draft.)

The whole game comes to a rest of sorts in the final stanza, in which the poet's salute to "my chosen envoys" now references—finally—the

4. Letter, AH to Harry Ford, 1 September 1989, in which Hecht changes the punctuation from a semi-colon to a colon.
5. Glyn Maxwell, *On Poetry* (London: Oberon Books, 2012), 29. By the same logic: "In poems, the black is someone." Maxwell wrote the entry on Hecht for *The Oxford Companion to Twentieth-Century Poetry*, ed. Ian Hamilton (Oxford: Oxford University Press, 1994).

poem's title but with a frisbee-like spin on "Envoi": a final signing-off by sending off his messengers into the dark beyond of outer space. "Final," though, not because the poem is in any sense a traditional "envoi" placed at the end of a work ("go, little book"), but because it imagines the present brief moment in light of how it will be seen retrospectively as but a faint echo of a richer past. (To make this interpretation even stronger, Hecht rewrote the earlier phrase, "A chiming, in the future, of the past" as "Posterity's faint echo of its past.") From this distant prospect in time, "Envoi" turns out to be epochal. Hecht might be out of date, a dodderer (a tweeter, to summon up the wobbly internal rhyme), but in his belatedness not as outdated as might seem to be the case with some other "dancing lads" if his "chosen envoys" carry as their offering a "payload lifted into haloed air,"—the odd internal rhyme of "payload" with "haloed" (emphasizing the long *a*) serving as a not-so-faint echo, a "piss-elegant trajectory," of the past in the present, a golden nimbus that reminds us of the frisbee saucer carrying the small voice at the poem's beginning.

"Envoi" is one of Hecht's most charming and curious later poems. Seemingly arriving from nowhere and on its way to somewhere, the lyric everywhere toys with its own evanescence, and yet, in doing so, it reminds us of its place in a literary tradition in which the concept of the "Envoi" is still alive. That concern with evanescence, eccentricity, and continuity, indeed with continuation and the happenstance of occasion, I take to be part of the larger story of the later poetry, which is also shaped and accentuated, inevitably, by a further reckoning of mortality in the particular. We have already had occasion, in Chapter 4, to discuss the moving elegy to James Merrill in *Flight Among the Tombs*, a volume that closes with another to Joseph Brodsky, who like Yeats, died in the dead of winter. So, too, *The Transparent Man* has a mortician's corner to it, in the section announced by the eerie lyric, "Crows in Winter." There, in the company of "The Book of Yolek," we uncover elegies to fellow friends and travelers in poetry, David Kalstone, James Wright, and L. E. Sissman, none of whom can be said to have died from aging but from diseases; and the same is true for the two dramatic monologues in the volume, the title poem, "The Transparent Man" and the longest poem in the volume, "See Naples and Die," which concentrate on different visions associated with dying. I want to consider both before turning to Hecht's last two volumes of poems.

Someone, the poet Irving Feldman, in fact, once said that Hecht's poems, like jumbo jets, sometimes need a long runway, and such is the case with "The Transparent Man," which deliberately idles around in something of a southern folksy idiom before setting off on not one but two ascents into the sublime. Idling around in order to establish "the sense of a spoken voice," as Hecht remarked to his editor Harry Ford, who had queried the use of "mighty" in the opening line: "I'm mighty glad to see you, Mrs. Curtis"; but also because Hecht wanted "the sense of someone beginning casually and building up to eloquence"[6]—classic Hecht strategies when it comes to dramatic monologue. "Building up" in this case means establishing the person's character in terms of her charitable concern for others, especially for her father; her simple dignity and matter-of-fact courage in facing her fate ("But with leukemia things don't improve"). The speaker is only thirty years old, we discover, and, because of her condition, we learn of her perfectly understandable disinclination toward reading books, which do produce "endings" but which seem rather irrelevant to her present circumstances and the "absent narrative . . . in which our fate is written," as Mark Strand has suggested in a different context.[7]

Nothing, however, in the chatty narrative, quite prepares us for what really occupies her thoughts (or Hecht's)—not in this poem, nor in the many other visionary moments that haunt Hecht's poetry:

> What I do instead is sit here by this window
> And look out at the trees across the way.
> You wouldn't think that was much, but let me tell you,
> It keeps me quite intent and occupied.
> Now all the leaves are down, you can see the spare,
> Delicate structures of the sycamores,
> The fine articulation of the beeches.
> I have sat here for days studying them,
> And I have only just begun to see
> What it is that they resemble. One by one,
> They stand there like magnificent enlargements
> Of the vascular system of the human brain.
> I see them there like huge discarnate minds,

---

6. Letter, AH to Harry Ford, 1 September 1989; see also letter, Harry Ford to AH, 30 August 1989.
7. Strand, "Narrative Poetry," in *The Weather of Words: Poetic Invention* (New York: Alfred Knopf, 2000), 63–4.

Lost in their meditative silences.
The trunks, branches and twigs compose the vessels
That feed and nourish vast immortal thoughts.
So I've assigned them names. There, near the path,
Is the great brain of Beethoven, and Kepler
Haunts the wide spaces of that mountain ash.
This view, you see, has become my Hall of Fame.

Hers is the patience of the visionary artist contemplating her subject, watching it slowly reveal itself in the manner of a poem: the "Delicate structure of the sycamores / The fine articulation of the beeches," right down to the act of naming, with our participating in the process of the revelation itself: the mind, Pygmalion-like, imagining other minds into being through language. And not just any mind, but those exceptional ones capable of "vast immortal thoughts" deserving the names of Beethoven and Kepler. The moment is primal, the intimacy redirected, not punctured ("you see"), by the wry reference to the vision as "my Hall of Fame."

There is no other speaker in Hecht who seems quite so imaginatively alive, so drawn to the heroically human—and, of course, also so near death. The pathos of "The Grapes" stems from a mid-life vision that arrests a sense of further development. Here, it is achieved through the proximity of the speaking voice to the surrounding silence, "the sleeving snows" that will come "within a month," and from the speaker's studious attempt to subject her first vision to further interpretation: to take the emblem of the plastic birthday toy, the figure of the transparent man, with its "fine-haired, silken-threaded filiations / That wove, like Belgian lace, throughout the head," in a direction that, with Frost-like skepticism, knowingly resists "transparency," the beautifully woven lines of the artifact, recapitulated as well at the end of the poem in the "fine books" Mrs. Curtis has offered the speaker:

> But this last week it seems I have found myself
> Looking beyond, or through, individual trees
> At the dense, clustered woodland just behind them,
> Where those great, nameless crowds patiently stand.
> It's become a sort of complex, ultimate puzzle
> And keeps me fascinated. My eyes are twenty-twenty,
> Or used to be, but of course I can't unravel
> The tousled snarl of intersecting limbs,
> That mackled, cinder grayness. It's a riddle
> Beyond the eye's solution. Impenetrable.

"Mackled cinder grayness," like the earlier "huge discarnate minds, / Lost in their meditative silences," reminds us, in its fullness of expression, of the "payloads lifted into the haloed air" in "Envoi," phrases that will prevent any easy assimilation of the complex into the simple:

> If there is order in all that anarchy
> Of granite mezzotint, that wilderness,
> It takes a better eye than mine to see it.
> It set me on to wondering how to deal
> With such a thickness of particulars,
> Deal with it faithfully you understand,
> Without blurring the issue. Of course I know
> That within a month the sleeving snows will come
> With cold, selective emphases, with massings
> And arbitrary contrasts, rendering things
> Deceptively simple, thickening the twigs
> To frosty veins, bestowing epaulets
> And decorations on every birch and aspen.
> And the eye, self-satisfied, will be misled,
> Thinking the puzzle solved, supposing at last
> It can look forth and comprehend the world.
> That's when you have to really watch yourself.
> So I hope that you won't think me plain ungrateful
> For not selecting one of your fine books,
> And I take it very kindly that you came
> And sat here and let me rattle on this way.

In one of the best readings of Hecht's later poetry, Robyn Creswell has noted that the narrator possesses "a submerged Christian sensibility"— perhaps because in writing the poem Hecht had in mind Flannery O'Connor, "someone I profoundly revered."[8] In any event, the quiet irony in the phrase, "I have found myself / Looking beyond, or through, individual trees / At the dense, clustered woodland just behind them, / Where those great, nameless crowds patiently stand," equates a possible reckoning of personal salvation ("I have found myself") with a vision of the nameless many patiently standing. But standing where? And patiently standing in what sense?

Hecht and his narrator studiously resist the temptation to transcendence, even under the pressure of an imminently imagined death, and the admonition to deal "faithfully" in response to the "thickness of

8. Letter, AH to Harry Ford, 21 July 1990. See Robyn Creswell, "Painting and Privacy: On Anthony Hecht," *Raritan* 21 (2002), 27.

particulars" "without blurring the issue" is, one senses, an artistic not theological credo, one that quite directly challenges notions of the merely decorative as anything other than "misleading." If we hear Hecht arguing against a formalizing version of himself (especially as seen and characterized by others), we might register his response to "the eye, self-satisfied" (which we also hear as "the self-satisfied I"), "thinking the puzzle solved," as presumptuous behavior requiring a further warning. "That's when you have to really watch yourself." The colloquial phrasing indicates "that the vision is receding," as Creswell suggests, and that the need to "really watch yourself"—to be careful—now includes, in its intensifier ("really"), the tense recognition that nothing less than artistic integrity is stake,[9] in this case remaining true to the opacity underlying or surrounding narrative and its desire for closure.

"See Naples and Die," the other lengthy narrative poem in *The Transparent Man*, is another "envoi" and one of the most puzzling poems in the volume, indeed in later Hecht more generally. At 488 lines, it too requires a long take-off, but it's not immediately clear where we land or, to some readers, why we're up in the air in the first place. The poem describes the dissolution of a marriage from the point of view of the husband, who is never named. His wife is called "Martha." The poem includes many fine passages, not of the continually exuberant and elevated order of its earlier Italian cousin, "The Venetian Vespers," but more along the lines of what an enthusiastic journalist or travel writer might record and make "poetic": a sumptuous meal in which oblique reference is made to a line from Wallace Stevens' "Esthétique du Mal," an arresting view of "Naples and its Bay," an entertaining escapade with a swindler, a restorative visit to a famous art gallery, some local festivities, a tour of a few notable ancient sites, and a landscape of "naked horrors," the last account stitched together from several letters by Pliny the Younger regarding his uncle's fatal decision to "satisfy / His scientific curiosity" and describe in detail the eruption of Mount Vesuvius.[10]

Indeed, the lower altitudes of journal or diary-writing, including the letter—not the Jacobean baroque flights of "Vespers"—are the

9. Creswell, "Painting and Privacy," 28–9.

10. See, *Pliny the Younger, Letters*, with an English translation by William Melmoth, revised by W. M. L. Hutchinson (London: W. Heinemann, 1952), Book VI, xvi and xx.

literary forms that most engage the narrator. At the outset of the poem, the speaker suggests, in fact, that what we are reading is from "my journal of that time"—the "time," or year, never specified but appears to be around the mid-twentieth century; and at the beginning of Section II, he alludes further to reading "a seventeenth-century diarist, / Candid and down-to-earth on Naples' Whores." Even when he remarks in the latter part of the poem that he is too depressed to continue putting his thoughts on paper, the narrative proceeds in the manner of a first-person travelogue, albeit of a disenchanted sort reflecting his increasing detachment from not just the "fabled" sites he is visiting but also of a marriage gone bad and his inability to understand, in much depth, the reasons for its failure. In the climactic, or rather purposely anticlimactic final section that precedes the Vesuvian passage, he observes, in a strange but characteristic mix of clinical detachment and theological melodrama:

> Marriages come to grief in many ways.
> Our own was, I suppose, a common one,
> Without dramatics, a slow stiffening
> Of all the little signs of tenderness,
> Significant silences, self-conscious efforts
> To be civil even when we were alone.
> The cause may be too deep ever to find,
> And I have long since ceased all inquiry.
> It seems to me in fact that Martha and I
> Were somehow victims of a nameless blight
> And dark interior illness. We were both
> Decent and well-intentioned, capable
> Of love and devotion and all the rest of it,
> Had it not been for what in other ages
> Might have been thought of as the wrath of God,
> The cold, envenoming spirit of Despair,
> Turning what was the nectar of the world
> To ashes in our mouths. We were the cursed
> To whom it seemed no joy was possible,
> The spiritually warped and handicapped.
> It seems, in retrospect, as I look over
> The pages of this journal, that the moments
> Of what had once seemed love were an illusion,
> The agreement, upon instinct, of two people
> Grandly to overestimate each other,
> An accord essentially self-flattering,
> The paradise of fools before the fall.

The passage works so well as "confession" that one of the questions bruited about the corridors, if not the criticism, is how much these sentiments might be attributed to an elderly Hecht reflecting back on the failure of his first marriage. Naples was the port from which the couple sailed to and from Ischia as well as to and from New York, although not in each other's company in their last voyage when returning to the States in 1955. But little else in the poem would seem to comport with this personal situation. Hecht's own comments about this poem—and there are only a few—lead in an altogether different direction. Made in the context of defending the poem against Joseph Brodsky's imputation that the "'narrative' is too thin to sustain a poem of such length," Hecht remarked, at some length, that this,

is the sort of complaint that might be made about Paradise Lost. I picked the comparison from Milton deliberately. My poem is intended as a commentary on the events in Genesis: the temptation, the fall, and the expulsion. It is also a commentary on the epigraph from Simone Weil. It is mainly, however, an account of the visions of paradise and of damnation that are glimpsed in the course of affairs. Its speaker is one of the damned; and one who fails to understand what has happened to him. He reveals more than he understands himself, like some of the characters in Henry James or Ford Madox Ford. He is figuratively "blind," and there is irony in his pride in being a careful observer, especially when he gets cheated during the "temptation" scene.[11]

There may be too much protestation here (it would be an understatement to say that Hecht was taken aback by his friend's negative response to the poem), but Hecht is not suggesting parity with Milton's epic, only offering an analogy with regard to its action being created out of a few events in Genesis. The temptation scene referred to in the letter involves, in the second section, a tourist's thinly veiled pride "Of wishing to exhibit worldly cunning" in a trickster world already infamous for being fully fallen, Naples' dark back alleys. And the error the narrator admits to making is priding himself "on being a keen observer" while, distracted by the looks of "two thuggish observers," he fails to see that the dazzling hands of the thief, young Ercole—"those adept, / Tapered,

---

11. See his letter dated in early 1990 in SL, 234–5. Brodsky's detailed criticisms are in an undated letter in the Hecht Archive, which includes the following comment: " 'See Naples and Die' is the way of making you pay for [the] magnificence of 'Venetian Vespers' and 'A Hill.' One always pays for visionary, not to mention revelatory jobs, with the hope of repeating the feat, and you get tricked into this hope by the poem's very background. Italy, Akhmatova used to say, is a dream that recurs to you for the rest of your life."

manicured, bejeweled hands"—had given him "folded newspaper" instead of money.

Once one catches on to the irony of the narrator being "figuratively blind," of revealing more than he knows, other sections of the poem come readily and more purposefully into focus, in particular the scene that immediately follows this one, centering on Bellini's famous painting, *The Transfiguration*. Apart from perhaps helping to date the action of the poem, I don't think it is significant that the speaker refers to the painting as being in the Museo Nazionale when it is now housed in the Capodimonte (the painting was moved sometime after 1950), but the narrator's reading of the painting is in important ways off-base. Addressing as he does the subject of the "Five dazzled apostles," he speaks of

> ... the two erect apostles, one being Peter,
> The other possibly John, both of them holding
> Fragments of scroll with Hebrew lettering,
> Which they appear just to have been consulting.
> Their lowered eyes indicate that, unseeing,
> They have seen everything, have understood
> The entire course of human history,
> The meaning and the burden of the lives
> Of Samson, Jonah, and Melchizedek,
> Isaiah's and Zechariah's prophecies,
> The ordinance of destiny, the flow
> And tide of providential purposes.
> All hope, all life, all effort has assembled
> And taken human shape in the one figure
> There in the midst of this afternoon.
> And what event could be more luminous?

This is a rhapsodic reading of the painting—a verbal parallel to the opening luncheon scene taking place "under a trellised roof of vines, / Light-laced and freaked with grape-leaf silhouettes / That romp and buck across the tablecloth, / Flicker and slide on the white porcelain." And also fundamentally quite wrong—in fact, figuratively quite blind. The narrator's ambitious understanding of "The entire course of human history" in the painting is undermined from the start when he misidentifies the two figures holding "Fragments of scroll with Hebrew lettering" with Peter and John. These figures are traditionally identified with Moses and Elijah, as the Hebrew lettering on the scrolls clearly indicates but the narrator doesn't seem to value. I don't think this is a mistake that the poet of the poem, Hecht, is likely to make—to erase the Old Testament in favor of the New—any more than the author of " 'More Light! More Light!' " and "The Book of Yolek" and any number of other poems in the plangent mode of "Meditation" is likely to consent to the typologically enthusiastic eye that sees "a day so glorious / As to explain and even justify / All human misery and suffering."[12] And then there is the conspicuous appearance of the hand at the end of the passage, not that of Ercole, whose costume is the *bella figura* of the poor, but of the painter: a "pastoral hand, moving in synchronous / Obedience to a clear and pastoral eye," a *bella figura*, for sure, and one to be wary of, however beautiful the painting.

Hecht is revealing a mind, an ego, an "I" or "eye" (yet again) that superimposes itself on reality, that doesn't see the "thickness of the particulars," or value the person; that, at the emotional climax at the end of Section IV, offers advice to his spouse Martha, in response "To the all-too-sad calamities of others, / The brute, inexplicable inequities, / To form for ourselves a carapace of sorts, / A self-preservative petrific toughness." "Petrific" is a loaded term. A rare word most memorably used by Milton and cited first in the *OED*, Death wields his "mace petrific" in *Paradise Lost* (10:294); but even if we don't catch the allusion, Martha's response tells us all we need to know—and more than the narrator fully understands:

> At this she raised her arm, shielding her eyes
> As if she thought I were about to strike her,
> And said *No* several times, not as a statement
> But rather as a groan. And then she gave me
> A look the like of which I can't describe.

Of course, he has, in effect, already struck her, and the "*No*" she groans, like earth feeling the wound at the Fall in Milton (9:782), marks the

12. Further evidence that the misreading belongs to the narrator and not the poet can be found in an essay Hecht was writing about the same time as "See Naples and Die," "St. Paul's Epistle to the Galatians," in which the subject of the Transfiguration is addressed in light of Paul's willful inclusion of himself in Jesus' messiahship. See Hecht, *Melodies Unheard*, 242. Hecht's essay was first published in Alfred Corn, ed., *Incarnation: Contemporary Writers on the New Testament* (New York: Viking, 1990): 148–61. In his solipsism, the narrator possesses an uncanny resemblance to Hecht's account of Paul. It may be of some significance that with regard to the cover design of the Waywiser edition of *The Collected Later Poems*, Hecht expressed a preference for Bellini's "Sacred Allegory" over his "Transfiguration" "both for its own sake, and because it is attractively enigmatic, less doctrinal and assertively Christian." See Letter, AH to Philip Hoy, 16 October 2003. I want to thank Gabriel Josipovici for calling my attention to this curious moment of blindness in the poem.

point of entry into the negative in this poem, into the underworld in all its tarnished meanings in the section that immediately follows, beginning with the "Grotta del Cane / Known in the ancient texts as *Charon's Cave*."

To return for a moment to the poem's beginning, when, without knowing it, we are first introduced to the already atrophying, spiritually dying speaker, we can see Hecht crafting, in a few words, the ground plan for the whole poem. The very first line of the poem reads, "I can at last consider those events / Almost without emotion." Yes, almost, but that word "consider" draws quiet attention to the fundamental problem or division in the poem that is played out in the narrative. The word "consideration" can summon nearly opposite meanings: consideration in the sense of looking closely at an event or person, and consideration in the sense of showing or feeling kindness toward another. Thoughtfulness, how contrastive that word can seem, even hair-splitting, had Hecht not already pointed to the differences in sense two poems earlier in his "Eclogue of the Shepherd and the Townie": "Kindness itself," remarks the Townie, "Depends on what we call consideration," and then, drawing on the other meaning, continues: "Think again. / Consider the perfect hexagrams of snow, / Those broadcast emblems of divinity." A poet given to "concentrating"—another double-edged word in Hecht—on the muse might well understand the potential conflict here.

Hecht's narrator is the very personification of "consideration," ultimately to the exclusion of Martha, and to himself as a person as well. He has no history, in contrast to the speaker of "The Venetian Vespers"; he spreads his wings and learning widely but rarely really "sees" anything. In this regard, he is the obverse of the speaker of "The Transparent Man," and in the end, reading Pliny on Vesuvius, he arrives at his solitary abrupt, where he is left to envision only,

> An endless beach littered with squirming fish,
> With kelp and timbers strewn on muddy flats,
> Giant sea-worms bright with a glittering slime,
> Crabs limping in their rheumatoid pavane.

We are reminded of the beginning images when "it is almost time for lunch." Now grotesquely rendered, the creatures have been vomited up by Vesuvius, as it were, and mark, shockingly, the poem's sudden end—a kind of continuous "still life" from which there is no relief, concluding the poem, as it does, with the present tense participle. (There is a visual analogue, if not a source, in the Capodimonte in a 1671 painting by Giuseppo Recco, *Natura Morta di Pesci e altri animali Marini*.) Yes, as Simone Weil urges in the poem's epigraph, "it *is* better to say, 'I'm suffering,' [my italics] than to say, 'This landscape is ugly.'" In fact, this is what the speaker of "The Venetian Vespers" can do, rather magnificently, and winning our sympathy in the process, but not the narrator of "See Naples and Die," thus leaving us in something of a limbo right down to the end of his story.

Hecht's remarks remain a helpful guide to his poem, to which we should add Gregory Dowling's fine essay, written before Hecht's commentary was generally available, especially for tracing out the connections with Stevens' "Esthétique du Mal."[13] But what of Brodsky's criticism, not so much that the narrative is "thin" as that the poem will seem a lesser remake of "The Venetian Vespers"? The comparison is surely inescapable, and Hecht must have anticipated it; but his comments suggest that he is also doing something quite different in the later poem by trying to present, sympathetically, a mind that is generally unsympathetic toward others, a mind that is in many ways attractive and interesting but in a purely literary sort of way, fundamentally disengaged as it is from an emotional life. He's not a self-aware Tyrannosaurus Rex sauntering toward extinction but a carapace incapable of love.

To press this point further, in the poem, and in "life," we should recall that Pliny the Younger wrote out of *consideration* for his uncle, Pliny the Elder. As his initial letter makes clear, he is invited by Cornelius Tacitus to send "a description of my uncle's death so that you can leave an accurate account of it for posterity."[14] By contrast, Hecht's nameless narrator writes largely out of self-consideration. He seems more concerned about his journal than "Martha," about reading than feeling, or even posterity. Perhaps in the end the narrative is "thin," not because the poem lacks either incident or a sense of progression. (At one poetry event, I'm told, when Hecht dared to read the entire poem, the room was so quiet you could hear the proverbial pin drop.) Nor because it fails to make use of those often-deepening Hechtian devices found in the contrasting use of light and

13. Gregory Dowling, "'Bewildered Tourists': Anthony Hecht's 'See Naples and Die'," *New Walk* 5 (2012–13), 18–25.
14. *Pliny the Younger, Letters*, xvi.

darkness, the counterpointing of Bellini against Bosch, in this case, but "thin" because structuring narcissism is itself a tightwalk rope over a void, the equivalent to, or variation on, writing a "Postcard from the Volcano," the other great Stevens poem besides "Esthétique du Mal" that haunts Hecht's poem, a poem also made rich through the contemplation of absence. A dramatic monologue, like its literary ancestor the soliloquy, as Hecht knew, always has the potential to be only about itself.

To hazard a biographical explanation but of a different kind than the one offered earlier in this chapter, the poem shows a narrator reflecting back on a situation perilously close to the poet's own in, say, 1955, and the kind of sterile, solitary, bookish life that could have been his future, but, in 1990, clearly had not materialized. Imagine the poet of *The Hard Hours* only becoming harder, like the giant tortoise in the poem of that title, turning into a carapace rather than into the author of *Millions of Strange Shadows*, and you have the petrific ingredients for "See Naples and Die."

"See Naples and Die" was one of the last poems completed before the 1990 publication of *The Transparent Man*. It was also Hecht's last venture with a long narrative poem, antipodal in almost every respect to the sentiments expressed in "The Transparent Man," but also a logical termination to the self-ruminations that began two decades earlier with "Green: An Epistle," in this case a rumination over an atrophied, stunted "self" that the author did not become. A surprising number of the poems, by contrast, stem from the early 1980s, capping a period of extraordinary creativity, as I've had occasion to mention more than once, including the title poem of the volume and the concluding poem, the aptly named and manifestly sibylline "Murmur" about a heart murmur, whose initial medical title, "Valvular Lesion," was rightly scrapped for giving away the ghost at the beginning. (Without spelling out the medical condition, each stanza describes a sonic variation on murmur.) The major later exceptions are "Terms," Hecht's ambitious canzone, attempted by only a few modern poets, that appeared in *The New Yorker* in April 1985, and the two poems mentioned earlier in this chapter as selected for inclusion in *The Best American Poetry*.

To these few we might add small gems like the Hardyesque "rarity in gray," "Curriculum Vitae," the introductory poem to *The Transparent Man* and first published in 1984 in a fine edition by Palaemon Press. It can only have been written by a poet who not only knows Hardy well but who understands intimately, as a parent, what it means for a child to set forth for school in a cold northern climate mythologized elsewhere as Rochester in "Sestina d'Inverno":

> Book-bagged and padded out, at mouth and nose
> They manufacture ghosts,
> George Washington's and Poe's,
> Banquo's, the Union and Confederate hosts',
>
> And are themselves the ghosts, file cabinet gray,
> Of some departed us,
> Signing our lives away
> On ferned and parslied windows of a bus.

The school bus reminds us of Charon's boat carrying its cargo into the gloom, the striking image of the signatures of the departed appearing as a nature's fateful mark and a final goodbye.

Whatever led to this reduced output—Hecht served as Consultant in Poetry to the Library of Congress from 1982–84, a period that coincided with an increasing and continuing emphasis on writing criticism—the reduction in verse making was not a reduction in quality. Nor was it permanent. Much of the renewed energy in the decade following the publication of *The Transparent Man* in 1990 can be attributed to the greater freedom afforded Hecht in retirement, time he continued to allocate to writing criticism; but he also returned to writing poems with increasing frequency and urgency. An important element in this renewal came from his teaming up, once again, with the prominent artist Leonard Baskin. Baskin had returned to the United States in the 1980s from a long residence in England, where he and the poet Ted Hughes had collaborated on a number of book projects, and, now a decade later, at Baskin's invitation, the collaboration with Hecht was renewed. The founder of the Gehenna Press in 1942, Baskin was known especially for the exceptionally fine quality of his book engraving. At his memorial service in 2000, Hecht described Baskin in a moving, thoughtful eulogy as,

a learnedly literary man, of a kind uncommon to the point of rarity among artists and sculptors. To be sure, Picasso, Matisse, Braque and Vuillard made illustrations for books; but they showed no interest whatever in type fonts, nor were they in love with the written word, as Leonard was. His appetite in this regard was extravagant and Elizabethan. He had a relish for orotundity, and employed it liberally in his writing. Yet this richness and baroque side of him was perfectly balanced by ruthless straightforwardness and detestation of sentimentality.[15]

On the basis of this brief sketch, we can see why Hecht found working with Baskin so appealing. Different in their talents, they were alike in sensibility and taste—to say nothing of their similarity in age and their common Jewish heritage, reflected, for instance, in their shared responsibilities in helping to produce the popular Passover Haggadah, edited by Rabbi Herbert Bronstein in 1974. Although Hecht was unhappy with the final version of the text of the Haggadah,[16] the prospect of a fruitful reunion with Baskin two decades later helped to inspire a fine late poem, written in expectation "about our project," the villanelle called "Prospects." Hecht typed out a copy as part of a 1993 letter to Baskin, with a typically understated comment that it is "on a topic that will interest you":[17]

> We have set out from here for the sublime
> Pastures of summer shade and mountain stream;
> I have no doubt we shall arrive on time.
>
> Is all the green of that enameled prime
> A snapshot recollection or a dream?
> We have set out from here for the sublime
>
> Without provisions, without one thin dime,
> And yet, for all our clumsiness, I deem
> It certain that we shall arrive on time.
>
> No guidebook tells you if you'll have to climb
> Or swim. However foolish we may seem,
> We have set out from here for the sublime
>
> And must get past the scene of an old crime
> Before we falter and run out of steam,
> Riddled by doubt that we'll arrive on time.
>
> Yet even in winter a pale paradigm
> Of birdsong utters its obsessive theme.
> We have set out from here for the sublime;
> I have no doubt we shall arrive on time.

15. Quoted from "Leonard Baskin: 1922–2000," *Proceedings of the American Academy of Arts and Letters* (2001), 70–5.
16. Letter, AH to Leonard Baskin, 25 July 1973, in which Hecht speaks of being "greatly disappointed" in the approved version of the text, "still largely written in fake-elegant English, riddled with 19th century pomposities, and inflated, unconvincing language that no child could take seriously."
17. Letter, AH to Leonard Baskin, 27 July 1993.

I am not suggesting that the "we" here is being used presumptively to refer to poet and artist in their new arrangement. That would reduce what is essentially a mysterious quest, which plays on the double meaning of prospects—in the sense of an act of looking forward and of a vista as seen from a particular vantage point—into a sentimental journey, and encourage an autobiographical reading that seems problematic and even insulting in a few places if taken literally. In this poem of considerable humility, quiet confidence, and prospective determination, rather, Hecht is imagining a more inclusively archetypal or allegorical journey, even biblical in the echoes from Psalm 23, a poem that might be profitably read against Longfellow's quest poem "Excelsior," whose excessive bravado amused both Housman and Hecht.[18]

Something of "Prospects" fineness of tone is registered when Eleanor Cook thought she noticed in Hecht's use of "enameled" in "enameled green" a possible echo of Milton's "L'Allegro," to which Hecht remarked, appreciative of her catching the Miltonic resonance, that he thought he had "'Lycidas' in mind" (presumably the great flower passage near the end, where "enameled" appears for the only time in the poem).[19] The point is not so much which Miltonic reference has priority—it's hard not to side with the poet. It's more that "Prospects" allows both a sense of the pastoral vitality associated with "L'Allegro" while retaining an element of pastoral elegy from "Lycidas." Setting out for the sublime, the sublime carrying inevitable suggestions of death, includes, as does the journey in "Lycidas," the prospect of poetic accomplishment—"Thus sang the uncouth Swain to th' oaks and rills"—but as registered in the more polished, quieter key of "L'Allegro," appropriate for a villanelle, and, we might further observe, enabled not simply by the hopeful progress registered in the repeating lines but also by the consonantal identity of all the endings and the near rhyme created in the middle line, usually the odd mate out in a villanelle.

The prospect of accomplishment seems the more rewarding, moreover, because of the experienced, indeed seasoned or wintry nature of the prospectors. As Hollander remarked about Hecht's poem, with admirable conviction regarding the importance of the creative act:

This is rather a remarkable glimpse of what art can mean. The absorption in it can make any prospect, even when glimpsed from a point toward an end of a

18. Hecht, *Melodies Unheard*, 95–6.
19. Letter, AH to Eleanor Cook, 5 October 1994.

journey, seem as if seen from *nel mezzo del cammin*. It is having great imaginative work to do, like that of a major poet, which initially affords such a prospect, and it is the true work of poetry to point this out to the rest of us.[20]

As it turned out—and Hollander didn't know the biographical context for this poem—the journey would issue in a series of twenty-two poems bearing the collective title of "The Presumptions of Death," thus helping to cinch the connection with "Prospects." The subject of death and achievement become one. The series, certainly Hecht's most ambitious single undertaking since "See Naples and Die," appeared initially in an expensive, limited, folio edition of sixty copies published in 1995 by the Gehenna Press, with some of Baskin's woodcuts done in color. The poems were then published in a trade edition as the first part of Hecht's *Flight Among the Tombs* (1996), with the woodcuts, now available to the general reader, appearing only in black and white. But the collaboration between artist and poet did not end here. Although a reader might assume this to be the case, three other "flower" poems published in *Flight Among the Tombs*, "Sisters," "A Pledge," and "*Là-bas*: A Trance," unaccompanied by woodcuts, are also the product of artist and poet collaborating, but this time for a fine press book, *The Gehenna Florilegium*, published in 1998, also as a folio. Baskin's boldly drawn images, all brilliantly colored, help to make the *Florilegium* a stunning visual feast. It is a shame the book is not more widely available for study since, in contrast to "Presumptions," it represents the only opportunity to view the poems and the drawings together. The collaborative *Florilegium* is, moreover, the source for the additional twelve flower poems in Hecht's final collection of poems, *The Darkness and the Light* (2001). This last volume includes as well a series of poems on biblical subjects, again without illustrations, for a joint project that was never brought to fruition because of Baskin's death in 2000.

All in all, an astonishing number of Hecht's late poems, some forty-five out of eighty poems in his final two books, might be regarded as "commissioned," the result, that is, of collaboration. But before we go very far down this numerical route and rope off these poems as necessarily lesser creations because not "inspired" in the Romantic sense, we might think of these individual topics as ones that, for different reasons, were naturally appealing to Hecht. Well versed in the Bible and long drawn to the subject of mortality, Hecht was a poet with an habitual

---

20. Hollander, "On Anthony Hecht," 151.

instinct for the florabundant. We should also recall Auden's cautionary view that,

all works of art are commissioned in the sense that no artist can create one by a simple act of will but must wait until what he believes to be a good idea for a work "comes" to him. Among those works which are failures because their initial conceptions were false or inadequate, the number of self-commissioned works may well be greater than the number commissioned by patrons.[21]

By this stage in his career, Hecht was certainly aware of initial conceptions that might prove to be false or inadequate, even if they required following out to some degree. He reported, at one point, for instance, eventually jettisoning a "death" poem in the manner of "Longfellow,"[22] and the several comments he made about the general challenges posed by his "limited" subject suggest a writer acutely aware of the need for invention. As he wrote to Daniel Albright about the Death poems:

In the traditional version [of the "Dance of Death" formula], Death remains the same indomitable figure and only his victims vary, and this makes for a certain limitation in terms of a reader's expectations. It was, I felt, essential to overcome this handicap insofar as it was possible. And the result was to have Death play all possible human roles (reserving to himself only his secret, ultimate purpose). He could therefore adopt any age or sex, present himself as alluring, amusing, friendly, childlike, anything that advanced his purpose; and this would allow a great variety of "voices," however insistent the central theme, as, for example, in Lydgate's *The Dance of Death*.[23]

By contrast, composing a substantial number of poems about flowers required an altogether different strategy. It involved indirection rather than impersonation, masking the individual assignments rather than creating different masks for each poem. "As you can see," Hecht wrote to Eleanor Cook, in conjunction with the flower poems in *Flight Among the Tombs*, "I've had to be very cunning in dealing with flowers in my poems, and have taken inordinate pains to avoid Victorian valentine arrangements, pinned with golden darts. The key to writing

21. Auden, *The Dyer's Hand* (1962), in *The Complete Works of W. H. Auden: Prose, Vol. IV*, ed. Edward Mendelson (Princeton: Princeton University Press, 2010), 465.
22. Letter, AH to Daniel Albright, 23 December 1993. A pattern poem, "Death the Analyst," in the shape of a skull, also never made it into the final collection, nor did "Cain the Inventor of Death." See, respectively, Letter, AH to Leonard Baskin, 8 October 1993, which includes a copy of the poem, and 29 October 1993.
23. Letter, AH to Daniel Albright, 4 January 1994 (*SL*, 261–2).

about flowers, I find, is to approach them very indirectly."[24] The poem that prompted these comments, "Sisters," stems, in fact, from a letter to Robert Frost by his sister, Jeanie Frost, "who spent most of her life in a state lunatic asylum in Maine." The flower, in this case, is the "cyclamen." Identified by name only as the poem's final word, the flower's "flame-white tongue" serves as an image for the "starched coifs" worn by the sisters of the title—not to be confused with Frost's sister, who is unnamed in the poem.

Whether the poem is read with special knowledge of its initial floral commission matters little in the end, although to know so in advance contributes to our sense of the poet's craftiness. "Sisters," for instance, is a remarkably moving description of the plight of the elderly, written by a prospective sympathizer. The poet knows the score; lets us hear the score in the quoted letter, which asks for "a small graphophone" for music and dance, for desiring to escape from the dark corridors of growing old, reflected in the residence itself, "this compound proctored by St. Vincent / De Paul in marble patience"; and then he picks up at the end the note of benediction sounded at the beginning in praise of the caregivers:

> And the youngest nurses, made beautiful with care,
> Sisters of Charity, escort the feeble
> Through inward terrors, through memories that disable,
> From dark brown hallways out into morning air,
>
> To agate swirls and citrines of the sun,
> Sparrows at their dust-baths, shameless, surprising
> These scrubbed, diligent girls, their starched coifs rising
> Like spinnakers, flame-white tongues of cyclamen.

A stunningly compacted, vital vision, it is impossible to know how much of this vision the feeble will actually see, but the "morning air" offers possibilities of change for all—and even a note of hope or at least release in the startling, apocalyptic image of the spinnaker sailing forth.

Impersonation and indirection: both involve different aspects of poetic wit or invention and distinguish these collaborative acts not only from each other but from Hecht's earlier sequence in *The Hard Hours* on the Seven Deadly Sins, for which Baskin had produced accompanying wood engravings. Those earlier poems, which have also been turned into grueling exercises for baritone by the American

---

24. Letter, AH to Eleanor Cook, 9 January 1997 (*SL*, 281–3).

composer Robert Beaser, are compactly epigrammatic and deliberately enigmatic, ranging from the tight tercets of "Lust" to the more spaciously greedy eight lines devoted to "Avarice." The seven poems are very much in the "emblem" poem tradition: dense, pointed, puzzling. Here's the one on "Pride," which appropriately is given pride of place, appearing first in the sequence:

> "For me Almighty God Himself has died,"
> Said one who formerly rebuked his pride
> With, "Father, I am not worthy," and here denied
> The Mercy by which each of us is tried.

The sentiments here might be said to fall into the category of damned if you do or damned if you don't. The phrase "For me," not "for mankind," keeps the speaker selfishly in the center of God's universe, just as the prayerful rebuke about worthlessness unwittingly seals his fate. Hecht had remarked on the overall rationale of the sequence that "the poems intend to justify the sins, not by making them attractive, but by showing that the alternatives are perhaps just as sinful or pointless."[25] Beaser's comments are perhaps even more to the point: "The musical rendering of these poems draws upon the irony, drama, and elliptical wit implicit in the text."[26]

Not only are the poems in "The Presumptions of Death" roomier in their own presumptive right, thus allowing the impersonations to be more fully realized than their allegorical ancestors from *The Hard Hours*, but in the aggregate this larger grouping should be regarded as a "suite" or "series" of poems—Hecht's descriptions[27]—rather than as a sequence. True, "Death Sauntering About" marks a plausible beginning, just as "Death the Carnival Barker" might be viewed as performing a loud "envoi," the one beginning on a note of expectation ("The crowds have gathered here by the paddock gates"), the other concluding by barking out the never-ending end of the subject or subjects in the final line: "Step forward, please! Make room for those in back!" But

25. Letter, AH to Donald Hall, n.d., probably 1959 (*SL*, 114).
26. Quoted from the liner notes for "Robert Beaser: The Seven Deadly Sins, Choral Variations, Piano Concerto," Decca Record Company Limited, 1994. Hecht makes it clear to Harry Ford that he intends the new poems "to be substantial in their own right; i.e., not epigrams, like the Seven Deadly Sins." Letter, AH to Harry Ford, 11 November 1993.
27. Letter, AH to Daniel Albright, 19 November 1993, and, respectively, Letter, AH to Charles Tung, 28 December 1993.

though attentive to local arrangements within the collection, the poems were conceived individually, in a great variety of forms, on topics of mutual interest to poet and artist, and are best read in relation to each other, not as fleshing out a narrative scheme of some kind.

In some cases the evidence of artistic collaboration is greater, or at least more revealing, than others. The first three woodcuts, for instance, accompanying respectively, "Death Sauntering About," "Death the Hypocrite," and "Death Demure," show little individuation, their faces not even visible under their cloaks, although one could certainly argue that these cloaked images are appropriate representations of the sauntering, hypocritical, and demure figure of death in these three poems.[28] But with "Peekaboo: Three Songs for the Nursery," artist and poet are clearly in step, one taking a cue from the other. Hecht's opening reference, "Go hide! Go hide! But through the latticework / Of my upraised bone hands / I see athlete and statesman, priest and clerk" creates a peekaboo image with the hands specifically reflected in Baskin's woodcut, although not in upraised position. And in the next poem, the "beautifully constructed" villanelle "All Out," a poem, as Hollander notes, that "exploits the hidden agenda of death lurking in repetition,"[29] death now faces us in full frontal view, mouth open, eye-sockets visible—all out, in other words, especially in contrast to the previous peekaboo image, which is of the upper torso only.

From here on (out), the Baskin images are more particularized in relation to the subject matter of the poem, the graphic figure often wearing the appropriate garb or bearing the symbol of the office. Two of the more elaborately depicted images, as we might anticipate, are those accompanying "Death the Poet: a Ballade—Lament for the Makers" and "Death the Painter" (Figures 8.1 and 8.2). The former image, which serves as the cover design for *Flight Among the Tombs*, presents two heads in profile facing each other, deadlocked, as if in a staring contest to the finish. One is of a poet possibly resembling Dante, thus continuing the volume's medieval connections. The other is of a skull, with prominently bared teeth and a half-illuminated skull cap resembling the moon in eclipse, the image reminding us as well of mutability's inescapable reign in this volume. Both figures wear a garland or laurel

28. The opening poems, as well as the series as a whole and the book in which it appears, are adroitly analyzed by Stephen Yenser, "Poetry in Review," *The Yale Review* 85.2 (1997), 161–76.
29. Hollander, "On Anthony Hecht," 150.

Figure 8.1. Leonard Baskin, *Death and the Poet*. (Reproduced courtesy of the estate of Leonard Baskin and the Galerie St. Etienne)

Figure 8.2. Leonard Baskin, *Death and the Painter*. (Reproduced courtesy of the estate of Leonard Baskin and the Galerie St. Etienne)

crown, perhaps in further homage to the ballade's great final stanza, when, as only poetry can show, the deadlock will mutate into a deadline, and one will be overtaken by the other:

> Archduke of Darkness, who supplies
> The deadline governing joy and woe,
> Here I put off my flesh disguise
> *Et nunc in pulvere dormio.*

The painter, by contrast, is on his own, a half-length view. Now bearing, it seems, beady eyes, the skull is set off by ruff and palette, and most of all by the fingers holding, against a large white space, the brush, the tool of his trade that also resembles a scalpel or "palette knife," as the poem makes pointedly clear. There is a Leonardo-like cartoon element to some of the engravings, like the one for "Death the Punchinello" (of which figure, Hecht later remarked, the younger Tiepolo "did some splendid...murals that are now in the Ca' Rezzonico in Venice")[30] to fit the dark comedy of that poem and the series as a whole. Several also are of considerable intricacy in the manner of early emblem literature. "Death the Archbishop" is a prize example of both artist and poet raiding the rich coffers of this tradition. Baskin's archbishop bears a substantial miter that discloses, immediately above his own skeletal head, the smaller figure of Christ's head, peering out, as the man of sorrows, from underneath a conspicuously large Byzantine (or German Iron) Cross declaring the Archbishop's lethal importance. Hecht's poem responds in kind by pointing in the last stanza to the "articles and emblems of my faith," in a poetic form reminiscent of the intricate manner of George Herbert. Attending acutely to the discordant ironies here, Peter Steele, the Jesuit poet and Australian friend of Hecht, confided to the author:

Knowing as my trade requires me to a few bishops and archbishops, I find a special starkness in "Death the Archbishop." But it is also one of those poems of yours in which the structural harmonies make all the more repellant the dark message which they modulate. It is as if George Herbert had taken license to articulate a nightmare, perhaps in the spirit of *diabolus simius Dei.* "How weak the serum of that serpent's tooth / The ignorant call *hope*" is a dictum which not even Lear had to attend to.[31]

30. Letter, AH to Philip Hoy, 12 January 2002.
31. Letter, Peter Steele to AH, 14 November 1994. Hecht Archive.

Those "structural harmonies," so nicely noted by Steele, could be given a further twist or turn in "Death the Copperplate Printer." If ever a poem were to rival the sharply edged form of an engraving, this would be it. The printer's emphatic strength, as it were, presses down on this poem with great force, leaving its mark in the combination of simple declarative sentences, crushingly harsh monosyllables, and elaborate stanzaic design, the precise pattern held resolutely together through the carefully appointed rhyme scheme. Lineal enjambment is rare, stanzaic release never. Meaning's press and screw is everything; the poem is a mirror of the persona's meanness:

> Slowly I crank my winch, and the bones crack,
> The skull splits open and the ribs give way.
>   Who, then, thinks to endure?
> Confess the artistry of my attack;
>   Admire the fine gravure,
> The trenched darks, the cross-hatching, the pale gray.

If the penultimate stanza here shades deliberately into artistic self-admiration, the final stanza seemingly waives art aside in one last casual turn of the screw:

> This is no metaphor. Margaret Clitherow,
> A pious woman, even as she prayed
>   Was cheated of her breath
> By a court verdict that some years ago
>   Ordered her pressed to death.
> I'm always grateful for such human aid.

This is a speaker who knows, plainly, about the cruelties of human history.

It also matters in what context a reader encounters the series. The English edition of the *Collected Later Poems*, published by Waywiser Press in 2004, departs from the original fine press edition and places the image above the poem rather than on the facing page as in the case of the Knopf edition. The difference is not insignificant. The Knopf woodcuts, always appearing on the verso or left-hand page, sometimes occupy a full page, and, along with their insistently binocular effect, they can occasionally dwarf the poem, as in the examples of "Death the Knight" or "Death the Society Lady." (Both are among the few colored prints in the Gehenna Press edition, thus further enhancing their visibility.) Those in the Waywiser edition are uniformly smaller, but with no loss in the quality of the reproductions, and their tight placement directly above the poem allows them to partake more immediately in the reading experience, with the eye initially able to view the two forms in tandem. The subsequent shift to the text then further inscribes the poem's character as a speaking picture in the manner of the earlier emblem tradition, in which the text both gives voice to the image and serves as a commentary on the image itself. Thus, with its first spoken line, "where have they gone, the lordly makers," the ballade of "Death the Poet" becomes a fine exercise in the memento mori tradition, in which the eye, seeing the two heads facing each other, also participates in the reduction of all things to a single denominator, solemnly sounded at the end of each stanza in the Latin refrain: "*Et nunc in pulvere dormio*" (And now I sleep in the dust).

Of course, the tonal possibilities, the shades and shading of meaning, are greater with the poems than the woodcuts—as in the instance quoted with the recurrent use of a refrain in Latin. As the Oxford scholar John Bayley observed, in relation to this refrain, "For Hecht learning is a part of poetry, as much an aspect of it as cadence and meter, which themselves bring many echoes from the past."[32] A woodcut can allude to its pictorial past by the very nature of its rough design, but it has no way to communicate the range of sonic references or allusions that are a distinctive feature of these poems. Nor can it very well represent what I take to be one of the chief tonal accomplishments of the series: their ability to speak out of both sides of the mouth, as it were, to deliver satiric portraits of mankind in general, in the Solomonic manner of the vanity of human wishes, while also serving themselves as satiric portraits of specific types, as in say the leisurely, roundabout, seemingly sympathetic manner of "Death the Archbishop":

> Ah my poor erring flock,
> Truant and slow to come unto my ways,
> Making an airy mock
> Of those choice pastures where my chosen graze,
> You loiter childishly in pleasure's maze,
> Unheedful of the clock.

32. Bayley, "Living Ghosts," *New York Review of Books* 44.5 (27 March 1997), 18–21.

Or as manifested in the superior, condescending remarks of "Death the Painter":

> Snub-nosed, bone-fingered, deft with engraving tools,
>   I have alone been given
> The powers of Joshua, who stayed the sun
>   In its traverse of heaven.
> Here in this Gotham of unnumbered fools
> I have sought out and arrested everyone.

Or as glimpsed in the desperate pathos of the human condition reckoned in "Death Riding into Town":

> Exalted manna is his name and sweet
>   To all the long suffering,
> Who kneel to embrace him, clasping his bone feet,
>   His scythe, ashes and sting,
>
> While to the light of heart and proud of purse
>   Encountered on his way
> He smiles his cryptic smile and bids a terse
>   "Go ahead, make my day!"

At some point in the not-so-distant future, the allusion to Clint Eastwood and his famous line from the movie *Dirty Harry* will join the Latinate refrain borrowed from John Skelton, England's first poet laureate—a line itself borrowed from an "anonymous Middle English Lyric" Hecht tells us in his note to "Death the Poet"—and require a footnote of its own from a future editor. Such are the sands of time, the snows of yesteryear, as the poet-turned-editor Hecht, under the weight of time, clearly understood.

In a few instances, as is often the case with satire, the poet leaves some tracks in the snow for a reader to guess the identity of the individual behind the mask, as in the case of "Death the Oxford Don."

> Sole heir to a distinguished laureate,
> I serve as guardian to his grand estate,
> And grudgingly admit the unwashed herds
> To the ten-point mausoleum of his words.
> Acquiring over years the appetite
> And feeding habits of a parasite,
> I live off the cold corpus of fine print,
> Habited with black robes and heart of flint.
> The word made flesh for me and me alone,
> I gnaw and gnaw the satisfactory bone.

One reader gets close to the mark when he notes that "death is not personified so much as the literary executor is satirized."[33] The identity is hinted at in the opening couplet and nearly turned into flesh in the ninth line, as the poem makes clear, in the last line, that the only need, or worth, of words is to offer its selfish keeper the sole opportunity to gnaw on them like a dog with a bone.

As a small riddle in the manner of a roman à clef, the poem hints at the larger place of riddles and the art of riddling in the series—in the collection and in later Hecht in general.[34] The poems in the series might be described, at their simplest, as positing a series of individual puzzles: how is x like y, death like a film director, or a carnival barker, or "a member of the Haarlem guild of St. Luke," to note some of the more obscure possibilities. And the poems disclose, in the manner of a riddle or a mystery, the reason for the comparison. Reason, of course, includes all sorts of linguistic possibilities for likeness that serve to flesh out the body of the poem. The answer to the question of how is death like "a member of the Haarlem guild of St. Luke" lies in the fact that they are both cabinet-makers; and the further joke—he is a master of intaglio, the art of the inlay, after all—now bending sharply in the direction of satire, is that most of his customers are too boorish to appreciate anything more than a "pine" box. Something of the grave-digger's riddling humor from *Hamlet* informs these poems, as well it might: "What is he that builds stronger than either the mason, the

33. Yenser, "Poetry in Review," 170.
34. Hecht writes elaborately about the relationship between riddles and poetry in his essay, "The Riddles of Emily Dickinson," in *Obbligati: Essays in Criticism* (New York: Atheneum, 1986), 85–117. The subject of riddles, enigmas, and mysteries—and the distinctions among them—is explored with great perspicuity by Eleanor Cook in *Enigmas and Riddles in Literature* (Cambridge: Cambridge University Press, 2006). Hecht traces his interest in riddles and mysteries back to childhood in the autobiographical poem "Apprehensions." The subject then appears with increasing frequency in his poetry. A partial list of poems would include " 'Auguries of Innocence,' " "The Venetian Vespers," Section IV (again as a childhood fascination), "Riddles" in *The Transparent Man*, almost all of the "Death" poems in *Flight Among the Tombs*, especially as the concept of riddle blends with games, including nursery rhymes, and is picked up in the teasing refrain from "All Out": "This is the way we play our little game," and reappears in the croupier's call in "To Fortuna Parvulorum." So deep and diverse is this interest that it is difficult to maintain the otherwise useful categories described by Cook. The concept of mystery in Hecht is likewise pervasive and evident in his interest in "wisdom" literature, both Sophoclean and scriptural, and becomes more pronounced in his later critical writings and last book of poems, *The Darkness and the Light* (2001), as we shall see in Chapter 9.

shipwright, or the carpenter?" Answer: "The gallows-maker, for that outlives a thousand tenants" (II.41–3).

"Death the Whore" takes us down the strangest byways in the series by making the identity of the speaker the central mystery of the poem. She doesn't give away her identity easily, even if, in her penchant for suicide, she is distantly reminiscent of people Hecht knew, including the poets Sylvia Plath and Anne Sexton.[35] Far more demure than "Death Demure," the lady only gradually reveals herself over the course of the 123 lines of blank verse, the longest poem in the collection, as a former but forgotten lover. But once having jostled that memory loose in the speaker—indeed quite vividly, with the initial help of some "glossy pages of *Victoria's Secret*," a reference to their past sex as "a little death," and the further mention of "my trial suicides" and her eventual success—she recedes into oblivion, or nearly so. All that remains is her "voice," but not the one the reader (or her lover-poet) will recall as we've come to know it, "but the weary voice shaped in your later mind / By a small sediment of fact and rumor, / A faceless voice, a voice without a body." These are not the final words of the poem, although they might well be. The final words, a couplet, return us to the beginning of the poem, but only to couple a mystery by turning it into an enigma: "As for the winter scene of which I spoke—/ The smoke, my dear, the smoke. I am the smoke." A ghostly sign of herself for sure, but precisely what the smoke signifies remains open to interpretation. From top to bottom, "Death the Whore" is a tease.

Late though they are in the poet's career, the "Presumptions of Death" makes an ideal introduction to this most sophisticated of poets. The woodcuts do their ancient work of appealing readily to the viewer's eye. The variety of poetic forms, the familiar topics and faces, further entice. The remaining fourteen poems in *Flight Among the Tombs* offer pleasures of a more seasoned kind—the element of seasoning here pointing in part to the strange way the second part functions as a kind of inverse mirror of the first. Forms reappear but now containing different matter. The villanelle "All Out," for instance, emerges in more optimistic dress as "Prospects." The ballade "Death the Poet" is now turned in the direction of romance in "A Pledge." And while death

35. *Anthony Hecht in Conversation with Philip Hoy* (1999; rev. 3rd edn. London: BTL, 2004), 109–13.

proves, as it always does, inescapable, as represented in the elegies to Merrill and Brodsky, Hecht's focus is more on the temporality of life, its evanescence for sure, but also on the curious incident, the odd detail that is part of life and can be made into art. Instead of the severe black-and-white images of the first part, the second part, we recall, houses "Matisse: Blue Interior with Two Girls—1947." Artist, painting, color, persons, and date: all point to the presence of the world, or what Hecht elsewhere calls, borrowing the phrase from Feste in *Twelfth Night*, "The Whirligig of Time," the title he chose for his marvelous translation of Horace's "Ode" (I.25) that rightly inaugurates the second part:

> They are fewer these days, those supple, suntanned boys
> Whose pebbles tapped at your window, and your door
> Swings less and less on its obliging hinges
> For wildly importunate suitors. Fewer the cries
> Of "Lydia, how can you sleep when I've got the hots?
> I won't last out the night; let me get my rocks off."
> Things have moved right along, and, behold, it's you
> Who quails, like a shriveled whore, as they scorn and dodge you,
> And the wind shrieks like a sex-starved thing in heat
> As the moon goes dark and the mouth of your old dry vulva
> Rages and hungers, and your worst, most ulcerous pain
> Is knowing those sleek-limbed boys prefer the myrtle,
> The darling buds of May, leaving dried leaves
> To cluster in unswept corners, fouling doorways.

So much for the wispy figure of "Death the Whore" in this starkly robust parable of aging. The poem begs to be judged, moreover, not so much in light of the original, as good a Latinist as Hecht was, but in relation to other efforts at translation. The Loeb version, for instance, politely titled "Lydia's Charms are Past," cries out for new life with its stilted Victorianisms and faux Shakespearean effects, almost as much as the phrases unwittingly conjured up by students in the comical Latin class Hecht describes in "The Mysteries of Caesar." "Caesar did with-hold his men from battle, / And he did have enough in presentness / To prohibit the enemy from further wastings, / From foragings and rap-ines." Hecht's wry insertion into the ode of a familiar line from Shakespeare's Sonnet 18 ("The darling buds of May") makes the fur-ther point, *pace* the Loeb translation, that Shakespeare can be a living presence ("he did have enough in presentness") if the reference fits into the current idiom.

Hecht hinted at this shift in emphasis between the two parts when he remarked on the dust jacket to *Flight Among the Tombs* that "The second part of the book, 'Proust on Skates,' expands on the themes and tones of the first part." "Expands" is a key word here and the reference to "Proust on Skates" illuminating. A favorite poem, Hecht had originally thought of using the poem's title to serve for the whole collection, but his editor, Harry Ford, wisely resisted this possibility, and in doing so not simply encouraged Hecht to find, as it turned out, in Christopher Smart a "slightly sinister" title that "beautifully matches the illustrations," but in effect freed up the Proust title for use as a subheading to indicate the thematic and tonal differences between the two parts.[36] With its dark, majestic, Hardy-like setting, "Proust on Skates" begins as if it could have been a poem headed for the first part but then swerves and indeed backtracks into the gloom a bit, before arriving at its true subject, expounding on the beautiful intricacies associated with Proust's style—an exemplary instance, as we shall see, on the page, in the present, of "Posterity's faint echo from the past."

Here are the first two of the ten stanzas:

> The alpine forests, like huddled throngs of mourners,
> Black, hooded, silent, resign themselves to wait
>   As long as may be required;
> A low pneumonia mist covers the glaciers,
> Spruces are bathed in a cold sweat, the late
>   Sun has long since expired,
>
> Though barely risen, and the gray cast of the day
> Is stark, unsentimental, and metallic.
>   Earth-stained and chimney-soiled
> Snow upon path and post is here to stay,
> Foundered in endless twilight, a poor relic
>   Of a once gladder world.

Into its magnificently belated and dark precincts worthy of Donne's "Nocturnal upon St. Lucy's Day"—"Spruces are bathed in a cold sweat, the late / Sun has long since expired"—the poem then admits people. Observers watch skaters execute various routines on "the polished soapstone lake." "A few tandem lovers, hand in hand / Perform their *pas de deux* along the edges / Oblivious, unconcerned." And as if

---

36. Letter, AH to Harry Ford, 26 November 1995; Letter, Harry Ford to AH, 28 November 1995, Hecht Archive.

we needed reminding, but we do, so oblivious are the lovers on the lake's edge: "This is a stony, vapor-haunted land /Of granite dusk, of wind sieved by the hedges,/ Their branches braced and thorned." All of this sumptuously melancholic description in turn becomes background itself for the arrival of "an odd party of three /Braided by silken ties," a party itself soon reduced in number leaving the sole image of a single person, who,

> as usual, all alone,
> And lacing on his skates,
> Steadies himself, cautiously issues forth
> Into the midst of strangers and his own
> Interior debates.

As our concentration turns to this one unnamed person, whose uncertainties and interior debates the poet seems to know so well, the lines then gradually issue forth in the most expressive gesture imaginable to capture a sense of the freedom suddenly experienced by the skater.

Over the course of three stanzas, in homage to the author—Proust, that is—a single sentence, probably the most extended and embroidered in all of Hecht, spreads itself across the white page:

> Sweatered and mufflered to protect the weak
> And lacey branches of his bronchial tree
>   From the fine-particled threat
> Of the moist air, he curves in an oblique
> And gentle gradient, floating swift and free—
>   No *danseur noble*, and yet
>
> He glides with a gaining confidence, inscribes
> Tentative passages, thinks again, backtracks,
>   Comes to a minute point,
> Then wheels about in widening sweeps and lobes,
> Large Palmer cursives and smooth *entrelacs*,
>   Preoccupied, intent
>
> On a subtle, long-drawn style and pliant script
> Incised with twin steel blades and qualified
>   Perfectly to express,
> With arms flung wide or gloved hands firmly gripped
> Behind his back, attentively, clear-eyed,
>   A glancing happiness.

The person who can be seen "lacing on his skates" is soon confident enough to produce "Large Palmer cursives and smooth *entrelacs*." The reference to the Palmer method of handwriting, popular in the United States in Proust's day, in which the writing instrument doesn't leave the page in making its curves, even when it comes to a "minute point," cinches the connection between skating and writing, and the freedom found in each, "floating swift and free—." Note the long dash, without a period, made in reference to Proust, of course, but also a reminder of the poet, who, in glancing fashion, has quietly pulled out all the stops curtailing each of the previous stanzas to form this single long, complex thought. So much incisory effort, it might seem, in retrospect, to arrive at that final line, and yet how effortless the process is in the reading, and momentarily triumphant, even if, as the final stanza concludes:

> It will not last, that happiness; nothing lasts;
> But will reduce in time to the clear brew
> Of simmering memory
> Nourished by shadowy gardens, music, guests,
> Childhood affections, and, of Delft, a view
> Steeped in a sip of tea.

The first line is true, almost to the point of sounding trite, until we see the melancholic remembrance of things past as providing the "bouillon of Proust's novel."[37] The reductions give us, as it were, the essence of a style that, like Vermeer's beautiful cityscape, a favorite painting of Proust's, the alpine forests are even required to respect. At the poem's end, they are still huddled on the sidelines, art momentarily giving us some comfort, like a cup of tea, whose steeped color reflects perfectly the radiantly alluring, variegated bronze of Vermeer's town.

From the poem on Proust to the elegies on Merrill and Brodsky, it is only a small step. In the "Adieu" to Merrill, Proust is among the "chosen band," with Dante, Rilke, and Mallarmé, who rejoice in "the rich polyphony of their latest friend"; and in the elegy to Brodsky, the last poem in the volume, we are reminded among many echoes— especially those from Auden's elegy on Yeats—of Proust's presence, the "Palmer cursives," now adjusted to fit the international circumstances of Brodsky's poetic identity: "In the Republic of Letters one fine hand, / Cyrillic, cursive, American, has been stilled." The metonymy of the hand points honorifically to Brodsky's signal literary achievements

---

37. Yenser, "Poetry in Review," 176.

spanning the old world and the new, from Leningrad to Brooklyn; and in Hecht's tribute to Brodsky's belief in "the lasting sovereignty of the word, / Beyond the grasp of politics or fashion," we are further reminded of the context of Proust's skillful act of writing as Hecht imagined it: "Escaped from the city's politics and fribble, / Hither has come an odd party of three," or four, if we include the poet. Or more if we follow out Hecht's footnote to Auden in the Brodsky elegy as part of posterity's accumulating echoes of the past.

No doubt these values are shared, if not trumpeted, by the seasoned poet of *Flight Among the Tombs*, whose interest in handwriting in the second part might be said to continue the graphic concerns of the first and the literariness of its twin creators, Baskin and Hecht. The second part is further marked by an unusual emphasis on literary references and sources, thus continuing "posterity's" promise in "Envoi." Poems serve as commentaries upon, expansions of curiosities of a kind found by the poet, as in the anecdote from Ronald Hayman's biography of Proust that provided the epigraph to the poem: "It really is rather odd to think of Proust on mule-back and on skates," Hecht remarked to Dana Gioia about the lines from Hayman that served as the epigraph to his poem. "In any case, it is an aspect of his life that rarely gets commented upon."[38] And so the tiny episode, mentioned only in passing by Hayman, becomes the seed for the poem and the central conceit of Proust's skating as a metaphor for the activity central to his life and identity: his writing.

These extended epigraphs are not so much decorative as probative, indeed part of the lyric's imaginary space linking the poem to the writings of another, in the manner we have already seen in the use made of the long quotation from Robert Hughes in the Matisse poem discussed in Chapter 6. We're invited to think about the reciprocally generative relationship between the two, an act of obbligato, to use a favorite metaphor of Hecht's, in which the poem now pays if not deference at least reference to its source.[39] A favorite passage of Hecht's from Aristotle's *Rhetoric*, for instance, appears as the extended epigraph

---

38. Letter, AH to Dana Gioia, 22 March 1996.
39. See page 175. I'm not suggesting a strict reversal and that the poems are subordinate to the texts that inspired them, merely that later Hecht seems more willing than ever to illustrate the complex set of obligations between reading and writing as a sign of the literacy he values so deeply, no doubt because he viewed it under threat from so many quarters, including, indeed especially, departments of English, where he taught for many years.

introducing "To Fortuna Parvulorum,"—the "Divinity of diminished expectations," as Hecht deliciously calls her. Another of the many poems in this volume measuring the ambitious follies of youth against the inevitable declinations of age, Aristotle's anecdote concludes on a note of plangent realism that "life on the whole is a bad business." But the poem's further surprise is to sound the bell through the croupier's call in French, in which the impoverished circumstance of age gives new meaning to the phrase "the chips are down":

> Now, having passed the obligatory stations,
>   I turn in turn to you,
> Divinity of diminished expectations,
> To whom I direct these tardy supplications,
>   Having been taught how few
>
> Are blessed enough to encounter on their way
>   The least chipped glint of joy,
> And learned in what altered tones I hear today
> The remembered words, "*Messieurs, les jeux sont faits,*"
>   That stirred me as a boy.

The poet is not so much a solitary maker here but a writer/reader of others in the process of making. Leaving a few tracks in the snow is a means of widening the radius of thought beyond a single point of the self as reference. "Go little poem in the company of others," we might imagine as the epigraph to the second part. To put the matter in the extreme, as Hecht does, it is to be a ruminant among ruminators, as in the case of what is surely the oddest poem in the volume: "A Ruminant." One ruminant (the poet) ruminates on the ruminations of "Sir Osbert Sitwell" (quoted from Martin C. D'Arcy, S.J.'s book, *The Mind and Heart of Love*, cited in the epigraph) on the habits of a ruminant, more commonly known as the camel (who is the further subject of Hecht's ruminations in "The Life of Crime," prompted by a passage, Hecht tells us in the notes, on Mayhew's *London Labour and the London Poor*). Short enough to quote in full, the first stanza of "A Ruminant" reads, rather stumbles into view, in the strange manner of something out of Dr. Seuss, or the Sir Thomas Browne of *Pseudodoxia Epidemica*, philological feet first and, a rarity in Hecht, without even the dignity of the left-hand margin in upper case:

> Out of the Urdu, into our instant ken,
> ambles the gross molester of the Sphinx,

> our *oont*, or camel,
> hunchbacked from failed exertions, poor Ur-Punch
> and brigand-clown of Noah's passengers,
>   the Hebrew *gimel*
>
> for the deformity it's luck to touch.
> Footpadded and austere, a temperance leader,
>   he slumps in torpid
> reverie over a sea of blistering dunes,
> yet easily is tamed, the Britannica says,
>   because he's stupid.
>
> Beware his soulful glances that conceal
> absence of thought and the ferocity
>   of a seasoned bigot,
> who nevertheless briefly became the bearer
> of kings and spices, the royal pattern of patience,
>   and wisdom's legate.

Dating back to "The Song of the Beasts" in *A Summoning of Stones* (1954), Hecht had often allotted a small space to beast fables: "Improvisations on Aesop" and "Giant Tortoise," for instance, in *The Hard Hours* (1967); and had the reprise here of this earlier interest been written in syllabic verse, we might readily add Marianne Moore and her penchant for exotic zoology to the company of Dr. Seuss and Dr. Browne, the former an early friend of the Hecht family, the latter a connoisseur of curiosities, whose *Pseudodoxia Epidemica* often engaged Hecht's inquiring mind. But Hecht's impulse, while sharing Moore's interest in arcane learning and a lower case left-hand margin, is basically comical and satirical, with the purposefully clumsy rhyme of "torpid" and "stupid" giving way to the more worrisome pairing of "bigot" and "legate." Not only might we think of "A Ruminant" as Aesop moralized, but in light of the Sitwell quotation, the poem amounts to something of a commentary on an Aesopian puzzle raised by one kind of ruminant about another kind. How can this most physically unattractive-looking beast be a mirror of mankind? Hecht's answer: not because it is unattractive but because this "gross molester of the Sphinx" gives off the appearance of ruminating, of thinking. If Proust on a mule is a strange sight, the "oont" is stranger still, and, as it turns out, far more dangerous, a threat we might understand to the value of thinking itself.

In Hecht's small republic of letters, the learning is too promiscuous to follow a straight and narrow classical line. The little curio called "The Message," "adapted," as we discover in the endnotes, "from a poem by Meleager in the Greek Anthology," seems like a snippet, in rhyming couplets, cut out of a longer poem by Pope.

> Fuscus, my friend, go tell that lying... Wait!
> Hold on a moment. Let me reformulate
> The sort of thing I'm after. Tell her she,
> Whether she likes the thought or not, will be...
> Or, rather, let me put it another way.
> Say that you left me reveling, and say
> Everyone says how good-natured I am.
> And let her know I'm happy as a clam.

That's all there is. Do we have a throwaway at last, contra Hollander? Or is the poem an act of recovery and re-covering? It catches our eye mainly because of the charming way the speaker fumbles over finding the right words for the situation—and then finally does in the last couplet, which has no place in the Greek original.

The poem that follows, another "classic," is promiscuous in an altogether different sense. "The Mysteries of Caesar" is probably the funniest single poem Hecht wrote since "The Ghost in the Martini." The comedy is not of the sexually rambunctious, psychological disruptive kind found in the earlier poem, but of a more genteel order, fit for the academic setting, and again engaging the familiar subject of youth versus age. The mysteries on hand refer to both the linguistic hash the boys make trying to render Caesar's Latin into sensible English and the mystique of the aptly named Mr. Sypher, whose mysterious identity as a repressed homosexual the boys also cannot fathom. The latter mystery, gently exposed in the final quatrain, lends a touch of pathos to the poem that balances, to a degree, the more comical rape and foraging of language going on in the classroom, which is rendered with precision and opportunistic flair by the poet. The latter quality is especially visible in his handling of the rhyming quatrains (*abba*), of which I quote only the introductory stanzas:

> Known to the boys in his Latin class as "Sir,"
> Balding, cologned, mild-mannered Mr. Sypher
> Defied his sentence as a highschool lifer
> With a fresh, carefully chosen boutonniere
>
> As daily he heard the Helvetians plead their cause
> In chains while captives were brought face to face
> With the impositions of the ablative case,
> The torts and tortures of the grammatic laws.

In the first stanza alone, Hecht mates "Sypher" with "lifer," framed by
"'Sir'" with "boutonniere," the two weak (feminine) interior rhymes
portending what? Followed by the more ostentatiously assertive
"'Sir,'" then finely qualified by its elaborately floral rhyming mate
"boutonniere." Mr. Sypher arrives each day prim but hopeful. After
which occur a more conventional pairing ("cause," "face," "case,"
"laws"), although a disturbing enough set of partners in today's liti-
gious world; then follow in the third stanza "impediments," "shackles,"
"freckles," and (hudibrastically) "pluperfect tense." And so it goes, with
surprise after surprise: "agonies," "*Gallic Wars*," "dishonorable scars,"
"'exercise'"—the punctuation adding to the variety, with a frequent
employment of enjambment and an occasional hyphenated rhyme,
"superb" with "imperturb-," to lend a further note of improvisation
and transitoriness to the whole escapade. In a 2001 letter, Richard
Wilbur complimented Hecht for being "the most resourceful rhymer
since George Gordon, Lord Byron,"[40] a remark whose primary effect
may be to cause other modern contenders to spring to mind (Auden?
Merrill? Wilbur himself?); but even in such lettered, literate company
(a republic within a republic), "The Mysteries of Caesar" offers plenty
of evidence of Hecht's virtuosic talents in this category.

I want to conclude this survey of later Hecht not as Hecht did, with
the elegy to Brodsky, but with the first of the flower poems he wrote:
"*Là-bas*: A Trance."[41] The poem has a number of splendid moments and
a rightful place in the curious itinerary of the second half as I have
been describing it. It also forms a link to the fuller exfoliation of flower
poems in Hecht's last volume of verse, *The Darkness and the Light*. The
title, of course, is French, meaning "over there" or, more ominously,
"Down There, or the Damned," in reference to the title of Joris-Karl
Huysman's scandalous, popular novel published in 1891; however the
figure at the center of the poem is a poet and, though unnamed, no
doubt Charles Baudelaire, the author of a single volume of poems
called *Les Fleurs du Mal*. Hecht's flower poem is appropriately placed
with the other "French" poems in the volume, thus forming something of a trio on poetry, painting, and prose fiction. And whereas
Brodsky's itinerary is a matter of history, the route here is a creation of

40. Letter, Richard Wilbur to AH, 22 March 2001. Hecht Archive. See also Hecht's
    wide-ranging essay "On Rhyme," in *Melodies Unheard*, 252–74.
41. Fax, AH to Leonard Baskin, 23 March 1996.

fancy, airing itself as such by beginning in exotic Samarkand, the ancient city (in the modern state of Uzbekistan) famous for its location on the Silk Road, and then, with its cargo of "emeralds and drugs," continuing on through "such ports of call as Amsterdam," and concluding in Paris in the "Hempen mirages and opium reveries / Crowding the mind of a Parisian poet." Along with a wonderful hallucinatory mirage of ship masts, these produce exotic reveries,

> Harvested from unfathomed depths of mirrors:
> Harems of young, voluptuous, sloe-eyed
>
> Houris, undressed, awaiting his commands,
> Untiring courtyard fountains casting jewels
> Thriftlessly into blue-and-white-tiled pools,
> Splashes mingled with languid sarabandes.

This is a travel poem made attractive by its easy movements and vivid descriptions. Its only requirement is somewhere and somehow the poet must tuck in a tulip along the way, which he does at the end, suddenly bringing together in the reflecting, dreaming mind of our Parisian poet the three geographical points the poem has traversed in a grammatical epiphany of resemblance—from Carpaccio to Carpet (caps intact) turned into "Holland's tulips" and then turned into its etymological origins in "turbans":

> Carpaccio's Middle East evokes an air-borne
> Carpet, a sash and headgear the color of flame
> Turned into Holland's tulips whose very name
> Comes to him from the Turkish word for turban.

Recalling Frost's advice for young poets not to "work up to a last line," Hecht once spoke of the dangers of beginning a poem backwards, that is starting from a "splendid coda and then be[ing] obliged to work backwards in order to justify it." He went on to surmise that Frost "probably also meant that to hit the reader over the head in the last line by arriving at a Metro-Goldwyn-Mayer finish is only one of the ways, and not necessarily the most subtle one, that a poem can achieve a major effect."[42] Much of the art of "*Là-bas*: A Trance" is not just keeping the tulip out of sight so the poem can go its own merry independent way, irrespective of the beautiful Baskin drawing it originally

---

42. Hecht, "On the Methods and Ambitions of Poetry," *The Hudson Review* 18.4 (1965–6), 498–9.

accompanied. It's also a matter of managing the closure, the moment when the tulip appears. Hecht clearly had a splendid coda in mind for this poem, probably initiated by looking up the flower in the *Oxford English Dictionary*—the holy ghost of Hecht's trinity of authorities that includes the Bible and Shakespeare—and seeing the word's rich migration westward from its Turkish roots in the sixteenth century. And yet the ending comes upon us with an air of surprise, as if floating in on an etymological carpet of its own, the kind of which poems are made, especially by a seasoned poet entranced by a prospect of flowers.

9

The Darkness and the Light and the Art of Reticence

It is easy to become sentimental about an author's last book—or "last look," as Helen Vendler has succinctly formulated the potentially overwrought equation between writing and dying.[1] At the extreme, we might think of this temptation as the John of Gaunt syndrome, in which the desire to say something big at the end by either poet or critic sweeps away any sense of the immediate audience and occasion. Such is not possible, or at least easy, with Hecht's last book of poems, *The Darkness and the Light* (2001). Not only does it not conclude his poetic life—Hecht would compose another half-dozen or so accomplished poems before his death in 2004—but the volume is itself marked by the continuation of his productive alliance with Leonard Baskin. To the dozen or so flower poems appearing in this collection, Hecht added another ten on biblical topics for what was to have been, rather grandly, a single copy of a fine press edition made for a wealthy Texan patron, had Baskin not died before the project's completion. The volume is then further fleshed out with another fifteen lyrics on a variety of topics, some commemorative, others occasional, often with a retrospective cast to them, and a gathering of translations from favorite authors—two by Baudelaire, three by Horace, two by Charles d'Orléans, and one each by Vaillant and Goethe.

Nonetheless, if not written out of the knowledge of being his last, the book is imbued with a sense of lateness, as how could it not be given the poet's advanced age memorably commemorated in "Sarabande on

---

1. Vendler, *Last Looks, Last Books: Stevens, Plath, Lowell, Bishop, Merrill* (Princeton: Princeton University Press, 2010).

Attaining the Age of Seventy-Seven." The book's dominant tenor is one of reticence and refinement. The poems are more given to meditation and the mysteries surrounding the unspoken than the drama of extended narration, more given, in fact, to an aversion of what dazzles in favor of an exploration of what is glimmering and dusky. Humility is a key note. The book certainly has some sharp edges, as we'll see, and some high flights and humor, but the blurb on the jacket, whoever composed it, rightly captures the chief characteristic of the volume, especially in relation to Hecht's previous books. Followers of Hecht's poetry, it observes, "will recognize an evolution of style in many of these poems—a quiet and understated voice, passing through darkness toward realms of delight."

Indeed, quiet and understated is the book's tonally atmospheric beginning and ending. The first poem, "Late Afternoon: The Onslaught of Love," begins not as an outpouring of passion as the subtitle might imply but with an invitation for the reader to listen carefully:

> At this time of day
> One could hear the caulking irons sound
> Against the hulls in the dockyard.
> Tar smoke rose between trees
> And large oily patches floated on the water,
> Undulating unevenly
> In the purple sunlight
> Like the surfaces of Florentine bronze.

The poem will end, as does this stanza, moving in the direction of pure silence. And so will the collection as a whole. The final poem, a prayer as metrically spare as anything Hecht ever wrote, is spun out of Psalm 139:12: " 'The Darkness and the Light are Both Alike to Thee,' " from which, in turn, the book derives its title:

> Like trailing silks, the light
> Hangs in the olive trees
> As the pale wine of day
> Drains to its very lees:
> Huge presences of gray
> Rise up, and then it's night.
>
> Distantly lights go on.
> Scattered like fallen sparks
> Bedded in peat, they seem
> Set in the plushest darks

Until a timid gleam
Of matins turns them wan,

Like the elderly and frail
Who've lasted through the night,
Cold brows and silent lips,
For whom the rising light
Entails their own eclipse,
Brightening as they fail.

We will return to these poems, but their presence here reminds us that Hecht, like Auden, always maintained a small place for the kind of purer lyric traceable back to Thomas Campion, as in the case of "Anthem," in *The Transparent Man*, or those more Herbertian lyrics interleaved in "Rites and Ceremonies" from *The Hard Hours*, or the lovely brief poem, "Retreat," in *Millions of Strange Shadows*, beginning, simply, "Day peters out." By purer lyric, I mean to underscore an idea proposed by Hecht when, in contradistinction to Donne's dramatic poetry, he speaks of a certain kind of lyric as being understood to be

a pure instant of perception captured in the course of its fleeting evanescence; it was a rapid sketch of some state of the soul, a hasty impression of the receptive mind, more inward than outward, often taking some grain of reality as a point of departure into a state of private rapture.[2]

Although this was not the kind of poetry Hecht generally favored, he was also not opposed to it "on any theoretical basis"; and, in this last book of poems, without altogether abandoning an interest in the dramatic monologue or associated notions of opposition and contrasts, he explored more fully this other kind of lyric, not hastily drawn or rapturously private, but still with an emphasis on the evanescent, on "lateness" in a variety of senses, as the two poems quoted suggest, in which, for the most part, Hecht attends to the smaller, often more private and mysterious moments in life. This is a difference in degree rather than kind, but the shift is a chief feature of his last, quieter, and more understated book and primarily responsible for what I think of as Hecht's "late style," his art of reticence affecting both the overall mood of the volume and the arrangement of poems.

2. See Hecht's remarks from *Anthony Hecht in Conversation with Philip Hoy* (1999; rev. 3rd edn. London: BTL, 2004), 72. As the comparison with Donne makes clear, the concept of purity, despite its sense, is always a relative value.

To follow out one strand of this argument: so discreetly titled and placed are the flower poems that their collective presence can readily escape critical awareness, thus achieving at least one of their creator's goals: the independent integrity of each poem as well as the volume as a whole. Only the poem called "Poppy" bears its floral origins openly, the last such poem in the collection, as if Hecht were leaving a belated key for the reader. Otherwise, as was the case with the flower poems in *Flight Among the Tombs*, the poems go their own way: a "strenuous excursion" in the ironic mode of the Romantic sublime in "A Fall," based on an episode mentioned in a letter by Byron, in which the rhododendron figures as a central image for describing the dense, head-spinning spray of a waterfall; a Herbertian-sounding definition poem called "Despair" that surprises us with associating the condition with "the full glare of relentless marigold sunshine"—until we understand more, that is, about the symbolic play of light and shadow in this last book of poems.

In a sense, their ingenuity is likewise a feature of their reticence. The poems take us by circuitous or devious routes to their originary floral circumstances. "Look Deep," for instance, never actually spells out its connection to the iris. The title invokes a session with a hypnotist (look deep in my eyes), with the eye containing a "pupil" and the iris present only by inference with regard to the pupil's "many-tinctured curtain / Of moiré silks." And as we look more deeply into the poem, we descend by way of refracted light from a beveled mirror, led by an unnamed multicolored messenger (Iris by another name), through a dreamscape of theatrical or operatic productions, of which the last, in reference to the biblical forty days of Noah's flood, finally delivers an image of an "*arc-en-ciel*," a rainbow in French but also associated in Greek mythology with the goddess from which the showy flower takes its name because of its wide variety of colors.

Subtle and indirect for sure, such acts of verbal bewitchery or "ensorcelment"—the word appears in the thematically related facing poem, the villanelle "Nocturne: A Recurring Dream"—deliver their secrets by compounding their message and therefore refusing to equate a poem with a single message or point of origin. The poem "Secrets," in fact, almost completely withholds its floral secret: another name for Foxglove is "witches thimble," Hecht tells Baskin[3]—the poem ending

<hr/>

3. Letter, AH to Leonard Baskin, 24 October 1997.

with the word "thimble" while describing the practices of witches throughout. A knowledge of folklore, helpful here, is explicitly summoned in a note to "The Hanging Gardens of Tyburn," which plays on ancient tales involving (again) the never-named mandrake plant, some of whose effects are familiar to students of literature in the works of Donne and Webster; and the association made by the Elizabethan herbalist, John Gerard, of the sunflower with "bodily lust" is put to work by Hecht, albeit in a different key, in the surging energy, the "Tumult of muscled currents," in "An Orphic Calling."[4]

As this poem suggests, indirection can enable rhetorical power or gusto. The poem is constructed in part out of a single, twenty-four-line sentence and is as baroquely energetic and linguistically playful as anything Hecht ever wrote. The opening lines begin in the present, *in medias res*, or midstream:

> The stream's *courante* runs on, a *force majeure*,
> A Major rippling of the pure mind of Bach,
> Tumult of muscled currents, formed in far
> Reaches of edelweiss, cloud and alpenstock.

Courante (suite or jig)/current; Bach (brook); a major rippling in A major; the stream's current is a metaphor for inspiration, even in late age, all followed by a modest single quatrain, classically simple in its reference to Orpheus and to the sunflower itself:

> An Orphic calling it is, one that invites
> Responsories, a summons to lute-led
> Nature, as morning's cinnabar east ignites
> And the instinctive sunflower turns its head.

Likewise, "Witness," Wilbur's favorite, is a tour de force of a different order. Writes Wilbur to Hecht: "It distils into a bearable strong draught all that cruelty and violence to which you have felt called to be a witness, and a true one."[5] As Hecht remarked, although to a different reader, the poem "undertakes a task I attempted once before in a poem called 'Poem without Anybody,' written in memory of James Wright. Both poems eliminate all human presence."[6] "Witness" is more severe still since the poem is without even a dedication:

4. Fax, AH to Leonard Baskin, 23 March 1996.
5. Letter, Wilbur to AH, 22 March 2001. Hecht Archive.
6. Letter, AH to John Van Doren, 16 February 2002 (*SL*, 331–2).

Against the enormous rocks of a rough coast
The ocean rams itself in pitched assault
And spastic rage to which there is no halt;
Foam-white brigades collapse; but the huge host

Has infinite reserves; at each attack
The impassive cliffs look down in gray disdain
At scenes of sacrifice, unrelieved pain,
Figured in froth, aquamarine and black.

Something in the blood-chemistry of life,
Unspeakable, impressive, undeterred,
Expresses itself without needing a word
In this sea-crazed Empedoclean Strife.

It is a scene of unmatched melancholy,
Weather of misery, cloud cover of distress,
To which there are no witnesses, unless
One counts the briny, tough and thorned sea holly.

Wilbur's response reminds us that we don't require knowing that the poem is part of a floral sequence to grasp its essence. And yet an important truth is gained, too, by concentrating on the figure of the sea holly, included in a modest after-the-fact matter ("unless / One counts") to conclude this exercise in military fustian. We reckon again, through the sharp contrast, how understated the conclusion is with regard to a subject of major importance to the poet. In the mundane image of the "briny, tough and thorned sea holly," the poet quietly engages (without quite engaging) the kind of engagé poetry-of-witness that Hecht distrusted in the writings of some of his contemporaries.[7] The sea holly is a veteran of its embattled environment, and anything but florid.

The biblical poems tell a different story. Their scriptural roots are immediately traceable in the notes. All stem from familiar Old Testament subjects, not the heroes of faith noted by Paul in Hebrews 11 (more about Paul down the line), but selective incidents balancing, roughly, women against men, in scenes that would readily lend themselves to graphic representation by an artist like Baskin. All are treated with a distinctly modernist, not postmodernist edge; most are delivered as brief dramatic monologues, some almost in the manner of a joke; a few feature sharp juxtapositions between past and present. Their success in part is that Hecht does not ask too much of his sacred text or its

---

7. See Letter, AH to Charles Tung, 2 February 1994 (*SL*, 263–4).

subjects, an act of compositional reticence only slightly surprising given the significance generally attached to scripture in much of his writings, whether verse or prose. In *The Hard Hours* alone, think of "Rites and Ceremonies," "The Vow," and "Behold the Lilies of the Field," or of the epigraph from Luther's translation of John that hovers demonically over "The Book of Yolek." But in *The Darkness and the Light*, the Bible is treated more in the manner of a literary text, after the writings of Robert Alter, whose critical studies of the Bible Hecht admired.

Most of the poems are deftly executed portraits or character studies, not untrue to their source but shaded by the poet for dramatic effect, the ironies often of a softer, sometimes comical sort. "I'm Haman the Hangman" begins "Haman" in something of a ridiculous fashion, and though he is clearly an analogue or type of the Nazi executioner, Hecht assumes that his readers will remember that Haman, in the Book of Esther, was hoist by his own petard, or, rather, hung on gallows of his own making. The ironic line on him begins early: "Let the Jews tremble and beware." The note of bravado recalls the irony of Shelley's Ozymandias, who boasts, "Look on my Works, ye mighty, and despair!"; and the narrowness, indeed rigidity of Haman's "us" versus "them" logic is adroitly captured in an alternating rhyme scheme that never deviates from its fundamental, sound-alike terms (engineer, structure; beware, capture, etc.). Haman is less than human.

In a different vein, loosely blank-verse "Judith" might be "The Dover Bitch" in reverse—or in revenge. She's never had much of an itch for men, she tells us, in a matter-of-fact narrative that immediately cuts against the frequently romanticized image of her as a sword-bearing biblical heroine: "It took less valor than I'm reputed for. / Since I was a small child I have hated men." The opening plain-spoken lines signal the abrupt beginning of her unvarnished anti-male tale, furthered by expressing her disappointment over her unwanted physical attractions. The brief saga concludes just as abruptly as it began, with a bar-room punch line about cleavage that ought to raise a smile in anyone but Holofernes:

> But at last, as fate would have it, I found a chance
> To put my curse to practical advantage.
> It was easy. Holofernes was pretty tight;
> I had only to show some cleavage and he was done for.

Hecht gives us "a certain slant" on these biblical episodes, to borrow an important image from a poem we'll turn to in more detail later in this chapter. Indeed, in an unrhymed sonnet, a down-in-the-mouth Miriam laments her disappearance from the limelight over the course of her brief three-book appearance in Exodus, Numbers, and finally Deuteronomy. Slanted but not untruthful: the poem fleshes out the story of her biblical decline—literally, in reference to her "white affliction" as a reminder of her punishment by God in Numbers, sometimes overlooked by readers concentrating only on her early biography: her glorious entry in Exodus 15 with timbrel in hand leading other women in song celebrating Israel's miraculous exodus from Egypt. And "Elders," which does include a brief epigraph from a Brahms song ("Ein dunkeler Schacht ist Liebe"—love is a dark shaft) offers a descent into the warped psychobiography and masturbatory practices of one of the elders, joined by another, "thrummed by the same impulse," to account for their perverse desire to spy on Susanna. It is as unattractive a portrait as Hecht ever produced, in sharp contrast to "Lot's Wife," the most sympathetic and "poetic" of these biblical studies.

This poem allows Hecht to voice a (nearly) unobstructed pleasure for "those childhood days," a rarity in his poetry because childhood is almost always shadowed by some grave malady or horrific event. But, of course, we all know what became of Lot's wife because she looked back, and although Hecht graciously elides this moment of judgment, her punishment for disobedience filters into the imagery in subtle ways (we have sugar and sand but no salt, for instance) and the recognition makes further exquisite the act of retrospection, as if all time has almost stopped, on its way to stopping completely once she is turned into salt. The poem, brief enough to quote, is an exercise in lyrical fullness:

> How simple the pleasures of those childhood days,
> Simple but filled with exquisite satisfactions.
> The iridescent labyrinth of the spider,
> Its tethered tensor nest of polygons
> Puffed by the breeze to a little bellying sail—
> Merely observing this gave infinite pleasure.
> The sound of rain. The gentle graphite veil
> Of rain that makes of the world a steel engraving,
> Full of soft fadings and faint distances.
> The self-congratulations of a fly,
> Rubbing its hands. The brown bicameral brain
> Of a walnut. The smell of wax. The feel
> Of sugar to the tongue: a delicious sand.

> One understands immediately how Proust
> Might cherish all such postage-stamp details.
> Who can resist the charms of retrospection?

On the verge of being without verbs, the poem quietly unfurls, "Puffed by the breeze to a little bellying sail." As the image suggests, the poem is almost but not quite a still life. Nature has been slowed down, not frozen in time, made more sensuous, fanciful, and immediate, as a child might remember, or rather as a poem about childhood memory might ideally recall, whether by Herbert, Vaughan, or Wordsworth. The spider's web, in this instance, is tethered but not fixed, made mobile by a breeze. Rain makes the world into "a steel engraving" and yet also "Full of soft fadings and faint distances." Hecht's fly is not crystallized in amber (à la Herrick) but seen "Rubbing its hands." Not just sand but the sands of time have been made delicious through art, as the surprising allusion to Proust at the end makes clear: surprising because until then it is possible to think that Lot's wife has been speaking. But the innocent "charms" clearly belong to our highly sophisticated poet, who has called nostalgia into being.

These biblical slants are made sharper and more acutely painful, however, through certain acts of juxtaposition, as in the case of "Samson," one of two biblical poems that show Hecht returning to familiar territory, violence and war. In "Samson," Hecht reworks the beginning few lines of the story in Judges, those dealing with the birth annunciation by the angel and the strictures against wine and the shearing of hair. In alternating fashion, these brief four-line scenes are set against modern redactions: a mother at the Boston Lying-In Hospital for women, with "with births defying expectation," and the "Hebrew shul at Lodz," one of the first cities in Poland overrun by the Nazis in September 1939, where,

> the little boys
> Studied the Torah, and let their sidelocks curl
> And sway to the rhythm of reading. They too have been
> Sacrificed, like Nazarites before them.

What's striking about "Samson" is all that is left unsaid. Hecht was never drawn to imagism as a movement, but these quatrains function like individual snapshots, their relational meaning a matter of interpretation by the reader. Having distilled a few crucial images, the poet steps back in order to let us puzzle out the connections between past and present, sacred and profane, light and darkness, the potential delusionary nature of the concept of the "miraculous" birth, and the precise sense in which "Sacrificed" is used at the end.

The absence of an explanatory narrative here points to an element of silence or mystery that Hecht will exploit more fully in the most ambitious poem in the volume. "Sacrifice" is composed in three parts, and Hecht was insistent that it form the centerpiece of the collection, a view honored as well in the cover design of the book produced by Chip Kidd juxtaposing a detail of a colorful Tiepolo painting, *Angel Preventing the Sacrifice of Isaac*, against a shadowy image from a newsreel of modern soldiers at war. (The precise sense in which we are to understand the poem's title represents one of the poem's chief puzzles.) The first two parts focus on the story of Abraham and Isaac, each adopting a deliberately archaic voice in different verse forms. Abraham faces the terrible decision of being asked to sacrifice his son. Isaac wrestles with accepting his role as the lamb being sentenced to slaughter. The third far longer part, set in 1945, at the end of World War II, then offers a lengthy, more discursive account of a German soldier, in retreat in France, threatening a family on a farm for a bicycle. None of the parts on its own is especially complicated—one doesn't feel the tension so tightly at work in these last poems—but their assembled meaning is puzzling. In what ways do the parts inform the whole? How do modern and ancient worlds interact, especially with respect to the concept of sacrifice?

In the best account of the poem to date, David Yezzi has argued that

the poem casts a bleak light on the biblical story, suggesting that God asks Abraham to sacrifice his son for no good reason, for a bicycle. Was Abraham right to agree to the sacrifice? God and the soldier call off the death in the end, but the resulting rift between father and son, the silence that ensues, mark both Hecht's poem and the biblical tale with extreme bitterness.[8]

And bleak the poem certainly ends up being. As with the biblical account, the war narrative is a temptation story, a trial again of the father with regard to saving or sacrificing his son, in this case for something as trivial as a bicycle, a trial we're made to see that he fails utterly. Although the soldier decides against shooting the boy for reasons that are left deliberately obscure, the "long silence" produced by the event

---

8. David Yezzi, "The Morality of Anthony Hecht," *The New Criterion* 22 (April 2004), 33.

is felt far into the future, with the father's shameful actions in this one
moment destroying any notion of family harmony:

> There followed a long silence, a long silence.
> For years they lived together in that house,
> Through daily tasks, through all the family meals,
> In agonized, unviolated silence.

The pauses enforced by the punctuation could hardly be heavier, the
verbal repetitions more tasking. In someone else's modern narrative,
war might create heroes, but not in Hecht's. There is nothing redemptive in the world of 1945, as was true, much earlier, in " 'More Light!
More Light!' "

But if "Sacrifice" invites us to think of parallels with the past, as
does " 'More Light!,' " its method of juxtaposition also asks us to regard
differences, again in the manner of the earlier poem. The Abraham
and Isaac story is a test of faith, in which, by contrast, Abraham agrees
with great reluctance to sacrifice his son, on behalf of someone, a
particular kind of God, who has shown him favors in the past; and the
sudden urging of this trial or temptation on the son poses a dilemma,
a central mystery worth exploring, debating, or representing in art, as
sculptors and painters, scholars and poets have done for centuries. In
a sense, this part of the poem represents Hecht's contribution to this
tradition. What the latter war narrative does, though, is open up the
biblical story to thought, as Yezzi has argued, in which the poet can
raise important religious questions without moralizing. If one story—
scripture—has priority over the other, its authority is not absolute in
the sense of being a transcription of the Word of God, but comparative; and by further dividing the scriptural story between father and
son, Hecht allows each his particular view on what both regard as a
terrifying moment, a moment about which Hecht, like Yeats before
him in Easter 1916, can only respond with ambivalence over events
bearing so fully on his heritage. "All changed, changed utterly: /
A terrible beauty is born." Yeats' refrain might serve as one gloss on
the Abraham and Isaac story, with all the troubled history the event
put in motion, including the "sacrifice" of the devout in the persons
of "the little boys" at Lodz. The other view, offered by the war narrative, tracks the element of change into one of those mysterious dark
corners of behavior during war that seems to defy explanation and
yet cannot be forgotten, or forgiven.

"Sacrifice" is a poem that doubly challenges, but for different reasons, the limits of human comprehension. One thing Hecht is not doing, however, by placing the war story *after* the biblical narrative, is interpreting the story of Abraham and Isaac typologically, that is, in anticipation of a New Testament emphasis on the sacrifice of Jesus and the insistent matter of personal faith in light of the Pauline interpretation of the Gospels that made the Hebrew Bible and its laws anachronistic. Hecht renders the comparison obsolete by removing the definite article from his poem, a revision made more radically complete in yet another biblical poem. "The Road to Damascus" brings into sharp, critical focus a view of Paul that has occasionally hovered around the edges of Hecht's poetry, appearing as Paul does at the end of "The Feast of Stephen" and by implication in the epigraph to "The Book of Yolek." Of even greater relevance to *The Darkness and the Light* in general is Hecht's late essay, "St. Paul's Epistle to the Galatians," a penetrating critique of the motives underlying Paul's rhetoric and character that concludes by making stunning, ironic use of the parable of Lazarus and Dives in Luke 16:19–31 to underscore the authority Jesus found in Moses and the prophets. Not only is the essay the most succinct expression of Hecht's theological predisposition; it also includes an illuminating summary of his thoughts about his growing up Jewish with an intense interest in a literature that was predominantly Christian.[9]

"The Road to Damascus" was not part of the biblical series with Baskin. It owed its initial inspiration to a painting by Francesco Ubertini that Hecht found "rather off-putting,"[10] but the poem, also off-putting but in a deliberately interesting way, has a strong place in a volume that explores a variety of biblical stories, including several involving the New Testament, with the "Road to Damascus" representing a crossroads of a sort. It is a poem of unbridled bitterness, of corrosive demystification. An initial query of just two words, "What happened?" sets the rest in motion, including several theories used to explain what happened

9. Originally published in Alfred Corn, ed., *Incarnation: Contemporary Writers on the New Testament* (New York: Viking Press, 1990), 148–61, the essay is collected in Hecht's *Melodies Unheard: Essays on the Mysteries of Poetry* (Baltimore: Johns Hopkins University Press, 2003), 238–51. Further page references are to *Melodies Unheard*.

10. Letter, AH to Philip Hoy, 18 June 1999. The poem was originally composed for Grant Holcomb, ed., *Voices in the Gallery: Writers on Art* (Rochester: University of Rochester Press, 2001).

to Paul at the moment of his supposed conversion in Acts. He was felled by an omen; his horse was startled by a snake; he was experiencing an epileptic episode, a condition he shared with a number of other famous people, as the notes to a draft of the poem make clear. The last described a medical condition in which Hecht had long taken a special interest because of his brother, Roger's, affliction; and he gives greatest attention to this theory:

> We are told by certain learned doctors that those
> Thus stricken are granted an inkling of that state
> Where *There Shall Be No More Time*, as it is said;
> As though from a pail, spilled water were to repose
> Midair in pebbles of clarity, all its weight
> Turned light, in a glittering, loose, but stopped cascade.

There are few moments in *The Darkness and the Light* more fully ironic than this one. The "learned doctors" refers not to biblical scholars but medical doctors; the invocation of an italicized line from Revelation (10.6) is used to gloss an effect produced by the seizure. And the beautiful simile that follows carries an allusion to "light" to describe a physical sensation only. But there is one moment more darkly and bitterly ironic than this, and it follows immediately, carrying with it a lifetime of contempt for an interpreter responsible, directly and indirectly, for so much pain done to others through the elevation of the New Testament over the Old:

> The Damascene culprits now could rest untroubled,
> Their delinquencies no longer the concern
> Of this fallen, converted Pharisee. He rather
> From sighted blindness to blind sight went hobbled
> And was led forth to a house where he would turn
> His wrath from one recusancy to another.

That last sentence has something of the dark wrath found in Milton's roll call of the fallen devils in *Paradise Lost* as they wander about committing various acts of desecration.

In light of this and the other biblical poems, we might readily agree that *The Darkness and the Light* is "Hecht's most Jewish book."[11] We might also recall the second of the two couplets quoted from Wallace

11. Robyn Creswell, "Painting and Privacy: On Anthony Hecht," *Raritan* 21 (Winter 2002), 30.

Stevens' "The Sun This March" that serve as epigraphs for the volume: "Oh! Rabbi, rabbi, fend my soul for me / And true savant of this dark nature be." The fact that it is quoted from Stevens tells an important truth about Hecht's last book: that its theology is not doctrinal but spiritual, and if biblically based not exclusively so on the Hebrew Bible. Across the page from "The Road to Damascus" is a curious poem in the manner of a Kafka-like parable but bearing the Yeatsian title, "The Ceremony of Innocence," thus inviting us to think of the poem as performing an adjustment on Yeats' apocalyptic "The Second Coming," with its famous line that "the ceremony of innocence is drowned." An adjustment, but of what kind? Hecht had puzzled over where to place this poem in putting together the collection,[12] but in retrospect its location seems both obvious and perfect for the light it casts on, and the illumination it receives from, the Pauline "Road to Damascus." Here is an unnamed someone who did participate with others in acts of brutality, as the poem's first ten lines recount, but also discovered— quietly—the errors of his ways:

> They learned that they had murdered the wrong man.
> And this made one of them thoughtful. Some years after,
> He quietly severed connections with the others,
> Moved to a different city, took holy orders,
> And devoted himself to serving God and the poor,
> While the intended victim continued to live
> On a walled estate, sentried around the clock
> By a youthful, cell phone-linked praetorian guard.

The laconic phrase, "and this made one of them thoughtful," speaks volumes here—and for the volume at large, indeed of the significant difference between two concepts so close in meaning: the "long silence" of shame encountered at the end of "Sacrifice" and the silence or quietude associated with reflection. No outward change of name here (from Saul to Paul) but an inward change of being, not the kind of alteration that will determine the destiny of a "new" people or a Second Coming but a conversion in the direction of goodness to help those in need. The unobtrusive modesty is part of the message—its wisdom—as well as the recognition of the evident limitations. "While" embraces the continuation of evil alongside good, just as the title of

---

12. Letter, AH to J. D. McClatchy, 6 February 2000.

Hecht's book of poems places the darkness and the light as part of the same continuous vision.

Stevens' "Rabbi," as Eleanor Cook has helped us to understand, is a figure for wisdom and knowledge, the poet's scholarly companion, and the same is true for Hecht—in this instance embodied in the unnamed figure in this poem and not, obviously, in the person of Paul who is, in effect, pre-empted or displaced by the scholarly rabbi. We might see this logic of transformed devotion further developed in one of the most artful poems in the volume, "Illumination." The title plays on an altogether different meaning of "Illumination" than that claimed to have been experienced by Paul on the road to Damascus: not violent or sudden light—what Hecht describes as "the full glare of relentless marigold sunshine" in "Despair"—but gradual and careful, the kind of "Illumination" associated with the time-consuming production of finely detailed works of art:

> Ground lapis for the sky, and scrolls of gold,
> Before which shepherds kneel, gazing aloft
> At visiting angels clothed in egg-yolk gowns,
> Celestial tinctures smuggled from the East,
> From sunlit Eden, the palmed and plotted banks
> Of sun-tanned Aden. Brought home in fragile grails,
> Planted in England, rising at Eastertide,
> Their petals cup stamens of topaz dust,
> The powdery stuff of cooks and cosmeticians.
> But to the camel's-hair tip of the finest brush
> Of Brother Anselm, it is the light of dawn,
> Gilding the hems, the sleeves, the fluted pleats
> Of the antiphonal archangelic choirs
> Singing their melismatic *pax in terram.*
> The child lies cribbed below, in bestial dark,
> Pale as the tiny tips of crocuses
> That will find their way to the light through drifts of snow.

Hecht takes us right into the making of a work of art, indeed into the studio itself, it would seem, as viewed from the admiring perspective of the illuminator. The language is necessarily quiet, although rich in sound and sense, as in the phrase "Celestial tinctures smuggled from the East." (Substitute "stolen" for "smuggled" and you lose a tincture of mystery associated with contraband.) A flower poem for the Baskin *Florilegium* in the form of a "notional" ekphrasis, one, that is, created by the poet and not based on a specific work, it redirects the motif of the

exotic itinerary described in "*Là-bas*: A Trance" to fit the more dedicated spiritual concerns of the present volume. "The tiny tips of crocuses," not the flaming headgear of tulips, mark the poem's final floral
destination, one associated with the birth of Jesus not the flying carpets
of Carpaccio, and produced with care, not flare.

The principal action of the poem is taken up with the process of
arriving at this final image. In this regard, "Illumination" is a Stevensian
work of and about the imagination, Brother Anselm's as well as Hecht's.
The gathering of materials is important, indeed impressive, as the first
part of the poem illustrates, but as the poet observes, "the camel's-hair
tip of the finest brush" transforms the powdery materials that go into
the production of art: the one tip giving bloom to the many in the
"tiny tips of crocuses," the artist's imagination illuminated by "the
light of dawn" to produce an illumination of his own. Compared to
Brother Anselm's quietly attentive craftsmanship, Paul's celebrated
declamation in 1 Corinthians 13:1 ("though I speak with the tongues
of men and of angels"), paraphrased by Hecht as "not by my skills or
merit am I made persuasive, but by the grace of God," has a distinctly
hollow ring to it.[13]

In a broad sense, we're hardly surprised by this sentiment. Attention
to skill or craft in the manner of an Anselm has always been a conspicuous feature of Hecht's art, in sharp contradistinction to the claims of
personal inspiration made by shaggy bearded bards in a manner not
dissimilar from Paul, Hecht's originary solipsist. One of the distinguishing features of this final collection is a return to writing a kind of poetry
more characteristic, in some ways, of the "impersonal" lyric venerated
by Eliot and the New Critical generation of poets, in which Hecht had
his beginnings, than with the large-scale imaginings of his middle years.
A return, of course, marked by a sense of difference, indeed of further
refinement, as in the case of his translation from the medieval poet
Charles d'Orléans, now titled, with an eye toward its revisionary status,
"Once More, with Feeling." Hecht had produced an earlier version in
A Summoning of Stones (1954), bearing the rather flat title "Springtime."
The new title with its marked emphasis on "feeling," however, should
not be confused with a sudden infusion of personal sentiment into the
poem: neither poem, in fact, uses the first-person pronoun. It has to
do with craft, with adding flare or gusto by heightening the vocabulary,

---

13. Hecht, "St. Paul's Epistle to the Galatians," 243.

strengthening the verbs, selecting the right nouns for the refrain, and enunciating more certainly the rhetorical, metrical, and rhyme patterns.

The poems, in the form of roundels, are short enough to compare briefly. The earlier version reads:

> The Weather hath put off his mien
> Of tearing winde and cold advance,
> And beareth new an elegance
> Yellow of sun and spritely greene.
> Nor bird nor wilde thing to be seen
> But shouteth in its own parlance:
> "The Weather hath put off his mien
> Of tearing winde and cold advance."
> And water where it spouteth e'en
> Weareth the colors of the dance,
> And everyone hath mayde quittance
> Of the dark wise of wrath and spleen.
> The Weather hath put off his mien.

It is not without its archaizing charms, nor its problems, beginning with the forced metrical stress on "hath," continuing with "mien" for "demeanor," which has more to do with behavior than clothing, and, finally, in the use of "advance" in the refrain, which puts pressure on its rhyming mates to stress, rather awkwardly, the last syllable in "parl*ance*" and "quitt*ance*." Hecht did not choose to include the translation in the selection of poems from *A Summoning of Stones* published with *The Hard Hours*.

The later version appears, by contrast, already more visually articulate in its division into stanzas:

> The world has doffed her outerwear
> Of chilling wind and teeming rain,
> And donned embroidery again,
> Tailored with sunlight's gilded flair.
>
> No beast of field nor bird of air
> But sings or bellows this refrain:
> "The world has doffed her outerwear
> Of chilling winds and teeming rain."
>
> Fountain, millrace and river spare
> No costly beading nor abstain
> From silvered liveries of grosgrain.
> All is new-clad and debonair.
> The world has doffed her outerwear.

This is a vision of nature in full dress, "Tailored with sunlight's gilded flair" (the verb strengthened through a trochaic substitution in the first foot), something about which to sing or—more startlingly—to bellow, to cite another of the many alterations that makes the poem more emphatically a celebration of seasonal change. The first poem is a statement about "elegance," the second inhabits its courtly subject, more in the manner of its regal creator, the poet who was also a duke.

A similar urge to return and improve is evident with the poem on the facing page, "Le Jet d'Eau." One of two translations from Baudelaire in this last volume, the original French version had long fascinated Hecht, and even though he attempted an early translation, "The Fountain,"[14] he clearly wasn't satisfied with the result, and seemed to mull over the poem until he thought he arrived as close as he could to a poem in the spirit of the original. With Baudelaire, we seem even closer to the realm of pure lyric than in the Orléans roundel, in the sense mentioned earlier by Hecht of a lyric being "a pure instant of perception captured in the course of its fleeting evanescence." The poem, beginning with the line, "My dear, your lids are weary," alternates direct address to a lover with a lyric refrain describing the fountain's flowing water. In the later version, there is a slight distancing of address achieved by removing the personal pronoun "my" from the first stanza, but the principal changes involve the refrain, which Hecht makes lighter and, if possible, more lyrical by a slight redisposing of diction, image, and line. Here is the earlier refrain:

> The sheer luminous gown
> The fountain wears
> Where Phoebe's very own
> Color appears
> Falls like a summer rain
> Or shawl of tears.

And the revised version:

> A spray of petaled brilliance
> That uprears
> In gladness as the Moon-
> Goddess appears
> Falls like an opulent glistening
> Of tears.

---

14. The poem appears among those included in "Uncollected Hecht," *Poetry* 198.5 (September 2011), 455–6; see also the comments by David Yezzi in his "Introduction," 443.

The earlier version is slightly hobbled by the "wears / Where" repetition, but the main difference between it and the later version comes from substituting "uprears" for "wears," which strengthens the fountain's upward movement in glad response to the moon's appearance and sharpens the later, crucial contrast with "Falls," in a line that recalculates the length, now eight rather than six syllables, in order to draw out the emphasis on "opulent glistening" followed, in the subsequent line, now by the sole image of tears, an image that recalls, in shape, the image of the delicately hyphenated "Moon," now hanging (like a tear?) at the end of the third line. Indeed, the image of the petal in "a spray of petaled brilliance"—a finer reckoning of the particular than the earlier "sheer luminous gown"—is carried through the refrain, undergoing, as it should, slight variations in meaning with each recurrence.

These are the small transformations in which a poet's art can be understood and appreciated. The disciplined impulse underlying the changes themselves bear out the "sterner test" of the poet Hecht described in his translation of Goethe, also included in this volume as "The Plastic and the Poetic Form":

> Let that Greek youth out of clay
> Mold an urn to fashion
> Beauty, gladdening the eye
> With deft-handed vision.
>
> But the poet's sterner test
> Urges him to seize on
> A Euphrates of unrest,
> Fluid in evasion.
>
> Duly bathed and cooled, his mind,
> Ardorless, will utter
> Liquid song, his forming hand
> Lend a shape to water.

If this poem provides a useful vocabulary to distinguish one form of making from another, sculpture from poesis, "Le Jet d'Eau" offers a perfect opportunity to reckon the challenge required of the poet in shaping, coolly and dispassionately, the movement of sound into the refrain's "liquid song."

Returns always involve difference, re-turnings, as verse teaches us to think, and if the translations allow a glimpse into the artistic values at the core of Hecht's thinking, the volume also includes an element of the autobiographical that characterizes change itself. "The exceeding brightness of this early sun / Makes me conceive how dark I have become." The other quotation in the epigraph from Stevens points to self-reflection accompanying an awareness of transition; and though Hecht does not include Stevens' lines about "a turning spirit in an earlier self," or the sentence immediately following, "That, too, returns from out the winter's air," there can be little doubt about the presence of winter in this last volume, as "Sarabande on Attaining the Age of Seventy-Seven" makes abundantly clear, or about the return (and re-turning) of earlier memories, some of a darkly bitter kind as in the case of "Circles."

This is a poem that belongs in *The Hard Hours*, it would seem, a circling back to Hecht's time as a "weakened, weekend father." The wordplay can't disguise the depth of the poet's feeling—"once more with feeling," we might say, in the sense of the return of passions that a reader of Hecht's poetry might well think locked in the distant past:

> Long inventories of miseries unspoken,
> Appointment books of pain,
> Attars of love gone rancid, the pitcher broken
> At the fountain, rooted unkindnesses:
> All were implied by her, by me suspected,
> At her saying, "I could not bear
> Ever returning to that village in Maine.
> For me the very air,
> The harbor smells, the hills, all are infected."

Like Dante's *Inferno*, whose *terza rima* is loosely recalled, the poem serves as a saga of personal punishment, meted out by the courts involving a divorced father's custody rights:

> All of us, in our own circle of hell
> (Not that of forger, simonist or pander),
> Patrolled the Olmsted bosks of Central Park,
> Its children-thronged resorts
> Pain-tainted ground,
> Where the innocent and the fallen join to play
> In the fields, if not of the Lord, then of the Law;
> Which decreed that love be hobbled and confined
> To Saturday,
> Trailing off into Sunday-before-dark;
> And certain sandpits, slides, swings, monkey bars
> Became the old thumbscrews of spoiled affection
> And agonized aversion.

In this dizzying and painstakingly tortuous descent, we appear to be nearing the bottom at the end of this long sentence; but a final circle remains:

> Of these, the most tormenting
> In its single-songed, maddening monotony,
> Its glaring-eyed and nostril-flaring steeds
> With perfect teeth, but destined never to win
> Their countless and interminable races,
> Was the merry, garish, mirthless carousel.

We've encountered this kind of glaring light on other occasions in this volume. But if we're searching for closure here, it's perhaps small comfort that we have to return nineteen lines to find the rhyme for "carousel" in "hell." "Oh! Rabbi, rabbi fend my soul for me / And true savant of this dark nature be."

Other memories are milder, quieter, especially those inspired by the late afternoon light. In the poem immediately following, called "Memory," Hecht offers another haunting still life, lavish with detail, of a room and its entrance, all gauged to invite us to wonder whose place it is and how is it that the poet knows it so well, since, as the title suggests, he seems to be describing it from memory. So vivid is it in his mind that he gives the illusion of returning to the place itself, after having been away for a long time, but the objects withhold their secrets and the room is eerily empty of people:

> Pink still were the shiny curling orifices
> Of matching seashells stationed on the mantel
> With mated, spiked, wrought-iron candlesticks.
> The room contained a tufted ottoman,
> A large elephant-foot umbrella stand
> With two malacca canes, and two peacock
> Tail-feathers sprouting from a small-necked vase.

Hecht never wrote a poem about his parents or their apartment, and this still may not be it. The closing lines reveal no more about "the family" than does the first, but steeped in memory it surely is and portentously astir with a sense of things as they were at some happier interval:

> On a teak side table lay, side by side,
> A Bible and a magnifying glass.
> Green velvet drapes kept the room dark and airless

> Until on sunny days toward midsummer
> The brass andirons caught a shaft of light
> For twenty minutes in late afternoon
> In a radiance dimly akin to happiness—
> The dusty gleam of temporary wealth.

More reticent and mysterious still is another "late afternoon" poem, "A Certain Slant," mysterious in part because of Hecht's own single annotation: "The poem had its origin in a sentence in a story called 'The Boys,' by Anton Chekhov." But readers of Hecht might well share Mary Jo Salter's puzzlement over the poet's decision not to annotate Emily Dickinson's famous poem beginning, "There's a certain Slant of Light."[15] There can be little doubt that Dickinson's poem was on Hecht's mind in composing *The Darkness and the Light*, perhaps too much so to require or bear commentary. In the conclusion to "Mirror," the speaker seems to rise out of the compressed depths of her famous lyric:

> It's when no one's around that I'm most truthful,
> In a world as timeless as before The Fall.
> No one to reassure that she's still youthful,
> I gaze untroubled at the opposite wall.

> Light fades, of course, with the oncoming of dusk;
> I faithfully note the rheostat dial of day
> That will rise to brilliance, weaken as it must
> Through each uncalibrated shade of gray,

> One of them that of winter afternoons,
> Desolate, leaden, and in its burden far
> Deeper than darkness, engrossing in its tones
> Those shrouded regions where the meanings are.

Dickinson's poem begins:

> There's a certain Slant of Light,
> Winter afternoons—
> That oppresses, like the heft
> Of Cathedral Tunes—

> Heavenly Hurt, it gives us—
> We can find no scar—
> But internal difference,
> Where the meanings are.

15. This and other comments from Salter are drawn from a talk she gave on Anthony Hecht at Amherst College, November 2007. I'm grateful to her for sending me a written version of her presentation.

In a draft version of Hecht's poem appears the date 16 January 2000, a reference not just to the new millennium but to the poet's birthday, and it seems to me entirely possible that the oppressive weight of a winter afternoon in Dickinson had a personal meaning to later Hecht, in much the same way that Dickinson's opening line pointed to a shared epistemology with regard to "where the meanings are," a common ground that expands if we recall, with Salter, another famous Dickinson poem, with a slightly different "slant," beginning:

> Tell all the truth but tell it slant—
> Success in Circuit lies
> Too bright for our infirm Delight
> The Truth's superb surprise
>
> As lightning to the Children eased
> With explanation kind
> The Truth must dazzle gradually
> Or every man be blind—.

If another poem were needed for additional support to counter Paul's sudden "illumination" on the way to Damascus, this would be it, with its pointed paradox that "The Truth must dazzle gradually / Or every man be blind—."

But too much Dickinson can also blind us to the originality of Hecht's "A Certain Slant," not simply because, as he says, its source lies in a sentence from a Chekhov story, a sentence he doesn't give but a careful reader like Salter can readily find in the translation by Harvey Pitcher: "A wintry sun penetrated the snow and tracery on the window-panes, played over the samovar and bathed its pure rays in the rinsing bowl." The reader who has been led this far will no doubt go on to the next sentence: "The room was warm, and the boys felt a tickling sensation in their numbed bodies as the warmth and chill competed for supremacy."[16] Hecht's poem grows out of the imagery of the first line, but the second, with its mention of "the boys," supplies a further context for the poem's setting and subject matter, which is a meditation on the mysterious evolution of "lives":

> Etched on the window were barbarous thistles of frost,
> Edged everywhere in that tame winter sunlight
> With pavé diamonds and fine prickles of ice

16. Anton Chekhov, *The Comic Short Stories*, trans. Harvey Pitcher (Chicago: University of Chicago Press, 1999), 163.

Through which a shaft of the late afternoon
Entered our room to entertain the sway
And float of motes, like tiny aqueous lives,
Then glanced off the silver teapot, raising stains
Of snailing gold upcast across the ceiling,
And bathed itself at last in the slop bucket
Where other aqueous lives, equally slow,
Turned in their sad, involuntary courses,
Swiveled in eel-green broth. Who could have known
Of any elsewhere? Even of out-of-doors,
Where the stacked firewood gleamed in drapes of glaze
And blinded the sun itself with jubilant theft,
The smooth cool plunder of celestial fire.

If the truth must dazzle gradually, then the poet must rely on parables at times, and so this poem does in its reckoning of "tiny aqueous lives" and their fates: the slop bucket and its "eel-green" broth reminding us of the aqueous origins of life in "Green: An Epistle." This later poem is less roiled and brooding, the autobiographical footprints less easy, if not quite impossible, to track. Its reticence is perfectly in keeping with the quiet, understated nature of this volume. In "A Certain Slant," some lives seem to do better than others in their upward ascent, but ultimately they join the rest as the late-afternoon sun bathes "itself at last in the slop bucket." What stands out in this parable is the initial question: "Who could have known / Of any elsewhere?" And, of course, the only person who could ask that question is the person who has been elsewhere, who has somehow left or escaped "our room," the poem's author. As with "Memory," the poem invites our curiosity about the identity of the place and the persons, an invitation furthered by Hecht's reference to "the story called 'The Boys.'" But if there is an answer, it only comes in the form of another question, in the reference to the "stacked firewood," reminiscent of the woodpile in Frost's poem of that name.

Frost's poem was of particular interest to Hecht, as his brief, subtle essay on the subject reveals, especially the enigmatical nature of the stack of wood itself: "How curious, how enigmatic, to find this perfectly stacked cord abandoned in the middle of nowhere." Frost's poem, of course, prompts this consideration; but in place of the deliberately "bland" explanation offered by the speaker himself—that the person who lived by the axe simply turned to other tasks—Hecht offers another possibility that the poet was "too reserved and careful to express": that the pile was left because the person had died, an explanation that grows in interest when Hecht adds the further gloss:

And if, as I urge you to consider, this "handiwork... on which he spent himself" were poems that had gone virtually unnoticed during the poet's lifetime and were to be chanced upon by some stray wanderer long after the poet's death, then this wood-pile might well signify for Robert Frost the secret fears he must have entertained when, a year earlier, his first book had been greeted by such discouraging reviews; and there he was, husband and father of four—it might have been father of six, but for the early deaths of two children—in a foreign country where his work had been briefly and summarily dismissed.[17]

To return to "A Certain Slant" after rereading the Frost essay is to see the conclusion of Hecht's poem in a different light: that the ending serves, as a rhetorical question will do, to offer an explanation for why the speaker left "our room." And one possibility is because of the irresistible lure of "stacked firewood" so different in character from Frost's forgotten handiwork that it had to be pursued with nothing less than Promethean flare. Frost's poem, from Hecht's perspective, is a parable about the worry of never being noticed, a worry that every poet must feel, but for some a worry that happily dissolves and certainly did in Frost's case given his subsequent spectacular visibility in the world of American letters. Here, in this last book of poems, is an equally discreet parable but of a different kind: a turn, a certain slant offered on Frost via Chekov by way of Dickinson, ignited by a touch or torch of Stevensesque vigor in the figure of art stealing life and light from the sun, the reflection even blinding the sun in the process. The only thing so bedazzling in this book of late afternoons could be the subject of poetry itself, which early on led one of "the boys"—the author of this poem—elsewhere.

At least one other poem is equally beguiling in its reticence, the poem that introduces the collection: "Late Afternoon: The Onslaught of Love." Some poems cannot be readily or easily fathomed, in part because they are so evidently a matter of surface, as in the case of this poem based on a famous passage from Flaubert's *Madame Bovary*.[18]

17. Hecht, "On Robert Frost's 'The Wood-Pile,'" *Melodies Unheard: Essays on the Mysteries of Poetry*, 154–8.
18. The passage from Flaubert's *Madame Bovary* can be found near the beginning of Part III, Chapter III. A comparison of Hecht's poem with its source suggests he was familiar with translations by both Eleanor Marx-Aveling (1888; rev. 1965) and Francis

Indeed, so closely does the poem hew to Flaubert that it's a bit puzzling that no mention is made of the source in the book or the notes, at least in the loose manner, say, of "After Flaubert," or, as in the case of "A Certain Slant," indicating a response to a particular sentence or episode. I suspect one possible answer is that Hecht knew that this was the right poem to introduce the collection: the lyrical mood of a late afternoon is picked up at various points in the collection and then finely—and finally—distilled in the last poem in the volume as afternoon moves into evening; but, by the same logic, he also didn't want to spoil the mood by raising the matter of translation at the outset. But there may have been another mood spoiler as well if the Flaubert connection became a primary focus for looking deep. So long as we read the poem in the high modernist mode (for which Flaubert was famous), in which artistic objectivity was the main, if not sole, focus of the work, then the poem could be justly appreciated on its own verbally ample terms—as exploiting to the fullest the lyrical moment ("At this time of day / One could hear..." etc.) and not as a commentary on the story of Flaubert's heroine, Madame Bovary herself and, as Hecht said in his letter to Sapinsley, "of the insatiable craving for experiences that were never hers because they were unreal and belonged entirely to the realms of her imagination"[19]—her unquenchable and ultimately delusional thirst for the material things associated with her aspirations to transcend her provincial life.

"A number of my poems have autobiographical elements," Hecht wrote on the publicist's questionnaire in anticipation of the publication of *The Darkness and the Light*, "but I prefer to leave unannotated which they are and how they bear upon my private life. In this I take the same liberties as some novelists."[20] It is impossible to read "Circles," the poem appearing immediately after "Late Afternoon," and not to think about his disastrous first marriage; but it is possible to read an "unannotated" "Late Afternoon" as a beautifully crafted poem about the onslaught of love in the high modernist mode of the impersonal, unless one learns or knows of *Madame Bovary*, in which case Hecht's

Steegmuller (1950). In a letter to Al Sapinsley, Hecht quotes at some length from Marx-Aveling; but some of the notable images and phrases in the poem, such as the splendid line "undulating unevenly," are present in Steegmuller only, 11 December 1998 (*SL*, 297–9).

19. Letter, AH to Al Sapinsley, 11 December 1998 (*SL*, 299).
20. Fax, AH to Jill Morrison, 30 November 2000.

poem becomes more apparent as a work of "double-colored taffeta" woven out of Flaubert's intricate verbal web, but containing autobiographical strands associated with the never named "she" of the poem, who resembles his first wife, but is now viewed with Flaubert-like objectivity. If the former connection was "bound to be discovered sooner or later," as Hecht remarked to Philip Hoy, who was preparing to give a paper on Hecht's sources at a conference,[21] the latter nonetheless remains "purely" in the realm of readerly conjecture, as is also the case with those other mysterious "late afternoon poems," "Memory" and "A Certain Slant." Privacy in Hecht shows itself to be a carefully guarded, shadowy space. And yet, as the mirror teasingly tells us, it's in "Those shrouded regions where the meanings are."

A poet who uses "purple" twice, as in "Undulating unevenly / In the purple sunlight / Like the surfaces of Florentine bronze," and again, "At this time of day / Sunlight empurpled the world," doesn't worry about being accused of excess. Likewise, a poet who concludes the volume with " 'The Darkness and the Light are Both Alike to Thee' " doesn't worry about going out on something of a grace note, indeed quoting a line verbatim from the King James version of Psalms 139:12, and thus carrying on a Herbertian legacy sounded two poems earlier in the epigraph to "Sarabande." Hecht's poem, quoted at the beginning of this chapter, is undeniably exquisite: classical in its purity of diction, elementally simple in its rhymes, plush with imagery, spare in design. The sun goes down, the sun comes up, a new day, another generation; but deeply elegiac, thus acquiring a place in Harold Bloom's canon of great last poems.[22]

Within this strict design, two moments in particular invite further attention: at the end of the first stanza, the sudden, startlingly swift movement into night, "Huge presences of gray / Rise up, and then it's night"; and the equally surprising appearance of the simile that begins the third stanza, "Like the elderly and frail / Who've lasted through the night," and turns the poem into an allegory of old age. The earlier shift into night now assumes, for all its simplicity, greater weight, and we see,

21. Letter, AH to Philip Hoy, 6 June 2004. "As to my use of Flaubert, you are welcome to point it out—though I think you would be the first to do so, no one else, to my knowledge, having spotted the source. Anyway, it was bound to be discovered sooner or later. And I'm glad it will be you to make it public, rather than some hostile critic."

22. Bloom, "Till I End My Song": A Gathering of Last Poems (New York: Harper, 2010).

retrospectively, how Hecht has managed the small drama of late aging by focusing on the temporal change from evening, when it is still possible to be poetic (through references to silk, olives trees, and wine), to the stark phrasing of "it's night" as the last words in that stanza. For those who are long-lived, there is nothing uncommon about this experience, as Hecht, at seventy-nine, writes to a younger poet:

I had of course plenty of reason to be prepared for this. Quite apart from seeing other elderly people, I found myself being described by [the poet] Tim Murphy as elderly, and I myself (with help) translated the great chorus on old age in *Oedipus at Colonos*. But it comes to everyone as a surprise when they grow old, a matter that is largely due to the gradualness of the process.[23]

Yes, that is exactly how the stanza is pitched—to underscore the illusion of extended time without overdramatizing the surprise.

At the same time, the latter part of the poem is less about surprise than stoic endurance, "Cold brows and silent lips," and generational change, but of what kind? Some readers have seen the reference to the "timid gleam / Of matins" in the second stanza as a purposeful diminishment of a younger generation of writers as lesser lights by a poet anxious about succession. But apart from being uncharacteristic of Hecht, the poem seems to be saying the reverse or at least something different: that the "rising light" associated with the next generation in the third stanza "entails" but does not cause the eclipse of the elderly. In effect, it is in the nature of things to change, for one generation to follow another, very like leaves on the tree in Homer's famous simile. There is also some purposeful ambiguity in the final line, "Brightening as they fail," as to whom it applies. Is it the rising lights who brighten as the elderly fail? Or is it the elderly who brighten as they fail, giving off a final glimmer? If in the case of the latter reading, there is a flash of recognition here by Hecht of his own continuing or renewed energies in his later years, even more specifically of the powers that went into the final collection, he is just as clearly resisting a John of Gaunt exclamatory ending, an overorchestrated "music at the close."[24] And if we read it in the former sense, then it points to a further consolation: the possibility that the art to which the poet has dedicated his life will continue. In either case, the suggestion that Hecht "deplores the next

23. Letter, AH to B. F. ("Pete") Fairchild, 9 January 2002.
24. *Richard II*, 2.1.12.

generation—or rather the fact that there must be a next generation"[25] is not an idea to be found in this poem.

"'The Darkness and the Light are Both Alike to Thee'" forms the right conclusion to Hecht's last book, in manner as well as statement. The title encapsulates major concerns of the volume and in Hecht generally. The poet rightly dispensed with a host of other possible titles: "Dusk and Dawn," "Wanings," "This Petty Pace," and "Diminishes." None does the job of elevating an observation of contrarieties into a universal principle—a law, as Hecht would say, even if his own poetry would continually describe how unlike light the darkness is.

But I want to close my own book with a last look at a poem slipped quietly between the finale and "Sarabande on Attaining the Age of Seventy-Seven." At first glance the poem seems unpromising, even deliberately puzzling, like so much else in this volume, bearing in epitaphic fashion the mysterious title, functioning like an inwrought rhyme, "I.M.E.M." The abbreviation alludes to a Georgetown University colleague of Hecht's: "In Memoriam Elias Mengel," if one filled out the initials. Mengel, a literary scholar of the eighteenth century and clearly of German ancestry, lived alone, in the narrowest house in Georgetown. So discreet in fact is the title that the person's identity can be discovered only by putting together a few facts from the poem in conjunction with the initials:

> To spare his brother from having to endure
> Another agonizing bedside vigil
> With sterile pads, syringes but no hope,
> He settled all his accounts, distributed
> Among a few friends his most valued books,
> Weighed all in mind and heart and then performed
> The final, generous, extraordinary act
> Available to a solitary man,
> Abandoning his translation of Boileau,
> Dressing himself in a dark well-pressed suit,

25. Jan Schreiber, "The Achievements of Anthony Hecht," *Contemporary Poetry Review*, posted on 1 December 2004. <http://www.cprw.com/the-achievements-of-anthony-hecht>. In response to the question, "is poetry alive and well in 2003?" put by Bruce Cole, Chairman of the National Endowment of the Humanities, Hecht remarked "I think it's in wonderful shape. I can offer into evidence the names of a good number of extraordinarily gifted young poets." He then lists seven poets as evidence that "poetry is thriving in this country and doing extremely well" (*Humanities: The Magazine of the National Endowment for the Humanities*, 25.2 (March/April 2004), 52.

> Turning the lights out, lying on his bed,
> Having requested neighbors to wake him early
> When, as intended, they would find him dead.

Careful readers of Hecht's poetry sometimes speak of the "nobility" of his voice, "so rare in contemporary poetry,"[26] and, in doing so, we are reminded of the large gestures in this direction: the full sweep of "The Venetian Vespers," the pathos of some of the dramatic monologues, the horrendous occasions of wartime suffering, the liebestod at the end of "Apprehensions," the onslaught of hard hours withstood, the final stanza of the ballade "Death the Poet"; but sometimes that voice is particularly resonant in the smaller, quieter moments, at least as these might appear to a detached observer. "To spare," the poem begins abruptly, signaling its own interest in classical simplicity, but then it slowly unfolds in a single, continuous, but ample thirteen-line sentence. "Spareness" and generosity or amplitude seem inseparable, the one a consequence of the other. The deceased spared his brother by not sparing himself. Hecht spares the reader by concentrating only on what seems important, the essentials, not the statistics, of a person's life, and not just any person as it turns out, but those of a "solitary man." This is a small slice of late Hecht, perhaps a partial view of how he might like to be viewed in retrospect, carefully ordering his concerns by noting the concerns of others. Books matter, as a way to designate a small group of friends, as does respect for a larger community of neighbors: the simple ease, not flourish, of the concluding "bed"/"dead" rhyme, the only rhyme in the poem and surely one of the oldest in the language, tells us as much, as does the careful preparation for the receivers to see the deceased, carefully clothed, without shock.

But perhaps most striking is what happens in the middle: how the unnamed he "Weighed all in mind and heart and then performed / The final, generous, extraordinary act / Available to a solitary man." Yes, "performed," but a performance from the head and heart, not an exercise in formality. The distinction is crucial. Abandoning his translation of Boileau is painful; few things could mean more, especially to a poet who had translated Voltaire, but not to be dwelt on at any length, since the point of the gathering energy in the succession of present participles is to prepare for the final act or action out of concern for others. As a poem, "I.M.E.M." is not "The Book of Yolek." Its scope is

---

26. J. D. McClatchy, *Anthony Hecht: Selected Poems* (New York: Alfred A Knopf, 2011), xiv.

smaller; it doesn't ask as much from its author or the reader, but there this passing was, nearly as unnoticed as Yolek's. Yet something in Hecht, some generosity of spirit in response to another, some interest in the thickness of the particular—of dealing "with it faithfully, you understand, / Without blurring the issue"—made him want to turn this moment into verse. And so he did, seeing in the mind's eye not a numeral tattoo this time but a spare yet stately inscription to honor, in kind and dignity, a scholar of eighteenth-century classicism.

Index